THE INDIAN BUDDHIST ICONOGRAPHY

THE INDIAN BUDDHIST ICONOGRAPHY

MAINLY BASED ON

THE SĀDHANAMĀLĀ

AND OTHER COGNATE TĀNTRIC TEXTS OF RITUALS

Benoytosh Bhattacharyya

PRINTWORLD

Publishers of Indian Traditions

Cataloging in Publication Data — DK
[Courtesy: D.K. Agencies (P) Ltd. <docinfo@dkagencies.com>]

Bhattacharyya, Benoytosh, 1897-1964, **author.**
The Indian Buddhist iconography : mainly based on the Sādhanamālā and other cognate tāntric texts of rituals / Benoytosh Bhattacharyya.
pages cm
"First published in 1920 by Humphrey Milford Oxford University Press" – Title page verso.
Includes bibliographical references and index.
ISBN 9788124613238 (HB)

1. Tantric-Buddhist art – India. 2. Buddhist art – India. 3. Art, Indic. 4. Gautama Buddha – Art. I. Sādhanamālā. II. Title.

LCC N8193.3.T3B43 2025 | DDC 704.9489430954 23

ISBN: 978-81-246-1323-8 (Hb)

First published in 1924 by Humphrey Milford Oxford University Press.
This reprint edition published in 2025

Printed and published by:
D.K. Printworld (P) Ltd.
Regd. Office: "Vedaśrī", F-395, Sudarshan Park
ESI Hospital Metro Station, New Delhi - 110015
Phones: (011) 4172 2626, 98713 94815
e-mail: indology@dkprintworld.com
Web: www.dkprintworld.com

THE INDIAN BUDDHIST ICONOGRAPHY

MAINLY BASED ON

THE SĀDHANAMĀLĀ

AND OTHER COGNATE TĀNTRIC TEXTS OF RITUALS

BY

BENOYTOSH BHATTACHARYYA, M.A. (*Calcutta*),

University Gold Medallist and Prizeman, Government Research Scholar in Iconography at the University of Dacca, Editor, Gaekwad's Oriental Series, and Librarian, Oriental Collection, Baroda State

(*WITH* 283 *ILLUSTRATIONS*)

1924

HUMPHREY MILFORD

OXFORD UNIVERSITY PRESS

LONDON NEW YORK TORONTO MELBOURNE

BOMBAY CALCUTTA MADRAS

Printed by
D. N. Banerjee,
at the Banerjee Press,
2, Maharani Sarnamayee Road,
CALCUTTA.

Haraprasād Shāstri

To

MAHĀMAHOPĀDHYĀYA PANDIT

HARAPRASAD SHASTRI, M.A., C.I.E.,

Honorary Member, Royal Asiatic Society of Great Britain and Ireland and Professor of Sanskrit in the University at Dacca,

This Volume is Dedicated as a mark of
Profound Devotion and Respect,
By his
Affectionate son,
Benoytosh Bhattacharyya.

Saṃgrahantu priyatvena
vistaradveṣiṇā mayā ।
Bhūriranuttame tasmin
kṣantavyaṃ vistarapriyaiḥ ॥

Advayavajra.

PREFACE

This volume represents part of the work done by me as a Government Research Scholar in Iconography for four years from 1920 to 1924. It is an attempt to write a comprehensive work on the Buddhist Iconography of India, and is mainly based on a Sanskrit text prepared from seven recensions of the Sādhanamālā *alias* Sādhanasamuccaya in the libraries of the Asiatic Society of Bengal, Nepal, and Cambridge University. This text so collated I hope to publish as soon as the opportunity presents itself. The text has been illustrated by pictures representing images in several museums in India and elsewhere and in the collections of numerous Nepalese monasteries. Where images could not be obtained or photographing was impossible or unsatisfactory the text has been illustrated with the help of drawings prepared by Nepalese Citrakāras of Buddhist origin from the ancient albums of their forefathers. Where no drawing could be obtained only the original text has been quoted with a translation.

The publication of this work necessitated, on my part, a prolonged visit to Nepal whither my father, Mahāmahopādhyāya Haraprasād Shāstrī, was proceeding on an invitation from His Highness the Mahārājā of Nepal. It also necessitated a visit to the museums of Calcutta, Dacca, Patna, Sarnath, Lucknow, Mathura, and Ajmere, to the Cave-temples at Ellora and Ajanta, to the excavations at Nalanda, and to Vikrampur, the seat of Bengal Buddhism.

In several ways I have been very fortunate in carrying out my researches. First, I have had the proud privilege of working under Professor A. Foucher, the accredited authority on Indian Buddhist images, during the period he was in charge of the Archæological Section, Indian Museum. Secondly, through the kindness of the Mahārājā of Nepal I was able to secure a number of MSS. from the Durbar Library for collation and study. Thirdly, through the kindness of Mr. P. J. Hartog, M.A., C.I.E., Vice-Chancellor of the Dacca University, I secured the loan of one of the three Cambridge MSS. of the *Sādhanamālā* which I had absolutely no chance of getting otherwise. Fourthly, during the first two years the most valuable library of the Asiatic Society of Bengal was thrown open for my use. Fifthly, the Dacca University gave me all facilities whenever applied for. Sixthly, the Government granted me, as a special favour, the Research Scholarship for a fourth year, a privilege not ordinarily granted under the rules.

Professor Foucher impressed upon me the fact that of the Buddhist Iconography, the most important and illuminating theme was its Indian section ; and that this was the fountain-head from which Tibet, China, and other countries drew their inspiration, which each amplified according to its own genius. The root of Buddhist Iconography is Indian, and Professor Foucher asked me to concentrate my attention on Indian images only. This advice has been of very great value to me ; it has enabled me to grasp some of the principles on which the whole fabric of Buddhist Iconography and methods of worship in later Buddhism is based. This Buddhist Iconography, for instance, is not idolatry ; the images do not represent objects of worship but represent the highest Buddhist ideal of Śūnya or Void, commingled with Vijñāna and Mahāsukha.

My grateful acknowledgments are due to His Highness Sir Chandra Shamsher Jung Bahadur Rana, Mahārājā of Nepal, for rendering me ungrudging help in all difficulties in a foreign land and for placing at my disposal the services of a Gubhāju and a Citrakāra, during our stay in Nepal.

I am deeply grateful to Mr. W. W. Hornell, M.A., C.I.E., M.L.C., until recently Director of Public Instruction, Bengal, for granting me the Research Scholarship I have been enjoying for four years ; and I am especially indebted to Mr. W. B. Finnigan, Personal Assistant to the Director of Public Instruction, for the interest he has taken in my affairs and for his sustaining encouragement. Without his kind help the work of printing would have been stopped long ago.

I have also to record my heartfelt thanks to Mr. P. J. Hartog, C.I.E., Vice-Chnacellor, Dacca University, for kindly procuring for collation one of the three Cambridge MSS. of the Sādhanamālā, and for his unceasing efforts to obtain for me *Rotograph* copies of the two other MSS in palm-leaf. My thanks are also due to Prof. G. H. Langley, M.A., I.E.S., Dr. S. W. Kemp, D. Sc., and Mr. K. N. Dikshit, M.A. for taking a keen interest in my work and for their sound advice.

In compiling the present work I have to acknowledge help from several other sources : I am indebted to Rai Bahadur P. N. Mookerjee, I.S.O., Principal N. N. Raye, M.A., Prof. M. G. Bhattacharyya, M.A., and Mr. B. B. Mittra, M.A. for revising portions of the manuscript and helping me in correcting the proofs ; to my friend, Mr. N. K. Bhattasali, M.A., Curator, Dacca Museum, for many acts of kindness and valuable suggestions ; and to Messrs. S. C. Mondol and A. B. Maitra for preparing a number of negatives for my use.

Lastly, it is not merely as a filial duty that I acknowledge the debt I owe to my father Mahāmahopādhyāya Haraprasād Śhāstri, M.A., C.I.E. for whose sustaining help in all matters of difficulty, domestic, educational and financial, I shall ever remain grateful, and to whom this book is dedicated as a mark of profound devotion and respect.

For various reasons this book had to be hurried through the press. I am aware that, in consequence, it is not free from errors. I much regret these and hope that the book may be so fortunate as to pass through the press again, since this will give me an opportunity of removing them.

BARODA,

29*th January*, 1924. BENOYTOSH BHATTACHARYYA

SYNOPSIS OF CONTENTS

PAGE

FOREWORD i

INTRODUCTION

§ 1. A Brief Historical Survey of Buddhism ix
§ 2. Evolution of the Doctrines xiv
§ 3. Evidence of Art xx
§ 4. The Pantheon xxiv

CHAPTER I

Buddhas, Buddhaśaktis and Bodhisattvas

§ I. Dhyānī Buddhas 1
Amitābha, Akṣobhya, Vairocana, Amoghasiddhi, Ratnasambhava, Vajrasattva

§ II. Divine Buddhaśaktis 7
§ III. Divine Bodhisattvas 8
§ IV. Mortal Buddhas 9
Gautama Buddha

§ V. Mortal Buddhaśaktis 12
§ VI. Mortal Bodhisattvas 12
§ VII. Maitreya, the Future Buddha 13

CHAPTER II

Mañjuśrī 15

§ 1. Emanations of Amitābha 17
Vāk, Dharmadhātu-Vāgīśvara

§ 2. Emanations of Akṣobhya 19
Mañjughoṣa, Siddhaikavīra, Vajrānaṅga, Nāmasaṅgīti-Mañjuśrī

§ 3. Emanations of the five Dhyānī Buddhas 24
Vāgīśvara, Mañjuvara, Mañjuvajra, Mañjukumāra

§ 4. Independent Forms 27
Arapacana, Sthiracakra, Vādirāṭ, Mañjunātha

CHAPTER III

Bodhisattva Avalokiteśvara 32
1. Ṣaḍakṣarī Lokeśvara 33
2. Simhanāda 35
3. Khasarpaṇa 36
4. Lokanātha 38
5. Hālāhala 40
6. Padmanartteśvara 41
7. Harihariharivāhanodbhava Lokeśvara 44
8. Trailokyavaśaṅkara 45
9. Rakta-Lokeśvara 46
10. Māyājālakrama Avalokiteśvara 47
11. Nīlakaṇṭha 48
12. Sugatisandarśana Lokeśvara 49
13. Pretasantarpita Lokeśvara 50
14. Sukhāvatī Lokeśvara 50
15. Vajradharma Lokeśvara 51

CHAPTER IV

Emanations of Amitābha
§ I. Gods 53
Mahāvala, Saptaśatika-Hayagrīva
§ II. Goddesses 55
Kurukullā, Bhṛkuṭī, Mahāsitavatī

CHAPTER V

Emanations of Akṣobhya
§ I. Gods 60
Caṇḍaroṣaṇa, Heruka, Buddhakapāla, Vajraḍāka
Hayagrīva, Yamārī, Jambhala

CHAPTER VI

Emanations of Akṣobhya (*continued*)
§ II. Goddesses 76
Mahācīnatārā, Jāṅgulī, Ekajaṭā, Parṇaśavarī, Prajñāpāramitā, Vajracarcikā, Mahāmantrānusāriṇī, Mahāpratyaṅgirā, Dhvajāgrakeyūrā Vasudhārā, Nairātmā

CHAPTER VII

Emanations of Vairocana 93
Mārīcī, Uṣṇīṣavijayā, Sitātapatrā-Aparājitā, Mahāsāhasrapramardanī, Vajravārāhī

CHAPTER VIII

Emanations of Amoghasiddhi 106
Khadiravanī Tārā, Vaśyatārā, Ṣaḍbhuja-Sitatārā, Dhanada-Tārā, Parṇaśavarī, Mahāmāyūrī, Vajraśṛṅkhalā

CHAPTER IX

Emanation of Ratnasambhava
§ I. Gods 113
Jambhala, Ucchuṣma Jambhala
§ II. Goddesses 116
Mahāpratisarā, Vasudhārā

CHAPTER X

Emanations of the five Dhyānī Buddhas
§ I. Gods 119
Jambhala, Mahākāla,
§ II. Goddesses 123
Vajratārā, Prajñāpāramitā, Māyājālakrama-Kurukullā, Sitatārā

CHAPTER XI

§ 1. Emanation of four Dhyānī Buddhas 129
Vajratārā
§ 2. Emanation of Vajrasattva 130
Jambhala, Cundā
§ 3. The Pañcarakṣā Maṇḍala 132
Mahāpratisarā, Mahāsāhasrapramardanī Mahāmāyūrī, Mahāmantrānusāriṇī Mahāsitavatī.
§ 4. The Tārās
(i) Ordinary.. 135
(ii) Extraordinary 136

CHAPTER XII

Independent Deities
§ I. Gods 141
Gaṇapati, Bighnāntaka, Vajrahuṅkāra, Bhūtaḍāmara, Vajrajjvālānalārka, Trailokyavijaya, Paramāśva, Nāmasaṅgīti
§ II. Goddesses 150
Sarasvatī, Aparājitā, Vajragāndhārī, Vajrayoginī, Grahamātṛkā, Gaṇapatihṛdayā, Vajravidāraṇī,

CONCLUSION 159

APPENDIX A.

Kiñcit-Vistara-Tārā-Sādhana (*Text with Translation*) .. 169

APPENDIX B.

Descriptions of One Hundred and Eight forms of Avalokiteśvara *appearing in the Macchandar Vahal, Kathmandu, Nepal* .. 177

GLOSSARY 189

BIBLIOGRAPHY 201

INDEX 204

LIST OF PLATES

The image reproduced on the cover is of Mahākāla ; see page 120, and plate XXXVIa.

		PAGE
PLATE I.	(*a*) First page of Sādhanamālā.	*iv*
	(*b*) Another page containing the alphabet.	
	(*c*) Last page of Pañcarakṣā.	
	(*d*) Guru Padmasambhava, (*Bauddh, Nepal*).	
	(*e*) Māyā's dream.	
PLATE II.	THREE CELEBRATED STUPAS OF NEPAL. ..	*xii*
	Simbhū.	
	Bauddh.	
	Kāṭhe Simbhu.	
PLATE III.	THE BUDDHIST TRIAD.	*xx*
	Dharma.	
	Buddha.	
	Saṅgha.	
PLATE IV.	SYMBOL WORSHIP.	*xxii*
	(*a*) Bodhi Tree, (Amarāvatī).	
	(*b*) Buddha's Headdress, (Bharhut).	
	(*c*) Buddha's Footprints, (Bharhut).	
	(*d*) The Wheel-of-the-law, (Bharhut).	
PLATE V.	ĀDI-BUDDHA, VAJRADHARA (*After a Nepalese Painting*).	*xxiv*
PLATE VI.	(*a*) Vajradhara yab-yum, (*Nepal*). ..	*xxviii*
	(*b*) Vajradhara yab-yum, (*Side View*).	
	(*c*) Buddha in different Mudrās, (*Java*).	
	(*d*) Buddha in different Mudrās, (*Nalanda*).	
PLATE VII.	(*a*) Amitābha. ..	2
	(*b*) Akṣobhya, (*Nepal*).	
	(*c*) Akṣobhya.	
	(*d*) Vairocana.	

			Page
PLATE VIII.	(*a*)	Vairocana, (*Nepal*)	4
	(*b*)	Amoghasiddhi.	
	(*c*)	Amoghasiddhi, (*Nepal*).	
	(*d*)	Ratnasambhava.	
PLATE IX.	(*a*)	Ratnasambhava, (*Nepal*).	6
	(*b*)	Vajrasattva, (*Nepal*).	
	(*c*)	Vajrasattva yab-yum, (*Nepal*).	
	(*d*)	Vajrasattva yab-yum, (*side view*).	
	(*e*)	Vajrasattva yab-yum, (*back view*).	
PLATE X.	(*a*)	Vajradhātvīśvarī.	8
	(*b*)	Locanā.	
	(*c*)	Māmakī.	
	(*d*)	Pāṇḍarā.	
PLATE XI.	(*a*)	Āryatārā.	10
	(*b*)	Samantabhadra, (*Nepal*).	
	(*c*)	Vajrapāṇi, (*Nepal*).	
	(*d*)	Ratnapāṇi, (*Nepal*).	
	(*e*)	Padmapāṇi, (*Nepal*).	
	(*f*)	Viśvapāṇi, (*Nepal*).	
PLATE XII.	(*a*)	Samantabhadra.	12
	(*b*)	Vajrapāṇi, (*Indian Museum*).	
	(*c*)	Vajrapāṇi, (*Nalanda*).	
	(*d*)	Seven Mortal Buddhas with Maitreya, (*Indian Museum*	
PLATE XIII.	(*a*)	Vajrāsana, (*Indian Museum*).	14
	(*b*)	Maitreya.	
	(*c*)	Vāk or Vajrarāga Mañjuśrī.	
	(*d*)	Siddhaikavīra, (*Sarnath*).	
PLATE XIV	(*a*)	Nāmasaṅgīti Mañjuśrī.	22
	(*b*)	Nāmasaṅgīti Mañjuśrī ? (*Nepal*).	
	(*c*)	Vajrānaṅga Mañjuśrī.	
	(*d*)	Mahārājalīlā Mañjuśrī, (*Indian Museum*).	
PLATE XV.	(*a*)	Vāgīśvara, (*Nepal*).	24
	(*b*)	Mañjuvara, (*Nalanda*).	
	(*c*)	Mañjuvara, (*Indian Museum*).	
	(*d*)	Mañjuvara, (*Birbhum*).	
PLATE XVI.	(*a*)	Mañjuvara, (*Indian Museum*). ..	26
	(*b*)	Dharmacakra Mañjuśrī, (*Nepal*).	
	(*c*)	Mañjukumāra.	
	(*d*)	Arapacana Mañjuśrī, (*Nepal*).	

			Page
PLATE XVII.	(*a*)	Arapacana, (*Java*). ..	28
	(*b*)	Arapacana, (*Dacca Museum*).	
	(*c*)	Arapacana, (*Nepal*).	
	(*d*)	Sthiracakra, (*Vaṅgīya Sāhitya Pariṣat*).	
PLATE XVIII.	(*a*)	Ṣaḍakṣarī Group, (*Sarnath*).	32
	(*b*)	Ṣaḍakṣarī Group, (*Indian Museum*).	
	(*c*)	Ṣaḍakṣarī Group, (*Birbhum*).	
PLATE XIX.	(*a*)	Ṣaḍakṣarī Lokeśvara, (*Nepal*).	34
	(*b*)	Ṣaḍakṣarī Mahāvidyā, (*Sarnath*).	
	(*c*)	Siṃhanāda, (*Magadha*).	
	(*d*)	Siṃhanāda, (*Nepal*).	
	(*e*)	Siṃhanāda, (*Nepal*).	
PLATE XX.	(*a*)	Siṃhanāda, (*Nepal*)...	36
	(*b*)	Siṃhanāda, (*Mahoba*).	
	(*c*)	Khasarpaṇa, (*Indian Museum*).	
	(*d*)	Lokanātha, (*Mahoba*).	
PLATE XXI.		KHASARPAṆA AVALOKITEŚVARA, (*Vikramur*). ..	38
PLATE XXII.	(*a*)	Lokanātha, (*Nepal*).	40
	(*b*)	Lokanātha, (*Sarnath*).	
	(*c*)	Padmanartteśvara.	
	(*d*)	Hālāhala Lokeśvara, (*Nepal*).	
	(*e*)	Padmanartteśvara, (*Nepal*).	
	(*f*)	Harihariharivāhana Lokeśvara, (*Nepal*).	
PLATE XXIII.	(*a*)	Harihariharivāhana, (*Nepal*).	44
	(*b*)	Harihariharivāhana.	
	(*c*)	Rakta-Lokeśvara.	
	(*d*)	Māyājālakrama-Lokeśvara, (*Nepal*).	
	(*e*)	Nīlakaṇṭha, (*Sarnath*).	
PLATE XXIV.	(*a*)	Last and first page of Abhiṣekavidhi. ..	48
	(*b*)	Sugatisandarśana Lokeśvara.	
	(*c*)	Pretasantarpita Lokeśvara.	
	(*d*)	Sukhāvatī Lokeśvara, (*Nepal*).	
	(*e*)	Vajradharma-Lokeśvara.	
PLATE XXV.	(*a*)	Caṇḍaroṣaṇa.	60
	(*b*)	Buddhakapāla.	
	(*c*)	Heruka, (*Dacca Museum*).	
	(*d*)	Hayagrīva.	

			PAGE
PLATE XXVI.	(*a*)	Yamāntaka, (*Nepal*).	72
	(*b*)	Yamāntaka, (*Nalanda*).	
	(*c*)	Jambhala.	
	(*d*)	Ucchuṣma Jambhala.	
PLATE XXVII.	(*a*)	Mahācīna Tārā.	76
	(*b*)	Mahācīna Tārā.	
	(*c*)	Jāṅgulī.	
	(*d*)	Ekajaṭā, (*Indian Museum*).	
PLATE XXVIII.	(*a*)	Ekajaṭā.	84
	(*b*)	Parṇaśavarī, (*Indian Museum*).	
	(*c*)	Prajñāpāramitā, (*Leiden*).	
	(*d*)	Vajracarcikā.	
PLATE XXIX.	(*a*)	Pratyaṅgirā.	88
	(*b*)	Pratyaṅgirā.	
	(*c*)	Pratyaṅgirā, (*Nepal*).	
	(*d*)	Dhvajāgrakeyūrā.	
PLATE XXX.	(*a*)	Nairātmā, (*Indian Museum*).	90
	(*b*)	Nairātmā, (Vaṅgīya Sāhitya Pariṣat).	
	(*c*)	Aṣṭabhuja-Mārīcī, (*Indian Museum*).	
	(*d*)	Aṣṭabhuja-Mārīcī, (*Indian Museum*).	
PLATE XXXI.	(*a*)	Aṣṭabhuja Mārīcī, (*Lucknow Museum*). ..	100
	(*b*)	Daśabhujasita-Mārīcī.	
	(*c*)	Uṣṇīṣavijayā, (*Indian Museum*).	
	(*d*)	Uṣṇīṣavijayā.	
	(*e*)	Sitātapatrā Aparājitā.	
PLATE XXXII.	(*a*)	Vajravārāhī.	104
	(*b*)	Vajravārāhī, (*Germany*).	
	(*c*)	Khadiravanī Tārā, (*Indian Museum*).	
	(*d*)	Khadiravanī Tārā, (*Mohoba*).	
	(*e*)	Khadiravanī Tārā, (*Dacca Museum*).	
	(*f*)	Khadiravanī Tārā, (*Indian Museum*).	
PLATE XXXIII.	(*a*)	Bhadrāsana Tārā.	108
	(*b*)	Ṣaḍbhuja-Sitatārā.	
	(*c*)	Dhanada Tārā.	
	(*d*)	Parṇaśavarī, (*Vikrampur*).	

PAGE

PLATE XXXIV. (*a*) Parṇaśavarī, (*Vikrampur*). 112
(*b*) Vajraśṛṇkhalā.
(*c*) Jambhala, (*Nepal*).
(*d*) Jambhala, (*Vikrampur*).
(*e*) Jambhala, (*Vikrampur*).

PLATE XXXV. (*a*) Ucchuṣma Jambhala, (*Sarnath*)... .. 116
(*b*) Mahāpratisarā, (*Dacca Museum*).
(*c*) Mahāpratisarā, (*Dacca Sāhitya Pariṣat*).
(*d*) Vasudhārā, (*Nepal*).

PLATE XXXVI. (*a*) Mahākāla, (*Nepal*). 120
(*b*) Vajratārā, (*Indian Museum*).
(*c*) Prajñāpāramitā, (*Indian Museum*).
(*d*) Vajratārā, (*Orissa*).

PLATE XXXVII. (*a*) Vajratārā, (*Nepal*). 130
(*b*) Cundā, (*British Museum*).
(*c*) Mahāpratisarā.
(*d*) Mahāsāhasrapramardanī.

PLATE XXXVIII. (*a*) Mahāmāyūrī. 134
(*b*) Mahāmantrānusāriṇī.
(*c*) Mahāsitavatī.
(*d*) Prasanna-Tārā.

PLATE XXXIX. (*a*) Mahattarī-Tārā, (*Nepal*). 144
(*b*) Bighnāntaka, (*Vaṅgīya Sāhitya Pariṣat*).
(*c*) Trailokyavijaya, (*Bodh Gaya*).
(*d*) Paramāśva.

PLATE XL. (*a*) Nāmasaṅgīti, (*Nepal*). 148
(*b*) Nāmasaṅgīti, (*Nepal*).
(*c*) Āryasarasvatī.
(*d*) Vajraśāradā.
(*e*) Vajraśāradā, (*Nalanda*).

PLATE XLI. (*a*) Mahāsarasvatī. 152
(*b*) Vajrasarasvatī.
(*c*) Aparājitā.
(*d*) Aparājitā, (*Nalanda*).

PLATE XLII. (*a*) Aparājitā, (*Indian Museum*). 156
(*b*) Vajrayogini Temple at Sāṅku, Nepal.
(*c*) Grahamātṛkā.
(*d*) Gaṇapati-Hṛdayā.
(*e*) Vajravidāraṇī.

			PAGE
PLATE XLIII.	1.	Hayagrīva, Lokeśvara.	178
	2.	Mojaghāñjavala (?) Lokeśvara.	
	3.	Hālāhala Lokeśvara.	
	4.	Hariharihariväthana Lokeśvara.	
PLATE XLIV.	5.	Māyājālakrama Lokeśvara.	178
	6.	Ṣaḍakṣarī Lokeśvara.	
	7.	Ānandādi Lokeśvara.	
	8.	Vaśyādhikāra Lokeśvara.	
PLATE XLV.	9.	Potapāda Lokeśvara.	178
	10.	Kamaṇḍalu Lokeśvara.	
	11.	Varadāyaka Lokeśvara.	
	12.	Jaṭāmukuṭa Lokeśvara.	
PLATE XLVI.	13.	Sukhāvatī Lokeśvara.	178
	14.	Pretasantarpita Lokeśvara.	
	15.	Māyājālakramakrodha Lokeśvara.	
	16.	Sugatisandarśana Lokeśvara.	
PLATE XLVII.	17.	Nīlakaṇṭha Lokeśvara.	180
	18.	Lokanātharaktāryyāvalokiteśvara.	
	19.	Trailokyasandarśana Lokeśvara.	
	20.	Siṃhanātha Lokeśvara.	
PLATE XLVIII.	21.	Khasarpaṇa Lokeśvara.	180
	22.	Maṇipadma Lokeśvara.	
	23.	Vajradharma Lokeśvara.	
	24.	Pupala Lokeśvara.	
PLATE XLIX.	25.	Utnauti (?) Lokeśvara.	180
	26.	Vṛṣṇācana Lokeśvara.	
	27.	Brahmadaṇḍa Lokeśvara.	
	28.	Acāta (?) Lokeśvara.	
PLATE L.	29.	Mahāvajrasattva Lokeśvara.	180
	30.	Viśvahana Lokeśvara.	
	31.	Śākyabuddha Lokeśvara.	
	32.	Śāntāsi Lokeśvara.	
PLATE LI.	33.	Jamadaṇḍa Lokeśvara.	182
	34.	Vajroṣṇīṣa Lokeśvara.	
	35.	Vajrahuntika Lokeśvara.	
	36.	Jñānadhātu Lokeśvara.	

			Page
PLATE LII.	37.	Kāraṇḍavyūha Lokeśvara.	182
	38.	Sarvaṇivaraṇaviṣkambhī Lokeśvara.	
	39.	Sarvaśokatamonirghāta Lokeśvara.	
	40.	Pratibhānakakūṭa Lokeśvara.	
PLATE LIII.	41.	Amṛtaprabha Lokeśvara.	182
	42.	Jālinīprabha Lokeśvara.	
	43.	Candraprabha Lokeśvara.	
	44.	Avalokita Lokeśvara.	
PLATE LIV.	45.	Vajragarbha Lokeśvara.	182
	46.	Sāgaramati Lokeśvara.	
	47.	Ratnapāṇi Lokeśvara.	
	48.	Gaganagañja Lokeśvara.	
PLATE LV.	49.	Ākāśagarbha Lokeśvara.	184
	50.	Ksītigarbha Lokeśvara.	
	51.	Akṣayamati Lokeśvara.	
	52.	Sṛṣṭikāntā Lokeśvara.	
PLATE LVI.	53.	Sāmantabhadra Lokeśvara.	184
	54.	Mahāsahasrabhuja Lokeśvara.	
	55.	Mahāratnakīrti Lokeśvara.	
	56.	Mahāśankhanātha Lokeśvara.	
PLATE LVII.	57.	Mahāsahasrasūryya Lokeśvara. ..	184
	58.	Mahāratnakula Lokeśvara.	
	59.	Mahāpaṭala Lokeśvara.	
	60.	Mahāmañjudatta Lokeśvara.	
PLATE LVIII.	61.	Mahācandrabimba Lokeśvara.	184
	62.	Mahāsūryyabimba Lokeśvara.	
	63.	Mahā-abhayaphalada Lokeśvara.	
	64.	Mahā-abhayakarī Lokeśvara.	
PLATE LIX.	65.	Mahāmañjubhūta Lokeśvara.	186
	66.	Mahāviśvaśūddha Lokeśvara.	
	67.	Mahāvajradhātu Lokeśvara.	
	68.	Mahāvajradhṛk Lokeśvara.	
PLATE LX.	69.	Mahāvajrapāṇi Lokeśvara.	186
	70.	Mahāvajranātha Lokeśvara.	
	71.	Amoghapāśa Lokeśvara.	
	72.	Devadevatā Lokeśvara.	

			Page
PLATE LXI.	73.	Piṇḍapātra Lokeśvara.	186
	74.	Sārthavāha Lokeśvara.	
	75.	Ratnadala Lokeśvara.	
	76.	Viṣṇupāṇi Lokeśvara.	
PLATE LXII.	77.	Kamalacandra Lokeśvara.	186
	78.	Vajrakhaṇḍa Lokeśvara.	
	79.	Acalaketu Lokeśvara.	
	80.	Śiriṣarā (?) Lokeśvara.	
PLATE LXIII.	81.	Dharmacakra Lokeśvara.	188
	82.	Harivāhana Lokeśvara.	
	83.	Sarasiri (?) Lokeśvara.	
	84.	Harihara Lokeśvara.	
PLATE LXIV.	85.	Siṃhanāda Lokeśvara.	188
	86.	Viśvavajra Lokeśvara.	
	87.	Amitābha Lokeśvara.	
	88.	Vajrasattvadhātu Lokeśvara.	
PLATE LXV.	89.	Viśvabhūta Lokeśvara.	188
	90.	Dharmadhātu Lokeśvara.	
	91.	Vajradhātu Lokeśvara.	
	92.	Śākyabuddha Lokeśvara.	
PLATE LXVI.	93.	Cittadhātu Lokeśvara.	188
	94.	Cintāmaṇi Lokeśvara.	
	95.	Śāntamati Lokeśvara.	
	96.	Mañjunātha Lokeśvara.	
PLATE LXVII.	97.	Viṣṇucakra Lokeśvara.	188
	98.	Kṛtāñjali Lokeśvara.	
	99.	Viṣṇukāntā Lokeśvara.	
	100.	Vajrasṛṣṭa Lokeśvara.	
PLATE LXVIII.	101.	Śaṅkhanātha Lokeśvara.	188
	102.	Vidyāpati Lokeśvara.	
	103.	Nityanātha Lokeśvara.	
	104.	Padmapāṇi Lokeśvara.	
PLATE LXIX.	105.	Vajrapāṇī Lokeśvara.	188
	106.	Mahāsthāmaprāpta Lokeśvara.	
	107.	Vajranātha Lokeśvara.	
	108.	Śrīmadāryyāvalokiteśvara.	

TRANSLITERATION

So many systems of transliteration are in existence that it is almost impossible to say which one is the standard. In the present work I have generally followed Professor Foucher, and the following examples of transcription in Roman are noteworthy in it :—

च	*represented as*	.. C
छ	..	.. CHH
च्छ	..	.. CCH
ष	..	.. Ṣ
श	..	.. Ś *or* Ṡ

FOREWORD.

All the three great religious systems of India developed well-filled pantheons, and it is not always easy to decide, to which of these three systems a particular image should be assigned. The importance of the study of Iconography which primarily concerns itself with the proper recognition of images will thus become apparent.

The difficulties of the investigator are again increased by the fact that free and frequent interchanges of deities took place among the three religious systems. Hindu deities Pārvatī and Indra are to be found among the Jainas* ; the latter, as well as Gaṇapati, Sarasvatī, Mahākāla, Nīlakantha, and the like, are famous in the Buddhist Pantheon. The Hindus are indebted to the Buddhists for borrowing gods like Mahācīnatārā, Jāṅgulī and Vajrayoginī under the names of Tārā, Manasā and Chhinnamastā respectively. Thus we have evidence that free interchanges of gods actually did take place first at the very outset of Buddhism and Jainism as well as in the more promiscuous Tāntric age. The Jainas and the Buddhists alike borrowed Hindu gods in their earlier stages, † but in the Tāntric age, the Buddhist gods were commonly exploited.

The problem of correct identification of images, therefore, presents a real difficulty, and great scholars have, more than once, attempted solutions. Professors Waddel, Grünwedel, Foucher, Burgess, Miss Getty, and many others have written useful works and gathered together a considerable amount of information on Buddhist Iconography.

But unfortunately the Pantheon of the Indian Vajrayānists has not been very much explored. Alice Getty and Deniker's work deals with Tibetan gods only, and the purely Indian gods seem to have attracted little notice from them. It is Professor Foucher who drew our attention first in 1900 and then five years later by the publication of his two parts of "Etude sur l'Iconographie Bouddhique de l'Inde," to a fruitful source of research in this direction. His curiosity was first aroused by a study of the illustrations given

* Indra appears in the Jaina Cave Temples at Ellora. For his image in Buddhist schools of sculptures, *see* Grünwedel : *Buddhist Art in India* p. 140 *et sqq.*

† The Jainas borrowed early Hindu gods like Brahmā, Kārttikeya, Kuvera, Gaurī, and Ambikā, (*See* I. A. Vol. XXXII, 159 *et sqq.*) and Buddhist Tāntric deities, such as, Yakṣeśvara, Vajraśṛṅkhalā, Gāndhārī, Bhṛkutī, Śyāmā and Aparājitā.

in many of the Nepal Manuscripts, and then he tried to identify the sculptures. For this purpose he hunted out Sādhanas from the Sādhanamālā and was surprised to find that the Buddhist gods tallied most accurately with the descriptions given in the Sādhanamālā. His second volume embodies a scrutinizing, though partial, study of the Sādhanamālā, and it was this book which first drew the attention of scholars to the necessity of referring to such Buddhist Tāntric texts of rituals, in order to make or justify any identification. When I was working under Professor Foucher in the Indian Museum as a Government Research Scholar he asked me to edit and study the different recensions of the Sādhanamālā and the Sādhanasamuccaya, and I began a systematic study, the result of which is embodied in this volume.

The Sādhanamālā, however, does not exhaust the materials for the study of Indian Iconography. The earliest manuscript of the Sādhanamālā belongs to the year A. D. 1167, and many of the later developments have been incorporated in the work, entitled, Dharmakoṣasaṅgraha by Paṇḍit Amṛtānanada who was the Residency Paṇḍit when B. Hodgson was the Resident of Nepal. A manuscript of this work is preserved in the Durbar Library, Nepal, and there is also a copy in the library of the Asiatic Society of Bengal in the Government Collection. The Niṣpannayogāmbara Tantra by Paṇḍit Abhayākara Gupta, who flourished in the 12th century A. D., contains details of no less than twenty-three Maṇḍalas with the descriptions of all gods constituting the Maṇḍala, the number sometimes being a very large one. Then there are the Heruka and Hevajra Tantras, Caṇḍamahāroṣaṇa-Tantra, Vajravārāhī-Tantra, Kriyā-Samuccaya, Vajrāvalī-Tantra, Yoginījāla-Tantra and numerous other Buddhist Tāntric works, the manuscripts of which are to be found either in the Durbar Library of Nepal, or in the University Library of Cambridge, or in the library of the Asiatic Society of Bengal. Thus there is still an extensive field for research in the direction indicated above.

It is admitted on all hands that the most urgent need of Buddhist Iconography is a thorough study and an accurate edition of the Sādhanamālā and similar collections. It contains about 300 Sādhanas enjoining the procedure for worshipping in the Buddhist Tāntric fashion, about 300 deities. Sometimes three or four Sādhanas describe the same deity ; when this is the case, we may assume that there is at least some slight difference either in the form or in the procedure of worship as elaborated in the different Sādhanas. The Sādhanas contained in the Sādhanamālā vary considerably in length. There are several copies of the manuscript, but there is no agreement between any two of the manuscripts as regards the number of

Sādhanas included. There is another similar collection, which goes by the name of Sādhanasamuccaya. Though the name is different, a comparative study revealed that the two collections were almost identical. For instance, if we compare the two lists of Sādhanas, one in the Sādhanamālā and another in the Sādhanasamuccaya, given on p. 181ff. under No. 112 and p. 179ff. under No. 111 in the Descriptive Catalogue of Sanskrit MSS in the Government Collection, Vol. I, Buddhist MSS, by Mahāmahopādhyāya Haraprasād Śhāstrī, it will be seen that except the Sādhana for Vajratīkṣṇa, a form of Mañjuśrī, the Sādhanasamuccaya has no difference from the Sādhanamālā. Similarly the two lists given by the same scholar on p. 264ff and 200ff in his Catalogue of Palm-leaf and Selected Paper MSS belonging to the Durbar Library, Nepal, Vol. II, may be compared. The result would be that the Sādhanas Nos. 59, 73, 76, 154 in the Sādhanasamuccaya would be different from the Sādhanamālā. There are also several lists of Sādhanas in the two Collections given in pp. 372-299, Vol. I, and pp. 1-66, Vol. II, of the "Catalogue du Fonds Tibetain de la Bibliotheque Nationale" by P. Cordier. A perusal of these lists would show how Sādhanas once extant in India are now lost to it and preserved in the pages of the Tibetan Tangyur. Scholars knowing Tibetan can do immense service to Indian Buddhist Iconography by studying the Tibetan translations of the Sādhanas.

There are altogether six Sanskrit MSS of the Sādhanamālā and Sādhanasamuccaya in India. Out of these, three are in the Government Collection now under the care of the Asiatic Society of Bengal, and three others are in the Durbar Library, Nepal. There are three manuscripts also in the University Library, Cambridge (Nos. ADD. 1593, 1648, 1686). Out of these nine, seven were used by me in preparing the text on which the present work in based. Mr. P. J. Hartog, M.A., C.I.E., Vice-Chancellor of the Dacca University, kindly obtained for me the loan of MS No. 1593 of Cambridge. I hope to utilize the other two MSS also, (if available), before the text of the Sādhanamālā is finally edited for printing.

Out of the nine manuscripts referred to, one is as old as 1167 A. D.* as the Colophon asserts ; it is in palm-leaf and belongs to the University Library, Cambridge. The next important MS also in palm-leaf belongs to the Durbar

* About this date there is no controversy. There is another MS. (No. Add. 1648) which in dated in N. S. 226 or A. D. 1106 as given in Appendix IX in Wright's *History of Nepal*, p. 323. C. Bendall reads the date as 336 N. S. or 1216 A. D. This date also is retouched and therefore doubtful. The date on which we can rely is the date on the cover, viz., N. S. 458 or A. D. 1338. Bendall : *Cambridge Catalogue*, p. 154.

Library, Nepal and may be assigned to the end of the 13th century on palæographical grounds. It is written in Bengali character and the writing exactly corresponds to the writing of the MS of Pañcarakṣâ, which was written in the reign of Madhusena, king of Gauḍa in Śaka 1211 * corresponding to A. D. 1289. Two pages, (one containing the alphabet), of the Sādhanamālā and one of Pañcarakṣā (Plate I, a-b-c) are reproduced side by side for ready reference. Other MSS however, do not call for further comments beyond those given in the respective Catalogues of MSS. I am sure, numerous other MSS of Sādhanamālā and Sādhanasamuccaya would be discovered if a thorough search is made in Nepal. For, it was at one time so popular that the priests of every monastery kept one for constant use and the number of monasteries at Kāṭhmāṇḍu alone is no less than five hundred.

We have already described the MS materials that are extant for the study of the Sādhanamālā, which is a collection of the Sādhanas. I would now endeavour to give an idea as to what a Sādhana means. The word 'Sādhana' has been translated by C. Bendall as 'charm' † but the real meaning should be 'procedure for worship.' The Mantra may be translated by the word 'charm,' but as the Sādhanas contain sometimes many of them besides numerous other things, it cannot be translated by the word 'charm.' Professor Foucher has indeed given an idea in the second part of his *Etude sur l'Iconographic Bouddhique de l'Inde* by summarising a Sādhana. Here also a Sādhana is translated in Appendix A. It will appear from a look at this translation that such a long procedure cannot be translated away by the short word 'charm'. The Sādhanas generally begin with a salutation to the Tathāgatas or to the deity for whose worship the Sādhana is composed or to the Guru of the writer. At the end also there is a Maṅgala Śloka expressing the pious wish that all sentient beings may attain salvation. The Sādhanas are composed in a very defective Sanskrit ‡; they contain sometimes old Ben-

* *See* description of the MS of Pañcarakṣā, A. S. B. Library No. 4078, Catalogue No. 77, in Śhāstrī's *Buddhist Volume* p. 117 ; also his paper entitled, " Vāṅgālār Purāṅa Akṣara " in the Vaṅgīya Sāhitya Pariṣat Pātrikā, B. S. 1327, p. 9.

† *See* for instance, Bendall : *Cambridge Catalogue*, p. 154.

‡ A word should be said about the language of the Sādhanas, which is full of grammatical errors of metre and spelling. The defective Sanskrit sometimes makes the meaning very obscure. But the Buddhists never cared for correct Sanskrit as is evident from the following quotation from the *Vimalprabhā*, A. S. B. Library No. 4727, Cat. No. 66. " Teṣāñca suśabdavādīnāṃ suśabdagrahavināśāya arthaśaraṇatāmāśritya kvacit vṛtte apaśabdaḥ kvacit vṛtte yatibhaṅgaḥ. Kvacit avibhaktikaṃ padaṃ, kvacit varṇasvaro lopaḥ, kvacit vṛtte dīrgho hrasvaḥ, hrasvo'pi dīrghaḥ kvacit pañcamyar the saptamī caturthyarthe ṣaṣṭhī kutracit parasmaipadini dhātau ātmanepadaṃ. kvacit ekavacane vahuvacanaṃ, vahuvacane ekavacanaṃ. . . . *See* Śhāstrīs *Des. Catal.* Vol. 1 (Buddhist Mss), p. 78.

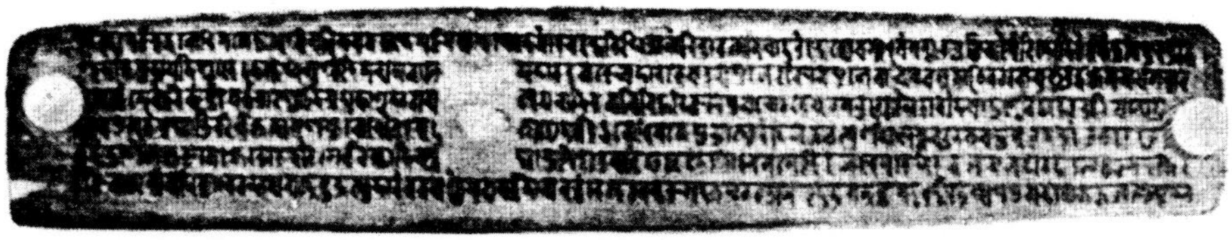

(a) First page of Sādhanamālā (Palm-leaf MS from Nepal)

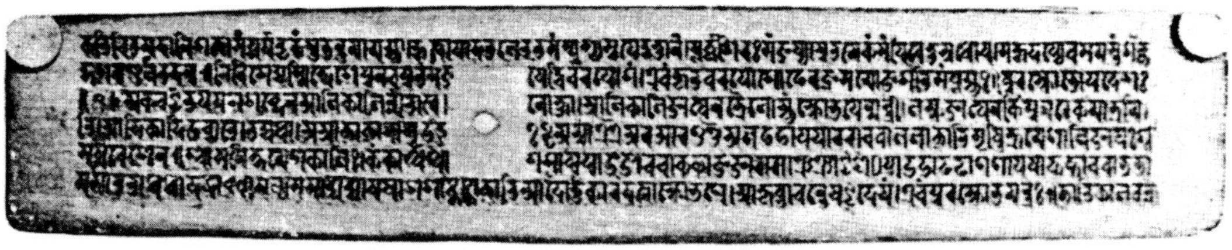

(b) Another page containing the alphabet (Palm-leaf MS from Nepal)

(c) Last page of Pañcarakṣā (MS in A.S.B.)

(d) Guru Padmasambhava (Bauddh)

(e) Māyā's Dream (Bharhut)

Plate I

gali songs of the same nature as those recorded by Mahāmahopādhyāya Hara-prāsād Śhāstrī in his " Bauddha Gān O Dohā." *

For the purpose of Iconography, the Dhyānas or the descriptive conceptions of the deity, are most important. In the specimen Sādhana translated in the Appendix, the Dhyāna has been omitted as practically all the Dhyānas on the types of the deities have been quoted and translated in the body of the book. In understanding the Dhyānas one thing must be remembered that the Buddhists unlike the Hindus did not believe in the separate existence, or the duality, of the worshipped and the worshipper—at least in the time of meditating on the form of the deity. The Sādhanamālā is always particular in saying that the worshipper should meditate (dhyāyāt) himself (ātmānam) as the god (Bhagavantaṃ) or the goddess (Bhagavatīṃ). The Hindus, however, so far as the ritual is concerned, generally postulate a separate existence of the worshipped from the worshipper. In rare cases, however, they regard the non-duality as essential ; but then, the Hindus in such cases must be disciples of the Buddhists.

Sometimes the Sādhanas state the names of the authors in the Colophons. The text that I have prepared contains the names of a good many authors. They are :—

1. Kumudākara, 2. Ratnākaragupta, 3. Padmākaramati, 4. Advayavajra, 5. Anupamarakṣita, 6. Sarahapāda, 7. Muktaka, 8. Cintāmaṇi Datta, 9. Harihara, 10. Śubhākara, 11. Prabhākarakīrti, 12. Nāgārjuna, 13. Ratnā karaśānti, 14. Garbhapāda, 15. Padmavardhana, 16. Asaṅgapāda 17. Manoratharakṣita, 18. Indrabhūti, 19. Sahajavilāsa, 20. Karuṇā, 21. Candramākaramati, 22. Kukkurīpāda, 23. Kalyāṇagarbha, 24. Durjayacandra, 25. Śāśvatavajra, 26. Trailokyavajra, 27. Virūpākṣa, 28. Guṇākaragupta, 29. Maṅgalasena, 30. Kumārākaragupta, 31. Abhayākaragupta, 32. Sujanabhadra, and 33. Sumatibhadra.

As these authors will have to be dealt with in the forthcoming edition of the text, I do not deal with them elaborately here. Suffice it to say, for our present purpose, that all these authors are well-known in Tibetan Tangyur, that they flourished in the Tāntric age in India, and that most of them hailed from Bengal.

* As in the Sādhana for Mahāmāyā. Mss. A—254, Na—94, C—199.—
" Phale sahi viasia kamalu paccohiu vajjeñ ।
Alalalalahoḥ mahāsuhena ārohiu nṛtyeñ ।
Ravikiraṇena paphullia kamalu mahāsuhena nṛtyeñ ॥ "

In the earlier phases of Buddhism we do not generally meet with the representations of gods. The scenes from Buddha's life, and the Jātaka stories were more or less depicted. Sculptures and railings of Sanchi and Bharhut are examples of this kind. It is in the Gandhara School of Art that images of Buddha and Bodhisattva Avalokiteśvara (?) first made their appearance. The sculptural remains at Amarāvatī are contemporaneous with the Gandhara School. The Mathura School followed closely and then came the sculptures of Sarnath, Magadha, Bengal, Java and Nepal in the Tāntric age. The paintings at Ajantā begin from the first century and continue down to the sixth century, and the sculptures of Ellora and some other Buddhist Cave Temples of Southern and Western India show that the influences of immature Tantra had begun to work. It has already been said that vigorous endeavour has been made to study and identify the sculptural remains of the Pre-Tāntric age, while those of the Tāntric age, up to now, have received little attention from scholars. Images are daily coming out from the ancient sites of Sarnath and Nalanda and we may well expect to discover a good many more from the other ancient sites, such as the Odantapuri, Vikramaśīla and Jagaddal monastaries, where Tāntric learning flourished most. That Bengal in the Mediæval period was practically Buddhist is well borne out by the still prevalent worship of Dharma, Mañjughoṣa, and by the numerous Buddhist sculptures that are constantly discovered in both Eastern as well as Western Bengal.

The Superintendents of the Archaeological Department, especially of the Eastern and the Central Circles often find it difficult to identify the new Buddhist finds, and in the absence of trustworthy materials, identifications are not always happy. Individual cases of what appeared to me to be wrong identifications I have referred to in the body of the book. I am sure that the authors themselves would not have hesitated to propose corrections had they the benefit of the new materials that are now given to the public. It is quite possible that many more instances of wrong identifications have escaped me. But I venture to hope that the work of rectification will now be facilitated by a reference to the many Dhyānas and the descriptions given in the present work. I do not, however, ask my readers to accept all my identifications, which are interspersed throughout the book. In all cases I have attempted to give my authorities and I shall welcome different interpretations and suggestions of new explanations.

The wealth of sculptural and bronze remains in Nepal have not yet received the attention they deserve. Nepal is the only place which presents an abundance of materials for the study of Iconography, especially Buddhist

Iconography. Some of the Buddhist monasteries at Patan are so rich in images that they can be said to constitute small museums by themselves. One hundred and eight sculptures alone appear in the Stūpa of Bauddhanāth (Vulgo-Baudh) in Nepal, and the art and technique of the sculptures and occasional images of Guru Padmasambhava bespeaks the Tibetan character of this temple. Out of these one hundred and eight images, forty-seven are in yab-yum and the rest are single. About ten of the single images represent Siddhapuruṣas of Tibet,—Mila-ras-pa, Padmasambhava and others. Though these images are Tibetan in character, they contain, nevertheless, some of the purely Indian Buddhist gods of the Vajrayāna Pantheon, for example, the images of Ṣaḍakṣarī Lokeśvara, Vāk, Heruka, Yamāntaka, and the like. There is a statement in a Tibetan work that in the matter of Art, the Bengal Art is the best, next to it is the Art of Nepal and the worst are those of Tibet and China. A specimen of Tibetan Art,—an image of Guru Padmasambhava from Baudh,—is illustrated in Plate I, d.

In the present work, endeavour has been made to identify the images of Buddhist deities by means of the Dhyānas given in the Sādhanamālā. Where images could not be procured, we have tried to illustrate the Sādhana with the help of sketches or drawings. These drawings have been copied from the ancestral albums of the native Citrakāras of Nepal, who are Buddhists. We have been able to secure a good number of drawings through the kind offices of Gubhāju Siddhiharṣa and Vīramān Citrakāra, both belonging to Kathmandu, Nepaḷ. Where the sketches present a wide variation from the Dhyāna we have not ventured to reproduce them ; thus we had to reject about fifty drawings brought from Nepal.

The great majority of Buddhist deities are believed to have emanated from one or the other of the five Dhyānī Buddhas, and Iconographists will agree with me in holding that the most scientific classification of the Buddhist deities is to sort out and classify them according to their parental Dhyānī Buddhas. As Mañjuśrī and Avalokiteśvara, the two most important Bodhisattvas each have a very large number of Sādhanas applicable to himself, they have been treated in separate chapters. The divinities who cannot be definitely stated to be emanations of any Dhyānī Buddha, have been termed as *Independent* and dealt with in a separate chapter.

Dhyānas have been quoted from the Sādhanamālā and translations have been given in each case. Dhyānas of the same deity without any marked variation have not been quoted, but the variations have been noted in all cases. It is necessary here to point out that Professor Foucher has given a number of Sādhanas from the Sādhanamālā with translations in French in the second part of his *Etude sur l'Iconographie Bouddhique de l'Inde.* These Sādhanas have not been omitted from the present work to ensure completeness,—also because Prof. Foucher's work is in French, and English is more readily understood in India than French.

As the complete text of the Sādhanamālā as collated from seven manuscripts in different collections is now ready and will be published in due course, we consider it useless to burden the present work with different readings given in different MSS while quoting the text. Different readings have, however, been given in cases where they involve a marked difference in meaning. The reading which seemed to me to be correct has always been given in the body of the text while the variants have been noted in the footnotes. Folia references of the following three MSS only are given when quoting the text of Sādhanamālā.

N. MS in palm-leaf belonging to the Durbar Library, Nepal. It is divided into two parts with two sets of pagination. In the first part, references are given as 'N—1,' and in the second, as 'Na—1.'

A. MS in paper belonging to the Government Collection in the Library of the Asiatic Society of Bengal, serial No. 8051 and Catalogue No. 74.

C. MS No. Add. 1593 in paper belonging to the University Library, Cambridge.

When a Dhyāna is quoted all the three references in Folia are given, for instance, N—1, A—1 and C—1.

When the images do not exactly correspond to the description given in the Dhyānas the difference is duly noted. Minor differences do not stand in the way of identification, as will be found in the cases of Siṃhanāda Lokeśvara, Mañjuvara, Ucchuṣma Jambhala, and several others, and they have been passed over.

In the *Introduction*, an attempt has been made to trace the history of Buddhism from the birth of Buddha down to its fall in India with the coming of the Muhammadans. This history has been traced in three different aspects, —(1) Doctrine, (2) Art, and (3) Literature.

The photographs in all cases, unless otherwise stated, have been reproduced from my negatives. But some have also been taken from the publications of the Archaeological Department and similar other publications.

THE AUTHOR.

INTRODUCTION.

§ I. *A Brief Historical Survey of Buddhism.*

Buddha was born during a period of intellectual ferment. The bold speculations of the old seers in the Āraṇyakas and the Upaniṣads were confined within the circle of the Brahmanical society. But soon after these speculations were ventilated, there appeared to have grown a large and extensive Āryāvarta which geographically included nearly the whole of Northern India, and no more comprised exclusively of the Brahmins and their followers, but included within its fold, some of the nomadic tribes just settling down to an ordered and civilized state of existence.

These tribes were, as they called themselves, the Kṣattriyas. They were fond of war, and after reducing the original inhabitants into the condition of the serfs, they remained there in right royal style, living in splendid cities and indulging in all sorts of moral, intellectual and artistic pursuits. Their number was very large towards the East and North-East of the old Aryan land, and the Śākyas, Vṛjjis, Videhas and Mallas, all belonged to this sort of unincorporated Kṣattriyas. The Kurus, the Pāñcālas, the Saurāṣṭras and the Ikṣvākus were more or less influenced by the culture of the Brahmins. As a result of the great upheaval in the domain of intellect and temperament mentioned above, some of the choicest spirits sprung from among the Kṣattriyas—men who profoundly influenced the subsequent Indian thought. Seven names stand forth as the most prominent in the matter of philosophy and religion. These are—Buddha, Mahāvīra, Gosālā Maṅkhāliputtra, Sañjaya Bellaṭṭhiputtra, Kakuda Kātyāyana, Pūrṇa Kāśyapa and Ajitakeśakambala. We are, of course, here concerned only with Buddha, and the system of philosophy of which he is the founder.

The ethical system of Buddha was based mainly on the Śāṅkhya, but profoundly modified by his own speculations. The boldness of the speculation, the grandeur of the moral idea set forth, and the strictness of discipline gave his system an attractive and engaging character. People of all shades of thought came to him and he incorporated them within his own fold and kept them in harmony as long as he lived.

But with the death of Buddha things changed and dissentions crept in, and though the Elders for a time succeeded in checking all schismatic efforts of the Youngers, it was at Vaiśālī that they parted company, never to be united again, on points which to the modern historian appear exceedingly minor and trifling. The Youngers, however, thought, as we learn it from the *Mahāvastu Avadāna,* that the difference was fundamental and far-reaching.

Thus the whole camp was divided into two parties. Those who stuck to Ethics and moral discipline were called the Therāvādins, and those who trifled with Ethics and discipline but stuck to metaphysical and altruistic doctrines were called the Mahāsāṅghikas. One point of difference is very marked,—the Youngers were all Lokottaravādins and believed in the superhuman character of Buddha. But schisms bring forth further schisms, and in the course of a century, the two parties split up into eighteen principal sects, beside a number of minor ones.

One of the Therāvādin sects, the Vaibhajyavādin or the Analytical sect was favoured by Aśoka, and rose to prominence. They sent missionaries to all parts of India and outside and succeeded in converting a multitude of people. But with the dismemberment of the Maurya Empire, the Buddhists fell on evil days. The relentless persecution of three successive Brahmin dynasties proved too much for the new faith. Young and vigorous, bold and speculative as the Mahāsāṅghikas were, they sought new fields for their activities beyond the dwindling empire of the Brahmins. They were most active amongst the new settlers in India, the Śakas, the Yavanas, the Pahlavas, and the Kuṣāṇas. The Vibhajyavādins, losing their prestige under the persecuting zeal of Puṣyamitra and his successors, seem to have fled to South and made at last Ceylon their home, where their doctrines can even now be studied in all their pristine purity.

The Mahāsāṅghikas made a headway at the time of Kaṇiṣka. In the Council held in his time, the Thderāvādins were very feebly represented and the Vibhajyavādins were not existent. The Mahāsāṅghikas made a commentary on the sayings of Buddha called "Bibhāṣā." The whole literature is now lost in the original but fragments exist in Chinese translations. At the Council of Kaṇiṣka there was a small but pushing sect called the Mahāyāna, but at that Assembly they did not count. But two generations later they made a great headway under Nāgārjuna and his powerful disciple, Āryadeva. Both of them were absolute Śūnyavādins. Buddha himself did not go beyond Arhatship. He held out to his followers as a reward for their discipline Arhatship, or an escape from the miseries of birth, old age and death, in other words, from the evils of transmigration. All speculations beyond Arhatship Buddha discouraged as of no use. But bolder spirits after him could not resist the temptation of speculating, and their speculations ended in the time of Nāgārjuna in Śūnyavāda. But in a very short time Śunyavāda failed to satsify the hancquerings of the Mahāyānists and so Maitreyanātha, one or two generations after Nāgārjuna, added *Vijñāna* to it, and founded what developed later on as the Yogācāra System.

The *Aṣṭasāhasrikā Prajñāpāramitā* which Nāgārjuna is said to have rescued from the nether regions became the standard work of the Śūnyavādins, and the same work as modified by the ideas of Maitreyanātha became the *Pañcaviṃśati-sāhasrikā Prajñāpāramitā.* This again, became the standard work of the Vijñānavādins. The Aṣṭasāhasrikā is divided into thirty-two chapters, while the Pañcaviṃśati-Sāhasrikā is divided into eight only, following the chapters of Maitreyanātha's work.

The controversy between the Śūnyavādins and the Vijñāvādins raged for several centuries and many ranged themselves on both sides. But in the 8th. century people were not satisfied with Vijñānavāda. They imported into it another element called the Mahāsukhavāda, so that after ordinary Nirvāṇa there were three elements, nemaly, Śūnya, Vijñāna and Mahāsukha. It is form Mahāsukha that Vajrayāna originated, and Vajrayāna is the system rich in iconographical ideas.

To understand the rise of Vajrayāna we shall have to go back to the teachings of Buddha. He had two Yānas, the Śrāvakayāna and the Pratyekayāna. The Śrāvakas were to hear from a Buddha, but they had to wait till the advent of another Buddha, for their emanacipation. In the meanwhile the Śrāvakas could teach, but they could neither attain, nor help others in attaining Nirvāṇa. The Pratyekas were eminent men ; they could attain Nirvāṇa by their own efforts without the help of a Buddha ; but they could not impart Nirvāṇa to others.

Buddhism continued in this state till the rise of the Mahāyāna whose proper name is Bodhisattvayāna. The Mahāyānist contemptuously called the previous Yānas as Hīnayānas. They held that they could by their own exertion reach Nirvāṇa and even Buddhahood, and help others in attaining both. The distinction between the Mahāyāna and Hīnayāna is graphically described in the first book of the *Mahāyānasūttrālaṃkāra* attributed to Asaṅga.

Thus there were three Yānas in Buddhism about the 2nd. and 3rd. centuries A.D. But there were four Schools of Philosophy, Sarvāstivāda (Sautrāntika), Vāhyārthabhaṅga (Baibhāṣika), Vijñānavāda (Yogācāra) and Śūnyavāda (Mādhyamaka). How these four systems were distributed amongst the three Yānas is one of the vital questions of Buddhism. But no light has been thrown on it as yet by the extant European or modern Indian literature on Buddhism. Happily, the discovery of an ancient manuscript entitled,

Tattvaratnāvalī, by Advayavajra has dispelled the darkness. Advayavajra was a Bengali and he flourished in the 12th century. He was a Bengali because he commented upon the Bengali *Dohākoṣa* by Sarahavajra, who flourished in the 11th century. He says :—" There are three Yānas, Śrāvakayāna, Pratyekayāna and Mahāyāna. There are four theories, Baibhāṣika, Sautrāntika, Yogācāra and Mādhyamaka. Śrāvakayāna and Pratyekayāna are explained by the theory of the Baibhāṣikas. Mahāyāna is of two kinds, Pāramitānaya and Mantranaya. Pāramitās are explained by the theories either of Sautrāntika, Yogācāra or Mādhyamaka ; Mantranaya is explained by the theories of Yogācāra and Mādhyamaka only." *

So Mantranaya commences with the most abstruse theories of Śūnyavāda and Vijñānavāda. Advayavajra postpones the explanation of Mantranaya in one place, and says,—" Mantranaya is very abstruse. It concerns with men who seek emancipation by deep and solemn methods. It is also very extensive owing to the understanding of such theories as the four symbolic representations. Therefore, we are not fit to explain it".† He cites for his authority—" Mantraśāstra transcends all other Śāstras, because, though all Śāstras have the same common object, there is no fear of ignorance here. The means are many, and they are not difficult of attainment, but it can be attained only by men whose senses are sharpened to the highest degree. On this point we have written a work, *Sekanirṇaya*.‡

The *Sekanirṇaya* is a short work in the same bundle of manuscripts by the same author. It accepts the Mahāsukha theory and dilates upon the various stages of the development of Mahāsukha, which, according to the author, is not possible to attain without the Śakti, the embodiment of Karuṇā.

* " Tatra trīṇi Yānāni, Śrāvakayānaṃ, Pratyekayānaṃ, Mahāyānaṃ ceti. Sthitayaḥ catasraḥ, Vaibhāṣika-Sautrāntika-Yogācāra-Mādhyamakabhedena. Tatra Vaibhāṣikasthityā Śrāvakayānaṃ Pratyekayānañca vyākhyāyate. Mahāyānañca dvividhaṃ Pāramitānayo Mantranayaśceti. Tatra Pāramitānayaḥ Sautrāntika-Yogācāra-Mādhyamakasthityā vyakhyānayate. Mantranayastu Yogācāra-Mādhyamakasthityā vyākhyānayate,"

Tattvaratnāvalī in Advayavajrasaṅgraha, Fol. 9.

† " Mantranayastu asmadvidhairihātigambhīratvāt, gambhīranayādhimuktikapuruṣaviṣayatvācca caturmudrādi-sādhana-prakāsanavistarattvācca na vyākriyate."

Ibid, Fol. 14.

‡ Ekārthatve'pyasaṃmohāt vahūpāyādaduṣkarāt ।
Tīkṣṇedriyādhikārācca Mantraśāstraṃ viśiṣyate ॥
Kṛtaścaibhiratra *Sekanirṇayo* nāma granthaḥ."

Tattvaratnāvalī Ibid, Fol. 14.

Plate II: Three Celebrated Stūpas of Nepal

Simbhū

Bauddh

Kāṭhe Simbhū

In another of his short works entitled, Mahāsukhaprakāśa, he says—'from the right perception of Śūnyatā comes "Bīja." From "Bīja" is developed the conception of an icon and from that conception comes the external representation of the icon ; * so the entire iconography of the Buddhists proceeds from a correct understanding of the doctrine of Śūnyatā. The yab-yum conceptions were an outcome of the dual conceptions of Śūnyatā and Karuṇā, both of which were conceived and represented, but which ultimately proved to be one and the same.

* "Śūnyatābodhito bījaṃ bījāt vimbaṃ prajāyate ।
Vimbe ca nyāsavinyāsa tasmāt sarvaṃ pratītyajaṃ ॥
Mahāsukhaprakāśa in *Ibid*, Fol. 32.

§ II. *Evolution of the Doctrines.*

The pivot of distinction between the Mahāyāna and the Hīnayāna lies in the question of Nirvāṇa or the final goal of a Buddhist, though the actual split between the Mahāsāṅghikas and the Sthaviras was originally due to difference on ten minor points of discipline.* The Hīnayānist, whether a Śrāvaka or a Pratyekabuddha, is mean, selfish and always strives towards his own Nirvāṇa or emancipation, ignoring altogether all other beings of the world. The Mahāyānist, on the other hand, takes just the opposite view, makes Compassion (Karuṇā) his motto, and sets himself to work vigorously for the uplift of mankind, nay, all sentient beings from man to the smallest insect. In fact, he seems to be more solicitous about the emancipation of the latter than of his own self.

Both the Hīnayānist and the Mahāyānist agree in saying that Buddha as a Bodhisattva remained in the Tuṣita Heaven prior to his descent to this earth. They agree in holding that Buddha as Śākyasiṃha was born in the womb of Māyā, the queen of Śuddhodana the king of Kapilavāstu,—and Māyā in her dreams saw a white elephant entering into her womb. They also agree that his birth took place at the Lumbini garden, that he obtained his Enlightenment under the Bo-tree at Bodh-Gaya, preached his First Sermon at Sarnath and entered into Nirvāṇa at Kuśīnagara.

But they differ on the question of the divinity of Buddha. The Hīnayānist regards him as the Progenitor of the Law, and calls him a super-man, but nothing but a man with extraordinary intellect. But the Mahāyānist, on the other hand, looks upon him as a divinity,† and as such, an eternal being coming to earth only for the salvation or deliverance of the beings tortured by Mārā, the Evil One. The Hīnayānist believes in the Buddhist Triad and reveres and worships it in the order of Buddha, Dharma and

* H. Śāśtri : Bauddhadharma No. 14.—" Tāñhārā sakalei Daśavastur viruddhe mat dilen, kramei se mat pracār haila ; yāñhārā se mat grahan karilen tāñhāder nām haila Sthaviravādī, yāñhārā grahan karilen nā tāñhāder nām haila Mahāsāṅghik." (*in Bengali.*)

† Compare Mahāvastu Avadāna, Vol. I, p. 2.—" Ārya-Mahāsāṅghikānāṃ pāṭhena Vinayapitakasya Mahāvastuye ādi." Kern has taken the Lokottaravādins as a sect of the Mahāsāṅghikas. But the fact seems to be that the Lokottaravavādins are the same as the Mahāsāṅghikas, who attempted for the first time to establish the divinity or the eternity of Buddha. The Mahāsāṅghikas subsequently turned out to be the Mahāyānists. *Manual of Buddhism*, p. 3 *et sqq.*

Saṅgha, that is, the Promulgator of the Law first, the Law second and the recipients of the Law last. Every new recruit to the faith had to recite the Triśaraṇa in the above order. But the Mahāyānist changes the order into Dharma, Buddha and Saṅgha, attributing the first and highest place to the Law, and the next higher place to the Promulgator of the Law. According to a Mahāyānist, Dharma or Prajñā is eternal and the highest object in Buddhism ; Buddha is only the Upāya or the means of obtaining that knowledge, which is diffused into the masses through him. This idea bears a close resemblance to the Hindu conception of the Mantras,* which are supposed to be eternal and of which only a glimpse was obtained by the Vedic Ṛṣis. It took a considerable time, though we cannot definitely say how much, for the idea of Prajñā and Upāya to evolve from Buddha and Dharma. As a consequence the Saṅgha was also changed to a more dignified designation of ' Bodhisattva' † which meant in earlier times all members of the Holy Order, and later on, only the higher members‡, as is current even is now Nepal.

In the matter of Nirvāṇa, Mahāyāna has on entirely different development. The Hīnayānist will be satisfied if he is emancipated from the bond of worldly sufferings, from the evil of birth and rebirth. He does not look beyond his own salvation. But the Bodhisattva, on the other hand, being anxious to do good to the world, acquires a certain state of mind known as 'Bodhicitta' (Bodhi Mind), which makes him advance higher and higher. Simultaneously with his advancement he acquires merit and commences his march towards the Akaniṣṭha Heaven§, where Amitābha Buddha of Boundless Light resides. The Universe according to the Buddhists consists of twenty-six Lokas or Heavens divided into three broad divisions, (1) Kāma

* See Peterson's *Handbook to the Study of the Rig-Veaa*, Part I. pp. 31-24 and *Jaiminīya Nyāya Mālā-Vistara*, I, 2, 27-32.

† The compound word " Bodhisattva " may be expounded as *Bodhau yatante ye sattvāh i.e.* " Those who strives for the attainment of Bodhi." In primitive Buddhism, according to the Mahāyānists, therefore, all members were Bodhisattvas. *See* also Sujuki : *Outlines of Mahāyāna Buddhism*, p. 290 *et sqq.*

‡ As in Beal : Si-yu-ki. Cf. Āryadeva Bodhisattva, i, 189 ; Aśvaghoṣa Bodhisattva, ii 75, 100, etc. In Nepal now all Vajrācāryyas are called Bodhisattvas.

§ There is another intellectual movement by which the Bodhisattvas cross the ten Bhūmis, first enumerated and described in *Mahāvastu Avadāna* p. 78 *et sqq.* The word " Vivarta" has been taken by Senart to mean " returning back from a higher Bhūmi to a lower." But this word in Mahāvastu always refers to a forward movement.

(2) Rūpa and (3) Arūpa.* When the Bodhisattva remains in the Kāma Lokas he will be subject to sensuous desires ; in the second group of Heavens he will be above these desires but will nevertheless retain his form,—and in the third the form of the Bodhisattva will be lost. The Rūpa Heavens again are divided into four broad divisions ; † in the first of these, the Bodhisattva is not subjected to sensuous desires ; in the second, he gains absolute purity, in the third, he is freed from the cycles of rebirth ; and in the fourth, he reaches the Akaniṣṭha Heaven or Sukhāvatī and becomes a Buddha.

The Arūpa Heavens are four‡ in number and in these the form of the Bodhisattva is lost ; in the first of these, the Bodhisattva is able to conceive the idea of and to merge himself in Infinite Space ; in the second, he attains Infinite Intelligence ; in the third, he conceivas the idea of absolute Non-entity ; and in the fourth, he abides neither in consciousness nor unconsciousness. This is the highest state,—this is Nirvāṇa.§

But here arose a most baffling controversy. On the question whether Nirvāṇa meant absolute Void (Śūnya) or a conscious state (Vijñāna)—the Mahāyānists ranged themselves in two divisions. The Yogācāra School could not pursuade itself to believe that sentient beings after ages of striving should only end in Void. The followers of this School were known as the Vijñānavādins of whom Maitreyanātha in the chief, who held that even in Śūnya, the Vijñāna or consciousness remained. The Mādhyamikas were more radical. They held that Śūnya meant a transcendental state (not annihilation), about which neither existence, nor non-existence, nor a combination of the two, nor a negation of the two, can be predicated. ||

* Max Muller: *Dharmasaṃgraha*, p. 31. The three equivalents in Sanskrit are *Kāmāvacara*, *Rūpāvacara*, and *Arūpāvacara*.

† Morier Williams : *Buddhism* p. 211 *et. sqq*. The Rūpāvacara heavens are either eighteen or twenty-two. See also *Dharmasaṃgraha*, p. 31.

‡ The four Arūpa heavens are—Ākāśānantyāyatana, Vijñānānantyāyatana, akiñcanyānantyāyatana, Naivasaṃjñānāsaṃjñyāyatana.

§ Compare Aśvaghoṣa's conception of Nirvāṇa in *Saundarananda*.

"Dīpo yāthā nirvṛtimabhyupeto naivāvaniṃ gacchati nāntarīkṣaṃ ।
Diśaṃ na kāñcit vidiśaṃ na kāñcit snehakṣayāt kevalameti śāntiṃ ॥
Evaṃ kṛtī nirvṛtimabhyupeto naivāvaniṃ gacchati nāntarīkṣaṃ ।
Diśaṃ na kāñcit vidiśaṃ na kāñcit kleśakṣayāt kevalameti śāntiṃ" ॥

|| Sujuki is of opinion that the word, 'Śūnya' is used because the language does not furnish a more expressive word. *Cf.*—the statement in Mādhavācāryyas *Sarvadarśana-saṃgraha*—"asti-nāsti-tadubhayā-nubhaya-catuṣkoṭivinirmuktam śūnyarūpaṃ." pp. 23-24. Compare also *Advayavajrasaṃgraha*, Fol. 13.—

"Na san nāsan na sadasan na cāpyanubhayātmyakaṃ ।
Catuṣkoṭivinirmuktaṃ tattvaṃ Mādhyamikā viduḥ" ॥

These are in short, the main ideas underlying the divisions of the Mahāyāna doctrine which is always very abstruse. But Buddhism, we should not forget, was a mass-religion and the mass is not expected to be so intelligent as to grasp the real philosophical significance of Prajñā and Upāya or of Nirvāṇa. The priests found a great deal of difficulty in making the mass understand the meaning of Nirvāṇa, to the attainment of which every Boddhisattva strives. They invented a word for Śūnya ; it was Nirātmā, that is, something in which the soul is lost. The Boddhicitta merges in Nirātmā and there remains in eternal bliss and happiness (Mahāsukhavāda). The word. ' Nirātmā,' it may be noted, is in the feminine ; the Nirātmā is therefore a Devī. in whose embrace the Bodhicitta remains.* The masses well understood the significance of Nirātmā, and this feminine aspect—an outcome of Mahāsukhavāda—in the doctrine of Nirvāṇa, gave rise to what is known as Vajrayāna.

The word ' Vajrayāna' means the vehicle of obtaining Nirvāṇa through the medium of Vajra, which is another name for Śūnya, so called because it is a thing which cannot be destroyed, cannot be cut, cannot be burnt.† The position of the priests, the Gurus and the Vajrācāryyas in the Vajrayāna thus became very much magnified, because they invented other methods for the mass to attain an easy salvation. The mass could not master the sacred writings and could not even recite them. The Dhāraṇīs, which were mostly meaningless strings of words, were composed for them, and the recitation of these Dhāraṇīs‡ promised them great merit. These Dhāraṇīs were later on, shortened into equally unintelligible Mantras and Vījamantras. Individual Mantras were assigned to individual deities, who were held to take their origin from the Vījamantras or mystic syllables. How the deities originated from particular syllables is a matter for independent investigation. Those votaries who could not worship their gods in accordance with the prescribed procedure (Sādhana) were promised by the Gurus perfection

* H. Sāstri: *Bauddhadharma.* (No. 2.) " Nirvāṇa "—" Ei Śūnyake tāñhārā valilen ' Nirātmā.' Śudhu Nirātmā valiyā tṛpta hailen nā, valilen " Nirātmā-devI,' arthāt Nirātmā śabdaṭi strIlinga. Bodhisattva Nirātmādevīr kole jhāñp diyā padilen." (*in Bengali*)

† Cf.—*Advayavajrasaṃgraha*, Fol. 16.—

" Uktañca Vajraśokhare—

Dṛḍhaṃ sāraṃ asauśīryaṃ acchedyābhedyalakṣaṇaṃ ।
Adāhī avināśī ca Śūnyatā vajramucyate" ॥

‡ The Dhāraṇīs, Hṛdayasūtras and Mantras belong properly to the Mantrayāna, about which no details are forthcoming. According to H. Tsang the Dhāraṇī-or Vidyādhara-piṭaka belonging to Mantrayāna is as old as the time of the Mahāsāṅghikas. Beal. *Si-yu-ki*, II, 165. See also Kern's remarks in *Manual of Indian Buddhism*, p. 6.

only through the muttering of the Mantras*. Thus the position of the Gurus became paramount and as they showed the easy way or the adamantine path for Nirvāṇa, they were called the Vajrācāryyas.

It was an evil day for Mahayāna when Asaṅga in the sixth century went up to heaven and brought the Tantras down to earth and introduced the much expected aid of gods, the want of which was keenly felt,—into the religion of the Mahāyānists of his time ; they had already lost faith in their own exertions and required the help of the gods for their salvation, nay more, they even stooped so low as to crave for the ordinary worldly perfections (Siddhis) and were not satisfied if they could not secure them.

What the word "Tantra" really means is difficult to ascertain. Various scholars have explained the word in various ways. Mahāmahopādhyāya Haraprasād Śhāstrī says,† "The word Tantra is very loosely used. Ordinary people understand by it any system other than the Vedas. But it really means the worship of Śakti or female energy. The female energy is worshipped in conjunction with male energy. The union of male and female energy is the essence of Tantra."

The mentality of the mass and the mentality of the Vajrācāryyas was in a such a state that it readily grasped and assimilated the doctrines of Tantra and developed a form of religion, which, according to Bendall,‡ was brought to "the level of very thinly veiled Kāmaśāstra." Rājā Rājendralal, while commenting upon the *Guhyasamāja*,§ says, "but in working it out theories are indulged in and practices enjoined, which are at once the most revolting and horrible that human depravity could think of, and compared to which the worst specimens of Holiwell Street Literature of the last century would appear absolutely pure." Yet nevertheless, the feminine element in the doctrine attracted a large number of followers and made it extremely popular and the most exquisite art, which this school developed, made it doubly attractive.

Whatever might be the fault of the Vajrayānists it is to them we owe the legacy of a rich, varied and extensive Pantheon. The purely Tāntric

**Cf.* the statement, "khede sati Mantraṃ japet", very often repeated in the Sādhanamālā.

† H. Śāstri : *Introduction to Modern Buddhism*, p. 10.

‡ *See* C. Bendall's Introduction to *Sikṣāsamuccaya*, p. VI.

§ R. Mitra : *Sanskrit Buddhist Literature*, p. 261.

gods were invariably accompanied with their Śaktis, who were sometimes given a separate seat in sculptures, sometimes the same seat, sometimes a seat on the lap of the gods, and sometimes they were represented in the actual embrace of the gods. The sober form of Tantra generally adopted the first three courses. But the most thorough-going form worshipped the gods in the embrace, in union with their Śaktis, or as the Tibetans describe it—in *Yab-yum*.

§ III. *Evidence of Art.*

The Buddhist Universe is represented by a Stūpa and the Stūpas received worship from the Buddhists from the life-time of Buddha down to the present day (Plate II). Similar is the case with the Three Jewels, which came to be represented later, both in symbolic and in human form * (Plate III). As Buddhism was originally a religion of tolerance it incorporated many of the Hindu deities in the first stage ; when Buddha had attained Enlightenment and was about to retire from the world, Brahmā and Indra approached him suddenly and asked him to stay for a time to deliver the people of Magadha. Kuvera, the Hindu god of Wealth, who is usually represented with a bag of gems in the left hand was also incorporated ; so was the case with Vasudhārā, who became in later times, the consort of Jambhala, the Buddhist god of Wealth. The railings of Bodh Gaya, Sanchi, Bharaut and Amaravati dating from the 3rd. to the 1st. century B.C. show unmistakables signs of worshipping everything that Buddha made sacred by his magic touch. For instance, the Bodhi Tree (Plate IV,a), his turban (Plate IV,b), his footprints (Plate IV,c), the Wheel-of-the-law (Plate IV,d), and similar objects were revered by the later Buddhists in the absence of their Departed Master. The railings show further, bas-reliefs representing innumerable scenes from Buddha's life as recorded in the *Lalita-Vistara* or the *Mahāvastu Avadāna* (e. g. Dream of Māyā, Plate I,e) as well as stories from the Jātakas. The Nāgas and the Yakṣas are also to be seen everywhere, but whether they received any worship, is difficult to say.

For several centuries after the Mahāparinirvāṇa of Buddha we never meet with any representation of the Great Master himself. Perhaps his personality was too great to admit of a representation, or Was it owing to the religious bias of the Indian Buddhists ? Whatever might be the cause, it so happened that the Indians were not the first to carve out a statue of Lord Buddha, one of the greatest celebrities of India. In Mahāyāna we have seen,

* From the materials now before us we may safely hold that the Nepalese Buddhists were the first to conceive the Holy Triad in human form, in which the Triad is worshipped there even in modern days. When representated in art, Dharma shows the Añjali against the breast in the first pair of hands and carries the rosary and the double lotus in the second. Buddha shows either the Samādhi or the Bhūmisparśana Mudrā ; and Saṅgha, a male divinity, shows the Dharmacakra Mudrā in the first pair of hands and the rosary and the book in the second pair.

Plate III: The Buddhist Triad

Dharma

Buddha

Saṅgha

Buddha was assigned a subordinate position among the Three Jewels; time obliterated almost everything of his solemn personality, and the Graeco-Buddhists carved out his first statue in Gandhara.* The intermixture of the Greek with the indegenous plastic art gave rise to what we now call the Græco-Buddhist Art, popularly known as the Gandhara School of Sculpture. Buddha was the chief object of representation in this art; the events and stories from his life were represented; many of the Jātaka stories of his previous births were also represented. At Taxila, Peshwar, Sahri-Balhol and numerous other places in the North-West Frontier Province, heaps of stones have been unearthed bearing innumerable images of Buddha in different attitudes (Āsanas) and different gestures (Mudrās). Besides Buddhas images, we meet with the images of Jambhala, Maitreya, Hārīti, the Indian Madonna, and her consort, and other Bodhisattva images † in the Gandhara Art, besides numerous other things.

There is considerable disagreement among scholars as to be beginning of Gandhara Art. Prof. A. Foucher declares that the reign of Menander was perhaps most suited for such a school of art to begin. But the date he assigns to Menander is cir. B. C. 160.‡ There again, scholars are divided in their opinion. Dr. R. C. Mazumdar who has gone deep into the question, and has examined all the arguments in favour or against the date, has come to the conclusion that a date prior to 90 B. C. cannot be assigned to Menander. We take it, that the Gandhara Art began in the reign of Menander in 90 B.C. and that no image of Buddha was made before that time.

This art was carried over to Mathurā, where again the Gandhara Art coming in contact with the local art took a somewhat different development, which has been assigned the name of the Mathura School of Sculpture.§ This School also produced numerous Buddha and Bodhisattva images, the image of Kuvera,‖ the scenes depicting the four principal and the four minor scenes of Buddha's life generally, including other scenes also. The Yakṣas and the

* A. Foucher: *Beginnings of Buddhist Art and other essays*, p. 127.

† See V. A. Smith: *Fine Art in India and Ceylon*, figs. 62, 63, Pl. XXVIII. fig. 64, 65, also Garuḍa and Nāga images, fig. 70; refer also to the image of Kuvara, No. 3912 of Indian Museum.

‡ Foucher: *Beginnings of Buddhist Art*, p. 127.

§ Cf. Vogel: *The Mathura School of Sculpture*,—" This explains the mixed character of the Mathura School in which we find on the one hand a direct continuation of the old Indian art of Barahut (Bharaut) and Sanchi and on the other hand the elassical influence derived from Gandhara " A. S. I. Ann. Rep. 1906-7, p. 145.

‖ *Ibid* p. 144 and V. A. Smith's *History of Fine Art in India and Ceylon*, fig. 81.

Nāgas which are the common property of the Hindus and the Buddhists, are to be frequently met with in this art. The Mathura School is famous for its images of the Kuṣāṇa kings, and its flourshing period ranges from the first century A. D. to the early Gupta period,* for we do not meet here with any of the later Buddhist gods, Avalokiteśvara, Mañjusrī, Tārā and the like.

Next to Mathura we come to Sarnath which covers a period from the time of Aśoka down to the reign of the Pālas.† It is here that we meet with the representations of the varied and extensive Pantheon of the Vajrayāna Buddhists. The images of Ṣaḍakṣarī Lokeśvara, Ucchuṣma Jambhala, Mañjuśrī, Tārā, Vasudhārā, Mārīcī, the five Dhyānī Buddhas, Vajrasttva and many others,—point to a higher and later form of Vajrayāna. Though the gods are here represented for the first time with their Śaktis, they do not, nevertheless, belong to the most attractive form in which they are required to be represented in Sampuṭayoga, or in union, or as the Tibetans call it, in *Yab-yum.*

Further downwards the monastaries of Odantapuri, Nalanda and Vikramaśīla must have developed the latest form of Vajrayāna before Buddhism was finally wiped out at the advent of the Muhammadan invader Bukhtiyar Khilji and his warlike cavalry, who targetted the shaven heads of the innocent Buddhist priests mistaking them for soldiers.‡ Nalanda is being excavated and a large number of images belonging to the higher form of Tantra have been unearthed. The Vikramaśīla monastery has not been identified yet ; but if the Odantapuri site be also excavated, it will most assuredly, yield innumerable images of Vajrayāna gods.

The most flourshing period of the Bengal school of sculpture ranges from the tenth century or even earlier down to the settlement of the Muhammadans in Bengal. A large majority of the images that have up till now been discovered in Bengal belong to the Hindu form of religion, though Buddhist images are also to be extensively met with. The products of the Bengal school are undoubtedly the best specimens of Indian art, but unfortunately

* *Mathura Museum Cat.*, pp. 27-28.

† Vincent Smith : *History of Fine Art in India and Ceylon*, p. 146.

‡ Elliott's *History of India*, p. 306. In *Tabakat-i-Nasiri*, Minhaju-s-Siraj gives a graphic description of how Bakhtiyar conquered the peaceful Vihāra and massacred all the undefended inmates. He smelt of plunder and seems to have destroyed the Vikramaśīla Vihāra, Jagaddala Vihāra and probably the Nalanda Vihara also, which is only eight miles or so away from Odantapuri (mod. Bihar on the Bukhtiyarpur Bihar Light Railway). This Vihāra contained perhaps the last remants of the Mahāsāṅghikas.

(a) *Bodhi* Tree (Amarāvatī)

(b) Buddha's Headdress (Bharhut)

(c) Buddha's footprints (Bharhut)

(d) Wheel-of-the-law (Bharhut)

Plate IV: Symbol-Worship

the existence of this school has not even been acknowledged by scholars. Many of the specimens of the Bengal School are preserved in the three museums of Calcutta, Dacca, and Rajshahi, but a large number of them are scattered about in Parganah Vikrampur, and the Districts of Dinajpur and Comilla.

The images of gods at Ajanta, Ellora, and South-India show signs of immature Tantra and may be assigned a time prior to the Bengal School, though the paintings of Ajanta and other sculptures have a long antiquity. Veteran scholars have asserted Java's indebtedness to Bengal in the matter of Art and religion, and it is quite probable that the art and the later Mahāyānism was carried over by the sea from Tāmralipti to Java by the Bengalees.

In the later phase of Vajrayāna, after its destruction in India, the priests of the celebrated monasteries took refuge in Nepal, and thus kept the torch of Budhdism still burning, in India. The art of Bengal was carried over there, but it soon degenerated at the hands of the native artists. We need not dwell here on the question as to how the priests fled to Nepal, and how they built innumerable monasteries there. Suffice it to say, that the followers of Vajrayāna, in order to make sure of their existence, converted a good many of the natives and carved out innumerable images of gods both in stone and in wood, so much so, that a student of Iconography is overwhelmed at their wealth and variety.

§ IV. *The Pantheon.*

The Pantheon of the Northern Buddhists was not built in a day. This we have tried to show in the two previous sections from the point of view of Buddhist doctrine as well as from the point of view of extant images. Now we shall examine the evidence of the Mahāyāna literature in Sanskrit and the accounts of the Chinese Travellers, who were Buddhists and who have recorded their observations minutely in their works. From what follows, we come to the conclusion that all Sanskrit works mentioning the five Dhyānī Buddhas or Vajradhara or Vajrasattva or any of the later gods cannot belong to a period prior to the time of Indrabhūti (*cir.* 700-750 A. D.)

There is no mention of the five Dhyānī Buddhas in the literature of the Mahāyāna Buddhists prior to the time of Indrabhūti. But it cannot be held that they were invented all at once. We meet with none of them in the works of Aśvaghoṣa (1st century A. D.), Nāgārjuna (2nd century A. D.) and Āryadeva* (3rd century). We have evidence that during A. D. 148-170 A. D. the *Sukhāvatī-Vyūha* or the *Amitāyus Sūtra* was translated into Chinese. This Sūtra mentions for the first time the name of Amitābha, and his other name Amitāyus,† who resides in the Sukhāvatī or the Akaniṣṭha heaven, where he remains in constant meditation and where he is believed to have brought forth the Bodhisattva Avalokiteśvara into existence.‡ The smaller recen-

* It may here be mentioned that as the work Cittaviśuddhiprakaraṇa mentions the five Dhyānī Buddhas and other later Vajrayāna gods, the author of the work cannot be the same Āryadeva, the disciple of Nāgārjuna, who flourished in the third century A.D. He must be the later Āryadeva of the Tāntric age, not only because he mentions the later Vajrayāna gods, but also because his work breathes throughout the doctrines of Tantra. Furthermore, the Tangyur Catalogue attributes the same work, with a slightly different name, Cittaśodhanaprakaraṇa, to him, which fact convincingly pushes him forward into the Tāntric age. It may be noted, however, that the name *Cittaviśuddhiprakaraṇa* has not been given in the Colophon of the work published in J. A. S. B. 1898 p. 117 ff. but it was given on the authority of C. Bendall. The real name of the work is *Cittaśodhanaprakaraṇa* as given in the *Tangyur Catalogue.*

Nāgārjuna's *Dharmasaṃgraha* likewise mentions the five Dhyānī Buddhas. Either this Nāgārjuna is the later Siddhācāryya, Nāgārjuna, or the passage mentioning the Dhyānī Buddhas is an interpolation. We are more inclined to accept the latter theory, as the manuscript of *Dharmasaṃgraha* we have been able to find out in Nepal and of which we possess a copy—omits the passage altogether.

† *Sukhāvatī-vyūha*, pp. 1, 28, 32.

‡ There is however a faint reference to Avalokiteśvara in the word, '*Avalokita*' in *Mahāvastu Avadāna*, Vol. II. p. 294.

Ādi-Buddha, Vajradhara, the Highest God of Buddhist Pantheon

Plate V

sion of this *Amitāyus Sūtra,* which was also translated into Chinese between A.D. 384-417, mentions two more names, of Akṣobhya as a Tathāgata and Mañjuśrī as a Bodhisattva. It may be noted, however, that Fa-Hien (394-414 A.D.) mentions the names of Mañjuśrī, Avalokiteśvara and Maitreya; Hiuen Thsang (A.D. 629-645) the names of Avalokiteśvara, Hārīti, Kṣitigarbha, Maitreya, Mañjuśrī, Padmapāṇi, Vaiśravaṇa, Śākya-Buddha, Śākya Bodhisattva and Yama. Besides these, the latter refers to *Vidyādharapīṭaka* and *Vajrapāṇidhāraṇi* belonging to Mantrayāna. There is evidence also in his work that many of the saints were deified as Bodhisattvas, such as, Aśvaghoṣa, Nāgārjuna, Asaṅga, Sumedhas, and others. He refers to many of the previous Buddhas also. I-Tsing, another devout Buddhist traveller, (A.D. 671-695), came all the way from China to India during the last quarter of the seventh century. He mentions the names of Avalokiteśvara, Amitāyus or Amitābha, Hārīti, the Caturmahārājikas, Maitreya, Mañjuśrī and Yama besides several Hindu gods.

Let us next examine the works of Śāntideva of the Nalanda monastery, who has been assigned to the middle of the seventh century by Cecil Bendall. This date seems rather doubtful in view of the fact that I-Tsing does not mention him in his work. In any case, we cannot assign to him a date later than A.D. 800, as his book, Śikṣā-samuccaya, was translated into Tibetan in the reign of the celebrated Tibetan king, Khri-lde-sron-btsan, who reigned between A. D. 816 and 838.* In this work we meet with the names of Akṣobhya as a Tathāgata, Amitābha as a Tathāgata, Gaganagañja as a Bodhisattva, and Siṃhavikrīḍita as a Tathāgata. That in his time Tantra had just begun to weild its influence is evident from a fairly large number of references to Tāntric works. It gives the Dhāraṇīs for Cundā, Trisamayarāja and Mārīcī. The name of the book, Śrīmālā-Siṃhanāda, clearly speaks of Siṃhanāda, one of the numerous names of Avalokiteśvara. In his *Bodhicaryyāvatāra*, Śāntideva speaks of Mañjughoṣa, one of the many forms of Mañjuśrī.

After Śāntideva for nearly a century and a half we do not meet with dated manuscripts in Sanskrit belonging to the Buddhist faith except the Jñānasiddhi of Indrabhūti. But there is no doubt that during this period Vajrayāna developed in a marvellously rapid degree. Great many works

* C. Bendall's Introduction to Śikṣā-Samuccaya, p. V.

It seems to me likely that he flourished at a period prior to the time of Indrabhūti (C. 77-750) as he does not mention the five Dhyānī Buddhas in any of his works. The five Dhyānī Buddhas ware invented by Indrabhūti and had Śāntideva known it, he would have mentioned them, inasmuch as his Śikṣāsamuccaya mentions the two among them. Amitābha and Akṣobhya.

were written, and great many deities were added to the Pantheon. Yantras (magic diagrams) and Maṇḍalas (magic circles) were invented, Mantras (charms) and Vījamantras (germ-syllables) were assigned to individual deities, and the number of deites increased astonishingly.

In the reign of Rudradeva (1015 A.D.) we find manuscripts of *Aṣṭa-sāhasrikā Prajñāpāramitā* bearing a large number of miniature pictures of Buddhist Tāntric deities. Some illustrated manuscripts of *Pañcarakṣā* belong to the same period. The various copies of the *Sādhanamālā* that we have been able to gather, date from A.D. 1165 and in one of these no less than four hundred descriptions or Dhyānas of both minor and principal deities are to be found.

Though Tantrayāna was introduced into the Mahāyāna System, it did not weild a great influence on the minds of the Indians before 700 A.D. Tāranāth writing in the 16th century says plainly that the Tantras existed in an occult form in the period between the time of Asaṅga and Dharmakīrti (A.D. 645-71),* for naturally it takes rather a long time to assimilate an entirely foreign influence such as the Tantra. Tāranāth further says that during the reign of the Pāla Dynasty there were many Vajrācāryyas and Siddhapuruṣas, who performed many prodigious feats. It was during this period that the Vikramaśīla monastery was famous as a centre of Tāntric learning and culture.†

The very first thing that Vajrayāna brought with it was the five Dhyānī Buddhas and their Śaktis along with a number of deities as emanating from them in the same way as Avalokiteśvara emanated from Amitābha, and as Prajñāpāramitā emanated from Akṣobhya mentioned in a Sādhana attributed to Asaṅga in the Sādhanamālā. The creator of all this, in all probability, was Indrabhūti, the king of Uḍḍiyāna, who, according to Tibetan tradition‡, flourished in the first half of the eighth century A.D. The word Vajrayāna is first met with in his work, entitled, *Jñanasiddhi*, in which there is a chapter on *Pañcākāra* giving the origin and the forms of the Dhyāni Buddhas. This

* " Dharmakīrti is not mentioned by Yuan Chwang (travelled through India 629-645) but he is spoken of by I-Tsing (671-95). Consequently, Dharmakīrti's palmy days were in 645-71 "—Ui, *Vaiśeṣika Philosophy.* p. 17.

† Kern : *Manual of Buddhism.* p. 133.

‡ Indrabhūti's son is Guru Padmasambhava, who went to Tibet in 647 A. D., and his daughter is Lakṣīṃkarā, who is believed to have been the founder and a vigorous exponent of Sahajayāna. Waddel : *Lamaism*, pp. 380 ff. Śhāstrī : *Buddhists in Bengal*, in the *Dacca Review*, Vol. II, No. 7. p. 98. " Sahajayana was preached by one of the Udiya chiefs named Indrabhūti and his gifted daughter Laksmi Devi or Laksmimkara Devi." See also *Tangyur Cat.* 2e partie—pp. 55 and 211.

work breathes throughout the doctrines of Tantra and betrays the anxiety of the author to establish a definite school of Mahāyāna by means of learned discussions and arguments. The theory of Mahāsukha also appears for the first time in this work with all its various ramifications. There is a great deal of controversy regarding the identification of Uḍḍiyāna ; some hold that it is the same as U-Chang-na of Hiuen Tsang or Udyāna in the Swat Valley in the North-Western Frontier Province, but many others are of opinion that it is the same as Orissa. The latter theory seems probable, for Uḍḍiyāna must be a place where Vajrayāna flourished, and a place where we should expect to find some Vajrayāna images. Sādhanamālā mentions four Pīṭhas or sacred spots of Vajrayāna, namely, Kāmākhyā, Sirihaṭṭa, Pūrṇagiri* and Uḍḍiyāna, and Uḍḍiyāna must be a place not very far off from Kāmākhyā and Sirihaṭṭa. Moreover, in the Sādhanamālā there is a Sādhana for the worship of a four-armed variety of Kurukullā, which goes by the name of Uḍḍiyāna Kurukullā, or Kurukullā as worshipped in Uḍḍiyāna. Images of this deity is extremely rare and if we are to believe the testimony of Mr. N. N. Vasu the only image of this variety of Kurukullā has been discovered in Orissa†. Lastly in Buddhist MSS of the Tāntric period the variants, Oḍḍa, Oḍra, Uḍra, Oḍaviṣa, Oḍiyāna, are mentioned, and all these seem to be the variants of Uḍḍiyāna. All this evidence, combined together, points to the identification of Uḍḍiyāna with Orissa, where innumerable images belonging to the Vajrayāna School have been discovered. Against the first theory identifying Uḍḍiyāna with Udyāna several arguments may be brought forward. We have no evidence that Tantra in the form of Vajrayāna ever flourished in Udyāna, nor a single Tāntric image is reported to have been discovered there, though much earlier images of the Gandhara School are daily coming out from this site. It is, moreover, improbable that Uḍḍiyāna being one of the four Pīṭhas would be two thousand miles away from two others, Kāmākhyā and Sirihaṭṭa, which are contiguous. In view of these facts we may conveniently identify Uḍḍiyāna with Orissa and set aside its identification with Udyāna.

Alexander Csoma de Koros places the introduction of the conception of Ādi-Buddha in Central Asia in the last half of the 10th century. The conception of Ādi-Buddha originated at Nalanda by the first half of the 10th. century and no mention of Ādi-Buddha is made by Indian writers before that time. Ādi-Buddha is the Primordial Buddha from whom the five Dhyānī Buddhas are said to have taken their origin, and homage is paid to

* Pūrṇagiri has not been identified.

† N. N. Vasu : *Mayurbhanj Archaeological Survey.*

Ādi-Buddha in the shape of a flame, which the priests of Nepal consider eternal, self-born and self-existent. Ādi-Buddha first manifested himself in Nepal in the shape of a flame of fire, and Mañjuśrī is said to have erected a temple over it in order to preserve the flame.* This temple is known as the Svayambhū Caitya (Plate II) and the place derives its name from it.

The conception of Vajradhara in human form presupposes Ādi-Buddha and therefore later than the first half of the 10th. century. Vajrasattva, being a regular development of Vajrapāni, the Bodhisattva emanating from Akṣobhya, might be a little earlier. In Vajrayāna, Ādi-Buddha is regarded as the highest deity, the originator even of the Dhyānī Buddhas. When represented in human form (Plate V), Ādi-Buddha begets the name of Vajradhara and is conceived in two forms, single, and *Yab-yum*. Vajradhara is decked in princely ornaments and garments, sits in the Vajraparyaṅka attitude, with his two hands, carrying the Vajra in the right and the Ghaṇṭā in the left, crossed against the breast in what is known as the Vajrahuṅkāra Mudrā. When represented in *Yab-yum* (Plate VI,a-b-c) his form would be exactly the same as described above, with the difference that he should be embraced in *Yab-yum* by his Śakti, whose name, according to Getty, is Prajñāpāramitā. The Śakti is richly dressed and richly decked in ornaments, and carries the Kartri in the right hand and the Kapāla in the left.

The Ādi or the Primordial Buddha was accepted mainly in the Kālacakrayāna,† a later development of the Vajrayāna, and the *Svayambhū Purāṇa* which deals with the glories of the Svayambhūkṣettra " the place of the Self-born" or Ādi Buddha, belongs to the system of Kālacakrayāna. This Ādi-Buddha, it may be pointed out, is a generic name. It signifies Vajradhara, described above, in the Kālacakrayāna ; but the Vajrayānists were not slow to appreciate the theory of a Promordial Buddha. Some considered Akṣobhya to be the Ādi-Buddha, others considered in the same way other Dhyānī Buddhas as the Ādi-Buddha, after their own fashion. Thus the Vajrayānists were divided into so many cults, according as they accepted

* It is very curious that Mañjuśrī is connected with this tradition as recorded in the *Svayambhū Purāṇa*. Mañjuśrī is as old as 4th century A. D. if not earlier and the conception of Ādi Buddha first originated in the first half of the 10th century. We wonder how Mañjuśrī could ever come to erect a temple over the flame. See Oldfield : *Sketches from Nepal*, Vol. II. p. 90 and 156 ff. and 188. Hodgson's *Essays*, pp. 115 ff.

† The conception of Ādi Buddha originated at the Nalanda monastery in the beginning of the 10th century A.D. *See* J. A. B. S. Vol. II (1833), p. 57 *et sqq.* ; also my article on *Vajradhara vs. Vajrasattva* in J. B. O. R. S. Vol. IX, p. 114 *et sqq.*

(a) Vajradhara Yab-yum (Nepal)

(b) Vajradhara Yab-yum
(Side View)

(c) Buddha in different *mudrās* (Java)

(d) Buddha in different *mudrās* (Nālandā)

Plate VI

one or the other of the Dhyānī Buddhas as the Ādi-Buddha. The followers of different cults made their deities bear the image of their own Dhyānī or Ādi-Buddha on their crown, sometimes contrary to the directions laid down in the Sādhanas.* We have evidence in a work belonging to the Akṣobhya cult that even the Dhyānī Buddhas themselves bear the image of Akṣobhya on their head in order to show their origin.† In other words, the followers of different cults believed the other Dhyānī Buddhas to be the offsprings of that particular Dhyānī Buddha whom they considered as their own Ādi Buddha.

The Hindus say that the number of their deities is thirty-three *crores*, and it seems that the Buddhists can claim a similar figure. One single deity may have innumerable forms according to the number of hands, the number of faces and the number of legs. He will differ, again, according to colour, according as he is worshipped in different Maṇḍalas, the number of which it is no very easy matter to ascertain. He will differ again according as he is invoked in different Tāntric rites, according to his companions, in accordance with the Āsanas, and the different weapons that are held in his hands. A permutation and combination of these different categories will give innumerable forms to one single deity. Besides these, the deity varies according to the whims of the devotees, or the donors, and ignorance of the sculptors or the painters.

* This accounts for the image of Amitābha on the crowns of the Sarnath figure of Ucchuṣma Jambhala and the Lucknow Museum figure of Mārīcī, and also of Akṣobhya on the crown of the Indian Museum figure of Uṣṇīṣavijayā. According to the Sādhanas, the image either of Ratnasambhava or of Akṣobhya is prescribed for Ucchuṣma Jambhala, that of Vairocana for both Mārīcī and Uṣṇīṣavijayā. *See Infra.*

† Advayavajra, who flourished in the 11th century, was a follower of the Akṣobhya cult, and he makes all the Dhyānī Buddhas except Akṣobhya bear the miniature figure of the latter, in his work *Advayavajrasaṃgraha*, Fol. 16.

CHAPTER I.

BUDDHAS, BUDDHAŚAKTIS AND BODHISATTVAS.

I. DHYĀNĪ BUDDHAS.

The Buddhists are more scientific than the Hindus in the matter of determining the hierarchy of the gods in their Pantheon. They believe that all gods emanated from one or the other of the Dhyānī Buddhas, popularly known as the Divine Buddhas, or four or five of them collectively; and the images of such emanations invariably bear the effigies of their sires on their head, crown or on the aureole behind them.

The Dhyānī Buddhas are a peculiar kind of Buddhas who are not required to pass through the stage of a Bodhisattva ;* they were never anything less than a Buddha. Thev are always engaged in peaceful meditation, and they voluntarily restrain themselves from the act of creation. To create is the duty of their emanations, the Divine Bodhisattvas.

The Dhyānī Buddhas are five in number to which a sixth, Vajrasattva is sometimes added. Though some of them were known before A. D. 700 yet the idea of the full five seems to have developed in the first half of the eighth century during the time of Indrabhūti, the king of Uḍḍiyāna. That the five Dhyānī Buddhas might have owed their origin to the theory of the eternity of the five senses, seems to be borne out by a passage † in the *Cittaviśuddhiprakaraṇa* of Āryadeva.‡ But it may also be possible that the

* Kern : Manual of Buddhism, p. 64.

† The passage is :—

> Cakṣur-Vairocaṇo Buddhah śravaṇo Vajraśūnyakah
> Ghrāṇaśca paramādyaistu Padmanartteśvaro mukham
> Kāyah Śrī-Heruko rājā Vajrasattvañca mānasaṃ.

....J. A. S. B. 1898, p. 178.

‡ The author of this work is Āryadeva, who has been identified with the famous disciple of Nāgārjuna of the same name to whom Catuhśatikā is attributed, in J. A. S. B. 1898, p. 176. We respectfully differ from this statement on the following grounds, and identify him with the Tāntric author Āryadeva or Āyadeva ; the Tangyur Catalogue attributes the work, Cittaśodhanaprakaraṇa to him ; and the mention of Vajradhara, Vajrasattva, Heruka, and the five Dhyānī Buddhas in this work makes us confident that this Āryadeva cannot be so old as the 3rd. Century, but must be later than 700 A. D. in any case. It may also be pointed out that the name of the work was not given in the manuscript itself ; the name was suggested by C. Bendall.

five mudrās, which Buddha Śākyasiṁha made sacred by using on memorable occasions and which were constantly realized in the Buddhistic figures of the different schools of art—gave rise to the five Dhyānī Buddhas (Plate VIcd). Advayavajra who flourished in the 11th century has written in one of his works that the five Dhyānī Buddhas took their origin from the theory of the eternity of the five Skandhas (elements), or rather, that they were the embodiments of the Skandhas, which were held by Lord Buddha to be the constituents of a Being fused together by action. Vajrasattva,* the sixth Dhyānī Buddha who is generally regarded as the priest of the five Dhyānī Buddhas and is usually represented with the priestly symbols, the Vajra and the Ghaṇṭā, is an embodiment of the five Skandhas collectively and undoubtedly a later incorporation to the Pantheon of the Northern Buddhists.

We have already said that the number of the Dhyānī Buddhas is five to which a sixth is sometimes added. The order in which the Nepalese Buddhists worship them is as follows :—

1. Vairocaṇa
2. Akṣobhya
3. Ratnasambhava
4. Amitābha
5. Amoghasiddhi
6. Vajrasattva

Excepting the last, they appear all alike, but they vary according to the particular colour of their body and the different positions of their hands. The following verse in the Sādhanamālā gives the colour and the mudrā of each.

Jino Vairocaṇo khyāto Ratnasambhava eva ca ।
Amitābhāmoghasiddhir-Akṣobhyaśca prakīrtitaḥ ॥
Varṇāḥ amīṣām sitah pīto rakto haritamecakau ।
Bodhyaṅgī-Varado-Dhyānaṃ mudrā Abhaya-Bhūsprśau ॥

" The Jinas (victorious ones) are Vairocaṇa, Ratnasambhava Amitābha, Amoghasiddhi and Akṣobhya, whose colours respectively are white, yellow, red, green and blue and who exhibit the Bodhyaṅgī (Dharmacakra or Teaching), Varada (Gift-bestowing), Dhyāna (Meditative), Abhaya (Assurance) and Bhūsparśa (Earth-touching) attitudes of hands respectively."

When represented, the Dhyānī Buddhas closely resemble each other. The differences, as has already been said, depend besides their colour on the positions in which the hands are held, and on the Vāhanas which they ride. Every Dhyānī Buddha is always represented in a sitting posture on a full blown double lotus. This attitude is known as the Dhyānāsana or the medita-

* The word: Vajra ' means ' Śūnya ' or Void and ' sattva ' means ' essence,' and so Vajrasattva is a god whose essence is Sūnya or Void.

(a) Amitābha

(b) Akṣobhya (Nepal)

(c) Akṣobhya

(d) Vairocana

Plate VII

tive attitude, in which he is required to sit cross-legged, the right foot crossing over and in front of the left with the soles of both feet turned upwards. The hand which rests on the lap is sometimes empty but in most cases it carries a bowl. The head is bare, and hair curly, which radiates effulgence like a flame. The eyes are half closed in meditation. They are dressed in an under-garment reaching from the breast to the knees and tied by a scarf. The body is loosely covered by the habit of a monk, leaving only the right arm bare.

The Dhyānī Buddhas are generally represented on the four sides of a Stūpa, which is the symbol of the Buddhist Universe, facing the four cardinal points. Vairocaṇa is the deity of the inner shrine and is therefore generally unrepresented ; but exceptions to this rule are by no means rare. He is occasionally assigned a place between Ratnasambhava and Akṣobhya. Independent shrines are also dedicated to each of these Buddhas.

1. Amitābha.

Colour—Red. Mudrā—Samādhi.
Crest—Lotus. Vāhana—A pair of peacocks.

By far the most ancient in the group of the Dhyānī Buddhas is Amitābha, who is conceived as residing in the Sukhāvatī Heaven in peaceful meditation. He presides over the current Kalpa (cycle), which goes by the name of Bhadrakalpa. But it is not his business to create or to stir himself to action ; it is his Bodhisattva, Padmapāṇi who is the active energy or the creative principle. He faces the West and the Nepalese Buddhists regard him as the fourth Dhyānī Buddha. His two hands with palm open lie on his lap, one upon the other (Samādhimudrā or Dhyānamudrā). His colour is red and his Vāhana is a pair of peacocks. His crest or cognizance is the full-blown lotus.* (Plate VIIa).†

* The following description appears in Advayavajrasaṁgraha :—

" Paścime dale ravimaṇḍalopari rakta-Hrīḥ-kārasambhūto raktavarṇṇomitābhaḥ padmacinhasamādhimudrādharaḥ Saṁjñāskandhasvabhāvo....grīṣmarturūpaḥ āmlarasaśariraḥ Tavargātmā....jāpamantraścāyaṃ Oṃ Āḥ Ārolika Huṃ "....Fol. 27.

† This and the other four miniatures of the five Dhyānī Buddhas have been taken from an illuminated manuscript of Pañcarakṣā (about 400 years old) which was very kindly lent to me by Dr. W. Y. Evans Wentz, an American Anthropologist. In the miniatures it may be noticed that the Vāhanas are always in pairs, and on the open space between them is the crest of the Dhyānī Buddha.

2. Akṣobhya.

Colour—Blue. Mudrā—Bhūparśa.
Crest—Vajra. Vāhana—A pair of elephants.

Next in importance and antiquity is undoubtedly Akṣobhya who is first mentioned as a Tathāgata in the smaller recension of the Amitāyus Sūtra, which was translated into Chinese between A. D. 384 and A. D. 417. The Vajrayāna Pantheon shows that a large number of deities, both masculine and feminine, have emanated from him. Akṣobhya is regarded as the second Dhyānī Buddha by the Nepalese Buddhists and when represented in the Stūpas, he always faces the East. His colour is blue. His left hand rests on the lap, while the right rests upon the right knee with the tips of the fingers touching the ground with palm downwards (Bhūsparśa or Bhūmisparśana Mudrā.* (Plate VIIb). † His Vāhana is a pair of elephants and his crest or cognizance is the Vajra. (Plate VIIe).

3. Vairocana.

Colour—White. Mudrā—Dharmacakra.
Crest—Cakra. Vāhana—A pair of Dragons.

Whether the Vairocana mentioned in the Cittaviśuddhiprakarana of Āryadeva, really refers to the Dhyānī Buddha, is difficult to determine, but there it is clearly stated that Vairocana presides over the eyes. His antiquity is borne out by the fact that a fairly large number of deities emanates from him, Mārīcī being their chief, to whom again a large number of Sādhanas in the Sādhanamālā are devoted. He is regarded as the oldest and the first Dhyānī Buddha by the Nepalese Buddhists and his place is in the sanctum of the stūpa, where he is the master of the whole temple and its contents. Naturally, therefore, he cannot be represented outside the stūpa ; but exceptions to this rule are frequently met with in celebrated Caityas in Nepal, where he is represented in the space between Akṣobhya in the East and Ratnasambhava in the South. His colour is white and his two hands are held against the breast with the tips of the thumb and forefinger

* Compare Advayavajrasaṁgraha—" Nīla-Huṁ-kāraniṣpannadvibhuja ekamukho bhūṣparśamudrādharo vajraparyaṅkī......kṛṣṇavajracinhaḥ suviśuddhadharmadhātu-Vijñānaskandhasvabhāvaḥ....śiśiramadhyāhnakaṭuśrutiākāśaśabdacavargo. Āḥ Vajradhṛk Huṁ asya jāpamantraḥ "....Fol. 26.

† The reproductions of the three stone images of Akṣobhya, Ratnasambhava and Amoghasiddhi are from photographs of a Nepalese caitya.

(a) Vairocana (Nepal)

(b) Amoghasiddhi

(c) Amoghasiddhi (Nepal)

(d) Ratnasambhava

Plate VIII

of each hand united (Dharmacakramudrā)* (PlateVIIIa).† His Vāhana is a pair of dragons or gryphons and his crest is the Cakra or the discus (Plate VIId).

4. Amoghasiddhi.

Colour—Green. Mudrā—Abhaya.
Crest—Viśvavajra. Vāhana—A pair of Garuḍas.

A tolerably large number of deities emanates from this Dhyānī Buddha, who is regarded in some quarters as another form of Amitābha and is comparatively a later addition to the Pantheon. The Nepalese Buddhists consider him to be the fifth Dhyānī Buddha in order. His left hand lies open on his lap and the right exhibits the Abhayamudrā or the attitude of assurance.‡ When represented, his colour is green and he always faces the North. His Vāhana is a pair of Garuḍas and his crest is the Viśvavajra or the conventional double thunderbolt (Plate VIIIb). Sometimes a serpent with seven hoods forms the background and the expanded hoods form his umbrella. (Plate VIIIc). In front of his shrine therefore, is found a small square pit which represents the tank in which the serpent resides.

5. Ratnasambhava.

Colour—Yellow. Mudrā—Varada.
Crest--Jewels. Vāhana—A pair of lions.

A few deities only emanate from this Dhyānī Buddha and this fact accounts for his late incorporation into the Buddhist Pantheon. The Nepalese Buddhists regard him as the third Dhyānī Buddha in order, who always faces the South when represented on the Stūpas. His colour is yellow ; his left hand rests on the lap with open palm and the right exhibits the Varadamudrā or the gift-bestowing attitude § (Plate IXa). His Vāhana is a pair of lions and his crest is the jewel (Ratnacchaṭā) (Plate VIIId).

* Compare Advayavajrasaṁgraha—" Oṁkārajaḥ śuklavarṇṇaḥ Vairocanaḥ śukla [cakra] cinhaḥ Bodhyagrīmudrādharaḥ Rūpaskandhasvabhāvaḥ.... Hemantartuviśuddhaḥ madhurarasaśarīraḥ kavargavyāpī.... Oṁ Āḥ Jinajika Huṁ ityasya jāpamantraḥ." ....Fol. 26.

† This bronze belongs to the collection of Pandit Siddhiharṣa.

‡ Cf. Advayavajrasaṁgraha—" Uttaradale śyāma-Khaṁ-kārajaḥ [śyāmavarṇṇo-moghssiddhiḥ viśvavajracihnābhayamudrādharo saṁskāraskandhasvabbāvo varṣārturūpaḥ] ....tiktarasātmakaḥ pavargaviśuddhaḥ....asya ca mantraḥ Oṃ Āḥ Prajñādhṛk Huṁ iti "....Fol. 27.

§ Op. cit. Fol. 26-27—" Dakṣiṇadale sūryyamaṇḍalopari Trāṁ-kārajaḥ pītavarṇṇo Ratnasambhavo ratnacihnavaradamudrādharo vedanāsvabhāvapiśunaśarīraḥ.... vasantartulabaṇaśarīraḥ tavargavyāpī....Oṁ Āḥ Ratnadhṛk Huṁ asya jāpamantraḥ."

6. Vajrasattva.

Āsana—Vajraparyanka. Symbols—Vajra and Ghaṇṭā.

Vajrasattva, the sixth Dhyānī Buddha is regarded, at least by the Vajrācāryyas of Nepal, as the Purohita or the priest of the group of the five Dhyānī Buddhas. He is not represented in the Stūpa, but independent shrines are dedicated to his worship. His worship is always performed in secret and is not open to those who are not initiated into the mysteries of the Vajrayāna, and he is represented in two forms, single and Yab-yum (Anuttara-Vajrasattva).

The most notable feature of this Dhyānī Buddha is that he wears ornaments and princely garments instead of the three pieces of rags (tricīvara). Instead of bare head he has a gaudy Mukuṭa (tiara) over it. These would have suited a Bodhisattva quite well but the mere idea of a Dhyānī Buddha wearing ornaments and rich garments is altogether reprehensible.

He sits cross-legged (Dhyānāsana) and carries the Vajra in the right hand with palm upwards against the breast and the Ghaṇṭā in the left resting against the left thigh * (Plate IXb). When represented singly he is exhibited before the public. The Sādhanamāla has several Sādhanas in which there are short Dhyānas or descriptions of Vajrasattva both single and Yab-yum. One of the Dhyānas mentions him as bearing the effigy of Akṣobhya on the crown, thereby alleging that at least in some quarters he was regarded as an emanation of Akṣobhya, and his dress and ornaments supply ample materials for thinking so ; and in that case he would be another form of Vajrapāṇi. Whatever might be the fact, the modern Buddhists regard him as one of the highest among the gods of the Buddhist Pantheon.

When represented in Yab-yum he is closely associated with his Śakti in embrace. He carries the Vajra and the Ghaṇṭā exactly in the same way when represented singly ; but the Śakti carries the Kartri in the right hand and the Kapāla in the left. (Plate IXcde).

In identifying the images of Dhyānī Buddhas it should always be remembered that they must and shall be represented in the Vajraparyaṅka (Adamantine) pose or the Dhyānāsana (meditative pose), and if any image is

* Cf. Advayavajrasaṁgraha, Fol. 26—" Vajrasattvastu Huṁ-kārajanmā....dvibhuja ekavaktro vajravajraghaṇṭādharaḥ manaḥsvabhāvaḥ kāṣāyarasaśarīraḥ śaradṛtuviśuddhaḥ yaralavādyātmakaḥ "....Compare also the description given in the Dharmakoṣasaṅgraha of Amṛtānanda—" Ekavaktraḥ śuklavarṇṇaḥ jaṭāmukuṭī ṣaṇmudrālaṅkṛtaḥ dvibhujaḥ savyena hṛdayapradeśe ākuñcitena bhujena kuliśaṃ bibhrāṇaḥ yasmin kulīśe śatāni koṭayaḥ agrabhāgāḥ santi. Vāmena bhujena nābhipradeśe ākuñcitena ghaṇṭāṃ vādayamānaḥ....Mārāḥ palāyitāḥ. Kamalopari vajrāsanaḥ."

(b) Vajrasattva (Nepal)

(c) Vajrasattva Yab-yum
(Nepal)

(a) Ratnasambhava
(Nepal)

(d) Vajrasattva Yab-yum
(Side View)

(e) Vajrasattva Yab-yum
(Back View)

Plate IX

Tabular Statement showing the attributes of the five Dhyānī Buddhas.

Dhyānī Buddha	Colour	Mudrā	Crest	Vāhana	Skandha	Position	Vījamantra	Season	Rasa	Varga
1. Vairocana	White	Dharmacakra	Discus	Dragons	Rūpa	Centre	Oṃ	Hemanta	Madhura	Ka
2. Ratnasambhava	Yellow	Varada	Jewel	Lions	Vedanā	South	Trāṃ	Vasanta	Labaṇa	Ta
3. Amitābha	Red	Samādhi	Lotus	Peacocks	Saṃjñā	West	Hrīḥ	Grīṣma	Amla	Ṭa
4. Amoghasiddhi	Green	Abhaya	Viśvavajra	Garuḍas	Saṃskāra	North	Khaṃ	Varṣā	Tikta	Pa
5. Akṣobhya	Blue	Bhūsparśa	Vajra	Elephants	Vijñāna	East	Huṃ	Śiśira	Kaṭu	Ca

represented otherwise, we may at once reject its identification as a Dhyānī Buddha.*

The tabular statement in page 7A shows the colour, position, mudrā, crest the Vījamantra, the Skandhas, the seasons, tastes and the letters of the alphabet represented by the five Dhyānī Buddhas.

II. DIVINE BUDDHAŚAKTIS.

Next in rank, but not very widely represented is the group of the Divine Buddhaśaktis, five in number, to which a sixth is added. The Buddhaśaktis affiliate themselves to their respective Dhyānī Buddhas, whose figures or images they generally bear on their crown. Cases in which they are represented on the stupas, in full form to the left of their husbands, are rare but more often their symbols or the Yantras are represented each on a slab in a niche. They occupy the corners intermediate between the four cardinal points taken up by the four or five Dhyānī Buddhas as the case may be.† The Buddhaśaktis are :—

1. Vajradhātvīśvarī (Plate Xa).
2. Locanā (Plate Xb).
3. Māmakī (Plate Xc).
4. Pāṇḍarā (Plate Xd).
5. Āryatārā (Plate XIa).
6. Vajrasattvātmikā.

Each Dhyānī Buddha has a Śakti or consort associated with him through whom a Divine Bodhisattva is brought forth. The Buddhaśaktis when sculptured or painted are represented in a sitting posture, mostly in Lalitāsana on a full blown lotus. The two hands generally hold a lotus each. The left hand exhibiting the Varada pose and the right resting on the right foreleg. The figure wears a petticoat fastened round the loins and a tight-fitting jacket or a bodice. Each head is decorated with a bejewelled crown. Each Śakti has the colour and the Vāhana of the Dhyānī Buddha to whom

* In the stone image of Vajrasattva (Plate IXb) from Nepal, he sits in the Paryaṅka attitude instead of the Vajraparyaṅka attitude. There is an inscription on the pedestal purporting the image to be that of Vajrasattva. Nowhere else have we found Vajrasattva represented in the Paryaṅkāsana. All the images of Vajrasattva in the Indian Museum and the Sarnath Museum strictly follow the description given in the Dharmakoṣasaṅgraha. This Nepal image is the only exception to this rule.

† See Oldfield : Sketches from Nipal, II, p. 171-72.

she belongs. The Buddhśaktis are so alike in appearance that they can be recognized only by the crests that they bear on the lotus.*

III. DIVINE BODHISATTVAS.

The word, 'Bodhisattva' in earlier times was synonymous with Saṅgha or the Holy Order and every Buddhist of the Mahāyāna faith was entitled to be called a Bodhisattva. In the Gāndhāra School of sculpture we meet with innumerable Bodhisattva images, both standing and sitting, and we venture to think that these images represented the more influential ones of the Holy Order. In Hiuen Tsang's time the great savants only of the Mahāyāna faith went by the name of Bodhisattva. This is true at least in the case of men like, Nāgārjuna, Aśvaghoṣa, Maitreyanātha, Āryadeva and others. The Buddhist scriptures prescribe certain extraordinary qualities and characteristics for the Bodhisattva. The duty of the Divine Bodhisattvas however, is to do the duties of a Mortal Buddha during the period between the disappearance of one Buddha and the coming of the next. Thus Gautama Buddha has disappeared and at least 4000 years after his disappearance Maitreya Buddha who is now in the Tuṣita Heaven would descend to earth. During the interval Padmapāṇi Bodhisattva or Avalokiteśvara is doing the duties of a Mortal Buddha and thus he will continue so long as the Bhadrakalpa or the cycle of Amitābha continues.

The Divine Bodhisattvas are also five in number to which a sixth is likewise added. They affiliate themselves to one or the other of the Dhyānī Buddhas and their respective Buddhaśaktis. They are :—

1. Sāmantabhadra (Plate XIb).
2. Vajrapāṇi (Plate XIc).
3. Ratnapāṇi (Plate XId).
4. Padmapāṇi (Plate XIe).
5. Viśvapāṇi (Plate XIf).
6. Ghaṇṭāpāṇi.

They are sometimes represented as standing erect and sometimes in different sitting attitudes (e.g. Plate XIIbc) each on a full-blown lotus and usually as holding in each hand a long stem of the same plant on which is placed the crest of the spiritual father of each. Each is covered by a robe and the upper part is covered by a scarf. The hair is cut short and on the head is a jewelled

* The illustrations of the five Buddhaśaktis have been taken from Wright's History of Nepal, Plate VI. Mr. Wright reproduces in Plate VI several drawings prepared by the native Citrakāras of Nepal.

(a) Vajradhātvīśvarī

(c) Māmakī

(b) Locanā

(d) Pāṇḍarā

Plate X

tiara which bears in the centre the effigy of that Buddha to whom the Bodhisattva owes his existence.* In order to explain more clearly the relation between the Bodhisattvas, their Buddhaśaktis and the Dhyānī Buddhas a tabular statement is given below :—

Dhyānī Buddha	Divinc Buddhaśakti	Divine Bodhisattva
Vairocaṇa	Vajradhātvīśvarī	Sāmantabhadra
Akṣobhya	Locanā	Vajrapāṇi
Ratnasambhava	Māmakī	Ratnapāṇi
Amitābha	Pāṇḍarā	Padmapāṇi
Amoghasiddhi	Āryatārā	Viśvapāṇi
Vajrasattva	Vajrasattvātmikā	Ghaṇṭāpāṇi

The illustrations† represent the five Divine Bodhisattvas in bronze. They are perhaps unique of their kind in India and hail from the U Vahāl at Patan in Nepal. All these images exactly correspond to the dictum laid down above except in the cases of Sāmantabhadra and Vajrapāṇi. The former shows the Dharmacakra Mudrā like his spiritual father, Vairocana, while the latter carries the Vajra and the Ghaṇṭā, the symbols of Vajrasattva, though not exactly in the same fashion. But according to the dictum, Sāmantabhadra ought to have carried the stem of the lotus bearing the Cakra, the symbol of his father in his two hands, the right palm in Varadamudrā being stamped with the same cognizance (Plate XIIa). The image of Vajrapāṇi on the other hand would have been more consistent if it had carried the stem of the lotus bearing the Vajra, the symbol of his spiritual father, Akṣobhya and if one of his hands had been stamped with it. ‡ The Vajra and Ghaṇṭā are the symbols of Vajrasattva and Ghaṇṭāpāṇi carries them. We are likely to confuse the images of the two, but the only consolation is that Ghaṇṭāpāṇi is very rarely represented.

IV. MORTAL BUDDHAS.

Both the Mahāyānists and the Hinayānists hold that a Buddha is one who is endowed with the thirty-two major and eighty minor auspicious marks. These are known as the external characteristics enumerated in Dharmasaṁ-

* See also Oldfield : Sketches from Nipal Vol. II, p. 175.

† In Plate XI. ‡ See Plate XIIb.

graha, attributed to Nāgārjuna.* He must have in addition three kinds of mental characteristics, namely, the ten Balas or forces, eighteen Āvenika Dharmas or peculiar properties, and the four Vaiśaradyas or points of self-confidence or assurance.†

The Hinayānists recognized in the earliest state twenty-four past Buddhas each having a peculiar Bodhi tree. The Mahāyanists also give several lists, though not systematically, and thirty-two different names have been recovered. The last seven Tathāgatas are well-known and are designated by the Mahāyānists as Mānuṣī or Mortal Buddhas. These are, Vipaśyin, Sikhī, Viśvabhū, Krakucchanda, Kanakamuni, Kaśyapa and Śākyasiṁha.‡ It is still to be found out whether these Buddhas, excepting the last of course, have any historicity behind them. We may be certain, however, that Kanakamuni and Krakucchanda were historical personages.§

Attempts have been made to establish a fantastic connection between the last five Mortal Buddhas with the five Dhyānī Buddhas and their Bodhisattvas by holding that the Divine Boddhisattvas discharge their duties of creation through the agency of the five Mortal Buddhas. The theory may be current in Tibet; it may ingeniously establish a new connection and may find strong support from scholars, but we may rest assured that the theory is against all historical sense and traditions.

When represented, the last seven Mortal Buddhas appear all alike; they are of one colour and one form, usually sitting cross-legged with the right hand displaying the earth-touching attitude,** that is, the Mudrā of Akṣobhya and as a matter of fact we are unable to identify a sculpture of the latter unless it is coloured or if no other identification mark is present. When painted, the Mortal Buddhas generally have yellow or golden colour. The only possible chance of identifying them is when they appear in groups of seven.

Sometimes they are represented as standing, in which case they appear under a distinguishing Bodhi Tree and with a distinguishing mudrā. The Indian Museum image No. B. G. 83 (Plate XIId) is an image of this kind. It may be noted however that Maitreya, the future Buddha has been added to this group.

* Dharmasaṅgraha, pp. 53-60.

† Kern : Manual of Buddhism, p. 62.

‡ Ibid, p. 64.

§ Ibid, footnote 1.

** Colossal images of the seven Mortal Buddhas representing them in the Bhūmisparśa Mudrā appear in one of the Buddhist Cave Temples at Ellora. See Fergusson and Burgess: Cave Temples of India, p. 383.

(a) Āryatārā

(b) Samantabhadra (Nepal)

(c) Vajrapāṇi (Nepal)

(d) Ratnapāṇi (Nepal)

(e) Padmapāṇi (Nepal)

(f) Viśvapāṇi (Nepal)

Plate XI

GAUTAMA BUDDHA.

Gautama, the last of the group of the seven Mortal Buddhas, is widely represented both in sculptures and in paintings. His images date from a period anterior to the birth of Christ and the Indian sculptors never seem to have been tired of this one hackneyed subject. Innumerable images of Buddha in innumerable attitudes and expressions have been discovered in India and this is true also of countries beyond, where Buddhism penetrated. Images of Buddha, therefore, are an independent study by themselves.

The Sādhanamālā furnishes us with several descriptions of **Buddha in Vajrāsana**, who is represented as sitting in the Vajraparyaṅka attitude with his right hand displaying the Bhūmiṣparśana pose. The Dhyāna* as given in one of the Sādhanas in the Sādhanamālā is thus quoted below and translated :—

Savyakareṇa Bhūṣparśamudrāṁ utsaṅgasthitāvasavyahastaṃ kāṣāyavastrāvaguṇṭhanaṃ nīlagauraraktaśyāmacatur-Māropari viśvapadmavajrāvasthitaṃ śāntaṃ lakṣaṇavyañjanenānvitagātraṃ. Tasya Bhagavato dakṣiṇe Maitreya-Bodhisattvaṃ gauraṃ dvibhujaṃ jaṭāmukuṭinaṃ savyakareṇa cāmararatnadhāriṇaṃ avasavyena nāgakeśarapuṣpachhaṭādhāriṇaṃ. Tathā vāmato Lokeśvaraṃ śuklaṃ dakṣiṇakareṇa cāmaradharaṃ vāmakareṇa kamaladharaṃ Bhagavanmukhāvalokanaparau ca tau bhāvayet....

Iti Vajrāsanasādhanaṃ samāptaṃ."

Sādhanamālā. A—15, N—13, C—5.

" The worshipper should meditate on himself as [Vajrāsana] who displays the Bhūṣparśa Mudrā in his right hand while the left rests on the lap ; who is dressed in red garments and sits on the Vajra on a double lotus placed on the four Māras of blue, white, red and green colour ; who is peaceful in appearance and whose body is endowed with all the major and minor auspicious marks.

To the right of the God is Maitreya Bodhisattva who is white, two-armed and wears the Jaṭāmukuṭa, and carries the chowrie-jewel in the right hand and the Nāgakeśara flower in the left.

Similarly to the left is Lokeśvara of white complexion carrying in his right hand the chowrie and the lotus in the left.

These two gods should be meditated as looking towards the face of the [principal] god......

Here ends the Sādhana for Vajrāsana."

Images of this divinity are found in overwhelming numbers in almost all Buddhist centres in India. The Indian Museum image reproduced is an example of this form of Gautama in Plate XIIIa. †

* See also Foucher : L'Iconographie Bouddhique p. 15 ff.

† It may be noted that instead of sitting on the Vajra the seat of the god is stamped with a small thunderbolt.

V. MORTAL BUDDHAŚAKTIS.

Like the Dhyānī Buddhas, the Mortal Buddhas have also their respective Buddhaśaktis through whom they obtained the seven Mortal Bodhisattvas. The Buddhaśaktis are :—

1. Vipaśyantī
2. Sikhimālinī
3. Viśvadharā
4. Kakudvatī
5. Kaṇṭhamālinī
6. Mahidharā
7. Yaśodharā.*

We have not yet met with any representation of these anywhere in India.

VI, MORTAL BODHISATTVAS.

They were brought into existence by their respective Mortal Buddhas and their Śaktis. They are :—

1. Mahāmati
2. Ratnadhara
3. Ākāśagañja
4. Śakamaṅgala
5. Kanakarāja
6. Dharmadhara
7. Ānanda.†

The names of Yaśodharā and Ānanda are familiar names, the former being the name of Śākyasiṁha's wife and the latter, that of his most favourite disciple.

* See Oldfield : Sketches from Nipal, Vol. II, 163 and 185 ff.

† Ibid.

(a) Samantabhadra

(b) Vajrapāṇi
(Indian Museum)

(c) Vajrapāṇi (Nālandā)

(d) Seven Mortal Buddhas with Maitreya
(Indian Museum)

Plate XII

The relation between the Mortal Buddhas, their Buddhaśaktis and Bodhisattvas may be thus shown in a tabular form :—

Mortal Buddha	Mortal Buddhaśakti	Mortal Bodhisattva
Vipaśyī	Vipaśyantī	Mahāmati
Śikhī	Śikhimālinī	Ratnadhara
Viśvabhū	Viśvadharā	Ākāśagañja
Krakucchanda	Kakudvatī	Śakamaṅgala
Kanakamuni	Kaṇṭhamālinī	Kanakarāja
Kaśvapa	Mahidharā	Dharmadhara
Śākyasiṁha	Yaśodharā	Ānanda

VII. MAITREYA, THE FUTURE BUDDHA.

It would not be out of place to mention here the name of Maitreya, who partakes of the nature of a Mortal Buddha, though he is not a Buddha yet. He is passing the life of a Boddhisattva in the Tuṣita Heaven, preparatory to his descent to the earth in human form. It is said that he would come to earth, full 4000 years after the disappearance of Buddha Gautama, for the deliverance of all sentient beings. Asaṅga is said to have visited Maitreya in the Tuṣita Heaven and the latter initiated him into the mysteries of Tantra. He is the only Bodhisattva worshipped both by the Hinayānists and the Mahāyanists alike, and his images can be traced from the Gāndhāra School down to the present time. Hiuen Tsang records the existence of a colossal image of Maitreya in Udyāna (U-chang-na). The sculptor in order to ascertain his correct form, is believed to have gone several times to the Tuṣita heaven before carving it.

Maitreya may be represented as a standing figure richly decorated with ornaments holding in his right hand the stalk of a lotus. He is distinguished from Padmapāṇi mainly by the figure of a small caitya, which the former bears on his crown. Getty remarks * that in Indian sculpture his hands form the usual Dharmacakramudrā ; in the left there is a vase, round, oval

* Getty : Gods of the Northern Buddhism, p. 21.

or pointed, or there may be the stems of flowers which support his two characteristic symbols, the vase and the wheel. Maitreya may also be represented seated as a Buddha with legs interlocked or both dangling down. His colour is yellow and his images sometimes bear the figures of the five Dhyani Buddhas on the aureole behind them. The small caitya on the crown of Maitreya is said to refer to the belief that a stūpa in the mount Kukkuṭapāda near Bodh-Gaya covers a spot where Kaśyapa Buddha is lying. When Maitreya would descend to earth he would go direct to the spot which would open by magic and Kaśyapa would give him the garments of a Buddha.*

The Sādhanamālā furnishes us with only one description of Maitreya as a principal divinity and several others in which he is represented as a minor god. When as a minor god he accompanies others, he generally carries the chowrie in the right hand and the Nāgakeśara flower in the left. The Sādhana describing the procedure of his worship has the following Dhyāna. †

....Pīta 'Maiṃ'kārapariṇataṃ viśvakamalasthitaṃ trimukhaṃ caturbhujaṃ kṛṣṇaśukladakṣiṇavāmamukhaṃ suvarṇagauraṃ sattvaparyaṅkinaṃ vyākhyānamudrādharakaradvayaṃ aparadakṣiṇavāmabhujābhyāṃ varadapuṣpitanāgakeśaramañjarīdharaṃ nānālaṅkāradharaṃ ātmānaṃ Maitreyarūpaṃ ālambya......

Maitreyasādhanaṃ " Sādhanamālā, A-307, Na-28, C-286.

" The worshipper should meditate on himself as Maitreya who originates from the yellow germ syllable "Maim," who is three-faced, three-eyed and four-armed ; whose right and left faces respectively are of blue and white colour ; whose complexion is yellow like gold ; who sits in the Paryaṅka attitude on an animal ; whose two hands are engaged in exhibiting the Vyākhyāna Mudrā and who shows in his other right and left hands the Varada Mudrā and the sprout of a full-blown Nāgakeśara flower ; who is decked in many ornaments. Meditating thus......

This is the Sādhana for Maitreya."

A Nepalese drawing reproduced in Plate XIIIb, represents this form of Maitreya, which follows the Dhyāna in all its details except the Vāhana.

* Getty : Gods of the Northern Buddhism, p. 22.

† Also quoted in Foucher : L'Iconographie Bouddhique, part 2, p. 48

(a) Vajrāsana (Indian Museum)

(b) Maitreya

(c) Vāk or Vajrarāga Mañjuśrī

(d) Siddhaikavīra (Sārnāth)

Plate XIII

CHAPTER II.

MAÑJUŚRĪ.

There is no doubt, the scholars are agreed, that the place assigned to Mañjuśrī in the Buddhist Pantheon is one of the very highest. The Mahāyānists consider him to be one of the greatest Bodhisattvas. They believe that the worship of Mañjuśrī confers upon them wisdom, retentive memory, intelligence and eloquence and enables them to master many sacred scriptures; and it is no wonder that his worship was widely prevalent among the Mahāyānists. They conceived him in various forms and worshipped him with various mantras. Those who could not form any conception of him according to Tāntric rites, attained perfection by simply muttering the mantras.

It is difficult to fix the exact date when Mañjuśrī entered the Buddhist Pantheon. His image is not to be found in the Gandhara and Mathura sculptures, and Aśvaghoṣa Nāgārjuna and Āryadeva do not mention him in their works. His name occurs for the first time in the Sukhāvatī Vyūha or the Amitāyus Sūtra.* But here also his name appears only in the smaller recension of the work. This work was translated into Chinese between A.D. 384 and A. D. 417.† Since then we find mention of Mañjuśrī in the subsequent Buddhist Sanskrit works and in the accounts of the Chinese travellers, Fa-hien, ‡ Hiuen Tsang, I-Tsing and others, and his images are to be found in the sculptures of Sarnath, Magadha, Bengal, Nepal and other places.

Many details § about Mañjuśri are to be found in the Svayambhū Purāṇa dealing with the glories of the Svayambhūkṣettra in Nepal. The Ādi-Buddha manifested himself here in the shape of a flame of fire and so it is called the Svayambhūkṣettra or the 'Place of the Self-Born'. This place is consecrated with a temple of Ādi-Buddha and close to it is the Mañjuśrī Hill now known as the Sarasvatīsthāna. The information about Mañjuśrī as gleaned from the Svayambhū Purāṇa is given below in brief.

It is said in the Svayambhū Purāṇa that Mañjuśrī hailed from China where he was living on mount Pañcaśīrṣa (the Hill of Five Peaks). He was a

* Sukhāvati-Vyūha, p. 92 App. II.

† Ibid. Introduction. p. III, n. 4 (1).

‡ There is considerable difference of opinion as regards the divinity of Mañjuśrī mentioned by Fa-Hien. Legge, Travels of Fa-Hien p. 46.

§ An account of the story recorded in the Svayambhū Purāṇa with many details will be found in (1) R. Mitra; *Sanskrit Buddhist Literature*, pp. 249—258. (2) Hodgson's *Essays*. p. 115 ff. and (3) Oldfield: *Sketches from Nipal* Vol. II p. 185fl.

great saint with a good number of disciples and followers including the king of that country, Dharmākara by name. One day Mañjuśrī received divine intimation that the self-born Lord, Ādi-Buddha had manifested himself in the form of a flame of fire on a lotus rising from the Lake Kālihrada in Nepal. He forthwith started for Nepal to pay homage to the god and was accompanied by a large number of his disciples, his two wives and king Dharmākara of China. When he came to the lake he found the god inaccessible, being surrounded by the vast expanse of water. With great difficulty he approached the flame of fire and paid his homage. Then he cast about in his mind how to make the god accessible, and began to go round the lake. He then with his sword cleft asunder the southern barrier of hills and the water rushed through that opening, leaving a vast stretch of dry land behind, which is known as the Nepal valley. Through that opening the water of the Bāghmatī even now flows down and it is still called 'Koṭ-bār' or 'sword-cut.'

Mañjuśrī lost no time in erecting a temple consecrating the flame of fire, and very near to the temple on a hillock he made his own habitation. On the same hill he made a Vihāra (or monastery) still known as the Mañjupattana for his disciples. Lastly he made Dharmākara the king of Nepal. These and many other pious deeds are ascribed to Mañjuśrī in the Svayambhū Purāṇa. Putting everything in proper order Mañjuśrī returned home and soon obtained the divine form of a Bodhisattva, leaving his mundane body behind.

From the above it appears that Mañjuśrī was a great man who brought civilization to Nepal from China. He had extraordinary engineering skill and was a great architect. We are not sure when he came down to Nepal from China, but there is no doubt that in the fourth century A.D. he was well-known as a Bodhisattva. He wielded great influence on the minds of the Buddhists and the Mahāyānists worshipped him in various forms and various ways. He is known in almost all the countries in the continent of Asia where Buddhism made its way. Various countries conceived various forms of Mañjuśrī. But we are here concerned only with the images that are purely Indian and not with those that hail from outside the country.

We have already made it abundantly clear that the Buddhists believe their gods as emanating from one or the other of the Dhyānī Buddhas or four or five of them collectively. But it had not been possible to assign Mañjuśrī to one particular Dhyānī Buddha or to one particular group of the Dhyānī Buddhas. The reason is not far to seek. We have evidence that the list of the Five Dhyānī Buddhas was completed sometime after Śāntideva if not considerably later, though two or three of them were known prior to him. It is after Śāntideva that the priests of Vajrayāna conceived the idea that all gods should emanate from one or the other of the Dhyānī Buddhas or four or five of them collectively, in the same way as Avalokiteśvara emanated from Amitābha.

Mañjuśrī was introduced into the Buddhist Pantheon long after Avalokiteśvara and nobody has any doubt as to his human personality. But Avalokiteśvara was an abstract idea, and never a man, and it is said that Amitābha in his anxiety to create caused a golden ray of light to appear from his head and in it originated the Bodhisattva Avalokiteśvara.* With Mañjuśrī the case is otherwise. He was regarded as a Bodhisattva in the same way as Aśvaghoṣa, Nāgārjuna, Āryadeva, Asaṅga and many others were regarded as Bodhisattvas in the time of Hiuen Tsang. But this is no reason why we should not regard Mañjuśrī as an emanation of any of the Dhyānī Buddhas. As a matter of fact, some considered him to be an emanation of Amitābha, others of Akṣobhya, still others of the group of the five Dhyānī Buddhas. Cases are, however, on record where Mañjuśrī is not affiliated to any of the Dhyānī Buddhas, i.e., in other words, regarded as independent.

Thirty-nine Sādhanas in the Sādhanamālā are devoted to the worship of Mañjuśrī and forty dhyānas describe fourteen distinct forms of the Bodhisattva. In finding out the names of the different varieties, special stress has been laid on the mantras rather than on the colophons of the Sādhanas. It should always be remembered that in determining the names of gods the mantras are the safest guide, especially when one deity has a great many forms. The fourteen varieties have each a different name e.g., Vāgīśvara, Mañjuvara, Mañjughoṣa, Arapacana, Siddhaikavīra, Vāk, Mañjukumāra, Vajrānaṅga, Vādirāṭ, Nāmasaṅgīti, Dharmadhātu-Vāgīśvara, Sthiracakra, Mañjunātha and Mañjuvajra.

Ordinarily Mañjuśrī carries the Sword and the Book in his right and left hands. In representations we sometimes find these two symbols placed on lotuses. He is accompanied sometimes by Yamāri, or by his Śakti alone ; sometimes by Sudhanakumāra and Yamāri and sometimes again by the four divinities, Jālinīkumāra also called Sūryyaprabha, Candraprabha, Keśinī and Upakeśinī. Though the last four are required to be present with Arapacana, they are found represented in other places also.

I. EMANATIONS CF AMITĀBHA.

The following two varieties of Mañjuśrī should bear the effigy of their sire Amitābha, one on the tongue and the other on the crown. The former is Vāk and the latter is Dharmadhātu-Vāgīśvara.

* Getty : *Gods of the Northern Pantheon*, p. 54.

1. VĀK.

Mudrā—Samādhi. Āsana—Vajraparyaṅka.
Special characteristics—Ornaments and dress.

He is also known as Dharmasaṅkhasamādhi, Vajrarāga, and Amitābha-Mañjuśrī, and is one faced and two-armed. His two hands are joined in the lap forming the Dhyāna or Samādhi Mudrā. In this respect he is identical with his sire whom he bears on his tongue. But he may be distinguished by the ornaments he wears and by the image of his sire if represented on the crown. The Dhyānī Buddhas have no ornaments and being creators themselves they have no fathers. Images of this form of Mañjuśrī are extremely rare in India with the exception of the one at the temple of Bauddhanath in Nepal. The accompanying sketch (Plate XIIIc) gives an idea of what Vāk is like. The Sādhanamālā has the following Dhyāna :—

" Dvibhujaikamukhaṃ sitaṃ vajraparyaṅkopari samādhimudrāhastam aśeṣakumārābharaṇabhūṣitaṃ pañcacīrakaṃ Mañjuśrībhaṭṭārakaṃ......niṣpādya....vajrajihvopari Buddhaṃ Amitābhaṃ vicintya....Oṃ Vākyedannamaḥ iti japamantraḥ."

Vākśādhanaṃ " Sādhanamālā, A-68, N-51.*

" The worshipper should meditate on himself the form of Mañjuśrī Bhaṭṭāraka, who is two-armed and one-faced, has white complexion ; whose hands are joined in forming the Samādhimudra; who is decked in all princely ornaments, wears the five pieces of monkish garments....thus meditating.... he should conceive the figure of Buddha Amitābha on the adamantine tongue....“ Oṃ Vākyedannamaḥ ” is the mantra for muttering.

DHARMADHĀTU VĀGĪŚVARA.

Faces—Four. Hands—Eight. Āsana—Lalita.

The images of Dharmadhātu Vāgīśvara are by no means common either in stone or in bronze. The Citrakāras in Nepal, however, do even now prepare paintings of this god. When represented he is of white complexion, has four faces and eight arms, and bears the five jewels on his tiara; he is clad in celestial garments and displays amorous sentiment. The two principal hands carry the bow and the arrow, the second pair the noose and the goad, the third the book and the sword, and the fourth, the Ghaṇṭā and the Vajra. He may have another form † exhibiting the Dharmacakra Mudrā in the first pair instead of the bow and the arrow, and in the second pair the arrow and the vessel

* Omitted in C.

† *See* Foucher: *L'Iconographie Bouddhique* II, 47 lines 1—5. This form bears the images of the five Dhyānī Buddhas on the crown.

instead of the noose and the goad. The Dhyāna describing the former is given below :—

" ....Aṣṭabhujaṃ caturmukhaṃ mūlamukhaṃ raktagauraṃ dakṣiṇaṃ kuṁkumāruṇaṃ paścimaṃ padmaraktaṃ, uttaraṃ pītaraktaṃ, dvābhyāṃ hastābhyāṃ dhanurbāṇadharaṃ, aparābhyāṃ pāśāṅkuśadharaṃ, punaraparābhyāṃ Prajñāpāramitāpustakakhaḍgadharaṃ, tathāparābhyāṃ ghaṇṭāvajradharaṃ mahārāgasṛṅgārarasojjvalaṃ lalitāsanasthaṃ viśvapadmacandre divyavastrābharaṇaṃ Amitābhajaṭāmukuṭinaṃ....

Dharmadhātuvāgīśvarasādhanavaśyavidhiḥ "

Sādhanamālā, A-67. N-51, C-51.

The worshipper should meditate in himself the form of [Dharmadhātu-Vāgīśvara] who is eight-armed, four-faced, and of reddish white colour, with the right face of red colour, face to the West of lotus-red colour and the face to the North of yellowish-red colour; who holds the bow and the arrow in one pair, the noose and the goad in another pair, the Prajñāpāramitā and the sword in another and the Ghaṇṭā and the Vajra in the remaining pair; who is resplendent with intense sentiment of passion and sits on the moon on a double lotus in the Lalita attitude; who is decked in celestial garments and ornaments and bears in his crown of chignon the effigy of Amitābha.... "

II. EMANATIONS OF AKSOBHYA.

No less than four varieties of Mañjuśrī are distinctly said to bear the images of Akṣobhya on their crown. Out of these four, Mañjughosa and Siddhaikavīra have four Sādhanas each devoted to their worship. The third variety is known as Vajrānaṅga to whom three Sādhanas are ascribed, but is not known to have been represented either in stone or in bronze. Similar is the case with the fourth one, Nāmasaṅgīti Mañjuśrī.

MAÑJUGHOṢA.

Vāhana—Lion. Mudrā—Vyākhyāna.
Characteristic Symbol—Lotus in the left.

Four Sādhanas in the Sādhanamālā describe the form of this variety of Mañjuśrī, which is known by the name of Mañjughoṣa. When represented he appears almost similar to Mañjuvara with the difference that the lotus here does not bear the book. It may also be pointed out that Mañjughoṣa should have the lotus only to his left, but Mañjuvara may have it on either side bearing the book. He has golden complexion, rides the lion and is decked in all sorts of ornaments. He is two-armed and displays the Vyākhyāna Mudrā, and to his left rises the lotus. He is sometimes accompanied by Yamāri in the left and Sudhanakumāra in the right. The Dhyāna as given in one of the Sādhanas is given below :—

....“ Mañjughoṣarūpaṃ ātmānaṃ paśyet siṃhasthaṃ kanakagauravarṇaṃ sarvālaṅkārabhūṣitaṃ Vyākhyānamudrāvyagrakaraṃ vāmapārśve utpaladharaṃ Akṣobhyamukuṭinaṃ. Dakṣiṇe Sudhanakumāraṃ vāme Yamāntakaṃ paśyet....mantraṃ japet Oṃ Vāgīśvara Muḥ *.... ”

Sādhanamālā, A-56-7, N-43, C-43.

The worshipper should meditate in himself the form of Mañjughoṣa who is seated on the lion ; whose colour is golden yellow ; who is decked in all ornaments ; whose hands are engaged in forming the Vyākhyāna Mudrā ; who has the Utpala in his left side and bears the image of Akṣobhya on the crown. To his right Sudhanakumāra and to the left Yamāntaka † should be conceived....the mantra Om Vāgīśvara Muḥ should be muttered.”

Some of the Sādhanas mention that he should sit in Lalitāsana on the back of a lion, while others are silent about the particular pose. We may therefore, conclude that he may sit in other attitudes also, for instance the Vajraparyaṅka or the Ardhaparyaṅka attitudes. His colour is generally yellow, but he may have the colour of Kuṅkuma as well.

2. Siddhaikavīra.

Colour—white (or) red. Symbol—lotus. Mudrā—Varada.
Special characteristic—figures of Akṣobhya and other Dhyānī Buddhas on crown.

Four Sādhanas describe the form of Siddhaikavīra, and in one of the them he is said to bear the image of Akṣobhya on the crown (*Mauli*), and this fact naturally leads us to conclude that he is an offspring of Akṣobhya ;— this seems to be more probable when we notice the small figure of the Dhyānī Buddha on the crown of the standing figure of Mañjuśrī (Plate XIIId), in the Sarnath Museum. The same Sādhana again calls him ‘ Pañcavīrakaśekharaḥ ’ which means the ‘bearing the five heroic ones (Dhyānī Buddhas) on the crown.’ This word, therefore, we venture to suggest has nothing to do with the god's origin, but the Dhyānī Buddhas, excepting Akṣobhya have been used only as a part of the ornamentation which may or may not be used in actual representations.

* The Mantra of Mañjughoṣa here is “ Oṃ Vāgīśvara Muḥ,” but in other Sādhanas it is “ Oṃ Dharmadhātu-Vāgīśvara Muḥ.” Again, the variety of Mañjuśrī which has been named Vāgīśvara has uniformly the Mantra “ Oṃ Vāgīśvara Muḥ.” As there is a great deal of difference between the forms of Vāgīśvara and Mañjughoṣa, we are inclined to think that the Mantra “ Oṃ Vāgīśvara Muḥ ” in the case of Mañjughoṣa is a mistake for “ Oṃ Dharmadhātu-Vāgīśvara Muḥ.”

† For details about the forms of Sudhanakumāra and Yamāntaka see Foucher: *L'Iconographie Bouddhique* II, p. 41.

When represented he carries the blue lotus in the left hand and exhibits the Varada Mudrā in the right. The Dhyāna describes his form in the following terms :—

Siddhaikavīro Bhagavān candramaṇḍalasthaḥ candropāśrayaḥ jagadudyotakārī dvibhujaḥ ekamukhaḥ śuklaḥ vajraparyaṅkī divyālaṅkārabhūṣitaḥ pañcavīrakaśekharaḥ....vāme nīlotpaladharaḥ dakṣiṇe varadaḥ.... tato Bhagavato maulau Akṣobhyaṃ devatyaḥ * pūjāṃ kurvanti.†

Sādhanamālā, A-74, N-56, C-57.

" The God Siddhaikavīra is on the orb of the moon, is the support of the moon, illumines the world, is two-armed, one-faced and of white complexion ; he sits in the Vajraparyaṅka attitude, is decked in celestial ornaments, bears the effigies of the five Dhyānī Buddhas on the crown....and carries the Utpala in the left hand and exhibits the Varada pose in the right.... then the goddesses pay homage to Akṣobhya who is on the crown of the God.'

In another Sādhana the description of the Maṇḍala‡ for Mañjuśrī is given. The God in the form of Siddhaikavīra, painted red, is in the middle, and is accompanied by four divinities, Jālinīprabha, Candraprabha, Keśinī and Upakeśinī. These four goddesses more often accompany Arapacana, another form of Mañjuśrī, as we shall see later on ; but we must not forget that Keśinī and Upakeśinī both have equal rights to be represented by the side of their common husband, Mañjuśrī. The Sādhanas are not generally explicit as to the pose of the God, and we will not be surprised if he is found standing as in the Sarnath image.

A confusion in likely to take place between the forms of Lokanātha and Siddhaikavīra if they are both represented without companions and without the figure of the Dhyānī Buddha, Amitābha or Akṣobhya as the case may be, on their crown ; for both these worthies have the same symbol, the lotus and the same Mudrā, the Varada pose. In that case the image would generally be identified as Lokanātha, who, because of his being a variety of Avalokiteśvara, is represented widely. Images of Siddhaikavīra, we should add, are extremely rare.

3. Vajrānanga.

Āsana—Pratyālīḍha. Colour—yellow. Hands—six or four.

The third variety bearing the image of Akṣobhya on the crown is known as Vajrānaṅga, who is worshipped in the Tāntric rite of Vaśīkaraṇa or bewitching men and women. He is yellow in complexion, is in the fullness

* A reads "devebhyaḥ." † A omits "kurvanti."

‡ Mañjuśrī (in the form of Siddhaikavīra) should exhibit the Varada pose and carry the lotus ; Sūryyaprabha and Upakeśinī should hold the lotus and exhibit the Varada pose : Candraprabha and Keśinī should also have the same symbol and the same pose of hand. The four companions of Siddhaikavīra should resemble his replicas.

of youth, and bears the image of Akṣobhya on his Jaṭāmukuṭa. The two principal hands hold the fully expanded bow of flowers charged with an arrow of a lotus bud. The four remaining hands carry the sword and the looking-glass in the two right hands while the two left carry the lotus and the Aśoka bough with red flowers. In another Sādhanā the Aśoka bough is replaced by Kaṅkelli flowers. He may have an alternative form with four hands,* in which case the arms carrying the mirror and the Aśoka bough are dropped. The Dhyāna describing the six-armed variety of Vajrānaṅga is given below :—

...." Vajrānaṅgaṃ Ārya-Mañjughoṣaṃ pītavarṇaṃ saḍbhujaṃ mūlabhujābhyāṃ ākarṇapūritaraktotpalakalikāśarayuktakusumadhanurdharaṃ ; dakṣiṇadvayena khaḍgadarpaṇabhṛtaṃ vāmayugalenendīvararaktāśokapallavadharaṃ ; Akṣobhyādhiṣṭhita jaṭāmukuṭinaṃ, pratyālīḍhapadaṃ soḍaṣavarṣākāraṃ mahāsṛṇgāramūrtiṃ paśyet...."

Sādhanamālā, A-64, N-49, C-49-50.

"....The worshipper should conceive himself as Ārya-Mañjughoṣa in the form of Vajrānaṇga with yellow complexion, and six arms ; with the two principal hands he draws to the ear the bow of flowers charged with an arrow of a red lotus bud ; the two remaining hands to the right carry the sword and the mirror, while the two left hold the lotus and the Aśoka bough with red flowers ; he bears the image of Akṣobhya on his crown of chignon, stands in the Pratyālīḍha attitude, appears a youth of sixteen years, and displays the intense sentiment of passion...."

Vajrānaṇga, as the name implies, is the Buddhist God of Love and is the prototype of the Hindu God Madana, in the Buddhist Pantheon. The flowery bow and the arrow of flowers are strikingly common to both. Besides these, unlike the Hindu Anaṅga, several other weapons are also attributed to the Buddhist God of Love and below is given an account of how he makes use of them.

It is written in the Sādhanamālā that in the act of bewitching a woman, she should be imagined by the worshipper as being pierced by him in her bosom with the arrow of the lotus bud. The woman falls flat on the ground swooning. Seeing this the worshipper should conceive that she is bound down in her legs by the chain which is the bow. Then by the noose which is the lotus stalk, she is tied by the neck and is drawn to his side. Then he should think that he is striking her with the Aśoka bough, is frightening her with the sword, and subsequently she has only to be shown the looking-glass to be completely subdued. A short text is quoted below from the Sādhana in support of the statement.

Iṣuṇa tu kucham bidhvā aśokaistāḍayeddhṛdi ।
Khaḍgena bhīṣayet sādhyām darpaṇaṃ darsāyet tataḥ ।

* Text—"Athavā caturbhujam darpaṇāśokapallavadharaṃ dvibhujarahitaṃ dhyāyāt."

(a) Nāmasaṅgīti Mañjuśrī

(b) Nāmasaṅgīti Mañjuśrī (?)
(Nepal)

(c) Vajrānaṅga Mañjuśrī

(d) Mahārājalīlā Mañjuśrī
(Indian Museum)

Plate XIV

Utpalena padam badhvā ākarṣayet suvihvalām (a) ॥ *

Unfortunately no image of this divinity has yet been discovered and it is, therefore, that we reproduce a drawing (Plate XIVc) from an ancient album, though it does not consistently follow all the details in the Sādhanas.

4. Nāmasaṅgīti Mañjuśrī.

Colour—reddish white. Attitude—Vajraparyaṅka.
Faces—three. Arms—four.

The fourth variety of Mañjuśrī with the effigy of the Dhyānī Buddha, Akṣobhya, on the crown is known as Nāmasaṅgīti Mañjuśtrī, to whom only one Sādhana in the Sādhanamālā is assigned. In this Sādhana he is described as three-faced and four-armed, and as bearing the image of Akṣobhya on the crown. The first or the principal face is red, the second blue and the third white. Of his four hands the first pair holds the bow and the arrow and the second the Book and the Sword. He sits in the Vajraparyaṅka attitude on the lotus. The Dhyāna describes him in the following terms :—

...." Raktagauraṃ padmacandropari † vajraparyaṅkaniṣaṇṇaḥ ; prathamamukhaṃ raktaṃ, dakṣiṇaṃ nīlaṃ, vāme śuklaṃ iti trimukhaṃ, hastacatuṣṭayena yathāyogaṃ Prajñākhaḍgadhanurbāṇayoginaṃ ratnakirīṭīnaṃ dvātṛṃśallakṣaṇānuvyañjanavirājitaṃ kumāraṃ kumārābharaṇabhūṣitaṃ ātmānaṃ vibhāvya....‡ tadanu sarva-Tathāgatābhiṣekapūrvakaṃ Akṣobhyamaulinaṃ ātmānam vicintya.....

Ārya-Nāmasaṅgītisādhanaṃ samāptam." Sādhanamālā, A-84, C-65 §.

...." The worshipper should meditate on himself as Ārya-Nāmasaṅgīti, whose colour is reddish white, who sits in the Vajraparyaṅka attitude on the moon over lotus. His principal face is red, the right blue and the left white, that is, three-faces ; in his four hands he carries the Prajñā [pāramitā], the sword, the bow and the arrow in proper fashion ; he wears a bejewelled crown and is endowed with the thirty-two major and eighty minor auspicious marks ; he appears a prince with princely ornaments........then the worshipper after offering Abhiṣeka to all the Tathāgatas, should further meditate himself as bearing the effigy of Akṣobhya on the crown."

We have not come across any image of this form of Mañjuśrī, and the illustration (Plate XIVa) is only a copy of a drawing in an ancient Nepalese album. The illustration in Plate XIVb with one face and four arms may represent this form of Mañjuśrī.

* Sādhanamālā, fol. A-64, N-48, C-49.

† C. has *paryaṅka*. ‡ A, omits *tadanu....vicintya*.

§ Omitted in N.

III. EMANATIONS OF THE FIVE DHYĀNI BUDDHAS.

Altogether four varieties of Mañjuśrī are said to bear the images of the five Dhyānī Buddhas on their crown, thereby suggesting that Mañjuśrī is a 'Pañcavīrakumāra' or the 'offspring of the five Victorious Ones,' i.e. the five Dhyānī Buddhas. Out of these four varieties excepting Vāgīśvara three others are rarely represented.

1. Vāgīśvara.

Colour—red or yellow. Āsana—ardhaparyaṅka
Vāhana—lion. Symbol—utpala.

Vāgīśvara is a tutelary deity of the Nepalese Buddhists and is widely worshipped in Nepal; and his popularity is borne out by the fact that innumerable wheels of prayer in Nepalese temples bear in monumental Newari characters, the mantra, "Oṃ Vāgīśvara Muḥ."

One of the Sādhanas describes him as having red complexion, as wearing all princely ornaments and as seated on a lion in the Ardhaparyaṅka attitude. He carries the Utpala in his left hand and the right is displayed in an artistic attitude. He may have a yellow variety, which is known as the Mahārājalīlā Mañjuśrī and the Dhyāna describing his form has already been quoted and translated by Professor Foucher.* Let us now describe the form of the red variety of Vāgīśvara as given in the Dhyāna :—

...."Pañcavīrakaśekharaṃ kumāraṃ sarvābharaṇabhūṣitaṃ kuṅkumāruṇaṃ vāmenotpalaṃ dakṣiṇena līlayā sthitaṃ siṃhāsanasthaṃ ātmānaṃ kumārarūpena cintayet....Oṃ Vāgīśvara Muḥ."

Sādhanamālā, A-54, N-41, C-54.

"....The worshipper should meditate in himself the form of [Vāgīśvara] who bears the images of the five Dhyānī Buddhas on the crown, appears a prince, is decked in all ornaments, has the complexion of Kuṅkuma; who carries the Utpala in the left hand while the right is displayed artistically; who has his seat on a lion, and appears a prince ....Oṃ Vāgīśvara Muḥ."

The Indian Museum image (Plate XIVd) of this divinity carries a ghaṇṭā in the right hand and instead of sitting on the lion is represented as sitting on a lion throne. The other image in bronze (Plate XVa) is a recent one and represents the god a little differently.

* In his *L'Iconographie Bouddhique*, part II, 43-44.

(a) Vāgīśvara (Nepal)

(b) Mañjuvara (Nālandā)

(c) Mañjuvara (Indian Museum)

(d) Mañjuvara (Birbhum)

Plate XV

2. Mañjuvara.

Mudrā—Dharmacakra. Vāhana—lion.
Attitude—Lalita or Ardhaparyaṅka.
Identification mark—Prajñāpāramitā on lotus.

Two Sādhanas in the Sādhanamālā describe the procedure of the worship of Mañjuvara, who is rather widely represented. He is yellow in complexion, sits on the back of a lion in the Lalita or in the Ardhaparyanka attitude and displays the sentiment of passion. His two hands are joined over the breast forming the Dharmacakra Mudrā, as he eternally instructs the people in the secrets of Dharma ; he holds the lotus or lotuses on which appears the Prajñāpāramitā Scripture. The text of the Dhyāna in one of the Sādhanas is given below :—

...." Taptakāñcanābhaṃ pañcavīrakumāraṃ Dharmacakramudrāsamāyuktaṃ Prajñāpāramitānvitanīlotpaladhāriṇaṃ siṃhasthaṃ lalitākṣepaṃ sarvālaṅkārabhūṣitaṃ....Oṃ Mañjuvara Huṃ "

Sādhanamālā. A-58, N-43-44, C-44.

...." The worshipper should meditate on himself the form of Mañjuvara, whose colour is the colour of molten gold, who is the offspring of the five Dhyānī Buddhas, whose hands display the Dharmacakra Mudrā, who carries the blue lotus with the Prajñāpāramitā (above), sits on a lion in the Lalita attitude, and is decked in all ornaments....Oṃ Mañjuvara Huṃ."

According to a second Sādhana, Mañjuvara should have the lotus under his left armpit with the Prajñāpāramitā on it ; he may sit in the Ardhaparyaṅka attitude and may be accompanied by the fierce God, Yamāntaka of blue colour with his distorted face terrible with bared fangs. The latter carries the staff in one hand and touches the leg of the principal god with another.

The image (Plate XVd)* discovered at Bara in the District of Birbhum probably represents this form of Mañjuśrī with the miniature figures of the five Dhyānī Buddhas over head, and of the two divinities, one on either side. They probably represent Sudhana in the right and Yamāntaka in the left. Mañjuvara here displays the Dharmacakra Mudrā and bears, under his left armpit, the stem of the lotus on which appears the Prajñāpāramitā Scripture as required by the Sādhana. The lotus to the right has been sculptured simply to keep up the balance with the lotus to the left.

The lion-vehicle of Mañjuvara is sometimes absent and in later images, he may sit in the Paryaṅka and other attitudes, (Plate XVb). † The

* This image was first identified as that of the Hindu goddess, Bhuvaneśvarī in the Birbhum Bibarana, then as that of Siṁhanāda Lokeśvara (Vide—A. S. I. Eastern Circle, Annual Report, 1920-21, p. 27) and later on as that of Mañjuśrī (Vide—Ibid, Pl. I, fig. 2). As I have not personally examined the image I am not sure as to the sex of the figure. If it is a female figure we will have no other alternative than to identify the image as that of Prajñāpāramitā.

† A. S. I., Central Circle 1919-20. Pl. V (a).

lotus to the right, which is not expressly required by the Sādhana sometimes bears the book (Plate XVIa) and sometimes the sword in order to keep up the balance more precisely (Plate XVIb).*

The Indian Museum image (Plate XVc) of Mañjuvara has on either side of him two female companions who represent no doubt the two wives of Mañjuśrī, Keśinī and Upakeśinī.

3. Mañjuvajra.

Colour—red. Faces—three. Hands—six. Companion—Prajñā.

The reason why Mañjuvajra is dealt with along with the other emanations of the five Dhyānī Buddhas is this. In the Sādhana describing the procedure of his worship we find a word, which means that Mañjuvajra "serves the three worlds, being created by the host of the resplendent Buddhas," † apparently referring to the group of the five Tathāgatas, or the five Dhyānī Buddhas; for, in the Sādhanamālā the word, "Buddha" seldom refers to anything other than the five Dhyānī Buddhas.

The colour of his body including the principal face is red like Kuṅkuma, the second face is blue, and the third white. He has six arms, out of which the two principal ones are engaged in embracing his Śakti with one hand touching her face. The remaining four hands carry the sword and the arrow, and the bow and the Utpala. He sits in Vajrāsana or in the Vajraparyaṅka attitude on the moon supported by the lotus. The Dhyāna is in verse and runs as follows :—

Kuṅkumāruṇasaṁmurtirnīlasitatrayānanaḥ,
Bhujadvayasamāśliṣṭa-Svābha-Vidyādharāsyadhṛk.
Khaḍgabāṇabhujañcāpanīlotpalaparigrahaḥ,
Viśvadalābjacandrasthaḥ vajrāsanaśaśiprabhaḥ.

Sādhanamālā, A-86, Na-85, C-66.

His beautiful person is red like Kuṅkuma ; he has three faces of [Kuṅkuma], blue and white colour, embraces his Svābhā Prajñā with two arms, of which one touches her face, carries the Khaḍga, the arrow, the bow and the blue Utpala, sits on the moon over a double lotus in Vajrāsana, and has the radiance of the moon."

* This bronze belongs to the collection of Pandit Siddhiharṣa of Nepal and the image is popularly known as Dharmacakra Mañjuśrī.

† The passage in which the word occurs is—

"Sphurad-Buddhaugha-nirmāṇa-prasādhita-jagattrayaḥ.
Svatattvodbhavacihnottham Mañjuvajraḥ svayaṃ bhavet."

(a) Mañjuvara (Indian Museum)

(b) Dharmacakra Mañjuśrī (Nepal)

(c) Mañjukumāra

(d) Arapacana Mañjuśrī (Nepal)

Plate XVI

4. Mañjukumāra.

Colour—red. Vāhana—animal.
Faces—three. Arms—six.

One Sādhana only in the Sādhanamālā describes him as three-faced and six-armed, and as riding on an animal. In his three left hands he carries the Prajñāpāramitā, the Utpala and the bow, while the three right show the sword, the arrow and the Varada pose. The extract is given below :—

...." Mañjukumāraṃ trimukhaṃ saḍbhujaṃ kuṅkumāruṇaṃ nīlasitadakṣiṇetaravadanaṃ sattvaparyaṅkinaṃ Khaḍgabāṇavaradaṃ dakṣiṇakaratrayaṃ, Prajñāpāramitāpustakanīlotpalacāpavadvāmakaratrayaṃ saśṛṅgārakumārābharaṇanivasanādikaṃ nānāpuṣpamadhāśobhacīratrayavirājitaṃ Tathāgataparamānuparighaṭitaṃ * ātmānaṃ dhyātvā...."

Sādhanamālā, A-79-80, N-61, C-61.

" The worshipper should meditate in himself the from of Mañjukumāra, who is three-faced and six-armed, whose colour is the colour of Kuṅkuma, whose right and left faces have (respectively) the blue and white colour ; who has his seat on an animal ; whose three right hands show the sword, the arrow and the Varada pose, while the three left carry the Prajñapāramitā, blue Utpala and the bow ; who is decked in princely ornaments and dress as befitting the sentiment of passion he displays, wears the three Cīrakas, which are gaudily decorated with various kinds of flowers ; who is made of the particles of the Tathāgatas....Thus meditating....."

It would be apparent from the translation why Mañjukumāra has been assigned to the five Dhyānī Buddhas : because his essence consists of the 'paramāṇus' or particles of the Tathāgatas meaning the five Dhyānī Buddhas. He is not known to us either in sculptures or in ancient paintings. The accompanying sketch (Plate XVIc), which has been restored from an ancestral album of a Vajrācāryya, however, gives a true idea of his form. The Vāhana, it may be noted, is absent in the drawing.

IV. Independent Forms.

The reason why we get forms of Mañjuśrī without fathers or the Dhyānī Buddhas on the crown, is rather difficult to ascertain, nor are we entitled to attribute them to the omission of the authors or the compilers of the Sādhanas. For the worship of Arapacana alone, there are, in the Sādhanamālā as many as eight Sādhanas and in none of these there is any faint reference even as to the origin of the god. It cannot be a case of omission but is one of deliberate commission. What then is the reason of this silence as to the origin of several forms of Mañjuśrī described below ? The only reason we can adduce is a

* A reads "paramāṇḍa."

simple historical fact. We know Mañjuśrī was, in the fourth century, known as a distinguished Bodhisattva, when the conception of the five Dhyānī Buddhas was practically in the air, and at best the name of Amitābha only was in existence. But when the conception of the Dhyānī Buddhas and their emanations was established, some forms of Mañjuśrī, were assigned to Amitābha, some to Akṣobhya and a few to the group of the five Dhyānī Buddhas by the later Buddhists according to their cults and some were left as independent ; and we shall not be surprised if an attempt is made in the sculptures to assign the following four independent forms to any particular Dhyānī Buddha or a particular group of them.

1. Arapacana.

Colour—white, or red. Āsana—Vajraparjaṅka. Companions—four.

Identification marks—Book against breast (vāme hṛdi gṛhītapustakaṃ) and the brandishing sword in the right (dakṣiṇe udyatakhaḍgakaram).

Eight Sādhanas in the Sādhanamālā describe the form of this divinity, who is sometimes white and sometimes red. He sits always in the Vajraparyaṅka attitude, and when he sits on animal he is called Prajñācakra. He is accompanied by the four divinities, Keśinī, Upakeśinī, Candraprabha and Sūryyaprabha, and as the group originate from the five syllables, 'A,' 'R,' 'P,' 'C,' and 'N,' the principal god is called Arapacana. When represented, the four companions of Arapacana resemble the principal god in all respects.

None of the forms of Mañjuśrī are so widely represented both in stone and in bronze as Arapacana, sometimes with the four companions (XVIIab) * and sometimes without them (Plate XVId). In one (Plate XVIIb) of the sculptures, preserved in the Dacca Museum, we find the four Dhyānī Buddhas, Vairocana, Ratnasaṃbhava, Amitābha and Amoghasiddhi (besides the usual four companions), sculptured on the aureole behind, the middle position at the top being occupied by one of the companion deities namely Candraprabha resembling the principal god. The Nepal bronze (Plate XVIIc)† does not carry the book against the breast but holds the stem of a lotus, which bears the book.

Arapacana is also called Sadyonubhava-Arapacana, or Sadyonubhava Mañjuśrī. He is resplendent like the full moon, has a smiling face, is decked in all princely ornaments, and sits on a double lotus in the Vajraparyaṅka attitude. He brandishes the sword in his right hand and carries the Prajñāpāramitā

* First published and identified as Mañjuśrī in Grunwedel: Buddhist Art in India, p. 199

† This bronze belongs to the collection of Pandit Siddhiharṣa of Kathmandu.

(a) Arapacana (Java)

(b) Arapacana (Dacca Museum)

(c) Arapacana (Nepal)

(d) Sthiracakra
(Vaṅgīya Sāhitya Pariṣat)

Plate XVII

Book against the breast in the left. Jālinikumāra (or Sūryyaprabha) is in front of him, Candraprabha behind, Keśinī to the right and Upakeśinī to the left. All these four divinities are replicas of the principal god. The Dhyāna in one of the Sādhanas describes the principal god in the following terms :—

....“ Khaḍgapustakadhāriṇaṃ ākuñcitapañcacīraṃ, raktavastrayuga-yutaṃ śṛṅgāraveśadhāriṇaṃ smitavikasitavadanaṃ śaśāṅkāntitulyaśobhaṃ viśvadalakamalasthabaddhaparyaṅkaṃ Sadyonubhavārapacanarūpaṃ ātmānam īkṣyeta.”

Sādhanamālā, A-63, N-47-48, C-48.

“ The worshipper should conceive himself as Sadyonubhava Arapacana, who carries the Khaḍga and the Book, wears the five cīrakas which are slightly folded, whose garments are of red colour, and befit the sentiment of passion he displays ; whose face is radiant with a smile, and whose splendour is like the splendour of the moon ; who sits on the double lotus in the Vajraparyaṅka attitude.... ”

This Sādhana further goes on to say that the principal god should originate from the first syllable “ A,” Jālinīkumāra from the syllable “ R,” Cadraprabha from “ P,” Keśinī from “ C” and Upakeśinī from “ N.” Mañjuśrī should be in the middle, Jālinīkumāra in front, Candraprabha behind, Keśinī to the right and Upakeśinī to the left. All of them have white complexion and are identical with the principal god in appearance.*

2. Sthiracakra.

Symbol—sword. Mudrā—Varada. Companion—Śakti.

The Sādhana for the worship of Sthiracakra has a remarkable feature unlike other Sādhanas in the Sādhanamalā, inasmuch as it does not give the Dhyāna at a stretch, but the information about his form is intersperesd throughout the Sādhana, which is again in verse. From the information about his form, as gleaned from the Sādhana, it appears that, in one of his hands he carries the sword,† which spreading its rays destroys the darkness of ignorance, while the other in engaged in bestowing boons of all kinds,‡ or in other words, displays the Varada pose. His colour is white § and he is decked in garments of the colour of the bee ; || he sits on the moon over a lotus, we know not in what what Āsana or attitude, and wears the Cīrakas which makes his body resplen-

* The text is quoted—ādisvarapariṇataṃ....Mañjughoṣaṃ....tadagre ca Rephajaṃ ....Jālinīkumāraṃ Bhagavadrūpaṃ paśyet, tathā pṛṣṭhe tathaiva pañcamādyakṣareṇa Candraprabhaṃ dakṣiṇe tathaiva Cakāreṇa Keśinīṃ stanabharavirājitāṃ nātharupāṃ vāme copakesinīṃ nakāreṇa tathaiva ca.” MSS. A-63, N-48, C-48.

† Bibhrāṇam karavālaṃ—MSS. A 46, N-35, C-34.

‡ Sarvākāravarapradānanipunaṃ—Ibid.

§ Prodyadgauragabhastibimbavimalaṃ—Ibid.

|| Candrasthaṃ bhramarāṅgabhāsuratarair-udbhāsuraṃ cīrakaiḥ. Ibid.

dent. He wears princely ornaments and displays the sentiment of passionate love. He is accompanied by a female or Prajñā, who is beautiful, displays the sentiment of passionate love and laughs profusely.*

We have not met with any representation of this form of Mañjuśrī, unless the Bangīya Sāhitya Pariṣad image † No. C (d) 8/16, (Plate XVIId.) is indentified with this. The sculpture agrees in almost all the details with the description given above, except that here the sword appears on a lotus, the stem of which is held in the left hand of the God, while the right exhibits the Varada pose. He sits in Lalitāsana on the moon over lotus, and is accompanied by his Śakti, who according to the Indian custom. occupies a position to the left of her consort.

3. Vādirāt.

Āsana—Ardhaparyaṅka. Vāhana—Tiger. Mudrā—Vyākhyāna.

This form of Mañjuśrī is rarely to be met with in stone or in bronze. One Sādhana only is devoted to the worship of this divinity to show that this form was not very popular amongst the Vajrayānists. Vādirāt is of medium height, neither very short nor very tall and appears a youth of sixteen years. He sits in the Ardhaparyaṅka attitude with the left leg slightly raised, on the back of a tiger. He wears all ornaments and displays the Vyākhyāna Mudrā. The Dhyāna is in verse and describes the form of Vādirāt in the following terms :—

Svacchaṃ soḍaṣavatsarākṛtidharaṃ śārddūlapṛṣṭhasthitaṃ
Vyākhyāvyākulapāṇipadmayugalaṃ vāmārdhaparyaṅkinaṃ ।
Dīrghaṃ nāpi na cāpi kharvamasamaṃ saundaryarāśyāśrayaṃ
Ratnasvarṇamaṇiprakāravividhālaṅkāramālākulaṃ ॥

....Srīmad-Vādirāṭsādhanaṃ samāptaṃ. Kṛtiriyaṃ Paṇḍita-śrī-Cintāmaṇi-Dattasya."

Sādhanamālā, A-50. N-37, C-37.

* Lālityaśṛṅgārarasābhirāmāṃ
Vyajjṛmbhamānāmbūruhāsyalakṣmīṃ ।
Vīram kumārabharaṇam dadhānam
dhyāyāt padam tasya samīhamānaḥ ॥ Ibid.

† This image has been identified as that of Mañjuśrī and described in the "Handbook to the Sculptures in the Museum of the Bangiya Sahitya Parisad" on page 33. The attitude or the "Āsana" of the God is clearly Lalitāsana, but it has been designated therein as the Sukhāsana Mudrā, in which the word 'mudrā' has been wrongly applied after 'Āsana.' It must be added that the word, 'Sukhāsana' is altogether unknown in the Sādhanamālā. In the 'Handbook' unfortunately a confusion has been made all through between the Sukhāsana and the Lalitākṣepa attitudes. The author designates uniformly the Ardhaparyaṅka Asana by the term Lalitākṣepa Mudrā and Lalitākṣepa by the Sukhāsana Mudrā. The figure of the Śakti in the image has been identified as that of Yamāntaka —an identification for which, I am afraid, it would be difficult to quote any authority.

" The worshipper should meditate on himself as [Vādirāṭ] who is beautiful (lit. pure or transparent), and appears a youth of sixteen years ; who sits on the back of a tiger ; whose lotus-like hands are eagerly engaged in displaying the Vyākhyāna Mudrā ; whose left leg is slightly raised in the Ardhaparyaṅka attitude ; who is neither tall nor very short, is unparalleled by any, is the receptacle of all beauties in the world, and is decked in various ornaments consisting of jewels, gold, gems and other valuables.....Here ends the Sādhana for Vādirāṭ. The author of this is Śrī Cintāmaṇi Datta."

4. MAÑJUNĀTHA.

Faces—three. Hands—six.

Like Mañjukumāra he is also endowed with three faces and six arms. He carries the Cakra, Vajra, Jewel, the lotus, and the sword.* These five symbols are held in five hands but the dhyāna does not mention the symbol that should be carried in the sixth. It is therefore probable that the sixth remains empty.

Some of the varieties of Mañjuśrī bear such a close resemblance to Prajñāpāramitā that it is difficult sometimes to distinguish between them. The only point of difference is that one is male and the other female. The iconographist thinks his duty done if he can identify an image as that of Mañjuśrī. But what has been said before clearly indicates that Mañjuśrī has as many as fourteen varieties, and unless we can definitely mention the particular variety, the mere identification as Mañjuśrī would be altogether useless.

* The extract is—" Vyutthāya Mañjunāthasya vahan garvaṃ samāhitaḥ
..................trimukhaṃ saḍbhujaṃ tathā
Cakravajramahāratnapadmakhaḍgadharāyudhaṃ."
MSS. A-87, Na-86, C-67-8.

CHAPTER III.

BODHISATTVA AVALOKITEŚVARA.

Avalokiteśvara is famous in the Mahāyāna Pantheon as a Bodhisattva emanating from the Dhyānī Buddha, Amitābha and his Śakti, Pāṇḍarā. As Amitābha and Pāṇḍarā are the presiding Dhyānī Buddha and Buddhaśakti of the present Kalpa (cycle) namely, Bhadrakalpa, Avalokiteśvara is said to be the Bodhisattva who covers the period between the disappearance of the Mortal Buddha, Śākyasiṃha and the advent of the Future Buddha, Maitreya. The Guṇakāraṇḍavyūha * gives an account of his character, moral teachings and miracles. In it we find that he refused Nirvāṇa, until all creatures of the Universe were in possession of the Bodhi knowledge, and to that end he is still supposed to work and foster spiritual knowledge amongst his fellow creatures. One of the passages in Kāraṇḍavyūha † characterises him as taking the shape of all gods of all religions, nay even the shape of the father and mother,—in fact, the form of the worshipped of any and every worshipper, to whom he may impart knowledge. By a slow and gradual process the people and next the animals and other creatures would advance spiritually to obtain salvation. For all these reasons, Avalokiteśvara is characterised as the best of the Saṅgha, the Jewel of the Buddhist Church or Saṅgharatna.

The Sādhanamālā gives altogether thirty-one Sādhanas which describe Avalokiteśvara or Lokeśvara in a variety of different forms. Among these variations, a good many have been described, though partially, supported by quotations from original texts with their translations in French, by M. Foucher in his Etude sur L'Iconographie Bouddhique de L'Inde, parte 2, Chapter II, Section 1.

Besides all the eleven varieties mentioned in Prof. Foucher's work three more have been added in the author's paper entitled, " The Identification of

* R. Mittra ; Skt. Bud. Lit. p. 95.

† Extracts from the text is quotes below—" Yāvat Avalokiteśvarasya dṛḍhapratijñā na paripūritā bhavanti sarvasattāḥ sarvaduḥkhebhyaḥ parimokṣitāḥ, yāvat anuttarāyāṃ samyak sambodhau na pratiṣṭāpitā bhavanti....yena yena rūpeṇa vaineyāḥ sattvāḥ tena tena rūpeṇa dharmaṃ deśayanti. Tathāgatavaineyānāṃ Tathāgatarūpeṇa dharmaṃ deśayanti....Maheśvaravaineyānāṃ Maheśvararūpeṇa dharmaṃ deśayanti.... Vāyuvaineyāṇāṃ Vāyurūpeṇa dharmam deśayanti....Rājavaineyāṇāṃ sattānāṃ Rājarūpeṇa dharmaṃ deśayanti....mātāpitṛvaineyānāṃ sattvānāṃ mātṛpitṛrūpeṇa dharmaṃ deśayanti. Yathāyathāvaineyānāṃ sattvānāṃ tathātathārūpeṇa dharmaṃ deśayanti." Kāraṇḍavyūha, pp. 21-22.

(a) Ṣaḍākṣarī Lokeśvara with Ṣaḍākṣarī Mahāvidyā and Maṇidhara (Sārnāth)

(b) Ṣaḍākṣarī Group (Indian Museum)

(c) Ṣaḍākṣarī Group (Birbhum)

Plate XVIII

Avalokiteśvara Images " read before the Second Session of the Oriental Conference held in 1922 at Calcutta. For the sake of convenience, these two will also be dealt with here in their proper places. Paṇḍita Amṛtānanda's Dharmakoṣasamgraha gives the description of another variety of Avalokiteśvara, which goes by the name of Sukhāvatī Lokeśvara.*

So the total number of variants goes up to fifteen, but it may surprise our readers to learn that the different forms of Avalokiteśvara are no less than one hundred and eight. The Macchandar Vahal, one of the numerous Vihāras in Kāthmaṇḍu has paintings in many colours of one hundred and eight variations of the Bodhisattva on wooden panels surrounding the temple on three sides. The paintings appear to be at least two hundred years old, and they bear inscriptions in old Newārī, giving their respective names. Clearly, in the point of antiquity, the discovery has a lesser importance than the ones we are dealing with at present, but as the overwhelming number of forms will no doubt throw a considerable amount of light on the Iconography of Avalokiteśvara, and thus facilitate identification, we do not hesitate to give a description of all these varieties, with the respective sketches, in the Appendix.†

Fourteen, out of the fifteen different varieties of Avalokiteśvara mentioned above, bear the figure of the Dhyānī Buddha Amitābha on the crown, showing that they emanate from the latter. The fifteenth, Vajradharma by name, is said to bear the figures of the five Dhyānī Buddhas on the crown. Now, let us take up the varieties one after another. These will be dealt with in order of popularity, which, again, will be determined by the number of Sādhanas devoted in the Sādhanamālā to their worship.

1. Ṣaḍakṣarī-Lokeśvara.

Colour—white. Arms—four.
Mudrā—Añjali. Symbols—rosary and lotus.
Companions—Maṇidhara and Ṣaḍakṣarī Mahāvidyā.
Identification Symbol—the Añjali against the breast.

Four Sādhanas in the Sādhanamālā are devoted to the worship of this form of Avalokiteśvara ; two of them describe him in a group of three, one in a group of two in the company of Ṣaḍakṣarī Mahāvidyā, and one singly. In all these, the form of Lokeśvara is the same. Below is quoted the Dhyāna of the Sādhana describing him in a group of three :—

...."Ātmānaṃ Lokeśvararūpaṃ sarvālaṅkārabhūṣitaṃ śuklavarṇaṃ vāmataḥ padmadharaṃ dakṣiṇato'kṣasūtradharaṃ aparābhyām hastābhyāṃ

* See below, No. 14. † See Appendix B.

hṛdi samputāñjalisthitaṃ dhyāyāt. Dakṣiṇe Maṇidharaṃ tattadvarṇa*-bhujānvitaṃ padmāntaroparisthaṃ. Vāme tathaiva aparapadmasthāṃ † Ṣaḍakṣarīṃ Mahāvidyāṃ...."

Sādhanamālā, A-16, C-6, N-13-14.

...."The worshipper should realize himself as [Ṣaḍakṣarī]-Lokeśvara decked in all sorts of ornaments, white in colour, four-armed, carrying the lotus in the left hand and the rosary in the right. The other two hands join in forming the Mudrā of clasped hand against the breast. To his right is Maṇidhara with the same colour and the same hands, sitting on another lotus. To the left is Ṣaḍakṣarī Mahāvidyā with identical form sitting on another lotus...."

The Dhyāna of this god has been restored from the Kāraṇḍavyūha, as one of the Colophons asserts.‡ The mantra assigned to this form of Avalokiteśvara is the famous "Oṃ Maṇi-Padme Huṃ" consisting of six syllables. These six syllables are here deified in the form of Ṣaḍakṣarī Mahāvidyā.

A perfect and perhaps unique image § (Plate XVIII, a) of this group of three deities hails from the Saṅghārāma of Sarnath, and is now preserved in the Sarnath Museum with the label bearing the inscription "Unidentified Group." Mr. Oertel erroneously identified the group as the Tri-Ratna or the Three Jewels of the Buddhists,—Dharma, Buddha and Saṅgha.|| In the group, Ṣaḍakṣarī Lokeśvara is in the middle ; the figure to the right is Maṇidhara and the female figure to the left is Ṣaḍakṣarī Mahāvidyā. It may be noticed that under the seats of lotuses are four miniatures, who represent none but the four guardians of the gates of the Saḍakṣarī Maṇḍala, as prescribed in the Kāraṇḍavyūha.

Another artistic but mutilated image (Plate XVIII, b) of the Ṣaḍakṣarī group, which was discovered in Magadha by Waddell and illustrated on Plate II (2) with his article (J. R. A. S. 1894), depicts the goddess in what is called the Vīrāsana. Waddell calls the central figure as "Caturbhuj Lokeswara" and Saḍakṣarī Mahāvidyā as the "Mother of Six Syllables."** As he proceeded to make the identification through Tibetan he missed their actual Sanskrit names. The image is now in the Indian Museum, Calcutta.

The other image †† (Plate XVIII, c) found in the District of Birbhum by Mr. K. N. Dīkśit, is also of the Ṣaḍakṣarī group, though it is mutilated

* A reads 'tadvarṇa'. † 'Apara' is dropped in A.

‡ Kāraṇḍavyūhāmnāyena racitaṃ sādhanaṃ.

§ Sarnath Catalogue, No. B (e) 6. Pl. XIV (b). || Sarnath Catalogue, p. 137.

Kāraṇḍavyūha, p. 74—"tasya ca maṇḍalasya caturdvāreṣu catvāro mahārājāḥ kartavyāh".

** J. R. A. S. 1894, Pl. II (2).

†† Described in A. S. I. Eastern Circle, Annual Report 1920-21, p. 27 and illustrated in Pl. I (2).

(a) Ṣaḍākṣarī Lokeśvara (Nepal)

(b) Ṣaḍākṣarī Mahāvidyā (Sārnāth)

(c) Siṁhanāda (Magadha)

(e) Siṁhanāda (Nepal)

(d) Siṁhanāda (Nepal)

Plate XIX

practically beyond recognition. The central figure depicting Ṣaḍakṣarī Lokeśvara has lost two hands bearing the rosary and the lotus at some iconoclastic hand, but the marks are still there on the stone. The two hands exhibiting the Añjali (wrongly stated as Namaḥkāra) Mudrā contains the jewel.

Images of the Ṣaḍakṣarī Lokeśvara, both in groups and singly, abound in Nepal and almost every monastary at Kathmandu and Patan has got one in it. As far as is known to us, the only coloured image (Plate XIX, a) of this divinity appears in the Bauddhanātha Temple, one of the most famous places of pilgrimage of the Buddhists in Nepal.

When he appears in the group of two, according to the Sādhanamālā, the goddess may have another form depicting her in Vīrāsana, with yellow complexion and a bejewelled crown. In this case she has two hands only, of which the left holds the jewel, while the right is empty.* The Sarnath Museum image B (f) 4. (Plate XIX, b), though mutilated hopelessly must represent this form of Ṣaḍakṣarī Mahāvidyā, and she can be readily recognized by the peculiar Āsana, which is absolutely rare in Buddhist Iconography.

Another alternative is also prescribed in the Sādhanamālā for all the three deities, and the Sādhana goes on to say—"Sometimes in the Sādhana of Saḍakṣarī Mahāvidyā, Lokeśvara holds also the lotus bearing the jewel and the book. Maṇidhara may hold the jewel and the lotus and be without the book. Ṣaḍakṣarī may hold the book and the lotus and be without the jewel."†

2. Simhanāda.

Colour—white. Āsana—Mahārājalīlā.
Vāhana—lion. Special Characteristics—no ornaments.

Identification marks—(i) left—sword on lotus.
(ii) right—Triśūla entwined by a snake.

Four Sādhanas also are devoted to the worship of Siṃhanāda, who is regarded by the Mahāyānists as the curer of all diseases. He is one of the most popular forms of the Bodhisattva Avalokiteśvara and his images are by

* The text has—
"Āryāntu cintayet pitām vāme ratnacchaṭābhṛtāṃ
Rikta-savyakarāṃ ratnamauliṃ vīrāsanānugāṃ."

"Ityārya-Ṣaḍakṣarīmahāvidyā-Lokeśvara-Bhaṭṭārakopadeśa-paramparāyātasādhana-vidhiḥ." Sādhanamālā A—21, C—11, N—17.

† Sādhanamālā, A—21, C—11, N—17. "Kvacit Ṣaḍakṣarīsādhane Bhagavān samaṇipustakāṅkitapadmadharaḥ Maṇidharastu pustakarahita-maṇipadmadharaḥ, Ṣaḍakṣarī tu maṇirahita pustakapadmadharā."

no means rare in India. At Patan, in Nepal, all the more important Vihāras have two images of Siṃhanāda, either is stone or in bronze, on either side of the staircase leading to the sanctum. He appears in many forms with very slight differences. The four Sādhanas alike describe him as follows :—

" Ātmānaṃ Siṃhanāda-Lokeśvararūpaṃ bhāvayet, śvetavarṇṇaṃ trinetraṃ jaṭāmukuṭinaṃ nirbhūṣaṇaṃ* vyāghracarma-prābhṛtaṃ siṃhāsanasthaṃ mahārājalīlaṃ candrāsanaṃ † candraprabhaṃ bhāvayet. Dakṣiṇe sitaphaṇiveṣṭitaṃ triśūlam śvetaṃ, vāme nānāsugandhikusumaparipūrita-padmabhājanaṃ. Vāmahastāt ‡ utthaṃ padmopari jvalatkhaḍgaṃ."

Sādhanamālā, A-35, C-23, N-25.

" The worshipper should conceive himself as Siṃhanāda Lokeśvara of white complexion, with three eyes, with the crown of chignon, having no ornaments, clad in tiger-skin, mounted on a lion in the attitude of princely ease, seated on and glowing like the moon. To his right is the white trident entwined by a white serpent ; to his left is the lotus-bowl full of fragrant flowers. From his left hand rises the (white) lotus on which is the fiery (white) sword."

Generally, in the images of Siṃhanāda, the bowl of flowers to his left is absent (Plate XIX, c) § and in very rare cases the trident also. Sometimes the trident is held in his right hand ||. The pose in which he sits is here called the Mahārājalīlā pose, which is another name for the Ardhaparyaṅka attitude ; but in representations, he may sit in the Paryaṅka attitude also (Plate XIX, d),—or is even found in a standing attitude (Plate XIX, e). The lion, which is found in almost all the images, may also be absent in bronzes (Plate XX, a). The fact that Siṃhanāda wears no ornaments is very important because this distinguishes him from some of the varieties of Mañjuśrī. The artistic specimen of Siṃhanāda (Plate XX, b) discovered at Mahoba and described by Mr. K. N. Dīkṣit** carries a rosary in his right hand. None of the Sādhanas in the Sādhanamālā refers to the rosary, but some of the Tibetan specimens have got it.

3. KHASARPANA.

Colour—white. Symbol—lotus.
Mudrā—Varada. Āsana—Lalita or Ardhaparyaṅka.
Companions—Tāra, Sudhanakumāra, Bhṛkuṭī, Hayagrīva.

Khasarpaṇa also is described in a number of Sādhanas in the Sādhanamālā, which fact points to his popularity amongst the Mahāyānists. Many

* C reads 'vibhūṣaṇaṃ'. † dropped in A. ‡ N reads 'upasthitaṃ'.

§ J. R. A. S. 1894, Pl. I. || As in the standing image from Pātan, Pl. XIX, e. This bronze belongs to Paṇḍit Siddhiharṣa's collection.

** K. N. Dīkṣit : " Six sculptures from Mahoba " in the A. S. I. Memoir No. 8, pl. Ia. p. 2.

(a) Siṁhanāda (Nepal)

(b) Siṁhanāda (Mahobā)

(c) Khasarpaṇa (Indian Museum)

(d) Lokanātha (Mahobā)

Plate XX

images of this variety of Lokeśvara have been discovered and many Museums possess one. The peculiar feature of this god is that he is invariably accompanied by the four divinities, Tārā, Sudhanakumāra, Bhṛkuṭī and Hayagrīva. The principal figure is the same as Lokanātha, two-armed and one-faced, carrying the same symbol and exhibiting the same Mudrā. The difference is that Lokanātha may be flanked by two divinities, Tārā and Hayagrīva. whereas Khasarpaṇa must be accompanied by two more, Bhṛkuṭī and Sudhanakumāra. He is of white complexion and sits, either in Lalitāsana or the Ardhaparyaṅka attitude. Below is given a somewhat lengthy Dhyāna describing the god :—

" Ātmānaṃ Bhagavantaṃ dhyāyāt himakarakoṭikiraṇāvadātaṃ dehaṃ, ūrujaṭāmukuṭaṁ Amitābhakṛtaśekharaṃ, viśvanalinaniṣaṇṇaṃ śaśimaṇḍale, ardhaparyaṅkaniṣaṇṇaṃ sakalālaṅkāradharavigrahaṃ smeramukhaṃ dviraṣṭavarṣadeśīyaṃ dakṣiṇe varadakaram. vāmakareṇa sanālakamaladharaṃ, karavigalatpīyūṣadhārāvyavahārarasikaṃ tadadhaḥ samāropitordhvamukhaṃ mahākukṣiṃ atikṛśaṃ atiśitivarṇam Sūcīmukhaṃ tarppayantaṃ śrīmat-Potalakācalodaranivāsinaṃ karuṇāsnigdhāvalokanaṃ sṛṅgārarasaparyupāsitaṃ atiśāntaṃ nānālakṣaṇālaṅkṛtaṃ.

Tasya purataḥ Tārā dakṣiṇapārśve Sudhanakumāraḥ.

Tatra Tārā śyāmā, vāmakaravidhṛtaṃ sanālaṃ utpalaṃ dakṣiṇakareṇa vikāśayantī ; nānālaṅkāravatī abhinavayauvanodbhinnakucabhārā.

Sudhanakumāraśca kṛtāñjalipuṭaḥ kanakāvabhāsadyutiḥ kumārarūpadhārī vāmakakṣavinyastapustakaḥ sakalālaṅkāravān.

Pāscime Bhṛkuṭī Hayagrīva uttare.

Tatra Bhṛkuṭī caturbhujā hemaprabhā jaṭākalāpinī, vāme tridaṇḍīkamaṇḍaludhārihastā dakṣiṇe vandanābhinayākṣasūtradharakarā, trinetrā.

Hayagrīvo raktavarṇṇaḥ kharvalambodaraḥ ūrddhvajvalat-piṅgalakeśaḥ bhujagayajñopavītī kapilataraśmaśruśrenīparicitamukhamaṇḍalaḥ raktavartulatrinetraḥ bhṛkuṭīkuṭilabhrūkaḥ vyāghracarmāmbaraḥ daṇḍāyudhaḥ dakṣiṇakareṇa vandanābhinayī.

Ete sarva eva svanāyakānanapreritadṛṣṭayo yathāśobhaṃ avasthitāḥ cintanīyāḥ.....

Iti Khasarpaṇasādhanaṃ". Sādhanamālā, A-23, C-12-13, N-19.

" The worshipper should conceive himself as the god [Khasarpana]. His person is as resplendent as the rays of a crore of moons ; he wears the crown, of chignon, bears the image of Amitābha on head, and sits on the moon over the double lotus in the Ardhaparyaṅka attitude ; his body is decked in all ornaments ; he has a smiling face, is aged about twice eight years, exhibits the Varada pose in the right hand and holds the lotus with a stem in the left ; he is expert in bestowing the stream of nectar that flows from his hand, while Sūcīmukha who stands below with an uplifted face, a protruding belly and very pale appearance receives the same. [Khasarpaṇa] resides in the womb of the mount Potalaka ; looks beautiful with compassion, is full of the sentiment of passion is extremely peaceful and endowed with various auspicious marks.

" Before him is Tārā and to the right is Sudhanakumāra.

" Here Tārā is green ; she causes to blossom with her right hand the lotus flower with a stem held in her left ; she has many ornaments and is oppressed by her breasts caused by her recent youth.

"Sudhanakumāra, again, has his two hands joined (añjali), is resplendent like gold, has the appearance of a prince ; he carries the book under his left armpit and is decked in all ornaments.

" To the West of the God is Bhṛkuṭī and to the North, Hayagrīva.

" Here Bhṛkuṭī has four arms, is resplendent like gold, has matted hair, carries the staff with three horns and the Kamaṇḍalu in the left, and in the right, [one is raised] in the attitude of bowing and [the other] carries the rosary ; she has three eyes.

" Hayagrīva has red complexion, is short, with a protruding belly ; his hair rises upwards in the shape of a flame, he has a snake as his sacred thread ; his face is recognized by a deep brown pair of moustaches ; his eyes are red and round ; his eye-brows are distorted in the act of frowning ; he is clad in tiger-skin, has the staff as a weapon and his right hand exhibits the act of bowing.

"All these deities should be meditated as situated in a befitting and artistic manner with their eyes directed towards the face of the principal deity."

Here ends the Sādhana for Khasarpaṇa."

The finest image (Plate XXI) * of Khasarpaṇa has recently been discovered by Mr. N. K. Bhaṭṭaśālī in the Parganna of Vikrampur in Eastern Bengal. The sculpture is one of the best products of the Bengal School of art, and will do credit to any art, ancient or modern.

If the central image is mutilated like the one reproduced in Plate XX, c, we would still be able identify Khasarpaṇa by noticing the four companions to the right and left of the God.

4. Lokanātha.

Colour—white. Symbol—lotus.
Mudrā—Varada.

Four Sādhanas, again, are devoted to the worship of the Lokanātha variety of Avalokiteśvara. He is single in three Sādhanas, and only one Sādhana describes him as accompanied by Tārā and Hayagrīva. The same Sādhana, in one of the Asiatic Society Manuscripts of Sādhanamālā adds further that Lokanātha should be accompanied also by the eight gods, Maitreya, Kṣitigarbha, Vajrapāṇī, Khagarbha, Viṣkambhin, Sāmantabhadra, Mañjughoṣa and Gaganagañja ; by the four goddesses, Dhūpā, Puṣpā, Gandhā, Dīpā ; and

* I am obliged to Mr. N. K. Bhaṭṭasali for allowing me to take a copy of his negative for reproduction.

Khasarpaṇa Avalokiteśvara (Vikrampur, Dacca)

Plate XXI

by the four guardians of the gates, Vajrāṅkuśī, Vajrapāśī, Vajrasphoṭā and Vajraghaṇṭā. In other words, the manuscript gives the constitution of the whole Maṇḍala of Lokanātha. The principal god has two hands, which carry the lotus in the left and exhibit the Varada pose in the right,—exactly like Khasarpaṇa, previously described. Let us, therefore, take up the Sādhana which gives the description of the Maṇḍala. It is in verse and thus describes the principal god :—

" Pūrvavat kramayogena Lokanāthaṃ śaśiprabhaṃ ।
Hrīḥkārākṣarasambhūtaṃ jaṭāmukuṭamaṇḍitaṃ ॥
Vajradharma-jaṭāntaḥsthaṃ aśeṣaroganāśanaṃ ।
Varadaṃ dakṣiṇe haste vāme padmadharaṃ tathā ॥
Lalitākṣepasaṁsthantu mahāsaumyaṃ prabhāsvaram ।
Varadotpalakā saumyā Tārā dakṣiṇataḥ sthitā ॥
Vandanādaṇḍahastantu Hayagrīvotha vāmataḥ ।
Raktavarṇṇo mahāraudro vyāghracarmāmbarapriyaḥ ॥"

Sādhanamālā, A-28, N-23, C-17.

" Following the same procedure as before, the worshipper should conceive himself as Lokanātha, resplendent like the moon, as springing from the sacred syllable " Hrīḥ " and wearing the crown of chignon.

" He has within his matted hair the figure of the god, Vajradharma,* is the destroyer of all diseases, exhibits the Varada Mudrā in the right hand and carries the lotus in the left.

" He sits in the Lalita attitude, is peaceful and resplendent ; to his right is Tārā, who has a peaceful appearance, exhibits the Varada Mudrā and carries the lotus.

" To the left is Hayagrīva, who exhibits the act of bowing, and carries the staff in his two hands ; who has red complexion, appears terrible and is fond of the garment of tiger-skin."

The Dhyāna in all MSS. goes thus far and no farther, except in the Asiatic Society manuscript already referred to, which gives the details of how the Maṇḍala for the worship of Lokanātha should be constituted. The Ms. A adds further :—

" Tadvaraṭakāṣṭadale padme Maitreyādi vinyaset ।
Maitreyaḥ pītavarṇaśca nāgapuṣpavarapradaḥ ॥
Kṣitigarbhaḥ śyāmavarṇṇaḥ kalasaṃ cābhayaṃ tathā ।
Vajrapāṇiśca śuklābhaṃ vajrahastavarapradaḥ ॥
Khagarbho nabhaśyāmābho cintāmaṇivarapradaḥ ।
Mañjughoṣo kanakābhaḥ khaḍgapustakadhāriṇaḥ ॥
Gaganagañjo raktavarṇṇah nīlotpalavarapradaḥ ।
Viṣkambhī tu kṣāravarṇṇaḥ ratnottamavarapradaḥ ॥
Sāmantabhadraḥ pītābhaḥ ratnotpalavarapradaḥ ।
Dhūpādicaturddevī ca Vajrāṅkuśyādidvāragāḥ ॥
Varṇāyudhayathāpurvaḥ maṇḍalasyānusārataḥ ।
Evaṃ vidheh samāyuktaṃ Lokanāthaṃ prabhāvayet ॥"

Sādhanamālā, A-28.†

* Vajradharma here stands for Amitābha.

† Wanting in all other Mss.

" On the eight petals of the lotus (on which the god sits) should be placed the gods Maitreya and others. Maitreya is of yellow complexion, carries the Nāga[keśara] flower and exhibits the boon pose. Kṣitigarbha has green complexion, carries the Kalaśa and exhibits the Abhaya pose. Vajrapāṇi is whitish in complexion, carries the Vajra and exhibits the Varada Mudrā. Khagarbha has the colour of the blue sky, carries the Cintāmaṇi and exhibits the Varada Mudrā. Mañjughoṣa is of golden complexion and carries in his two hands the sword and the book. Gaganagañja is of red colour, carries the lotus and exhibits the Varada Mudrā. Viṣkambhin is ash-coloured, carries the best jewel and exhibits the Varada Mudrā. Sāmantabhadra is yellowish in complexion, carries the jewel on a lotus and exhibits the Varada Mudrā. The four goddesses Dhūpā and others [accompany Lokanātha] and the [four goddesses] Vajrāṅkuśī and others guard the gates, their colour and weapons being in accordance with the Maṇḍala. In this way Lokanātha should be conceived by the worshipper."

When represented, Lokanātha is generally alone and is occasionally accompanied by Tārā and Hayagrīva. But we have never come across an image in which all the surrounding deities, Maitreya and others, are represented. He may sit in three attitudes according to three different Sādhanas ; he may have the Lalita, the Paryaṅka or the Vajraprayaṅka attitudes. In the fourth the Āsana is not mentioned, and it is for this reason that we get images of Lokanātha in Ardhaparyaṅka (Plate XX, d) or even in a standing attitude (Plate XXIIa) as well. The standing image reproduced is of pure ivory and has silver foliage behind it.* The Sarnath image reproduced on Plate XXII, b represents the earliest image of Lokanātha with the miniature figure of Amitābha on the crown.

5. Hālāhala.

Colour—white.	Faces—three.
Hands—six.	Companion—Prajñā.

Three Sādhanas in the Sādhanamālā are devoted to the worship of Hālāhala Lokeśvara. Images of this divinity are rarely to be met with in India. But in Nepāl we have been able to find some, though they do not strictly follow the Sādhana. The distinguishing feature of Hālāhala is that he is generally accompanied by his Śakti or the female energy whom he carries in his lap. The Sādhanas all enjoin the presence of the Śakti, though at least two images, one in stone, (Plate XXII, c) another in bronze, have been discovered in Nepal, where the god has been represented alone. According to the Sādhanas, the god should be seated, but the two images

* It belongs to a wealthy Newārī merchant of Kāṭhmāṇḍu and I had access to it through the influence of Paṇḍita Siddhiharṣa Vajrācāryya.

(a) Lokanātha
(Nepal)

(b) Lokanātha
(Sārnāth)

(c) Padmanartteśvara

(d) Hālāhala (Nepal)

(e) Padmanartteśvara
(Nepal)

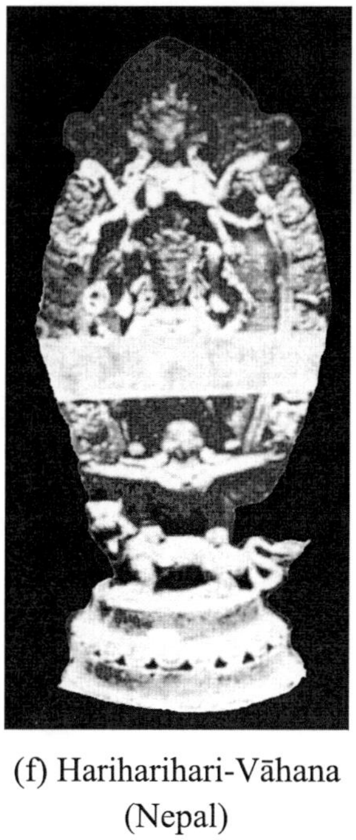

(f) Hariharihari-Vāhana
(Nepal)

Plate XXII

above referred to represent him in a standing attitude. The Dhyāna contained in one of the Sādhanas runs as follows :—

" Hrīḥkāravījaniṣpannaṃ Hālāhalaṃ mahākṛpaṃ ।
Trinetraṃ trimukhaṃ chaiva jaṭāmukuṭamaṇḍitaṃ ॥
Prathamāsyaṃ sitaṃ nīlam dakṣiṇaṃ vāmalohitaṃ ।
Śaśāṅkārdhadharaṃ mūrdhni kapālakṛtaśekharaṃ ॥
Jaṭāntaḥsthajinaṃ samyak sarvābharaṇabhūṣitaṃ ।
Sitāravindanirbhāsaṃ śṛṅgārarasasundaraṃ ॥
Ṣaḍbhujaṃ smeravaktrañca vyāghracarmāmbarapriyaṃ।
Varadaṃ dakṣiṇe pāṇau dvitīye cākṣamālikāṃ ॥
Tritīye śaranarttanaṃ vāme cāpadharam tathā ।
Dvitīye sitapadmañca tritīye stanameva ca ॥

Vāmajānunā sitāṃ Svābhadevīṃ dadhānaṃ ;.vāmena kamaladharāṃ dakṣiṇena bhujena Bhagavadāliṅganaparāṃ kusumaśobhitajaṭākalāpāṃ. Dakṣiṇe pārśve sarpaveṣṭitaṃ triśūlaṃ, vāmapārśve padmasthakapālaṃ nānāsugandhikusumaiḥ sampūrṇaṃ. Raktapadmacandre līlākṣepasthitam bhāvayet."

Sādhanamālā, A-37, N-26, C-25.

" The worshipper should conceive himself as Hālāhala, the great compassionate, originating from the sacred syllable 'Hrīḥ,' with three eyes, three faces and his matted hair rising upwards in the shape of a crown. The first (or the principal) face is white, the right blue and the left red. He bears on his head the crescent and the Kapāla. The Jina Amitābha is within his chignon and he is decked in all ornaments. He is resplendent like the white lotus and appears beautiful by the sentiment of passionate love he displays. He has six arms, a smiling face and is fond of garments of tiger-skin. He displays the Varada Mudrā in the first right hand, the second has the rosary, while the third flourishes the arrow. The first left hand carries the bow, the second the white lotus and the third touches the breast (of his Śakti). He carries the Śakti of his own emanation on the left lap. She shows the lotus in the left hand and the right is engaged in the act of embracing the god. Her chignon is decorated with flowers. To their right is the Triśūla entwined by a snake and on the left is the Kapāla on the lotus, full of a variety of fragrant flowers. The god sits in the Lalita attitude on the red lotus."

6. Padmanartteśvara.

(I)

Face—one. Arms—eighteen. Symbol—lotus.

Āsana—Ardhaparyaṅka (in a dancing attitude).

Identification mark—Double lotus in all hands.

Three Sādhanas in the Sādhanamālā are also devoted to the worship of this variant of Avalokiteśvara. But the three Sādhanas are entirely different, describing three widely different forms of the deity. It is therefore necessary that all the three Dhyānas should be quoted and translated. There is no difficulty in taking the three to be Padmanartteśvara bacause all doubt is set at rest by the fact that the mantras, where mentioned, are the same and that the Sādhanas always designate him as Padmanarttesvara.

Images of Padmanarttesvara are extremely rare even in Nepāl. So far as is known to us, only one image (XXII, e) of this divinity has up till now been discovered. It follows the Dhyāna given below :—

" Padmanarttesvarāmnāyena Ārya-Avalokitesvara-Bhaṭṭārakaṃ ātmānaṃ vibhāvayet ekamukhaṃ aṣṭādaśabhujaṃ ardhaparyaṅkinaṃ Amitābhajaṭājūṭamaṇḍalaṃ, sarvakaraih viśvapadmadhāriṇaṃ, yoginīvṛndaparivṛtaṃ dakṣiṇavāmaparśvasthita-Tārā-Sudhana-Bhṛkuṭi-Hayagrīvaṃ divyālaṃkāravastrabhūṣaṇaṃ...."

Sādhanamālā, A-39. N-28, C-27.

" The worshipper should conceive himself as Bhaṭṭāraka Avalokitesvara in the form of Padmanarttesvara, who is one-faced and eighteen-armed, who stands in the Ardhaparyaṅka attitude, on whose crown of chignon is the effigy of Amitābha, who carries the double lotus in all his (eighteen) hands ; who is surrounded by a host of Yoginīs ; whose right and left sides are occupied by Tārā, Sudhana, Bhṛkuṭi and Hayagrīva ; and who is decked in all kinds of ornaments...."

The Āsana that is prescribed in the Sādhana, we may notice, is the Ardhaparyaṅka. This Āsana may have two varieties ; the ordinary, which is also called the Mahārājalīlā, as in the cases of Vāgīsvara and Siṃhanāda and the second, the dancing variety, (ārdhaparyaṅkena nāṭyasthaṃ) as in the cases of Heruka Vajravārāhī and others. As the word 'narttesvara' means the " God of dances " or the " God in a dancing attitude," the Āsana of Padmanarttesvara may, therefore, be taken as the dancing variety of Ardhaparyaṅka, and this is borne out by the fact that the only image that we have got, shows the god in the same attitude. This image hails from the Sarasvatīsthān or the Mañjuśrī Hill in Svayambhūkṣettra in Nepal. Though the god has here been represented with only two of the companion deities, yet the principal figure minutely corresponds to the description given in the Sādhanamālā.

(II)

Colour—red. Companion—Śakti.
Mudrā—Sūcī. Symbol—lotus.
Vāhana—animal.

Another form of Padmanarttesvara is described in a second Sādhana and the Dhyāna contained therein runs as follows :—

" Padmanarttesvaraṃ ātmānaṃ bhāvayet sattvaparyaṅkaniṣaṇṇaṃ dvibhujaikamukhaṃ raktaṃ sakalālaṅkāradharaṃ Amitābhamukuṭaṃ, vāmaparśve Pāṇḍaravāsinīsamāśliṣṭaṃ āliṅganābhinayasthitavāmabhujena raktapadmadharaṃ, narttanābhinayena Sūcīmudrayā vikāśayadaparadakṣiṇakaraṃ...."

Sādhanamālā, A-29, N-28, C-27.

" The worshipper should conceive himself as Padmanarttesvara, who is seated on an animal, is two-armed and one-faced ; whose complexion is red and who is decked in all kinds of ornaments, bears the effigy of Amitābha on the crown and is embraced by Pāṇḍaravāsinī in the left ; whose left hand, which carries the lotus, is raised in the act of embracing [the Śakti], while the right exhibits the Sūcīmudrā in the act of dancing...."

The accompanying drawing (Plate XXII, d) is all that we could secure in Nepal, of this form of Padmanarttesvara. The right hand which ought to have shown the Sūcīmudrā, has been given a lotus in the drawing. Moreover, the Vāhana is altogether absent.

The same Sādhana from which the Dhyāna quoted above has been restored, contains the description of the Maṇḍala. The Sādhana in question further goes on to say that the lotus on which the God sits should have eight petals, each of which should contain one goddess. For instance, the East petal will have Vilokinī, white in colour and carrying the red lotus. The South is occupied by Tārā of green colour holding the Palāśa and the lotus flowers. Bhūriṇī who should be in the West, is yellow in complexion and carries the Cakra and the blue lotus ; Bhṛkuṭī in the North, whose complexion is white, holds the yellow lotus. In the North-East, there should be Padmavāsinī, who is yellow in complexion and holds the Māñjiṣṭhā and the lotus. South-East is occupied by Viśvapadmeśvari who is sky-coloured and holds the white lotus. The South-West is occupied by Viśvapadmā, who is white and carries the black lotus. The North-West is occupied by Viśvavajrā of variegated complexion, holding the black lotus.

(III)

Colour—red. Arms—eight.

Āsana—Ardhaparyaṅka in a dancing attitude.

Companions—Eight goddesses mentioned in (II).

The Nepal Manuscript No. 603 of Sādhanamālā, gives a third description of Padmanarttesvara, which is not to be found in any other manuscript. As the MS. No. 603 is full of mistakes and omissions, the Sādhana in question is not altogether free from them. As it is, the Sādhana may be restored as follows :—

" Namaḥ Padmanarttesvarāya.

Tatra visvapadmopari candre rakta-Hrīḥ-kārapariṇataṃ Padmanarttesvaraṃ raktavarṇaṃ ekamukhaṃ jaṭāmukuṭinaṃ trinetraṃ, aṣṭabhujaṃ, sarvālaṅkārabhūṣitaṃ sarpayajñopavītaṃ ardhaparyaṅkena tāṇḍavaṃ. Prathamabhujadvayena nṛtyābhinayanaṃ, dvitīyadakṣiṇabhujena vikāśayan sūcīmudrā, vāmabhujena raktapadmaṃ śirasi dhṛtaṃ, tritīyabhujadvayena vajravaddaṇḍatriśūladharaṃ, caturthabhujadvayena akṣasūtrakuṇḍikādharaṃ, aṣṭadevīparivṛtaṃ, evaṃ bhūtaṃ Padmanarttesvaram Lokanāthaṃ bhāvayet."

" Salutation to Padmanarttesvara.

Here the worshipper should conceive himself as Padmanarttesvara, on the moon over the double lotus, springing up from the sacred syllable 'Hrīḥ,' of red complexion, one-faced, having the crown of chignon, three eyes and eight arms ; as decked in all sorts of ornaments, wearing the sacred thread of a snake, and dancing in the Ardhaparyaṅka attitude. The first pair of hands exhibits the dancing pose, the second right exhibits the Sūcīmudrā against the breast, the second left holds the red lotus over head ; the third pair carries the staff and the Triśūla, surmounted by a Vajra, while the fourth pair carries the rosary and the water-pot. The principal god is surrounded by eight goddesses. In such a manner the god Padmanarttesvara Lokanātha should be conceived."

7. Harihariharivāhanodbhava.

Lokeśvara.

Colour—white. Arms—six.

Identification mark—Vāhana consisting of Siṃha, Garuḍa and Viṣṇu.

-There was a considerable difficulty in recognizing images of this divinity. The Sādhana gives the description of the principal god, but is practically silent as to why a peculiar name of this kind has been ascribed to this particular variety of Lokeśvara. India has not given us, up till now, any image of Harihariharivāhana and it is rare even in Nepal. There is only one sculpture (Plate XXIII, a) at Svayambhūkṣettra, and a bronze (Plate XXII, f) at Pāṭan, and both follow the Sādhana precisely. The lion is lowermost, on which rides Garuḍa. On the back of Garuḍa again, is the Hindu god, Nārāyaṇa with the four symbols, the conch, the discus, the mace and the lotus. Lokeśvara rides Nārāyana. The lion, the Garuḍa and Nārāyaṇa, all have 'Hari' as their synonym, and as three Haris are there, Lokeśvara is said to have the Vāhana of three Haris and thus to have acquired the name of Ḥariharihariväbana. Two Sādhanas in the Sādhanamālā are devoted to the worship of this form of Ārya-Avalokiteśvara and the Dhyāna in one of them describes the god in the following terms :—

" Harihariharivāhanodbhavaṃ Bhagavantaṃ Ārya-Avalokiteśvaraṃ sarvāṅgaśuklaṃ jaṭāmukuṭinam śāntaveśaṃ, dakṣiṇakareṇa Bhagavantaṃ Tathāgataṃ sākṣiṇaṃ kurvantaṃ, dvitīyena akṣamālādhāriṇaṃ, tritīyena duḥkuhakaṃ lokaṃ upadeśayantaṃ, vāmena daṇḍadharaṃ, dvitīyena kṛṣṇājinadharaṃ, tritīyena kamaṇḍaludharaṃ, siṃhagaruḍa-Viṣṇuskandhasthitaṃ ātmānam dhyātvā...."

Sādhanamālā, A-39-40, N-29, C-27-28.

" The worshipper should conceive himself as Harihariharivāhanodbhava or god Arya-Avalokiteśvara white in all limbs, with the crown of chignon, clad in peaceful garments, citing the Tathāgata as witness with one of his

(a) Harihariharivāhana (Nepal)

(b) Harihariharivāhana

(c) Rakta-Lokeśvara (Nepal)

(d) Māyājālakrama-Lokeśvara (Nepal)

(e) Nīlakaṇṭha (Sārnāth)

Plate XXIII

right hands, carrying the rosary in the second and instructing the deluded people with the third ; as carrying the staff in one of his left hands, the black deer's skin in the second and the Kamaṇḍalu in the third ; as riding on the shoulder of Viṣṇu [who rides on] Garuḍa, [who is again on the back of a] lion. Thus meditating...."

But all the images of this divinity are not made strictly in accordance with the directions laid down in the Sādhanas. There is an image of this god at Pāṭan with a snake entwining the legs of the lion, like the one reproduced in the Appendix. It is interesting to note that the word 'Hari' is also a synonym for snake and it is no wonder that the snake is present there ; but in that case the sculpture cannot be said to follow the Sādhana precisely. Sometimes, in the drawings, instead of the deer's skin in one of the hands of the god, we find an elephant (Plate **XXIII**, b).

8. Trailokyavaśaṅkara.

Colour—red. Āsana—Vajraparyanka.

This variety of Lokeśvara is also known as Oḍḍiyāna, Uḍḍiyāna or Ōdiyāna Lokeśvara, or Lokeśvara as worshipped in Orissa, which was, in the middle ages, a great centre of Tāntric learning. This form of Lokeśvara does not appear to have been very widely represented. We have met with only one bronze of this god in the Kva Vāhāl at Pāṭaṇ in Nepal. Here also, the image of the god does not follow the Sādhana precisely. Two Sādhanas only in the Sādhanamālā are devoted to the worship of Trailokyavaśaṅkara and the Dhyāna contained in one of them is given below :—

"Lokeśvaraṃ sarvāṅgamahārāgaraktaṃ ekamukhaṃ dvibhujaṃ trinetraṃ jaṭāmukuṭamaṇḍitaṃ vajrāṅkitapāśāṅkuśahastaṃ raktapadme vajraparyaṅkaniṣaṇṇaṃ divyābharaṇavastravibhūṣitaṃ ātmānaṃ vicintya...."

Sādhanamālā, A-41, N-30, C-29.

"The worshipper should realize himself as Lokeśvara (in the form of Trailokyavasaṅkara), whose limbs are reddened by the intense sentiment of passion, who is one-faced, two-armed, three-eyed ; who has the crown of chignon over head, carries in his two hands the noose and goad stamped with the Vajra ; who is seated on the red lotus in the Vajraparyaṅka attitude ; and is decked in celestial garments and ornaments. Thus meditating...."

The Dhyāna, it may be noticed, does not give the name of this variety of Lokeśvara as Trailokyavasaṅkara, but the Colophon* attributes the name to him. It further says that the Sādhana is composed by the great Tāntric savant, Sarahapāda. famous in the middle ages as one of the eighty-four Siddhapurusas.

* "Oḍḍiyānakrameṇa Trailokyavaśaṅkara-Lokeśvara-sādhanaṃ Sarahapādakṛtam."

9. Raktalokesvara.

(I)

Colour—red. Arms—four. Companions—Tārā and Bhṛkuṭī.

Two Sādhanas in the Sādhanamālā are devoted to his worship. But the two Dhyānas describe two widely different forms of the god. It is therefore necessary that both the Dhyānas should be quoted and translated. One of the Dhyānas describe him in the terms given below :—

" Dakṣiṇottarapārśve Tārā-Bhṛkuṭī-devīdvayasahitaṃ Ārya-Avalokiteśvara-Bhaṭṭārakaṃ raktavarṇṇaṃ raktamālyāmvarānulepanaṃ pāśāṅkuśa-dhanurbāṇadharacaturbhujaṃ raktakusumāyitāśokataroradhastat avasthitaṃ ātmānaṃ vicintayet.....

Raktalokeśvarasādhanaṃ". Sādhanamālā. A-43, N-31-32, C-31.

" The worshipper should conceive himself as Ārya-Avalokiteśvara, who is flanked in the South and North, by the goddesses Tārā and Bhṛkuṭī ; who has red complexion, wears red garments and is besmeared with red unguents ; who carries in his four hands the noose, the goad, the bow and the arrow,* and who places himself under the Aśoka tree, which has blossomed forth red flowers."

The Colophon attributes to him the name of Rakta-Lokeśvara, and this name has been given simply because his complexion is red. The only image (Plate XXIII, c) of this form of Lokeśvara, again, as far as we have been able to ascertain, appears in the Kva Vāhāl at Pāṭan in Nepal. This bronze bears an inscription in Newārī on the pedestal, which designates him as Raktalokeśvara. It may be noticed that he is not flanked in this image by his two companions, Tārā and Bhṛkuṭī. As there is no mention of the particular Āsana of the god, the standing attitude in the bronze is quite in keeping with the Sādhana.

(II)

Colour—red. Arms—two.
Symbol—lotus in the left hand. Mudrā—opening petals of lotus.

The next Dhyāna undoubtedly describes a second form of Raktalokeśvara, of whom no representation has yet been found. The Dhyāna runs as follows :—

"Raktavarṇṇaṃ Amitābhagarbhajaṭāmukuṭadharaṃ vāmakaragṛhīta-raktapadmaṃ tacca dakṣiṇakareṇa vikāśayantaṃ vividhālaṅkāravibhūṣitaṃ.:..

Raktalokeśvarasādhanaṃ" Sādhanamālā. A-43, N-32, C-31.

* These four weapons are held in the first and second pair of his hands.

" The worshipper should conceive himself as [Raktalokeśvara] of red complexion, having a crown of chignon bearing the effigy of Amitābha, carrying the red lotus in the left hand and opening its petals with the right,* and as decked in various ornaments...."

A reference may be made to the Dhyāna of Vajradharma, equally unpresented, whose form will be described under No. 15. The forms of Raktalokeśvara and Vajradharma are almost identical, with the difference that the Sādhana enjoins for Vajradharma the Vāhana of a peacock and the five Dhyānī Buddhas on the crown.

10. Māyajālakrama Avalokiteśvara.

Faces—five. Hands—twelve.
Āsana—Pratyālīḍha. Colour—blue.

As the Sādhana for the worship of this particular form of Avalokitesvara has been restored from the Māyājāla Tantra, this peculiar name has been given to the deity. This is the only fierce form of Lokeśvara known to the Indian Buddhists, though fiercer forms are also to be met with in the Tibetan Buddhist Iconography. The Dhyāna given in the Sādhanamālā describes him in the following terms :—

" Bhagavantaṃ Ārya-Avalokiteśvaraṃ kṛṣṇavarṇṇaṃ pratyālīḍhasthaṃ sūryyamaṇḍalasthitaṃ pañcamukhaṃ triṇetraṃ dvādaśabhujaṃ sitarakta-dakṣiṇamukhadvayaṃ tathā pītaharitavāmamukhadvayaṃ dakṣiṇabhujaih ḍamaru-khaṭvāṅga-aṅkuśa-pāśa-vajra-śaradharaṃ, vāmabhujaiḥ tarjanī-kapāla-raktakamala-maṇi-cakra-cāpadharaṃ daṃṣṭrākarālasakalavadanaṃ ṣaṇmudropetaṃ muṇḍamālālaṅkṛtaśarīraṃ nagnaṃ sarvāṅgasundaraṃ ātmānaṃ jhaṭiti pratyākalayya.... "

Sādhanamālā, A-45, N-33, C-32.

" The worshipper should conceive himself as Ārya-Avalokiteśvara, who has blue colour, who stands in the Pratyālīḍha attitude on the orb of the sun ; who is five-faced, three-eyed, twelve-armed, with the two right faces of white and red colour, and two left of yellow and green colour ; who carries in his right hands the Ḍamaru, Khaṭvāṅga, goad, noose, Vajra and the arrow, and in the left hands the raised index finger, the Kapāla, the red lotus, jewel, cakra and the bow ; whose faces look terrible with bare fangs ; who is endowed with the six auspicious ornaments ; † whose person is embellished by the garlands of heads, who is nude and appears beautiful in all limbs. Thus quickly meditating...."

* The word 'vikāśayantaṃ' may also mean 'exhibiting', which would have suited the context well in this case. If that meaning is accepted, the god will have the lotus in both of his hands.

† These six ornaments have been enumerated in the following verse in the Sādhanamālā :—

" Kaṇṭhikārucakaṃ ratnamekhalāṃ bhasmasūtrakaṃ ।
Ṣaṭ vai Pāramitā etā mudrārūpeṇa yojitāḥ ॥"

The image reprodueed (Plate XXIII, d) is perhaps the only one of its kind in India, and belongs to the Svayambhūkṣettra (vulgo-Simbu) in Nepal. It is sculptured in an obscure corner, on one of the panels of a miniature caitya, and corresponds exactly to the description given in the Sādhanamālā; the only deviation is that the god has not been represented as nude in this image.

11. Nīlakantha.

Colour—yellow.	Āsana—Vajraparyaṅka.
Mudrā—Samādhi.	Symbol—bowl of jewels.
Companions—two serpents on either side.	Identification mark—no ornaments.

One Sādhana only is devoted to the worship of this form of Lokesvara which is almost the same as that of Amitābha, whom he bears on his head with the difference that here the former wears the sacred thread and bears the effigy of his sire on head. Amitābha being a Dhyānī Buddha, has no father. Nīlakaṇṭha, according to the Sādhana, is accompanied by two serpents. The Dhyāna is given below :—

" Bhagavantaṃ pītavarṇṇaṃ ardhacandrāṅkitajaṭāmukuṭinaṃ Amitābhopalakṣitaśiraḥpradeśaṃ raktapadmoparisthitaṃ; kṛṣṇasāraharinacarmaṇi vajraparyaṅkinaṃ; samādhimudropari nānāratnaparipūrṇakapāladhāriṇaṃ, eneyacarmakṛtayajñopavītinaṃ, vyāghracarmāmbaradharaṃ nirābharaṇaṃ Nīlakaṇṭhaṃ nilaguṭikāviśiṣṭakaṇṭhaṃ : parasparābhisambaddhapuccha-samaṇiphanāviśiṣṭa-Bhagavadavalokanaparordhvamukha-kṛṣṇasarpadvayopalaksitaṃ ātmānaṃ evam vibhāvayet.....

Nīlakaṇṭha-Ārya-Avalokiteśvara-sādhanaṃ samāptam."

Sādhanamālā, A-44. N-32. C-32.

" The worshipper should conceive himself as the god Nilakaṇtha, whose complexion is yellow, who wears the crown of chignon decorated with the crescent ; on whose head is to be noticed the effigy of Amitābha, who sits in the Vajraparyaṅka attitude on a red lotus, on which is spread the skin of a black deer ; who exhibits the Samādhi Mudrā with his two hands carrying the Kapāla (bowl) filled with a variety of gems ; whose sacred thread consists of the deer-skin (eneya) ; who wears the tiger-skin, and bears no ornaments [on his person] ; whose throat shows the blue pill [of poison] : on either side of whom and looking towards him are to be seen two cobras with jewels on their hoods, and with tails entwined with each other."

Apparently the model of this god has been taken from the Hindu deity Śiva, who is said to have saved the world from destruction by swallowing the poison that came out from the mouth of Vāsuki, the lord of serpents, while the gods and demons were churning the ocean together. The poison, if it could enter Śiva's stomach, would surely have destroyed him. But it remained in his throat, and as the colour of the poison is said to be blue, there is a blue spot in the white throat of the god. That is the reason why the name Nīlakaṇṭha has

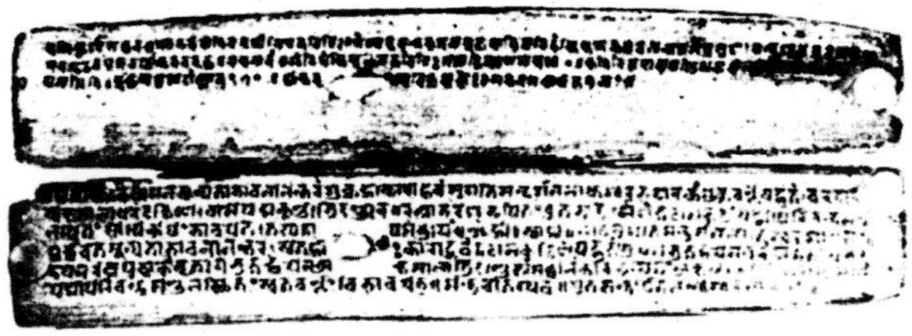

(a) Last and first page of Abhiṣekavidhi
(MS in Durbar Library, Nepal)

(b) Sugatisandarśana Lokeśvara

(c) Pretasantarpita Lokeśvara

(d) Sukhāvatī Lokeśvara (Nepal)

(e) Vajradharma Lokeśvara

Plate XXIV

been attributed to Śiva. As this particular form of Lokeśvara has also the same name, it is not unreasonable to suppose that the model for this variety has been taken from the Hindu god, Śiva Nīlakaṇṭha.

A confusion is likely to occur in the identification of the images of Nīlakaṇṭha and Vāk, the latter being a variety of Mañjuśrī, if their respective fathers are not represented. The only point of distinction in that case would be the total absence of ornaments and luxuriant dress in the case of Nīlakaṇṭha. If the image bears princely ornaments and dress, it must be identified as that of Mañjuśrī.

In the temple of Bauddhanātha (Vulgo-Baudh) in Nepal, one image of this god in colours has been discovered, but here the god appears alone without the serpents. The other image (Plate XXIII,e) hails from the monastery at Sārnāth, though we are not certain how far the identification proposed elsewhere* is acceptable to scholars.

12. Sugatisandarśana-Lokeśvara.

Colour—white. Arms—six.

How we came across the two Sādhanas describing the two varieties, the Sugatisandarśana and the Pretasantarpita Lokeśvara has already been narrated elsewhere.* The obverse side of the first leaf of the Abhiṣekavidhi of the Guhyasamāja containing the two Sādhanas along with the last page is reproduced herewith (Plate XXIV,a) for ready reference. The Dhyāna for Sugatisandarśana given there is quoted below :—

" Sugatisandarśana-Lokeśvara-Bhaṭṭārakaṃ śuklavarṇṇaṃ ṣaḍbhujaṃ varadābhayākṣamālādharaṃ dakṣiṇe, vāme padmakuṇḍītridaṇḍī ca ratnābharaṇabhūṣitaṃ vratasūtradhāriṇaṃ jaṭāmukuṭī[na]ṃ padmopari candramaṇḍale sthitaṃ bhāvayet."

" The worshipper should conceive himself as Bhaṭṭāraka Sugatisandarśana-Lokeśvara, white in complexion, six-armed, showing the Varada and Abhaya poses and the rosary in the [three] right hands, and carrying the lotus, the water-pot, and the staff with three horns in the [three] left ; as decked in ornaments and jewels, wearing the sacred thread, and having a crown of chignon over head ; as situated on the moon over lotus, and as peaceful in appearance."†

* In my paper entitled "The Identification of Avalokiteśvara Images " read before the Second Session of the Oriental Conference held at Calcutta, in the year, 1922, and printed in its proceedings.

† In my paper referred to above an attempt has been made to identify one of the Sarnath images with this particular variety of Lokeśvara. But as there are discrepancies of a serious nature, I have since abandoned the identification.

The Citrakāras of Nepal still draw pictures of this deity and a drawing is reproduced (Plate XXIV,b), to give our readers a fair idea as to his form, so that when we actually meet with one of its representations in stone or metal, it may readily be recognized.

13. Pretasantarpita Lokeśvara.

Colour—white. Arms—six.

The Sādhana for the worship of this deity, likewise, has been furnished by the obverse side of the first leaf of the Abhiṣekavidhi, which was appended to the Nepal MS. in palm-leaf of the Sādhanamālā. We have not met with any representation of this deity anywhere except the one at Macchandar Vahal in Nepal. The Dhyāna has been expressed in the following terms :—

" Jaṭāmukuṭinaṃ ṣaḍbhujaṃ prathamabhujadvayena varadau, dvitīyabhujadvayena ratnapustakau, tṛtīyabhujadvayena akṣamālātridaṇḍikaṃ, sarvālaṅkārabhūṣitaṃ * vratasūtradhāriṇaṃ saumyamūrtiṃ, padmopari candramaṇḍale sthitaṃ, śvetavarṇṇaṃ bhāvayet—

Pretasantarpita-Lokeśvara-sādhanaṃ."

" The worshipper should conceive himself as [Pretasantarpita Lokeśvara], who wears the crown of chignon, is six-armed, exhibits in the first pair of hands the Varada poses and carries, in the second pair the jewel and the book, and in the third the rosary and the Tridaṇḍī ; who is decked in all sorts of ornaments, wears the sacred thread, has a graceful appearance, stands on the orb of the moon over the lotus, and is white in complexion."

The illustration in Plate XXIV,c shows how the Citrakāras of Nepal still prepare drawings of this deity, and it is important in suggesting many minor features which the little Dhyāna does not mention.

14. Sukhāvatī Lokeśvara.

Faces—three. Arms—six.

Āsana—Lalita. Companion—Śakti (Tārā).

Colour—white.

We have not been able to find out the Sādhana for this deity in the Sādhanamālā, but the Dharmakoṣasaṅgraha of Amṛtānanda, however, gives a description of the god. Nepal abounds in the images of this deity (for instance, in Plate XXIV,d) both in stone and in bronze, though he is not found anywhere else. The description above referred to runs as follows :—

" Trimukhaḥ śvetavarṇṇaḥ ṣaḍbhujaḥ, dakṣe, mudrāḥ, śarakṣepajapamālāvaradāni, vāmeṣu dhanuḥkamala-Tārorūsamarpaṇāni lalitāsanaḥ kamalopari, Vajratārā, Viśvatārā,-Padmatārābhiḥ parivṛtaḥ. Upari caityaḥ.

Sukhāvatī Lokeśvaraḥ."

* The Ms. has "akṣa" after "bhūṣitaṃ."

" Sukhāvatī Lokeśvara is three-faced, white in colour, and six-armed ; one of his right hands exhibit the act of shooting an arrow, the remaining two have the rosary and the Varada pose ; in two of the left hands he carries the bow and the lotus and the third is placed on the thigh of Tārā ; he sits in Lalitāsana on the lotus and is surrounded by goddesses, Vajratārā, Viśvatārā, Padmatārā and the like. Above is the Caitya."

15. Vajradharma Lokeśvara.

Colour—reddish white. Vāhana—peacock.

Identification mark—opening the lotus against the breast.

It has already been pointed out that Vajradharma is the only variety of Avalokiteśvara who is regarded as the offspring of the five Dhyānī Buddhas instead of Amitābha only. The distinguishing feature of this god is that he rides a peacock. The Sādhana devoted to his worship is almost wholly in verse and we give below the portion dealing with his form. This has been omitted by Dr. Foucher, and was first pointed out by the present writer in his paper on the " Identification of Avalokiteśvara Images " :—

" Taṃ sitaṃ raktavarṇṇaṃ tu padmarāgasamadyutiṃ I
Pañcabuddhamukuṭadharaṃ harṣeṇotphullalocanaṃ II
Vāmato spardhayā nālam dhṛtvā ṣoḍaśapatrakaṃ I
Padmaṃ vikāśayantañca hṛdi dakṣiṇapāṇinā II
Mayūropari madhyasthe niṣaṇṇaṃ candramaṇḍale I
Sattvaparyaṅkamābhujya saśṛṅgārarasotsavaṃ II
Caityāntaḥstha-mahākarma-kūṭāgāra-vihāriṇaṃ I
Bhāvayet Vajradharmāgryaṃ nityaṃ Bodhiṃ avāpnuyāt II"

Sādhanamālā, A—20, N—16, C—10.

" The worshipper should conceive himself as excellent Vajradharma, of reddish white complexion with splendour like that of the Padmarāga gem, who bears the effigies of the five Dhyāni Buddhas on the crown ; whose eyes beam with delight ; who holds with pride the stem of a lotus with sixteen petals and with the right causes it to blossom against the breast ; who sits on the moon over lotus on the back of a peacock, enjoys his seat of the animal and displays the delightful amorous sentiment ; who moves in the sanctum inside the Caitya, the place for great performances. He (the worshipper) certainly receives the Bodhi who meditates [upon him] in this manner."

The illustration in Plate XXIV,e shows the form of Vajradharma as drawn by the artists of Nepal in modern days. The right hand which ought to have been empty carries a book.

* * * *

The conception of Avalokiteśvara is as old as the third century B.C. He was first ushered into existence by the Mahāsāṅghikas, about the time of Aśoka, in their work, entitled Mahāvastu Avadāna, where he has been characterised* as the " Bhagavān who takes the form of a Bodhisattva, whose duty

* Senart ; Le Mahāvastu, Vol. II, p. 294.

it is to look round (Avalokita) for the sake of instructing the people and for their constant welfare and happiness." This Avalokita Bodhisattva no doubt gave rise to the concrete form of Avalokiteśvara, even before the second century A. D. and his images can be traced from the Gupta period, onwards. He appears in a concrete form first in the Sukhāvatī-Vyūha*, so far as our present information goes. The very great number of forms of Avalokiteśvara have undoubtedly a bearing on the passage† in the Kāraṇḍa-vyūha, where he is said to take all possible forms of godhead in order to instruct the people and to put them in the way of salvation. As different people were of different religions, this Compassionate Bodhisattva had to assume the shape of all gods of all religions, nay even the shape of the father and the mother. As we are not sure how far these one hundred and eight forms are authoritative, it is desirable that these forms should be treated in an Appendix.‡

* This work was first translated into Chinese between A.D. 148 and 170 while the smaller recension was first translated into the same language between A.D. 384 and 317. Max Muller: Sukhāvatī Vyūha. Introduction pp. III—IV.

† Quoted above, p. 32, footnote.

‡ See Appendix B.

CHAPTER IV.

EMANATIONS OF AMITĀBHA.

I. GODS.

Besides Avalokiteśvara and two forms of Mañjuśri, only two male divinities in the Sādhanamālā emanate from the Dhyānī Buddha Amitābha. One is Mahāvala and the other is Hayagrīva. Images of these we have not yet come across . So we must content ourselves at present with only the Dhyānas and their translations.

1. Mahāvala.

Āsana—Pratyālīḍha. Colour—red. Appearance—terrible.

One Sādhana only is devoted to the worship of this particular emanation of Amitābha. The Dhyāna is given below :—

" Mahāvalaṃ ekamukhaṃ caturbhujaṃ sarvāṅgaraktaṃ ūrdhvapiṅgala-sarppāvabaddhakeśaṃ dakṣiṇabhujābhyāṃ sitadaṇḍacāmaradharaṃ* vāmabhujābhyāṃ vandanābhinayatarjanīdharaṃ vyāghracarmanivasanaṃ sarpābharaṇaṃ pratyālīḍhaṃ daṃṣṭrākarālavadanaṃ sūryyamaṇḍalaprabhāmālinaṃ Amitābhamukuṭinaṃ dhyāyāt ".

Sādhanamālā. A—278, Na—86, C—216.

" The worshipper should realize himself as Mahāvala with one face, four arms and red complexion ; whose brown hair rises upwards and is tied round by a snake ; who carries in his two right hands the white staff and the chowrie, while the two left show the Namaskāra and the Tarjanī Mudrā ; who is clad in tiger-skin, wears ornaments of snake, and stands in the Pratyālīḍha attitude ; whose face looks terrible with bare fangs ; who is resplendent like the orb of the sun, and bears the effigy of Amitābha on the crown."

2. Saptaśatika Hayagrīva.

Colour—red. Appearance—terrible.

Symbols—Vajra and Daṇḍa (staff).

Identification mark—The horse's head over head.

He has several other forms, but in only one he is said to bear the image of Amitābha on his crown. Another is said to bear that of Aksobhya, and in the third, there is no indication as to who should appear on his head. So, the three different forms should be dealt with in three different places. The particular name by which the third variation of

* C reads, "sitacāmara ".

Hayagrīva goes is Paramāśva, while the other two are given the name of Hayagrīva simply. As the prēsent Sādhana which describes the form bearing the Dhyānī Buddha Amitābha on the crown, has been, according to the Colophon, restored from the Saptaśatika Kalpa, we designate this particular form of Hayagrīva as Saptaśatika Hayagrīva. In this case also we have not met with any representation in stone or bronze, and the drawings that have been brought from Nepal present so wide a difference that we do not venture to reproduce them here. The Dhyāna as presented in the Sādhana is given below :—

"Raktavarṇṇaṃ mahābhayānakaṃ trinetraṃ kapilaśmaśruṃ raudraṃ vṛhadudaraṃ daṃṣṭrākarālinaṃ dantauṣṭhakapālamālinaṃ jaṭāmukuṭinaṃ Amitābhaśiraskaṃ, dvitīyamukhaṃ nīlaṃ hayānanaṃ hihikāranādinaṃ, brahmāṇḍaśikharākrāntaṃ, dvitīyena bhavāgraparyantaṃ, aṣṭanāgopetaṃ kharvavāmanākāraṃ vyāghracarmanivasanaṃ sarvālaṅkārabhūṣitaṃ sakaladevāsuraṃ tarpayantaṃ gṛhītavajradaṇḍaṃ....vicintayet.

Saptaśatikakalpoktaṃ Hayagrīvasādhanaṃ samāptaṃ."

Sādhanamālā. A—279, C—217.

The worshipper should conceive himself as [Saptaśatika Hayagrīva] of red complexion, who is terribly awe-inspiring, three-eyed, with brown beard ; who is angry and has protruding belly ; whose face appears terrible with bare fangs ; who wears garlands of skulls with teeth and lips, bears on his head the crown of chignon, and the figure of Amitābha ; whose second face is distorted like that of a horse, which is blue in colour and neighs incessantly ; who tramples on the top of the universe with one leg and the end of the world with the other ; who is deeked in (ornaments of) eight serpents, is short and dwarfish, is clad in tiger-skin and decked in all ornaments ; who pleases all the gods and Asuras, and holds the Vajra and the staff (in his two hands)."

It may be noticed that the Dhyāna is not clear about the number of hands and faces ; but it seems from the description that Hayagrīva is endowed with a principal face, terrible in appearance over which is the horse's head. This horse's head over the principal one is found only in the case of Hayagrīva, and distinguishes him from all other Buddhist deities. But when, as a minor god, he accompanies others, we do not, as a rule, notice the horse's head. In such cases, the Daṇḍa or the staff serves as the identification mark. From the Dhyāna it also appears that he is two-armed and carries the Vajra and Daṇḍa. The Vajra is generally held in the right hand, while the Daṇḍa is carried in the left. About the name, however, the Colophon is certain, and it asserts that this Sādhana has been restored from the Saptaśatika Kalpa, meaning a ritual work, consisting of words, that can make up seven hundred ślokas in the Anuṣṭubh metre.

II. GODDESSES.

The feminine divinities that emanate from the Dhyānī Buddha Amitābha are three in number, the most important and popular being Kurukullā, to whose worship no less than fourteen Sādhanas are devoted in the Sādhanamālā. Two Sādhanas are devoted to Bhṛkuṭī and one Sādhana only to Mahāsitavatī, who is also known as one of the Pañcarakṣās or the five Great Protectresses. None* of these goddesses we have been able to find out in stone or bronze ; but paintings are, however, made by the Nepalese Artists even in modern times. Let us take up the goddesses one by one :—

1. Kurukullā.

She is one-faced and may have two, four, six or eight arms. When she is endowed with six arms, she bears the effigies of the five Dhyānī Buddhas on her crown, or in other words, she is then regarded as the offspring of the combination of the five Dhyanī Buddhas. When two-armed she is called Śukla Kurukullā, and when she has four arms, she is called by the names of Tārodbhava Kurukullā, Oḍḍiyāna Kurukullā, Hevajrakrama Kurukullā and Kalpokta Kurukullā.

Kurukullā is said to confer success in the Tāntric rite of Vaśīkaraṇa or the rite of subduing or bewitching men, women, ministers or even kings. Many interesting processes are given in some Sādhanas for bewitching in different cases. The mantra of Kurukullā is "Oṃ Kurukulle Huṃ Hrīḥ Svāhā". If this mantra is muttered ten thousand times, all men will be bewitched ; thirty thousand would be sufficient for subduing a minister and one lakh for a king. She can even confer on her devotees the power of subduing all ministers and all kings.

(i) Śukla Kurukullā.

Colour—white.	Symbols—rosary and the bowl of lotus.
Vāhana—animal.	Āsana —Vajraparyaṅka.

Only one Sādhana in the Sādhanamālā furnishes us with the manner of her worship. The Dhyāna contained therein is a long one and runs as follows :—

"Ātmānaṃ Bhagavatīṃ akṣasūtrotpalāmṛtakuṇḍīṃ savyāvasavyābhyāṃ dadhānāṃ, trinetrāṃ Padmadhṛkpramukhaiḥ sarva-Tathāgataiḥ Vīnādiṣoḍaśadevībhiḥ abhiṣiktāṃ, Amitābhavirājitanānāpuṣpaśobhitajaṭāmukuṭāṃ śṛṅgārādirasopetāṃ, kiñcit savyapāṇipallavasthākṣasūtraṃ ālokamānāṃ,

* Some Tibetan forms of Kurukullā, however, are noticed in Getty and Deniker's "*Gods of the Northern Buddhisim*".

kṣīrāmbhodhiśvetavarṇṇābjasthāṃ amṛtāṅkopari sattvaparyaṅkāsanasthaṃ, kaṅkana-keyūra-kuṇḍala-nūpura-muktāhāra-divyavastrādivibhūṣitāṃ, nīl-Anantabaddhakeśīṃ, pīyūṣavarṇṇa-Vāsukikṛtahārāṃ, rakta-Takṣakakṛtavarṇṇograkuṇḍalāṃ, dūrvāśyāma-Karkkoṭakakṛtayajñopavītāṃ, śukla-Padmanāgendrakṛtahārāṃ, mṛṇālavarṇṇa-Mahāpadmakṛtanūpurāṃ, pīta-Śaṅkhapālakṛtakaṅkanāṃ, dhūmābhravat-Kulikakṛtakeyūrāṃ, śubhravarṇṇāṃ sravadamṛtavigrahāṃ karuṇārdracittāṃ bhāvayet.

Śukla-Kurukullā-sādhanaṃ ". Sādhanamālā. A—191, N—106, C—155.

" The worshipper should conceive himself as the goddess (Kurukullā), who carries the rosary and the cup of Utpala full of nectar in the right and left hands respectively ; who is three-eyed and is offered bathing water by (the Bodhisattva) Padmapāṇi and others, by all the Tathāgatas and the sixteen damsels beginning from Vīṇā ; who wears the crown of chignon, which is decorated with various flowers and the miniature figure of Amitābha ; who displays the sentiment of passionate love, and other sentiments ; who turns slightly to have a look at the rosary which she carries in her leaf-like hand ; who sits on an animal and rests on the nectar-like lap of the white lotus, that rises from the ocean of milk ; who is decked in bracelets, armelts, ear-rings, anklets, pearl-necklace, and is clad in celestial garments ; whose hair is tied up by the serpent Ananta of blue colour, whose necklace is formed by the milk-coloured Vāsuki, and the prominent ear-ornament (Kuṇḍala) of red Takṣaka ; whose sacred thread is the green Karkkoṭaka ; whose girdle is the white Padma, the lord of serpents ; whose Nūpura (anklet) is the serpent Mahāpadma of the colour of the lotus stalk ; whose bracelet is yellow Śaṅkhapāla ; whose armlet is Kulika of the colour of smoky clouds ; whose complexion is white, and who seems to diffuse nectar and possesses a heart whieh is melted with compassion."

From this somewhat long description, the form of Śukla-Kurukullā would be sufficiently vivid. The other varieties have many features in common with the form described above and will now be noticed briefly. It is not necessary to quote and translate all the Dhyānas given in the Sādhanamālā.

(ii) Tārodbhava-Kurukullā.

Colour—red. Arms—four. Āsana—Vajraparyaṅka.
Vāhana—Kāmadeva and his wife riding upon Rāhu.

Five Sādhanas describe the goddess with very slight differences. She has red complexion, red garments, red ornaments and a seat of red lotus. She is four-armed and shows in her two left hands the Abhaya pose and the arrow, while the two right carry the bow and the red lotus. She sits in the Vajraparyaṅka attitude and under her seat of lotus appears Kāmadeva and his wife riding on Rāhu. She has red aureole behind her, wears the effigy of Amitābha on the crown and resides in the Kurukulla mountain. She is in the fulness of youth and displays amorous sentiments. Sometimes she charges an arrow on the bow and is ready to strike.

(iii) Oḍḍiyāna-Kurukullā.

Appearance—terrible. Colour—red.
Āsana—Ardhaparyaṅka. Vāhana—corpse.

This variant of Kurukullā may be called the Oḍiyāna or Uḍḍiyāna or Oḍḍiyāna Kurukullā, or Kurukullā as worshipped in Orissa. This form of the goddess presents rather a fierce form in as much as she has the garland of heads, the five skulls on her head, protruding teeth and tongue, garments of tiger-skin, and brown hair rising above her head in the shape of a flame. Her eyes are three in number which are red, round and moving. She is four-armed ; the principal pair of hands is engaged in drawing to the full the flowery bow charged with an arrow of red lotus. The second pair holds the goad of flowers and the red lotus. She has red complexion and sits in the Ardhaparyaṅka attitude on a corpse.

(iv) Aṣṭabhuja Kurukullā.

Arms—eight. Colour—red.
Āsana—Vajraparyaṅka. Mudrā—Trailokyavijaya.

As has previously been pointed out, Kurukullā may have another form with eight arms also emanating from the Dhyānī Buddha Amitābha, though it is not expressly mentioned in the only Sādhana devoted to her worship. This Sādhana is attributed in the Colophon to the great Uḍiyā Siddhācāryya, Indrabhūti, who flourished about 700 A. D., and who had a more illustrious daughter, Lakṣmīṅkarā by name, well-versed in the doctrines of both Vajrayāna and Sahajayāna. The goddess described in this Sādhana is not of a terrible appearance like the six-armed Māyājāla Kurukullā or the four-armed, Oḍiyāna Kurukullā, but is mild, youthful and compassionate. The most important feature of the Sādhana is that it gives the description of a complete Maṇḍala which comprises of the principal goddess and twelve surrounding divinities. For a better understanding of the form of this goddess and of the constitution of the Maṇḍala, it is desirable that the Dhyāna should be quoted and translated :—

" Kurukullāṃ Bhagavatīṃ aṣṭabhujāṃ raktavarṇṇāṃ raktāṣṭadalapadmasūryye Vajraparyaṅkaniṣaṇṇāṃ kūṭāgāramadhyanivāsinīṃ, prathamakaradvayena Trailokyavijayamudrādharāṃ, avaśiṣṭadakṣiṇakaraiḥ aṅkuśaṃ ākarṇapūritaṃ śaraṃ varadamudrāṃ dadhānāṃ, pariśiṣṭavāmabhujaiḥ pāśaṃ cāpaṃ utpalaṃ dadhānāṃ, sakalālaṅkāravatīṃ bhāvayet.

Pūrvadale Prasannatārāṃ, dakṣiṇadale Niṣpannatārāṃ, paścimadale Jayatārāṃ, uttaradale Karṇatārāṃ, aiśānadale Cundāṃ, āgneyadale Aparājitāṃ, nairtyadale Pradīpatārāṃ, vāyavyadale Gaurītārāñca dhyāyāt. Etāśca sarvāḥ raktavarṇṇāḥ Pañca-Tathāgatamukuṭyaḥ vajraparyaṅkaniṣaṇṇāḥ dakṣiṇabhujābhyāṃ varadamudrā-ākarṇapūrita-śaradharāḥ, vāmabhujābhyāṃ utpalacāpadharāḥ.

Pūrvadvāre Vajravetālīṃ lambodarāṃ vikṛtamukhīṃ raktavarṇṇāṃ Akṣobhyamukuṭāṃ, dakṣiṇahastābhyāṃ tarjanī-aṅkuśadharāṃ, vāmakarābhyāṃ vajraghaṇṭāpāśadharāṃ.

Dakṣiṇadvāre Aparājitāṃ pītavarṇṇāṃ Ratnasambhavamukuṭāṃ dakṣiṇahastābhyāṃ daṇḍāṅkuśadharāṃ, vāmahastābhyāṃ ghaṇṭāpāśadharāṃ.

Pāścimadvāre Ekajaṭāṃ kṛṣṇavarṇṇāṃ ūrdhvakeśāṃ lambodarāṃ dantāvaṣṭabdhauṣṭhāṃ Amitābhamukuṭāṃ, dakṣiṇakarābhyāṃ vajra-aṅkuśadharāṃ, vāmakarābhyāṃ ghaṇṭāpāśadharām.

Uttaradvāre Vajragāndhārīṃ kanakasyāmāṃ Amoghasiddhimukuṭāṃ vikṛtamukhīṃ lambodarāṃ, dakṣiṇabhujābhyāṃ khaḍga-aṅkuśadharāṃ vāmabhujābhyāṃ ghaṇṭāpāśadharāṃ vicintayet.

Etāḥ catasraḥ ālīḍhapadasthāḥ ".

Sādhanamālā. A—183-4, N—101, C—150.

" The worshipper should conceive himself as goddess Kurukullā, who is eight-armed, has red complexion, sits on the Vajraparyaṅka attitude on the disc of the sun over the lotus with eight petals and resides in the sanctum ; who displays the Trailokyavijaya mudrā in her first pair of hands, and shows in the other right hands the aṅkuśa, the arrow drawn up to the ear and the Varada pose, and in the other left hands the noose, the bow and the Utpala; and who is decked in all kinds of ornaments.

On the east petal is Prasannatārā, on the south is Niṣpannatārā, on the west Jayatārā, on the north Karṇatārā ; on the north-east petal is Cundā, on the south-east Aparājitā, on the south west Pradīpatārā, and on the north-west Gaurītārā. All these deities have red complexion and five Dhyānī Buddhas on the crown ; they sit in the Vajraparyaṅka attitude and show in the two right hands the boon pose and the arrow drawn up to the ear, and in the two left hands the Utpala and the bow.

In the eastern gate is Vajravetālī, who has protruding belly, distorted face, red complexion, the effigy of Akṣobhya on tiara, and carries in the two right hands the Tarjanī and the goad, and in the two left the Vajraghaṇṭā and the noose.

In the southern gate is Aparājitā, who has yellow complexion, the effigy of Ratnasambhava on tiara, and carries in her two right hands the staff and the goad, and in the two left the bell and the lasso.

In the western gate is Ekajaṭā, who has blue colour, hair rising upwards over head, and protruding belly ; who bites her lips with her teeth, bears the image of Amitābha on tiara, and carries in her two right hands the Vajra and the goad, and in the two left the bell and the lasso.

In the northern gate is Vajragāndhārī, who has golden complexion, bears the image of Amoghasiddhi on tiara, has distorted face, and protruding belly and carries in her two right hands the sword and the goad, and in the two left the bell and the lasso.

All these four goddesses stand in the Ālīḍha attitude."

2. Bhṛkuṭī.

Arms—four. Colour—yellow.

We are, no doubt, familiar with the name of Bhṛkuṭī, who accompanies, as a minor goddess, some varieties of Avalokiteśvara. When she accompanies Khasarpaṇa, she is yellow in complexion and four-armed, carrying in the two left hands the Tridaṇḍi and Kamaṇḍalu. One of the two right hands is raised in the attitude of doing homage, while the other carries the rosary.

Bhṛkuṭī is also worshipped by the Buddhists as a principal goddess and two Sādhanas in the Sādhanamālā are devoted to her worship. She is described in the following words :—

" Caturbhujaikamukhīṃ pītāṃ trinetrāṃ navayauvanāṃ varadākṣasūtradakṣiṇakarāṃ, tridaṇḍikamaṇḍaludharavāmakarāṃ Amitābhamudritāṃ padmacandrāsanasthāṃ Bhagavatīṃ dhyātvā....

Bhṛkuṭīsādhanaṃ." Sādhanamālā, A—178, Na—3, C—145-6.

" The goddess (Bhṛkuṭī) should be conceived as four-armed, one faced, yellow in complexion, three-eyed, blooming with youth ; as showing the Varada Mudrā and the rosary in her two right hands and carrying the Tridaṇḍī and the Kamaṇḍalu in the two left ; as stamped with the effigy of Amitābha (on head) and as sitting on the moon supported by the lotus. Thus meditating.... "

Another Sādhana adds that she should have a peaceful appearance and should wear the crown of chignon on head.

The illustration printed on Plate LXI,b (*Sic.* correct to 'a'. 'b' is a picture of Vasudhārā) as that of Bhṛkutī in Getty's *Gods of Northern Buddhism*, is in reality that of Grahamātṛkā, which deity will be described later.

3. Mahāsitavatī.

Arms—four. Colour—red. Āsana—Ardhaparyaṅka.

All the five goddesses constituting the Mahāpañcarakṣā group are said to emanate from one or other of the Dhyānī Buddhas. Mahāsitavatī is attached to Amitābha. The short Sādhana is as follows :—

" Mahāsitavatī caturbhujaikamukhī raktā dakṣiṇabhujadvaye akṣasūtravaradavatī vāmabhujadvaye* vajrāṅkuśahṛtpradeśasthapustakavatī Hrīṃbījā Amitābhamukuṭī ardhaparyaṅkasthitā nānālaṅkāravatī sūryyāsanaprabhā ceti."

Sādhanamālā. A—215, Na—17, C—171.

" Mahāsitavatī is four-armed and one-faced, of red complexion, shows in her two right hands the rosary and the Varada pose and in her two left hands the goad surmounted by a Vajra and the book against the breast ; she originates from the syllable ' Hrīṃ,' bears the effigy of Amitābha on tiara, sits in the Ardhaparyaṅka attitude, is decked in various ornaments, sits on the disc of and glows like the sun."

* A Omits " vāmabhujadvaye....nānālaṅkāravatī ".

CHAPTER V.

EMANATIONS OF AKṢOBHYA.

I. GODS.

The number of deities that emanate from the Dhyānī Buddha, Askṣobhya is rather large,—larger than the emanations from any other Dhyānī Buddha. The reason is that Akṣobhya was one of the earliest Tathāgatas to enter the Buddhist Pantheon. The blue colour of Akṣobhya is associated with the terrible deities in the Sādhanamālā and with the gruesome rites in the Tantra. The deities emanating from this Dhyānī Buddha have generally the blue colour and they are usually terrible both in appearance and in deeds. Excepting perhaps Jambhala all other male emanations of Akṣobhya have terrible appearance with distorted face, bare fangs, three eyes, protruding tongue, garland of heads and skulls, the tiger-skin and ornament of snakes.

Besides seyeral forms of Mañjuśrī, male deities emanating from Akṣobhya are nine in number, each having a large number of Sādhanas devoted to his worship. The deities to wit, Caṇḍaroṣaṇa, Heruka, Buddhakapāla, Samvara, Hayagrīva, Raktayamāri, Kṛṣṇayamāri, Jambhala and Ucchuṣma-Jambhala. Let us take them up one by one.

1. CAṆḌAROṢANA.

Colour—yellow. Appearance—terrible.
Symbols—sword and Tarjanīpāśa.
Identification Mark—left leg touching the ground (avaninihitajānuḥ).

Caṇḍaroṣaṇa is also called Mahācaṇḍaroṣaṇa, Caṇḍamahāroṣaṇa and Acala. Four Sādhanas are devoted to his worship and he is always represented in yab-yum. Prabhākarakīrti is said to be the author of one of the Sādhanas a major portion of which is in verse. As there is no mention of the crest of Akṣobhya in this Sādhana we take up another which is in prose. The Dhyāna* describing the god runs as follow :—

"Śrīcaṇḍamahāroṣaṇaṃ Bhagavantaṃ atasīpuṣpasaṅkāśaṃ Acalāparanāmānaṃ dvibhujaṃ kekarākṣaṃ daṃṣṭrākarālamahāghoravadanaṃ ratnamaulinaṃ daṃṣṭrānipīḍitādharaṃ muṇḍamālāśiraskaṃ āraktacakṣudvayaṃ dakṣiṇe khaḍgadharaṃ tarjanīpāśahṛdayasthavāmakaraṃ sitasarpayajño-

*. According to other Sādhanas, he may have blue colour and the effigies of the five Dhyānī Buddhas on the crown. The significance of the two symbols is that the noose is required to bind the host of the Māras, all of whom should be conceived as nude with hair dishevelled and as crying in utter helplessness, while the sword cuts them through.

(a) Caṇḍaroṣaṇa

(b) Buddhakapāla

(c) Heruka (Dacca Museum)

(d) Hayagrīva

Plate XXV

pavītaṃ vyāghracarmanivasanaṃ nānāratnaviracitābharaṇaṃ bhūmilagna-vāmacaraṇaṃ īṣadunnatadakṣiṇacaraṇaṃ sūryyaprabhāmālinaṃ ātmānaṃ vicintya....Akṣobhyamukuṭinaṃ dhyāyāt."

Sādhanamālā. A—91, Na—20-21, C—70.

" The worshipper should meditate on himself as Śrī-Caṇḍamahāroṣaṇa, whose colour is like that of the Atasī flower, and who is also called Acala; who is one-faced, two-armed, and squint-eyed, whose face appears terrible with bare fangs, who wears a bejewelled head-dress, bites his lips with the teeth, and wears on his crown a garland of heads, whose eyes are slightly red, who carries the sword in his right hand and the noose round the raised index finger against the breast, whose sacred thread consists of a white snake, who is clad in tiger-skin, whose ornaments consist of various gems; whose left leg touches the ground, while the right is slightly raised, and who has the radiance of the sun. Thus meditating....he should also be conceived as bearing the effigy of Akṣobhya on his crown.

It should be noticed that the Dhyāna is silent about the Śakti in whose embrace the god should remain in yab-yum. But if the Buddhist priests are to be believed and if the testimony of the Buddhist Citrakāras may be held to be of any value, we must assume that he is always represented in yab-yum, and can never be represented singly. The accompanying sketch (Plate **XXV**, a) meets all the requirements, but we have not yet succeeded in discovering any representation of the deity either in stone or in metal. Caṇḍaroṣaṇa is the most important figure in the celebrated Caṇḍamahāroṣaṇa Tantra. His worship is always performed in secret, and the god is kept secluded from public gaze. Even if there be a bronze image, it is practically inaccessible to any one else except the initiated.

2. Heruka.

Varieties—single or yab-yum.
Arms—two (single); two or four (yab-yum).
Āsana—Dancing in Ardhaparyaṅka.

Heruka is one of the most popular deities of the Buddhist Pantheon. His name is generally associated with his Śaktis, who embrace the god and remain in yab-yum. He is also worshipped singly and in that case he will have two arms only. When represented in yab-yum, he will have two or four arms. No less than five Sādhanas are devoted to his worship.

(i) Dvibhuja Heruka.

Colour—blue. Vāhana—corpse (not always).
Āsana—Dancing in Ardhaparyaṅka. Symbols—Vajra and the Kapāla.
Identification mark—Khaṭvāṅga with flowing banner hanging from the left shoulder.

Three out of the five Sādhanas are devoted to this particular form of Heruka. Two of these are in prose and one is in verse. His worship cenfers Buddhahood on his worshippers and Heruka is said to destroy all Māras of the world. His images are extremely rare even in Nepal. We know of only two images ; one appears in the Bauddhanātha Temple in Nepal and another has recently been discovered at Comilla and is deposited in the Dacca Museum, Dacca. The Dhyāna describes his form in the following terms :—

" Śavastham ardhaparyaṅkaṃ naracarmasuvāsasaṃ ।
Bhasmoddhūlitagātrañca sphuradvajrañca dakṣiṇaṃ ॥
Calātpatākākhaṭvāṅgaṃ vāme raktakaroṭakaṃ ।
Śatārdhamuṇḍamālābhiḥ kṛtahāramanoramaṃ ॥
Īṣaddaṃṣṭrākarālāsyaṃ raktanetravilāsinaṃ ।
Piṅgordhvakeśaṃ Akṣobhyamukuṭam karṇakuṇḍalaṃ ॥
Asthyābharaṇaśobhaṃ tu śiraḥ pañcakapālakaṃ ।
Buddhatvadāyinaṃ dhyāyāt jaganmāranivāraṇaṃ ॥

Herukaśādhanam."

Sādhanamālā. A—258, Na—50-51, C—20.

" The worshipper should conceive himself as (Heruka) who stands on a corpse* in the Ardhaparyaṅka attitude, who is well-clad in human skin ; whose body is besmeared with ashes, who wields the Vajra in the right hand ; in whose left is the Khaṭvāṅga with a moving flag (hanging from his shoulder like the sacred thread), and who carries in his left hand the Kapāla full of blood ; whose necklace is beautified by a chain of half-a-hundred heads ; whose face is only slightly distorted with bare fangs and who revels in his blood-shot eyes ; whose brown hair rises upwards and on whose tiara is the effigy of Akṣobhya ; whose ear-ornament is the Kuṇḍala and who is decked in ornaments of bones ; on whose head are the five skulls, who bestows Buddhahood and protects the world from the Māras."

In another Sādhana for the worship of this particular kind of Heruka, the Khaṭvāṅga is described as being surmounted by a Vajra of five thongs and as decorated with the flag with moving bells, man's head and the double lotus, the lower half of the Khaṭvāṅga resembling the Vajra with one thong. This Sādhana does not mention the number of heads in the necklace, but says simply that it is sewn by guts. His left leg rests on the double lotus (and not on the corpse), while the right is placed on the left thigh in a dancing attitude.

The image (Plate XXV, c) that has been discovered by Mr. N. K. Bhaṭṭaśālī and deposited in the Dacca Museum, agrees in all details with the description just given. Though the hands are broken it can yet be discerned that the right weilded the Vajra and the left carried the Kapāla against the breast. The attitude in which he stands is called the dancing attitude in Ardhaparyaṅka. His head-dress is decorated with five skulls and the effigy of Akṣobhya. The Khaṭvāṅga has an overflowing banner attached to it and the ends of the banner are decorated with small bells.

* The corpse on which Heruka dances is prostrate on the ground and lies on its breast. His Śaktis, when represented singly on corpses, will also have this peculiar kind of corpse with its face down. As a matter of fact, this serves as a distinguishing symbol in the case of Heruka and his Śaktis.

(ii)

Variety—yab-yum. Companion—Prajñā.

Only one Sādhana in the Sādhanamālā gives the procedure for the worship of the two-armed Heruka in yab-yum, who is also known as Trilokyākṣepa. The god varies a little from the description of single Heruka given above. He also has two arms, which carry the Vajra in the right and the Kapāla in the left. The Khaṭvāṅga, as usual, hangs from his left shoulder and resembles a sacred thread. He wears ornaments of bones and is embraced by his Prajñā, who is one-faced and two-armed, carrying the Kartri in the right hand and the Kapāla in the left. He has bare fangs, wears garlands of heads and feasts on human flesh, as is evident from the following Namaskāra given in the Sādhana :—

"Daṃṣṭrotkaṭamahābhīmamuṇḍasragdāmabhūṣitaṃ ।
Bhakṣyamānaṃ mahāmāṃsaṃ Śrī-Herukaṃ namāmyahaṃ ॥ "

An image in colours of this variety of Heruka appears in the Bauddhanātha Temple in Nepal.

(iii) Caturbhuja Heruka.

Variety—yab-yum. Arms—four. Companion—Svābhā Prajñā.

One Sādhana also is devoted to the worship of this particular form of Heruka ; here he is four-armed and is embraced by his Prajñā who is identical with him in all respects. The four-armed Heruka is similar in all other respects to the two forms described above, except that he carries in his four hands the black Vajra, the sword, the Khaṭvāṅga and the jewel. The Khaṭvāṅga this time does not hang from his left shoulder but is carried in one of his hands. The Sādhanas in all these three cases are particular in saying that they all bear the image of Akṣobhya on their tiara.

3. Buddhakapāla.

Variety—yab-yum. Arms.—four.
Colour—blue. Companion—Prajñā.
Āsana—dancing in Ardhaparyanka.

Only one Sādhana gives the description of this god, who is, in all probability, another form of Heruka. The Sādhana says that when Heruka is embraced by Citrasenā he gets the name of Buddhakapāla. He has one face and four arms carrying the Khatvāṅga, the Kapāla, the Kartri and the Damaru ; he is embraced by his Prajñā, Citrasenā and remains in yab-yum. He is slightly different from the four-armed variety of Heruka as the following Dhyāna in the Sādhana will show :—

"Mahāviro ghorasaṃhārakārakaḥ nīlavarṇṇaḥ mahāvapuḥ asthyābharaṇārdhaparyaṅkaṃ nṛtyasthaṃ muṇḍamālāvibhūṣitaṃ mukuṭe Akṣobhyadhāriṇaṃ ekavaktraṃ caturbhujaṃ, vāme khaṭvāṅgakapālaṃ, dakṣine kartriḍamarukaṃ, Prajñāliṅgitaṃ ; vāme Citrasenā mattā muktakeśī sarvabhayarahitā devī cumbayantī muhurmuhuḥ evam ātmānaṃ dhyātvā....

Iti Śrīmato Buddhakapālasya Sādhanaṃ ".

Sādhanamālā, A—275, Na—47, C—214.

" The worshipper should meditate on himself as (Buddhakapāla) who is a great hero, the supreme destroyer, of blue complexion and gigantic stature ; who has ornaments of bones, stands in Ardhaparyaṅka in a dancing attitude, is decked in garlands of heads, holds the effigy of Akṣobhya on the crown, is one-faced and four-armed ; who carries the Khaṭvāṅga and the Kapāla in the left hands and the Kartri and the Ḍamaru in the right, and is embraced in the left by the Prajñā, Citrasenā by name, intoxicated, nude, and fearless, who with dishevelled hair kisses the god incessantly. Thus meditating...."

The same Sādhana later on gives the details of the Maṇḍala and further goes on to say that Buddhakapāla is surrounded by twenty-four goddesses arranged in three circles. The first circle has Sumālinī (blue) in the East, Kapālinī (yellow) in the North, Bhīmā (green) in the West and Durjayā (white) in the South. The next circle has Śubhamekhalā (east), Rūpinī (north), Jayā (west) and Kauverī (south) ; Kāminī (north-east), Mahodadhi (north-west), Kariṇī (south-west) and Māriṇī (south-east). The outermost circle has Bhīmadarśanā (east), Ajayā (north), Śubhā (west), Ostārakī (south) ; Surakṣinī (north-east), Vikālarātri (north-west), Mahāyaśā (south-west) and Sundarī (south-east). Besides these, there are the four guardians of the gates, Sundarā (East), Subhagā (North), Priyadarśanā (West) and Nairātmā (South). Excepting the four deities of the innermost circle, all other goddesses have blue complexion, two arms, one face, ornaments of bones, brown hair rising upwards but no garland of heads. They carry the Kapāla in the left and the Kartri in the right and dance in the Ardhaparyaṅka attitude.

The accompanying sketch (Plate XXV, b) represents the main god in the embrace of his Śakti Citrasenā, but without the attendants. The remarks made about the yab-yum representations of Caṇḍaroṣaṇa apply to this case also, and we shall have to be satisfied in the case of this deity with a mere sketch drawn by a Nepalese artist.

4. Vajraḍāka.

Variety—yab-yum. Companion—Vajravārāhi.

When Heruka is embraced by the Ḍākinī Vajravārāhi in yab-yum, he is called Vajraḍāka. Vajraḍāka has three varieties, Samvara, Saptākṣara and Mahāmāyā. Samvara is one-faced and two-armed, the second Saptākṣara is three-faced and six-armed and is surrounded by six goddesses, and the third variety, Mahāmāyā is four-faced and four-armed and is surrounded by four goddesses.

(i) Samvara.

Colour—blue. Āsana—Ālīḍha.
Vāhana—Kālarātri. Symbols—Vajra and Ghaṇṭā.
Prajñā—Vajravārāhī.

One Sādhana only in the Sādhanamālā describes the procedure for the worship of this variety of Vajraḍāka. He is two-armed and one-faced and bears the effigy of Akṣobhya on his crown. He appears terrible with his garment of tiger skin, the garland of heads, a string of skulls round the head, three eyes and the Ālīḍha attitude, in which he tramples upon Kālarātri. The Dhyāna is in verse and describes the god in the following terms :—

" Lalāṭāsthaṃ kapālamālām candrārdhaṃ mūrdhni dhārayet ।
Ṣaṇmudrā muṇḍamālī ca viśvavajrī trilocanaḥ ॥
Ālīḍhapadavinyāso viśvākṣaravivartinīḥ ।
Sabhairavāṃ Kālarātriṃ ārūḍho vyāghracarmabhṛt ॥
Akṣobhyaśekharaḥ kṛṣṇo vajraghaṇṭājaṭānvitaḥ ।
Vīro'sau Vajravārāhī vajrāsṛkpūrṇakapālabhṛt ॥
Khaṭvāṅgamekhalā raktā trinetrā muṇḍamālinī ।
Pañcamudrā muktakeśī digvastrā Buddhaśekharā ॥
Dvibhuja-Samvaropadeśaḥ samāptaḥ."

Sādhanamālā, A—277 C—214.*

"The worshipper should conceive himself as (Samvara) who has a garland of heads round his forehead, the crescent on the top of his head, is endowed with the six auspicious symbols, wears a necklace of heads, has the Viśvavajra on his headdress, is three-eyed, stands in the Ālīḍha attitude, originates from a combination of all the letters of the alphabet, tramples down the fierce Kālarātri, is clad in tiger-skin, has the crest of Akṣobhya, is blue in colour, carries the Vajra and the Ghaṇṭā, has matted hair, displays heroism and is embraced by Vajravārāhī holding the Vajra, and the Kapāla full of blood. Her girdle is the Khaṭvāṅga, complexion is red, and eyes are three; she wears the garland of heads, is endowed with the five auspicious symbols, has dishevelled hair and nothing but the four quarters as her garment (*i.e.* she is nude) and wears the image of Buddha [Vairocana] on the crown.

(ii) Saptākṣara.

Faces—thre Arms—six.
Asana—Ālīḍha. Prajñā—Vajravārāhī.

This variety of Vajraḍāka is called Saptākṣara or the 'seven-syllabled' one, because his Mantra † consists of seven syllables. Like Dvibhuja-Samvara mentioned above, he is also embraced by Vajravārāhī, who

* Wanting in N.

† " Oṃ Hrīḥ Ha Ha Huṃ Huṃ Phaṭ."

is identical with her consort in all respects. Like Samvara this god also tramples upon Kālarātri and holds the Viśvavajra on the crown. He has also the crescent on his head, is endowed with the six auspicious symbols, stands in the Ālīḍha attitude on the orb of the sun. He has three faces of blue yellow and green colours and carries the Vajra, the Ghaṇṭā and the human skin in the three left hands and the Kapāla, the Khaṭvāṅga and the Triśūla in the three right hands.*

The Sādhana adds further that on each of the six spokes of the wheel of the sun on which the god stands, there should be six deities, namely, (commencing from the right) Herukī, Vajrabhairavī, Ghoracaṇḍī, Vajrabhāskarī, Vajraraudrī and Vajraḍākinī. They should have respectively blue, yellow, red, green, smoky and white colour. All of them have dishevelled hair, fierce appearance, three eyes, and the quarters as garments. They carry the sounding Damaru and the Ghaṇṭā in the first pair of hands and the human skin in the other pair. They stand on the sun which is on the corpse, their headdress is decorated with a row of skulls, and they stand in the Ālīḍha attitude.†

In another Sādhana devoted to the worship of Saptākṣara, a slight variation is to be noticed. In it, we find that the god should, in the first pair of hands which are engaged in embracing the Prajñā, carry the Vajra and the Ghaṇṭā ; in the second pair, the human skin only ; and in the third pair, the

* The text of the Sādhana is as follows :—

> "Ṣaḍbhujaṃ trimukhaṃ tryakṣaṃ sarvalakṣaṇalakṣitaṃ ।
> Vyañjanāśitisaṃyuktaṃ ālikālyudbhavaṃ prabhuṃ ॥
> Vajraghaṇṭāsamāpannaṃ naracarmārdradhāriṇaṃ ।
> Vāṃe kapālakhaṭvāṅgatriśūlaṃ dakṣiṇe kare ॥
> Kapālamālāmukutīṃ viśvavajrajaṭādharaṃ ।
> Ardhenduśekharaṃ caiva ṣaṇmudrādehabhūṣaṇaṃ ॥
> Nīlapītaharitavaktraṃ vyāghracarmāmbarāvṛtaṃ ।
> Ālīḍhākrāntasūryyasthabhairava-Kālarātrikāṃ ॥
> Yathā nāthasya tathā Vajravārāhyāpi bhujādibhiḥ ।
> Devī jānu samāveṣṭya paramānandavihvalā ॥

Durjayacandroddhṛtaṃ Saptākṣarasādhanaṃ Samāptaṃ."

Mss. Na-60, C-208, A-267.

† The goddesses constituting the Maṇḍala of Saptākṣara—

> Herukī prathamā devī dvitiyā Vajrabhairavī ।
> Tṛtīyā Ghoracaṇḍī syāccaturthī Vajrabhāskarī ॥
> Pañcamī Vajraraudrī ca ṣaṣṭhī syād-Vajraḍākiṇī
> Nīlapītaraktaharitadhūmrasitā devyāḥ ॥
> Muktakeśā mahāraudrā trinetrāśca digambarāḥ ।
> Raṇaḍḍamaru ghaṇṭā ca hastetarakaradvaye ॥
> Dadhānā naracarmāṇi pretasūrryoparisthitāḥ ।
> Kapālamālāmukutā āliḍhāsanasaṃsthitāḥ ॥
> Ṣaḍakṣarabhavābhavyā devyah sarvvāḥ yathākramaṃ ॥

Ibid.

Kapāla and the Triśūla. The Khaṭvāṅga hangs from his shoulder as usual. Vajravārāhī is identical with the Prajñā mentioned before with the difference that here she should have in the second pair of her hands the bow and the arrow instead of the human skin.

(iii) Mahāmāyā.

Colour—blue.	Prajñā—Buddhaḍākinī.	Companions—four.
Arms—four.	Faces—four.	Appearance—terrible.

Āsana—Dancing in Ardhaparyaṅka.

Mahāmāyāhvayaṃ devaṃ caturmukhaṃ caturbhujaṃ ı
Aṅke yasya tathā devī catasro dikṣu cāparāḥ ıı

Heruka goes by the name of Mahāmāyā when he is embraced by Buddhaḍākinī (another name for Vajravārāhī) and remains in yab-yum. This variety of Heruka has four faces and four arms and is accompanied by four goddesses in the four cardinal points. Two Sādhanas in the Sādhanamālā are devoted to the worship of this deity. One of these is attributed to Kukkurīpāda, celebrated as one of the eight Siddhas who flourished in the mediæval age in India. Below is given a summary of the description of the Maṇḍala * for Mahāmāyā.

Mahāmāyā has a terrible appearance : his person is besmeared with ashes and his hair streams upwards in the shape of a flame. He has blue complexion and his headdress is decorated with a row of skulls. His four faces have blue, yellow, white and green colour and he carries in his four hands the Kapāla, arrow, the Khaṭvāṅga and the bow. He possesses the five auspicious symbols, has the torque round the neck and bracelets in his hands. He is clad in human skin, has three eyes in each head and fiery flames radiate from his

* The following Dhyāna has been given in the Sādhanamālā :—

"Karuṇācalvajraṃ nīlapītasitaśyāmacaturmukhaṃ caturbhujaṃ dakṣiṇabhuje[ṣu] kapālaśaradharaṃ vāme khaṭvāṅgadhanurdharaṃ raudrāsanasthaṃ trinetraṃ sārdramuṇḍasragdāmamālinaṃ kapālamālābhiḥ śirasi bhūṣitaṃ asthyālaṅkāravibhūṣitaṃ īṣaddaṃṣṭrākarālavadanaṃ piṅgalordhvakeśaṃ....svābhā-Prajñāliṅgitaṃ vyomāvakāśinaṃ Vajradharābhiṣekinaṃ....Tatra pūrvadale Vajraḍākinī nīlavarṇā nīlapītaraktaśyāmacaturmukhā caturbhujā. Vāmabhuje khaṭvāṅgaghaṇṭā dakṣiṇe vajrakapālahastā.... Dakṣiṇadale Ratnaḍākinī pītavarṇā pītanīlaraktaśyāmacaturmukhā caturbhujā vāmabhuje patakākañcukañca ḍakṣiṇe triśūlaratnahastā....paścimadale Padmaḍākinī sitāruṇavarṇā, raktapītanīlaśyāmacaturmukhā caturbhujā vāmabhuje dhanuḥkapālaṃ dakṣiṇe śaraviśvapadmahastā....uttaradale Viśvaḍākinī śyāmavarṇā, śyāmapītaraktanīlacaturmukhā caturbhujā, vāmabhuje pāśakapālaṃ, dakṣiṇe khaṭvāṅga-(or khaḍga-)ḍamaruhastā ....devyaḥ sarvā raudrāsanasthāḥ kapālamālāḥ śirasi vibhūṣitāḥ sārdramuṇḍasragdāmamālinyaḥ trinetrāḥ, īṣaddaṃṣṭrākarālavadanāḥ jvalitorddhvakeśāḥ sphuradraśmīmālinyaḥ ....—Mahāmāyāsādhanopāyikā samāptā." Sādhanamālā, A-225, Na—48, C-200.

body. He appears beautiful in his sentiment of mixed anger and delight, and stands in the Ardhaparyaṅka in a dancing attitude. He is embraced by Buddhaḍākinī,† who is red, and carries the same weapons and has the same appearance and symbols as those of Mahāmāyā. Her four faces are red, yellow, white and green.

The four petals in the four cardinal directions of the lotus seat are occupied by the following goddesses.

(1) Vajraḍākinī in the East who is of blue colour, with four faces of blue, yellow white and green colour and carries the Khaṭvāṅga and Ghaṇṭā in the two left hands and the Vajra and the Kapāla in the two right.

(2) Ratnaḍākinī is on the South, of yellow complexion, with four faces of yellow, blue, red and green colour. She carries the flag and the jackal in the two left hands and the Triśūla and the jewel in the two right.

(3) Padmaḍākinī on the West, of reddish-white complexion, who has four faces of red, yellow, blue and green colour and who carries the bow and the Kapāla in the two left hands and the arrow and the double lotus in the two right.

(4) Viśvaḍākinī on the North, of green colour, who has four faces of green, yellow, red and blue colour and who carries the Pāśa and the Kapāla in the left and the Khaṭvāṅga (or the sword) and the Ḍamaru in the two right hands.

These four deities display wrathful attitudes, have their heads decorated with a number of skulls, have garlands of heads still wet with blood, three eyes, protruding teeth, brown hair streaming upwards in the shape of a flame and fiery flames radiate from their persons.

5. Hayagrīva.

Colour—red.	Faces—three.	Arms—eight.
Āsana—Lalita.	Appearance—terrible.	

One form of Hayagrīva with Amitābha on the crest has already been discussed in the previous Chapter. There is another form of the god that emanates from the Dhyānī Buddha Akṣobhya. The Dhyāna describing him runs as follows :—

Ārya-Hayagrīvam raktavarṇaṃ trimukhaṃ aṣṭabhujaṃ pratimukhaṃ trinetraṃ nīlasitadakṣiṇetaravadanaṃ sarpābharaṇaṃ lalitākṣepapadanyāsaṃ

† The Dhyāna for Buddhaḍākinī (Prajñā) is given in another Sādhana :—

Priyatulyāyudhā raktā tatkaṇṭhāśleṣī dordvayā ।
Srī-Buddhaḍākinī raktapītaśvetaharinmukhī ॥

sakrodhadṛṣṭinirīkṣamānaṃ, prathamamukhaṃ smeraṃ lalajjihvaṃ, dakṣiṇamukhaṃ daṃṣṭrāvaṣṭabdhauṣṭhaṃ, vyāghracarmanivasanaṃ vajradaṇḍakaraṇamudrāśarodyatadakṣiṇakaracatuṣṭayaṃ tarjanikāsvakucagrahapadmadhanurudyatavāmakaracatuṣṭayaṃ Akṣobhyamauliṃ dhyāyāt."

Sādhanamālā. A –279, Na—87, C—217.

"The worshipper should conceive himself as Ārya Hayagrīva, who has red complexion, eight arms, and three faces, each face with three eyes ; whose right and left faces are of blue and white colour, who has ornaments of snake, whose legs are so placed as to resemble the Lalita attitude, who has angry looks, whose first face has a smiling appearance, the right has a protruding tongue and the left bites the lips ; who is clad in tiger-skin ; who shows in his four right hands the Vajra, the staff, the Karaṇa pose and the raised arrow. Of the four left hands, one has the Tarjanī, another hand touches his own breast, and the lotus and the bow are in the remaining two. He bears the image of Akṣobhya on his crown."

The accompanying drawing (Plate XXV,d) shows how this god is represented now-a-days in Nepal. It varies a little from the description given in the Sādhana. The hand that ought to have touched the breast displays a different Mudrā ; and the hand that ought to have displayed the raised index finger only, has a noose round it. Nevertheless, the sketch is important as it shows a miniature neck of a horse set above the head, to prove that the representation is really of Hayagrīva, that is, the god possessing the neck of a horse. The Karaṇa pose, generally absent in other Sādhanas, of which a correct representation has been given, should also be noted.

6. Yamāri.

Identification mark—head of a buffalo. Vāhana—buffalo.

No less than fourteen Sādhanas describe the procedure in which the deity should be worshipped. In one of the Sādhanas it is said that in accordance with the different functions discharged by the deity, he gets different colours ; for instance, in the Śāntikavidhi, he is white and faces the East ; in Pauṣṭika, he is yellow and faces the North ; in Vaśyavidhi, he is red and faces the West ; and in Ākarṣaṇa, he is blue and faces the South, and so on. Of these varieties, the red and the blue are more popular ; in other words, his worship is mostly performed with a view to enchanting men and women (Vaśyavidhi), and to forcibly subduing them and bringing them to the worshipper (Ākarṣaṇavidhi). Yamāri or Yamāntaka may be worshipped alone or in conjunction with the Prajñā. He should have the head of a buffalo on his shoulders and should ride on a buffalo. Getty * records a tradition current in Tibet, which gives the origin of this fearful god.

* Getty : *Gods of the Northern Buddhism* p. 136.

There was once a holy man who lived in a cave in deep meditation for fifty years, after which he was to enter into Nirvāṇa. On the night of the forty-ninth year, eleventh month and twenty-ninth day, two robbers entered the cave with a stolen bull and slaughtered it there. But when they discovered the presence of an ascetic, a witness to their crime, they beheaded him,—and lo ! his body assumed the ferocious form of Yama and taking up the bull's head, he set it up on his headless shoulders. He then killed the two robbers and drank their blood from the cup made out of their skulls. In his fiery and insatiable thirst for victims he threatened to depopulate the whole of Tibet. The Tibetans appealed to their Tutelary deity, Mañjuśrī, whereupon the latter assumed the fierce form of Yamāntaka and defeated Yama in a fearful struggle.

Whatever might be the truth of the tradition, it sufficiently explains the presence of eulogies of Mañjuśrī in the Sādhanas for Yamāntaka. It may be noted, however, that the Sādhanamālā is absolutely silent about Yama, both as a principal deity or as an opponent of Yamāntaka.

(i) Raktayamāri.

Asana—Pratyālīḍha. Variety—yab-yum.
Appearance—terrible. Companion—Prajñā.
Colour—red.

Six Sādhanas are devoted to the worship of this variety of Yamāntaka. He is one-faced and two-armed and is embraced by the Prajñā who is identical with him in appearance. The Dhyāna describing his form is given as follows :—

"Ātmānaṃ Yamāntakaṃ ekamukhaṃ dvibhujaṃ pratyālīḍhapadaṃ raktaparipūrṇakapālavāmakaraṃ sārdrapītamuṇḍāṅkitasitadaṇḍadakṣiṇakaraṃ nāgābharaṇavibhūṣaṇaṃ piṅgalordhvakeśaṃ vyāghracarmāmbaradharaṃ Akṣobhyamukuṭinaṃ svābha-Prajñāliṅgitaṃ mahiṣopari viśvadalakamalasūryyasthaṃ dhyāyāt. Bhagavatīñca dvibhujaikamukhīm, vicitrābharaṇām, ālīḍhapadasthitām, madavihvalām, skhalatvyāghracarmāṃśukām, Bhagavatā saha samputayogena pratyālīḍhenāvasthitaṃ evaṃ vicintya...."

Sādhanamālā. A—288-9, Na—35, C—224.

"The worshipper should realize himself as Yamāntaka, one-faced and two-armed, who stands in the Pratyālīḍha attitude, carries the Kapāla full of blood in the left hand and in the right the white staff surmounted by a yellow head still wet with blood ; who is decked in ornaments of snakes ; whose brown hair rises upwards, who wears garments of tiger-skin, bears the image of Akṣobhya on the crown, is embraced by his Svābhā-Prajñā, ane stands on the sun over the double lotus on the back of a buffalo. He (the worshipper) should also meditate upon the Bhagavatī (Prajñā), who is one-faced, two-armed, has variegated ornaments, stands in the Pratyālīḍha attitude, is intoxicated with wine, wears garments of tiger-skin that are slipping from her waist and remains in yab-yum,—both standing in the Pratyālīḍha attitude. Thus meditating...."

(ii) Kṛṣṇayamāri.

Colour—blue. Varieties—four.

Eight Sādhanas in the Sādhanamālā describe his different varieties. He may have (*a*) one face and two arms, or (*b*) three-faces and four-arms, or (*c*) three or six faces and six arms. In all other respects the god is the same; but even when he is two-armed, the symbols are different. He is represented singly and also in yab-yum.

(*a*)

Asana—Pratyālīḍha. Symbol—the staff surmounted by a Vajra.
Mudrā—Tarjanīpāśa against the breast. Variety—single.

This form of Yamāri is sometimes met with in representation. He has no attendants and the Dhyāna describes his form in the following terms :—

" Yamāriṃ vicintayet ātmānaṃ pratyālīḍhapadasthitaṃ ekamukhaṃ dvibhujaṃ nīlavarṇaṃ dakṣiṇakare vajrāṅkitodyatanīladaṇḍaṃ, vāmakare tarjanīpāśaṃ hṛdi; evaṃ bhūtaṃ Yamāriṃ....viśvadalakamalopari sūryyasthaṃ mahisārūḍham bhāvayet "

Sādhanamālā. A—299, Na—39, C—231.

" The worshipper should conceive himself as (Kṛṣṇa)-Yamāri who stands in the Pratyālīḍha attitude, is one-faced and two-armed, and is blue in colour; who carries the brandished staff stamped with a Vajra in the right hand, and in the left the Tarjanī and the Pāśa against the breast. In this form, Yamari....should be conçeived as standing on the sun over the double lotus and as riding a buffalo ".

The illustration (Plate XXVI,a) shows a two-armed form of Yamāri and the image is in the possession of Pandit Siddhiharṣa Vajrācāryya of Nepal. It may be noticed, however, that the right hand which ought to have carried the staff according to the Sādhana, carries a Cakra instead.

(*b*)

Appearance—terrible. **Variety—yab-yum.**
Faces—three. **Arms.—four.** **Companion—Prajñā.**

The form of Yamāri with three faces and four arms looks terrible and awe-inspiring. He is represented in Yab-yum and the Dhyāna describes his form as follows :—

"........................Yamāriratibhīṣaṇaḥ ।
Kaṭhoravarhikaṇṭhābho savye śuklāruṇetaraḥ ॥
Krodhaparyaṅkayogena viśvābjaravisaṃsthitaḥ ।
Svābha-Vidyādharāsvādarasāyanamahāsukhaḥ ॥
Kaṭhorordhvajjvalatkeśaḥ piṅgabhrūśmaśrulocanaḥ ।
Phaṇīndravṛndanepathyo mṛṇāladhavaladvijāḥ ।
Mudgarāsidharaḥ savye vāme rājīvaratnadhṛk ॥"

Sādhanamālā, A—297, Na—83, C—229.

"Yamāri is terribly fierce, has the deep (blue) colour of the neck of a peacock, with his right and left faces of white and red colours (respectively). He stands on the sun over a double lotus in an angry attitude. He enjoys the bliss of partaking the nectar which, a sip from the lips of the Prajñā of his own emanation gives. His hair stands on his head in the shape of a flame, and his brows, beard and the eyes are of brown colour. His ornaments are the host of the lords of twice-born serpents, who are white like the stalk of a lotus. He carries in his right hands the Mudgara and the sword and in the left the lotus and the jewel."

(*c*)

Āsana—Ālīḍha. Faces—three or six.
Arms—six. Variety—single.

The form of Yamāri with three faces and six arms, though equally fierce in appearance as the previous one, is not represented in yab-yum but appears singly. As the information given is of a similar character, we refrain from quoting the Dhyāna. In this case, all the three faces have a protruding tongue, canine teeth, three eyes and contortions of the brows. He has a big belly, is short and dwarfish and wears a garment of tiger-skin. He carries the Vajra, the sword and the Mūṣala in the three right hands and the goblin (Vetālī) the axe and the lasso in the three left. According to a second statement in the Sādhana, he is said to carry the sword, the Mudgara and the **Vajra** in the three right hands and the Ghaṇṭā, the Vajrapāśa and the **Mūṣala** in the three left. The same Sādhana further says that

(a) Yamāntaka (Nepal)

(b) Yamāntaka (Nālandā)

(c) Jambhala

(d) Ucchuṣma Jambhala

Plate XXVI

though he is represented generally as three-faced. and six-armed, he may also have six faces and six legs with the same weapons.. The **Dhyāna** for the worship of this six-faced and six-legged variety of Yamāntaka runs as follows :—

Yamāntakaṃ kruddhaṃ ūrddhvakeśaṃ kṛṣṇaṃ ṣaḍmukhaṃ ṣaḍbhujaṃ ṣaṭcaraṇañca mahiṣārūḍhaṃ pratyālīḍhasthitaṃ naramuṇḍacūḍairvibhūṣitaṃ* atibhayānakākāraṃ vyāghracarmanivasanaṃ dakṣiṇe khaḍga-mudgara-vajrāni, vāme ghaṇṭā-vajrapāśa-mūṣalān dhārayantaṃ, mukuṭe Akṣobhyaṃ vibhāvayet."

Sādhanamālā, A—299, Na—39, Ç—280.

" The worshipper should realize himself as Yamāntaka, who has angry looks, whose hair rises upwards, who is six-faced, six-armed and six-legged ; who rides the buffalo, stands in the Pratyālīḍha attitude, is embellished with severed human heads has a very ferocious appearance, is clad in garments of tiger-skin ; who carries in the right hands the Khaḍga, Mudgara and the Vajra and in the left the Ghaṇṭā, the Vajrapāśa, and the Mūṣala and who bears the effigy of Akṣobhya on the crown."

Excepting one stone image from Nalanda (Plate XXVI,b)† no other representation has yet been found of this form of Yamāri.

7. Jambhala.

Variety—yab-yum. Faces—three.
Arms—six.

Jambhala has undoubtedly a great antiquity behind him and we have evidence that he existed at a time when the conception of the five Dhyānī Buddhas had not yet been accomplished. This was why he could not be assigned to one particular Dhyānī Buddha from whom he might have originated. In other words, Jambhala is to be taken as a parallel of Mañjuśrī, who, similarly, could not be assigned to one particular Dhyānī Buddha. In the Sādhanamālā we find that he may bear the images of Ratnasambhava, Akṣobhya, the five Dhyānī Buddhas or Vajrasattva on his head. So, Jambhala will have to be discussed under each of these headings. Images of Jambhala are to be met with in the Gandhara, Mathura, Sarnath, Magadha, Bengal and Nepal sculptures. Here we are concerned only with that variety of Jambhala which bears the image of Akṣobhya on the tiara. He

* Most of the Mss. read —naramuṇḍaruṇḍair— ; but I have accepted Prof. Fouchers' reading as it seems to be in keeping with the extant images, in which Ruṇḍas or headless bodies are absent altogether.

† First published in A. S. I., Central Circle, *Annual Report*, 1920-21, Plate I, and described on P. 39.

is here three-faced and six-armed and is represented in yab-yum. Though the Dhyāna does not mention his colour, we may suggest that this variety of Jambhala has the blue colour,—the colour of the Dhyānī Buddha Akṣobhya from whom he originates. The Dhyāna in the Sādhanamālā runs as follows :—

" Jambhalaṃ trimukhaṃ ṣaḍbhujaṃ Akṣobhyajaṭāmukuṭinaṃ dakṣiṇa-tribhujaiḥ mātuluṅgāṅkuśabāṇadharaṃ prathamabhujena vāmapārśvasthita-Prajñāliṅgitaṃ aparavāmabhujābhyāṃ sapāśanakulakārmukadharaṃ ātmānaṃ niṣpādya. . . . "

Sādhanamālā, A—309, Na—25, C—237.

" The worshipper should conceive himself as Jambhala, three-faced and six-armed, whose crown of chignon bears the image of Akṣobhya ; who carries in his three right hands the citron, the goad and the arrow ; who embraces in one of his left hands the Prajñā situated in his left and in the other two carries the mongoose [tied round] with a lasso and the arrow. Thus meditating. . . . "

The accompanying drawing (Plate XXVI,c) though it does not agree in all details with the description given in the Dhyāna, shows how this deity is pictured in modern days by the Newari artists.

(ii) Ucchuṣma-Jambhala.

Appearance—terrible.	Vāhana—Kuvera vomitting jewels.
Āsana—Pratyālīḍha.	Identification mark—nude.

Ucchuṣma, being a variety of Jambhala, bears also the image of Akṣobhya on his crown ; he may, however, have the image of Ratnasambhava instead. Several Sādhanas are devoted to his worship, and the Dhyāna describing him with the image of Akṣobhya on his crown runs as follows :—

"Ātmānaṃ Bhagavantaṃ Ucchuṣmaṃ pañcavarṣakumārākṛtiṃ kharvaṃ viśvapadmasthaṃ candropari sarpābharaṇabhūṣitaṃ ratnamukuṭīṃ muñcadratnamukhapītāṅgasupta-Dhanadasya [caraṇadvayaṃ dakṣiṇena caraṇena]* vāmenākrāntamūrdhvaṃ pratyālīḍhapadaṃ ; nagnaṃ ūrddhvaliṅgaṃ lambodaraṃ ; hṛdi dakṣiṇapāṇisthaṃ raktapūrṇakapālābhimukhadṛṣṭiṃ ; vāmajaṅghāsaktavāmakareṇa ratnacchaṭodgāryyadhomukhanakulīṃ aviddhaḍhollakarṇadvayaṃ ardhenduśekharaṃ daṃṣṭrākarālavadanaṃ raktavarttulatrinetraṃ kṛtabhṛkuṭīlalāṭaṃ piṅgorddhvakeśaṃ bhūsparśamudranīl-Ākṣobhyamunimastakaṃ [dhyāyāt] ".

Sādhanamālā, A—217, C—242.†

* All the mss. read " dakṣiṇena caraṇena caraṇadvayaṃ."

† Wanting in N.

" The worshipper should meditate on himself as the god Ucchuṣma, who appears like a child of five years, is dwarfish, stands on the double lotus on the moon, is decked in ornaments of snakes and a bejewelled headdress; who, standing in the Pratyālīḍha attitude, tramples with his right leg upon the legs of the sleeping Dhanada of yellow complexion with his mouth vomitting out jewels, while the left leg rests upon the head; who is nude, and whose *membrum virile* is pointed upwards; who has a protruding belly, and has eyes fixed on the Kapāla which he carries in his right hand against the breast; who carries in his left hand touching the left thigh the mongoose vomitting out jewels, whose ears are large and unpierced; who has a crescent on the crown, whose face is distorted with bare fangs and three eyes red and round; whose forehead is distorted owing to the contortions of the brow, whose brown hair rises upwards, and who bears on his tiara the image of Akṣobhya of blue colour displaying the earth-touching attitude."

The accompanying sketch (Plate XXVI,d) shows how this god is represented now-a-days in Nepal, though it differs in certain minor details from the description given above.

CHAPTER VI.

EMANATIONS OF AKSOBHYA (*Continued*).

II. GODDESSES.

Comparatively a very large number of goddesses emanate from Akṣobhya. Some of the goddesses are well-known and extremely popular, but to none of these a large number of Sādhanas is assigned. We have already seen that the male emanations of this Dhyānī Buddha are always, except in a very few cases, of a terrible and awe-inspiring character. Most of the female emanations also are blue in complexion and partake of the fierce nature of the male ones, though we notice, among others, genuinely peaceful forms, such as, Prajñāpāramitā, Vasudhārā and Mahāmantrānusāriṇī. No less than eleven goddesses emanate from the Dhyānī Buddha Akṣobhya and we shall discuss their forms one by one.

1. Mahācīnatārā.

Āsana—Pratyālīḍha. Appearance—terrible.
Vāhana—corpse. Arms—four.
Symbols—*rt.* Sword, Kartri, *lt.* Utpala, Kapāla.

Two Sādhanas are devoted to the worship of Mahācīnatārā or Tārā of Mahācīna (Great China), and two Dhyānas, one in prose and the other in verse, describe the goddess in precisely identical forms. She is also known in Buddhist Tāntric literature as Ugratārā and the Vajrayoginī temple at Sāṅku in Nepal contains in the sanctum a figure of Ugratārā. The principal image is always covered under costly garments and with costly ornaments, but when the priests began to recite the Dhyāna, we were left in no doubt whatever that the image was that of Ugratārā. This Ugratārā or Mahācīnatārā of the Buddhists has been incorporated by the Hindus in their Pantheon under the name of Tārā and the latter count her among the ten Mahāvidyā goddesses. The Dhyāna in the Sādhanamālā describes her form in the following words :—

"Pratyālīḍhapadāṃ ghorāṃ muṇḍamālāpralambitāṃ ı
Kharvalambodarāṃ bhīmāṃ nīlanīrajarājitāṃ ıı
Tryambakaikamukhāṃ divyāṃ ghorāṭṭahāsabhāsurāṃ ı
Suprahṛṣṭāṃ śavārūḍhāṃ nāgāṣṭakavibhūṣitāṃ ıı
Raktavarttulanetrāñca vyāghracarmāvṛtāṃ kaṭau ı
Navayauvanasampannāṃ pañcamudrāvibhūṣitāṃ ıı

(a) Mahācīna Tārā

(b) Mahācīna Tārā

(c) Jāṅgulī

(d) Ekajaṭā (Indian Museum)

Plate XXVII

Lalajjihvāṃ mahābhīmāṃ sadaṃṣṭrotkaṭabhīṣaṇāṃ ।
Khaḍgakartrikarāṃ savye vāmotpalakapāladhāṃ ।
Piṅgograikajaṭāṃ dhyāyāt maulav-Akṣobhyabhūṣitāṃ ॥

....Mahācīnatārā Sādhanaṃ."

Sādhanamālā, A—112, N—80, C—87.

"The worshipper should conceive himself as [Mahācīna-Tārā] who stands in the Pratyālīḍha attitude, is awe-inspiring, has garland of heads hanging from the neck, is short and has a protruding belly ; who has terrible looks, whose complexion is like that of the blue lotus ; who is three eyed, one-faced, celestial and laughs horribly ; who, in an intensely pleasant mood, stands on the corpse, is decked in ornaments of snakes, has red and round eyes, wears the garments of tiger-skin round her loins, is in youthful bloom, is endowed with the five auspicious symbols, and has a protruding tongue ; who is most terrible, appears fierce with bare canine fangs, carries the sword and the Kartri in the two right hands and the Utpala and the Kapāla in the two left ; whose crown of one chignon is brown and fiery and bears the image of Akṣobhya within it."

This is the Dhyāna we find in the Sādhanamālā, the earliest manuscript of which belongs to A. D. 1165. According to the Colophon, the Sādhana for Mahācīnatārā has been restored from the Mahācīna-Tantra, which should, therefore, be earlier than the earliest extant manuscript of Sādhanamālā. As the Sādhana in verse is attributed to Śāśvatavajra, we may be certain that the Dhyāna we have just quoted was not in existence before Śāśvatavajra. Now, in the Tārārahasya of Brahmānanda who flourished in the middle of 16th century * and in the Tantrasāra of Kṛṣṇānanda Āgama vāgīśa we find almost an identical Dhyāna describing a goddess of the name of Tārā.—

" Pratyālīḍhapadāṃ ghorāṃ muṇḍamālāvibhūṣitāṃ ।
Kharvāṃ lambodarīṃ bhīmāṃ vyāghracarmāvṛtāṃ kaṭau ॥
Navayauvanasampannāṃ pañcamudrāvibhūṣitāṃ ।
Caturbhujāṃ lolajihvāṃ mahābhīmāṃ varapradāṃ ॥
Khaḍgakartrisamāyukta-savyetarabhujadvayāṃ ।
Kapālotpalasaṃyuktasavyapāṇiyugānvitāṃ ॥
Piṅgograikajaṭāṃ dhāyenmauläv-Akṣobhyabhūṣitāṃ ।
Bālārkamaṇḍalākāralocanatrayabhūṣitāṃ ॥
Jalaccitāmadhyagatāṃ ghoradaṃṣṭrāṃ karālinīṃ ।
Sāveśasmeravadanāṃ stryalaṅkāravibhūṣitāṃ ॥
Viśvavyāpakatoyāntaḥ śvetapadmoparisthitāṃ ।
Akṣobhyadevīmūrdhanyastrīmūrtirnāgarūpadhṛk ॥ "

Tantrasāra, p. 415 *et sqq.*

* Brahmānanda's direct pupil, Pūrṇānanda Paramahaṃsa wrote his work, Tattva-Cintāmaṇi in the Śaka year 1199 *i.e.* A. D. 1577. Brahmānanda has therefore been placed in the middle of the 16th century. See M. M. Haraprasad Shastri : *Notices of Sanskrit mss.* Second series. Vol. I. p. 139.

A comparison of the two Dhyānas will at once reveal how the original composition of Śāśvatavajra has been modified in the Tantrasāra in the light of a Hindu Tāntric Paṇḍit. Some lines have been added to the original Dhyāna and all the grammatical errors have been rectified : and this seems to be the process of Hinduizing a Buddhist Tāntric deity. It is remarkable that the Hindus retained in their Dhyāna the crest of Akṣobhya which fact at once bespeaks the Buddhist origin of the goddess , for, we know for certain that none of the Hindu gods or goddesses are in the habit of wearing a miniature figure of their sires on the crown. Moreover, Akṣobhya is unknown in the Hindu Pantheon except when he is borrowed from the Buddhists,—and the Hindus fail to explain the desirability of putting in his figure on the crown of Tārā.

The accompanying sketches (Plate XXVII,a-b) portray the Buddhist form of Tārā or Mahācīnatārā and shows in what different forms she is represented in Nepal in modern times. It may be pointed out that the corpse under the feet of the Hindu Tārā is not a corpse properly speaking, but it is the form of Mahādeva's deadbody, to whom she is attached as a Sakti.

2. Jāṅgulī.

Jāṅgulī is widely worshipped amongst the Buddhists as a goddess who cures snake-bite and can prevent it. According to a Saṅgīti in the Sādhanamālā she is as old as Buddha himself, and the secret of Jāṅgulī and the mantras for her worship are said to have been imparted to Ānanda by Lord Buddha. Besides, the Saṅgīti, four Sādhanas describe the procedure of her worship and give elaborate mantras for the extraction of poison from the body of the snake-bitten. These four Sādhanas describe three entirely different forms of Jāṅgulī, two with one face and four arms and one with three faces and six arms.

(i)

Colour—white. Identification Symbol—Vīṇā in the two principal hands.
Symbol—snake. a Mudrā—Abhaya.

In two Sādhanas Jāṅgulī is described as having one face and four arms. In both cases she is alike in all respects except in the matter of the weapons she carries in her hands. In one, the Dhyāna is as follows :—

"Ātmānaṃ Ārya-Jāṅgulīrūpāṃ sarvaśuklāṃ caturbhujāṃ ekamukhāṃ jaṭāmukuṭinīṃ śuklottarīyāṃ sitaratnālaṅkārabhūṣitāṃ śuklasarpavibhūṣitāṃ sattvaparyaṅkamāviṣṭāṃ, mūlabhujābhyāṃ vīṇāṃ vādayantīṃ, aparadakṣiṇenābhyapradāṃ candrāṃśumālinīṃ dhyāyāt...."

Sādhanamālā. A—133, N—97, C—106.

"The worshipper should meditate himself as Ārya Jāṅgulī who is all white in complexion, four-armed, one-faced, has the crown of chignon, wears white scarf, is decked in white ornaments of gems and white serpents and rests on an animal; who plays on the Vīṇā with the two principal hands, carries the white snake in the second left and exhibits the Abhaya mudrā with the second right and is radiant like the moon."

In a second Sādhana she is said to exhibit the Varada Mudrā in the second right hand. The accompanying sketch (Plate XXVII,c) shows how she is represented in Nepal.

(ii)

Colour—green. Mudrā—Abhaya.

Symbols—Triśūla, peacock's tail and snake.

The second variety resembles the first in many respects. But in the Sādhana there is no mention of the animal-seat or the particular Āsana in which Jāṅgulī should stand or sit. The symbols are also different. In this case she will carry the Triśūla, the peacock's tail, the snake and exhibit the Abhaya Mudrā.

(iii)

Faces—three. Arms—six.

Vāhana—snake. Colour—yellow.

The third variety of Jāṅgulī will have three faces and six arms. Two Sādhanas in the Sādhanamālā, one in prose and the other in verse, describe this form. The Dhyāna contained in one of these runs as follows :—

"Arya-Jāṅgulīṃ ātmānaṃ jhaṭiti niṣpādayet, pītāṃ trimukhāṃ ṣaḍbhujāṃ nīlasitadakṣiṇetaravadanāṃ khaḍgavajrabāṇadakṣiṇahastatravāṃ satarjanīpāśaviṣapuṣpakārmukavāmakaratrayāṃ sphītaphanāmaṇḍalaśiraḥsarpasthāṃ divyavastrābharaṇabhūṣitāṃ kumārīlakṣaṇojjvalāṃ Akṣobhyākrāntamastakāṃ dhyātvā...."

Sādhanamālā, A—131, N—95, C—104.

"The worshipper should quickly conceive himself as Ārya Jāṅgulī, who is yellow in complexion, three-faced, and six armed; whose faces to the right and left are blue and white; who carries the sword, the Vajra, and the arrow in the three right hands, and the Tarjanī with the noose, the blue lotus and the bow in the three left hands; who rests on the expanded hood of the serpent, is decked in celestial ornaments and dress, is resplendent with the auspicious marks of a virgin and bears the image of Akṣobhya on head. Thus meditating...."

The Hindu goddess Manasā or Viṣaharī has a marked resemblance to the appearance of Jāṅgulī, and some of the Dhyānas in the Hindu Tāntric works for the goddess distinctly give her the epithet of "Jāṅgulī."

3. Ekajaṭā.

Colour—blue. Appearance—terrible.
Attitude—Pratyālīḍha.

Ekajaṭā is one of the most powerful goddesses in the Vajrayānic Pantheon. If a man listens to her Mantra but once, he is at once freed from all obstacles and is attended always with good fortune; his enemies are destroyed and he becomes religiously inclined, even attaining the level of a Buddha.* Four Sādhanas in the Sādhanamālā devoted to the worship of Ekajaṭā, describe four different variations of the goddess. She may have one face with two, four or eight arms, or she may be twelve-faced with twenty four arms.

The main features of the goddess are given in one of the Sādhanas, the Colophon of which asserts that the Sādhana has been restored from Tibet by Ārya Nāgārjuna,† who was famous in the mediaeval ages as one of eight Siddhapuruṣas of India. The general description of the goddess appearing in it is quoted as follows :—

"Kṛṣṇavarṇāḥ matāḥ sarvāḥ vyāghracarmāvṛtā kaṭau ।
Ekavaktrā trinetrāśca piṅgordhvakeśamūrdhajāḥ ॥
Kharvā lambodarā raudrāḥ pratyālīḍhapadasthitāḥ ।
Saroṣakarālavaktrāḥ muṇḍamālāpralambitāḥ ॥
Kuṇapasthā mahābhīmā maulāv-Akṣobhyabhūṣitāḥ ।
Navayauvanasampannāḥ ghorāṭṭahāsabhāsurāḥ ॥
.. ..
Viśvapadmopari sūryya cintanīyāḥ prayatnataḥ ॥"

Sādhanamālā. A—141, Na—13-14, C—112.

* Cf.—"Devyā Ekajaṭayāstu mantrarājo mahāvalaḥ ।
Asya śravaṇamātreṇa nirbighno jāyate naraḥ ॥
Saubhāgyaṃ jāyate nityaṃ vilayaṃ yānti śatravaḥ ।
Dharmaskandho bhavennityaṃ Buddhatulyo na saṃśayaḥ ॥"

† The Colophon is—"Ārya-Nāgārjunapādaiḥ Bhoṭeṣūddhṛtaṃ iti."

"All these [three] variations [of Ekajaṭā] are of blue colour, have the tiger-skin round their loins, are one-faced, three-eyed, have brown hair rising upwards on head, are short, pot-bellied, wrathful and stand in the Pratyālīdha attitude; they have faces distorted with anger, and garlands of heads hanging from their necks, rest on corpses, have terrible appearance, bear the image of Akṣobhya on the crown, have youthful bloom and laugh horribly; and they should be conceived on the orb of the sun over the double lotus."

This general description only applies to the following three varieties of Ekajaṭā with one face and two, four or eight arms—

(i) When two-armed, she will carry the Kartri and the Karota (skull cup) in her two hands. (Plate XXVII,d).*

(ii) When four-armed, Ekajaṭā carries the arrow and the sword in the two right hands and the bow and the skull in the two left. In two other Sādhanas describing the four-armed variety, she is represented with slight modifications. Here she holds in the first pair of hands the Kapāla and the Kartri while the other pair shows the Utpala and the sword; she may hold also the rosary instead of the sword. (Plate XXVIII,a).†

(iii) When eight-armed, she carries the sword, the arrow, the Vajra and Kartri in the four right hands and the bow, the Utpala, the Paraśu and the skull in the four left hands.

(iv) Vidyujjālākarālī.

Faces—twelve.	Arms—twenty-four.
Colour—blue.	Āsana—Pratyālīḍha.

Vāhana—Indra, Brahmā, Viṣṇu, and Śiva.

Symbols—

Right.		*Left.*	
1. Khaḍga.	7. Dart.	1. Bow.	7. Caṣaka.
2. Vajra.	8. Mudgara.	2. Noose.	8. Utpala.
3. Cakra.	9. Mūṣala	3. Tarjanī.	9. Bell.
4. Jewel.	10. Kartri.	4. Banner.	10. Paraśu.
5. Aṅkuśa.	11. Ḍamaru.	5. Mace.	11. Brahmaśiraḥ.
6. Arrow.	12. Rosary.	6. Triśūla.	12. Kapāla.

The fourth variety of Ekajaṭā is known as Vidyujjvālākarālī, who is said to have originated from the sweat of Buddha. This form of Ekajaṭā with

* The photograph represents Ekajaṭā as the companion of Khadiravanī Tārā in an image belonging to the Indian Museum (*Infra.* Pl. XXXIII,c).

† A Nepalese drawing of the four-armed variety of Ekajaṭā is reproduced as a specimen.

twelve faces and twenty-four arms is rarely met with in sculptures or in bronzes.* The Dhyāna is somewhat long and it describe the goddess in the following terms :—

"Dvādaśamukhāṃ mahākṛṣṇavarṇāṃ caturviṃśatibhujāṃ caturmārasamākrāntāṃ śvetakapālopari pratyālīḍhapadāṃ mahāpralayāgnisamaprabhāṃ vivṛtāsyāṃ hāhākārāṃ lalajjihvāṃ saroṣāṃ vikṛtakoṭibhīmataṭabhrūnetracaladvartulāṃ, bhayasyāpi bhayaṅkarīṃ, kapālamālā śirasi bhūṣitāṃ, vyāḍairalaṅkṛtāṃ ṣaṇmudropetāṃ, prathamamukhaṃ mahākṛṣṇaṃ, tathā dakṣiṇamukhapañcakaṃ sitapītaharitaraktadhūmravarṇañca, vāmamukhapañcakam raktasitapītaharitasitaraktañca; ūrdhvamukhaṃ dhūmraṃ, vikṛtaṃ, kruddhaṃ; sarvamukhāni daṃṣṭrākarālavadanāni, trinetrāni, jvalitordhvapiṅgalakeśāni; kharvalambodarīṃ pīnonnatapayodharāṃ vyāghracarmanivasanāṃ; dakṣiṇadvādaśabhujeṣu khaḍga-vajra-cakra-ratnacchaṭāṅkuśa-śara-śakti-mudgara-mūṣala-kartri-ḍamaru-akṣamālikāñca, vāmadvādaśabhujeṣu dhanuḥ-pāśa-tarjanī-patākā-gadā-triśūla-caṣaka-utpala-ghaṇṭā-paraśu-Brahmaśiraḥ-kapālāñca—

> Suprahṛṣṭāṃ śavārūḍhāṃ nāgāṣṭakavibhūṣitāṃ ।
> Navayauvanasampannāṃ hāhāṭṭahāsabhāsurāṃ ॥
> Piṅgograikajaṭāṃ dhyāyāt maulāv-Akṣobhyabhūṣitāṃ ॥

Iti Vidyujjvālākarālīnāmaikajaṭasādhanaṃ."

Sādhanamālā. A—136-37, Na—12, C—108-9.

"The worshipper should conceive himself as [Vidyujjvālākarālī], who has twelve faces, deep blue colour and twenty-four arms; who tramples upon the four Māras [Brahmā, Viṣṇu, Śiva and Indra], stands on the white skulls in the Pratyālīḍha attitude, is terrible like the Fire of Destruction, has a wide open mouth from which comes the sounds of 'hā,' 'hā;' who has protruding tongue, is wrathful, has eyes round and moving, and whose forehead is distorted owing to the frequent contortions of the brows; who is more awe-inspiring than Awe itself, whose head is decorated with a garland of skulls. who is decked in ornaments of snake, and is endowed with the six auspicious symbols; whose first face is of deep blue colour and the five faces to the right have respectively white, yellow, green, red and the colour of smoke. while the five faces to the left have red, white, yellow, green and whitish red colour; the face on the top is of the colour of smoke, distorted and displays anger; all his faces look terrible with bare fangs and three eyes; whose brown hair rises upwards in the shape of a flame, who is short and has protruding belly; whose breasts are full and heaving; who is clad in tiger-skin, carries in her twelve right hands, the sword, the thunderbolt, the discus, the jewel, the elephant-goad, the arrow, the dart, the hammer, the pestle, the saw, the drum and the rosary, and in the twelve left hands the bow,

* I brought, however, a painting of this goddess from Nepal and published it in tri-colour with my remarks, in the vernacular monthly, Māsika Vasumatī, Vol. I, part 12.

the noose, the raised index finger, the flag, the mace, the trident, the bowl, the blue lotus, the bell, the axe, the severed head of Brahmā,* and a skull...... ; who is extremely happy, rides a corpse, is decked in ornaments of eight snakes, is youthful, appears resplendent with terrible laugh, wears the crown of one chignon, which is brown and fiery, and which bears the image of Akṣobhya on it."

Here ends the Sādhana for Vidyujjvālākarālī, another form of Ekajaṭā."

4. Parṇaśavarī.

Colour—yellow. Faces—three. Arms—six.
Symbols—*rt.* Vajra, Paruśu, arrow ; *lt.* Tarjanīpāśa, cluster of leaves, bow.
Āsana—Pratyālīḍha. Vāhaṇa—*Bighnas.*
Identification mark--pleasant smile in the face.

The worship of Parṇaśavarī, it is believed, is efficacious against the outbreak of epidemics and it assures safety to the terror-stricken. The epithet 'Piśācī ' given in the Mantra shows that she was regarded as one of the semi-human supernatural beings. Two Sādhanas in the Sādhanamālā describe two forms of this goddess, one with the image of Akṣobhya on the crown and the other with that of Amoghasiddhi. In one, her faces depict pleasant smile and in another she smiles but has an irritated expression all the same. The followers of the Akṣobhya cult believed her to be an emanation of Akṣobhya, while the followers of the Amoghasiddhi cult believed her to be an emanation of Amoghasiddhi. Curiously enough, the two images that we have been able to discover in Eastern Bengal both have the image of Amoghasiddhi on the crown. It may also be possible that she has been associated with Amoghasiddhi because of her green colour ; while the form with yellow colour has been assigned to Akṣobhya. It would have been more reasonable to assign the latter to Ratnasambhava, who has yellow complexion and whose emanations generally have the yellow colour. The Dhyāna describing Parṇaśavarī with yellow colour and the image of Akṣobhya on crown, runs as follows :—

" Bhagavatīṃ pītavarṇāṃ trimukhāṃ trinetrāṃ ṣaḍbhujāṃ prathamamukhaṃ pītaṃ, dakṣiṇāṃ sitaṃ, vāmaṃ raktaṃ, lalitahāsinīṃ sarvālaṅkāradharāṃ parṇapicchikāvasānaṃ navayauvanoddhatāṃ pīṇāṃ, dakṣiṇabhujaiḥ vajraparaśuśaradhāriṇīṃ, vāmabhujaiḥ satarjanīkāpāśaparṇapicchikādhanur-

* Brahmā, it may be pointed out, belongs to the Hindu Pantheon, and is endowed with four faces. He is one of the three highest gods of the Hindus, and the Buddhists, in their hatred towards them, makes sevaral of their deities trample upon Brahmá and others, or carry his severed head in one of their hands.

dhāriṇīṃ puṣpāvabaddhajaṭāmukuṭastha-Akṣobhyadhāriṇīṃ sūryyaprabhā-maṇḍalinīṃ, adho bighnān nipātya sitapadmacandrāsane pratyālīḍhasthāṃ, hṛdvāmamuṣṭitarjanyādho bighnagaṇān santarjya dakṣiṇavajramuṣṭiprahārā-bhinayāṃ....bhāvayet....

Parṇaśavarīsādhanaṃ." Sādhanamālā, A—161, N—122, C—130.

"The worshipper should conceive himself as [Parṇaśavarī] of yellow complexion, with three faces, three eyes and six arms ; whose first face is blue, the right white and the left red ; who smiles in a pleasing manner, is decked in all sorts of ornaments, wears the apron of leaves, is haughty with youthful bloom, is stout in appearance, carries in her right hands the Vajra, the Paraśu and the arrow and in the left the Tarjanī with the noose, the cluster of leaves and the bow ; whose crown of chignon is decorated with flowers and the image of Akṣobhya ; who has the effulgence of the sun as her aureole, stands in the Pratyālīḍha attitude on the moon over the white lotus, trampling under her feet the *Bighnas*, threatens the host of [other] Bighnas with the clenched fist of the left hand exhibiting the Tarjanī against the breast, and who shakes her right fist at [the host of the *Bighnas*]...."

The mutilated image (Plate XXVIII,b) in the Indian Museum with three faces and six arms trampling upon Gaṇeśa probably represents this form of Parṇaśavari as the word "Bighna" in the Sādhanamālā often refers to Gaṇeśa.*

The Sādhana, referred to above, further gives us the information that Parṇaśavarī may have an alternative form with four arms and the image of Akṣobhya on the crown. In that case she will carry the Vajra and the Parasu in the two right hands and the Tarjanī with the noose, and the cluster of leaves in the two left, omitting the bow and the arrow.

5. Prajñāpāramitā.

Prajñāpāramitā is the embodiment of the Mahāyāna Scripture of the same name which was, according to the Buddhist tradition, restored from the nether regions by Nāgārjuna in the second century A. D. Buddha is said to have kept this Book of Transcendental Knowledge under the care of the Nāgas in the nether regions, as in his time people were not sufficiently intelligent to grasp the true meaning of the doctrines embodied in it. The worship of Prajñāpāramitā was very popular among the Buddhists, and Ārya Asaṅga is credited to have composed one of the Sādhanas for her worship, which is said

* See for instance, the image of Bighnāntaka (Plate XXXIX,b) trampling upon "Bighna" or Gaṇeśa.

(a) Ekajaṭā

(b) Parṇaśavarī (Indian Museum)

(c) Prajñāpāramitā (Leiden)

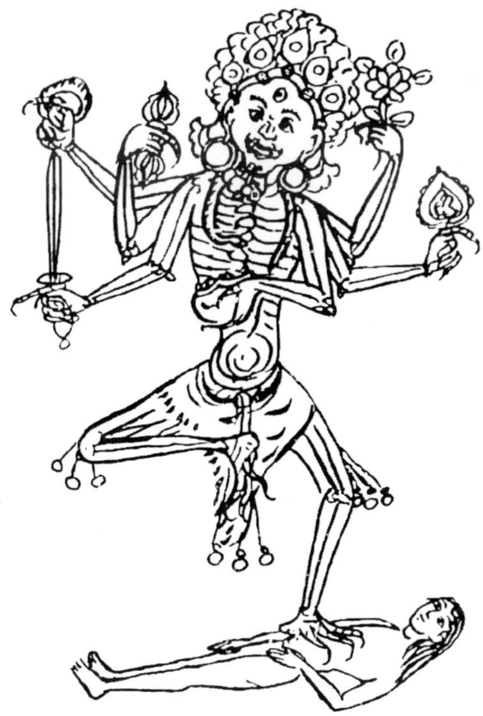

(d) Vajracarcikā

Plate XXVIII

to confer wisdom and erudition to her devotees. Nine Sādhanas in the Sādhanamālā describe the procedure of her worship, and out of these only two are assigned to the cult of Akṣobhya. Like Mañjuśrī, she has also a long antiquity and it is for this reason that she could not likewise be assigned to one particular Dhyānī Buddha, as the conception of the Dhyānī Buddhas was not in existence when Prajñāpāramitā scripture was restored from the nether regions by Nāgārjuna. The two Sādhanas describe the white and the yellow varieties of the goddess.

(i) Sitaprajñāpāramitā.

Colour—white. Āsana—Vajraparyaṅka.
Symbols—lotus and book.

Only one Sādhana in the Sādhanamālā describes the form of white Prajñāpāramitā with the image of Akṣobhya on the crown. She is two-armed, one faced, sits in the Vajraparyaṅka attitude on the white lotus and carries the red lotus in the right hand and the Prajñāpāramitā Book in the left. She is decked in all sorts of ornaments and has a beautiful and pleasant appearance unlike other emanations of Akṣobhya. The Dhyāna runs as follows :—

"Dvibhujāṃ ekavadanāṃ sitavarṇāṃ manoramāṃ ।
Ardhacarcarakeśīñca śvetāmbhoruhasaṃsthitāṃ ॥
Padmaṃ dakṣiṇahaste tu raktavarṇāṃ vibhāvayet ।
Prajñāpāramitāṃ vāme vajraparyaṅkasaṃsthitāṃ ॥
Sarvālaṅkārasampūrṇṇāṃ bhāvayennābhimaṇḍale ।
Aṅkarajñānasambhūtāṃ paramānandakāriṇīṃ ॥

....Akṣobhyamudritā ceyaṃ. Sitaprajñāpāramitāsādhanaṃ."

Sādhanamālā. A—163, N—123, C—132.

The worshipper should meditate on the form of Sita-Prajñāpāramitā in the navel, as two-armed, one faced, white in colour, and beautiful in appearance, with half curly hair ; as sitting on the white lotus, carrying in her right hand the red lotus and the Prajñāpāramitā Book in the left ; as sitting in the Vajraparyaṅka attitude, decked in all ornaments, originating from the knowledge of the letter 'Aṃ' and bringing in immense delight....This goddess is stamped with the image of Akṣobhya [on the crown]."

(ii) Pītaprajñāpāramitā.

Colour—yellow. **Mudrā—Vyākhyāna.**
Distinctive mark—Book on lotus to the left.

The yellow variety of Prajñāpāramitā with the crest of Akṣobhya is identical in form with the one described above, except with regard to the colour and the Mudrā She is yellow in complexion, bears the crest of Akṣobhya on her crown of chignon, wears celestial ornaments and garments, and displays the Vyākhyāna pose in her two hands. On a lotus in her left rests the scripture, Prajñāpāramitā.

The celebrated image of Prajñāpāramitā (Plate XXVII,c)* of Java belongs to this variety, and tallies in all details with the description given in the Dhyāna.

6. VAJRACARCIKĀ.

Asana—Dancing in Ardhaparyaṅka. Arms—six.
Symbols—*right.* Vajra, Khaḍga, Cakra. *left.* Kapāla, jewel, lotus.
Colour—red. Distinctive feature—emaciated body.
Vāhana—corpse. Appearance—terrible.

Only one Sādhana in the Sādhanamālā describe the form of Vajracarcikā, and the Dhyāna contained therein runs as follows :—

Vajracarcikāṃ trinetrāṃ ekamukhīṃ ardhaparyaṅkatāṇḍavāṃ mṛtakāsanasthāṃ kṛśāṅgīṃ daṃṣṭrotkaṭabhairavāṃ naraśiromālāvibhūṣitakaṇṭhadeśāṃ Akṣobhyamukuṭinīṃ vyāghracarmanivasanāṃ muktakeśīṃ ṣaḍbhujāṃ, dakṣiṇe vajrakhaḍgacakradhāriṇīṃ, vāmc kapālamaṇikamaladharāṃ raktavarṇāṃ, karmānurūpataḥ śuklādıvarṇayuktāñca dhyātvā. . . .''

Sādhanamālā, A—211, Na—14-15, C—169.

" The worshipper should conceive himself as Vajracarcikā, who is three-eyed and one-faced, dances in the Ardhaparyaṅka attitude on a corpse, is emaciated in appearance and looks terrible with bare fangs; whose neck is embellished by a garland of human heads, who is decked in ornaments of bones, is endowed with the five auspicious symbols, bears the image of Akṣobhya on the crown, is clad in garments of tiger-skin and has dishevelled

* Published in Havell : *Indian Sculpture and Painting*, Plate XIV.

hair; who is six-armed and carries in her three right hands the Vajra, the sword and the Cakra, and in the left the Kapāla, the jewel and the lotus; who has red complexion but gets white and other colours in accordance with the different purposes for which she is invoked. Thus meditating...."

From the accompanying sketch (Plate XXVIII,d) her terrible form with emaciated body would at once be apparent. The skeleton of the fleshless body shows through the skin in all its nakedness. She appears more fierce because of her vulture-like claws.

7. Mahāmantrānusāriṇī.

Colour—blue. Arms—four. Mudrā—Varada.
Symbols—Vajra, Paraśu and noose.

The remarks made in the case of Mahāsitavatī, an emanation of Amitābha and one of the Pañcarakṣā goddesses, apply to the case of Mahāmantrānusāriṇī also. This goddess is another of the Pañcarakṣā goddesses and as her colour is blue, she affiliates herself to the Dhyānī Buddha Akṣobhya. Only one short Sādhana describe her form and the Dhyāna contained therein is as follows :—

Mahāmantrānusārīṇī caturbhujaikamukhī kṛṣṇā dakṣiṇabhujadvaye vajravaradavatī vāmabhujadvaye paraśupāśavatī Huṃkāravījā Akṣobhyakirīṭinī sūryyāsanaprabhā ceti."

Sādhanamālā, A—215, Na—17, C—171.

"Mahāmantrānusāriṇi is four-armed and one-faced, is blue in complexion, shows in her two right hands the Vajra and the Varada Mudrā and in the two left the Paraśu and the noose; she originates from the syllable "Huṃ,' bears the image of Akṣobhya on the crown, sits on and glows like the sun."

8. Mahāpratyaṅgirā.

Colour—blue. Arms—six.
Symbols—*right.* Khaḍga, Aṅkuśa, Varadamudrā,
left. Tarjanīpāśa, red lotus, Triśūla.

One short Sādhana in the Sādhanamālā is assigned to Mahāpratyaṅgirā. The Dhyāna describing her form is as follows :—

"Mahāpratyaṅgirā kṛṣṇā ṣaḍbhujaikamukhā khaḍgāṅkuśavaradadakṣiṇahastā raktapadmatriśūlahṛdayasthasapāśatarjanīyuktavāmahastā Huṃvījā Akṣobhyamukuṭā sarvālaṅkāravatī rūpayauvanasampannā...."

Sādhanamālā, A—215-16, Na—18, C—172.

"Mahāpratyaṇgirā is blue in colour, six-armed, one-faced, carries in her right hands the sword, the goad and exhibits the Varada Mudrā, and in the left the Tarjanī with the noose against the breast, the red lotus and the trident; she originates from the syllable 'Huṃ', bears the image of Akṣobhya on the crown, is decked in all ornaments and is young and beautiful."

The accompanying sketches (Plate XXIX,a-b) represent Mahāpratyaṅgirā and answers to the description given in the Sādhana. The Nepalese image reproduced in Plate XXIX,c with innumerable heads and arms is also worshipped as Mahāpratyaṅgirā. But we have not yet succeeded in finding a Dhyāna for Mahāpratyaṅgirā which corresponds to the image illustrated.

9. Dhvajāgrakeyūrā.

Two Sādhanas in the Sādhanamālā describe two widely different forms of Dhvajāgrakeyūrā. In one, the crest of Akṣobhya is mentioned but in another, it is not expressly mentioned. The weapons in both cases are different. In one, she is three-faced and in another four-faced. The two forms agree, however, in all other respects.

(i)

Colour—blue. Faces—three. Arms—four.
Appearance—terrible. Asana—Pratyālīḍha.
Symbols—*right* Khaḍga and Pāśa. *left* Khaṭvāṅga and Cakra.

The Dhyāna describing Dhvajāgrakeyūrā with three faces and four arms and with the crest of Akṣobhya runs as follows:—

"Dhvajāgrakeyūrā kṛṣṇā trimukhī caturbhujā raktaśyāmadakṣiṇavāmamukhī khaḍgapāśadhārīdakṣiṇakaradvayā vajrāṅkitakhaṭvāṅgacakravāmahastadvayā ūrddhvapiṅgalakeśī śuṣkapañcamuṇḍālaṅkṛtaśiraskā vyāghrājinavasānā daṃṣṭrākarālamukhī pralambodarī pratyālīḍhapadā sūryyāsanaprabhā pītavastrakañcukinī Huṃbījā Akṣobhyamukuṭā."

Sādhanamālā. A—216, Na—18, C—172.

(a) Pratyaṅgirā

(b) Pratyaṅgirā

(c) Pratyaṅgirā (Nepal)

(d) Dhvajāgrakeyūrā

Plate XXIX

" Dhvajāgrakeyūrā is blue in colour, three-faced, and four-armed with the right and left faces having red and green colour (respectively). She carries the sword and the noose in the two right hands, and the Khaṭvāṅga surmounted by a Vajra and the Cakra in the two left, has brown hair rising upwards on her head which is embellished by a row of five shrivelled up heads, wears garments of tiger-skin, and has faces distorted with bare fangs. She has protruding belly, stands in the Pratyālīḍha attitude, has the seat of and glows like the sun, wears yellow garment and jacket, originates from the syllable ' Huṃ ' and bears the image of Akṣobhya on the crown."

(ii)

Faces—four. Arms—four. Colour—yellow.
Symbols—*right* sword, Cakra. *left* Tarjanīpāśa and Mūṣala.

As already pointed out, Dhvajāgrakeyūrā may have another form, with four faces and four arms. She has yellow complexion instead of blue, carries the sword and the Cakra in the two right hands and the Tarjanīpāśa, and the Mūṣala surmounted by a Vajra in the two left. A Triśūla hangs from her left shoulder. Her first face is yellow, left red, right white and the face above is distorted and has the colour of the smoke. In all other respects, she is identical with the one described before.

The accompanying drawing (Plate XXIX,d) portrays Dhvajāgrakeyūrā as she is represented in Nepal in modern times.

10. Vasudhārā.

Mudrā—Varada. Symbol—ears of corn. Colour—yellow.

Vasudhārā figures in the Pantheon of the Mahāyāna Buddhists as the consort of Jambhala, the Buddhist God of Wealth. Only three Sādhanas are devoted to her worship, and in one of these only is she said to bear the image of Akṣobhya. In two others, she is assigned to the Dhyānī Buddha Ratnasambhava. It may be noticed by the way that Vasudhārā has a greater antiquity than the Dhyānī Buddhas themselves.* The Dhyāna describing the goddess with the figure of Akṣobhya on the crown runs as follows :—

* This is the reason why she has not been assigned to one particular Dhyānī Buddha. Followers of different cults assigned Vasudhārā to different Dhyānī Buddhas.

[Ātmānaṃ] Vasudhārāṃ Bhagavatīṃ dhyāyāt, kanakavarṇāṃ sakalālaṅkāravatīm dviraṣṭavarṣākṛtiṃ, dakṣiṇakareṇa varadāṃ, vāmakareṇa dhānyamañjarīdharāṃ, Akṣobhyadhāriṇīṃ. Purato Bhagavatīṃ Śrīvasuṃ, dakṣiṇato Vasuśriyaṃ, paścimataḥ Śrivasumukhīṃ, vāmato Vasumatiśriyaṃ ; etāścādyakṣaravījāḥ svanāyikāsamānarūpāḥ cintānīyāḥ."

Sādhanamālā. A—228, Na—1, C—181.

"The worshipper should conceive himself as the goddess Vasudhārā of golden complexion, who is decked in all sorts of ornaments, appears like a young girl of twice eight years, exhibits the Varada Mudrā in the right hand, carries the ears of corn in the left, and bears the image of Akṣobhya (on the crown). In front of the goddess should be conceived Śrīvasu, in the right Vasuśrī, in the west Śrīvasumukhī and in the left Vasumatiśrī. These four goddesses originate from the first syllables of their names and are identical in form with the principal goddess."

11. Nairātmā.

Āsana—Dancing in Ardhaparyaṅka.	Colour—blue.
Appearance—terrible.	Vāhana—corpse lying on its back.
Symbols—Kartri and Kapāla.	Identification symbol—Khaṭvāṅga to the left.

Two Sādhanas in the Sādhanamālā describe her form, which is in many respects, similar to the form of Vajravārāhī with the Kartri and the Kapāla. In fact we can only distinguish between the two by noticing the corpse only. When it lies on its breast we must identify the goddess as Vajravārāhī. But if the corpse lies on its *back* the goddess is Nairātmā. There are, however, other features also for distinguishing between their forms. Vajravārāhī, being an emanation of Vairocana, should bear the image of Vairocana on the crown ; but Nairātmā being an emanation of Akṣobhya should bear the image of Akṣobhya on the crown. Moreover, the excrescence near the right ear of Vajravārāhi must also be absent in the case of Nairātmā. In all other respects the two resemble each other remarkably. The Dhyāna in one of the two Sādhanas describes the form of Nairātmā in the following terms :—

"Śavahṛccandrasthārdhaparyaṅkena nāṭyasthitāṃ Nairātmāṃ kṛṣṇāṃ ekamukhāṁ ūrddhvapiṅgalakeśāṃ Akṣobhyamukuṭinīṃ daṃṣṭrākarālalalajjihvāṃ, dakṣiṇena kartridhārinīṃ, vāme kapālakhaṭvāṅgadhāriṇīṃ, raktavartulatrinetrāṃ pañcamudrāvibhūṣaṇāṃ [dhyāyāt.] "

Sādhanamālā. A—244, Na—56, C—193.

"The worshipper should conceive himself as Nairātmā who stands in Ardhaparyaṅka in a dancing attitude on the moon over the breast of a corpse,

(a) Nairātmā (Indian Museum)

(b) Nairātmā
(Vaṅgīya Sāhitya Pariṣat)

(c) Aṣṭabhuja Mārīcī
(Indian Museum)

(d) Aṣṭabhuja Mārīcī
(Indian Museum)

Plate XXX

is blue in complexion, has brown hair rising upwards, and bears the image of Akṣobhya on the crown ; whose face looks terrible with bare fangs and protruding tongue ; who carries the Kartri in the right hand and bears the Kapāla and the Khaṭvāṅga in the left ; whose three eyes are red and round, and who is endowed with the five auspicious symbols."

The word ' Nairātmā ' means ' having no soul ' and is another name for Śūnya in which the Bodhisattva merges when the Nirvāṇa has been attained. Gradually the conception of Śūnya took the form of a goddess in whose embrace the Bodhisattva is said to remain in eternal bliss and happiness. Nairātmā gets the blue colour, because the colour of Śūnya according to the Buddhist tradition, is like the colour of the sky, which is blue.

The Indian Museum image. No. 3941 (Plate XXX,a)* is the only image that we know, of this goddess. Here the goddess, in accordance with the Dhyāna, has a terrible appearance with canine teeth, garland of heads and three eyes rolling in anger. She stands on the corpse lying on its back and dances in the Ardhaparyaṅka attitude. Burning flames radiate from her person, and her hair rises upwards in the shape of a flame. She is decked in the five auspicious symbols, the Kaṇṭhikā (torque), Rucaka (bracelets), Ratna (jewels), Mekhalā (girdle) and Bhaṣma (ashes) or the Sūtra (sacred thread) in the form of a garland of heads. She bears the image of her sire, Akṣobhya on the crown, and carries the menacing Kartri in the right hand. The left hand

* I offer this identification with some diffidence in view of the fact that Mr. B. C. Bhattacharyya, M.A. has identified the image differently in his recent treatise on *Indian Images* Part 1, " *Based on Genetic, Comparative and Synthetic Principles*," published by Messrs. Thacker Spink & Co. The Kartri carried in the right hand of the goddess has been transformed by Mr. Bhattacharyya as Karṇikā (not kartrikā ?) or the branch of a palm tree. I am afraid it is a rather cruel strain on the credulity of the readers to ask them to see a palm leaf where nothing else but a clear knife is to be seen. The Dhyānas quoted by Mr. Bhat acharyya in support of his identification of the goddess as Kāli hardly explain a single feature of the figure. The attitude, the rod that hangs from her left shoulder, the miniature figure on the crown of the goddess—none has been explained by the Dhyānas. The failure of Mr. Bhatt charyya to recognize the figure of the Dhyānī Buddha Akṣobhya on the crown of the image is indeed amazing ! In this connection the following quotation from his *Preface* would be of considerable interest to Iconographists : " The experience of the author has gone far to confirm this statement. It is not that the *layman* who holds this view has any special *penchant* for things Buddhist, spiritual or physical ; it is simply that he is unable to distinguish a Hindu image from a Buddhist image,.... The author in the following pages has attmepted a systematic and critical study of those images which on fundamental grounds cannot be designated otherwise than as purely Hindu or Brahmanic." Preface p. e. pp. 40-41, and Pl. XXV.

The above is only another instance of the danger of working in hurry in a difficult field with insufficient materials and training, of the ludicrousness of a pompous display of ' *Genetic, Comparative and Synthetic* ' principles, where such mistakes can be committed, and of the unavailing vanity of roundly condemning laymen, without oneself being sure that he has risen above the level.

carrying the Kapāla is broken. The Khaṭvāṅga as usual, hangs from her left shoulder.

The Vaṅgīya Sāhitya Pariṣat bronze (Plate XXX,b) herewith illustrated for the first time, presents an interesting problem to Iconographists. It was at first taken to be an image of Vajravārāhī,—but as the Kartri is not surmounted by a Vajra, the excrescence near the right ear is absent, and as the corpse on which the goddess stands does not lie on its breast, the identification could not stand. The suggestion that the image might be one of Vajrayoginī did not also find favour, as the corpse in this case also should lie on its breast. Moreover, all the Dhyānas for Vajrayoginī unanimously attribute the Ālīḍha attitude, instead of the dancing attitude in Ardhaparyaṅka, which is to be seen in this bronze figure. The fact seems to be that the image really represents Nairātmā without the crest of Akṣobhya, and that the Khaṭvāṅga which should hang from her left shoulder is lost, in the same way as small weapons in Nepalese or Darjeeling bronzes are often found missing.

CHAPTER VII.

EMANATIONS OF VAIROCANA.

According to the Sādhanamālā, all emanations of Vairocana are feminine and no male deity emanates from him. Five goddesses are given the image of Vairocana on the crown, thereby showing that they are all emanations of that particular Dhyāni Buddha. Some of these goddesses are expressly stated in the Sādhanas to be "Vairocanakulodbhavā," meaning, "born of the family of Vairocana." The goddesses that emanate from this Dhyānī Bhddha are said to reside in the interior of the Caitya. Vairocana, it may be remembered, is the lord of the sanctum of the temples, and it is natural for the deities emanating from him to reside therein. Among the five goddesses emanating from Vairocana, Mārīcī is most important and popular, who is sometimes believed to be the consort of Vairocana. Vairocana is distinguished from the other Dhyānī Buddhas by the white complexion and the Dharmacakra Mudrā displayed in his two hands.

1. Mārīcī.

Mārīcī is invoked by the Lāmās of Tibet at the advent of the morning, showing her connection with the sun. Like the Hindu Sun-god, she has also a chariot, but the chariot of Mārīcī is drawn by seven pigs while the chariot of the sun is drawn by seven horses. Again, the charioteer of the sun is Aruṇa with no legs, but in the case of Mārīcī the charioteer is either a goddess with no legs or Rāhu,—only a head without a body.

There is a belief that Mārīcī is the same as Vajravārāhī, but there is very little basis for the theory. Vajravārāhī is actively associated in yab-yum with her consort Heruka or Samvara, an emanation of Akṣobhya. Mārīcī is, on the contrary, regarded as a consort of Vairocana himself and not of any emanation of a Dhyānī Buddha. She is never known to be associated with him in yab-yum, but always appears singly. Heruka rides a corpse lying on its breast and accordingly such a Vāhana has been given to Vajravārāhī, but Mārīcī is never known to tread upon a corpse or even the prostrate form of a man. The images of Vajravārāhī always represent her as one-faced with an excrescence near the right ear, but

Mārīcī, though rarely represented as one-faced, is never known to have any excrescence anywhere in her body. Vajravārāhī, according to the Dhyāna, may have four arms but Mārīcī can never have four arms: she must have either two, eight, ten or twelve arms according to the Sādhanas. Mārīcī is always said to reside in the womb of a Caitya, whereas Vajravārāhī being an abbess may reside anywhere. The Mantra for Vajravārāhī is "Oṃ Sarva-Buddhaḍākinīye Vajravarṇanīye huṃ huṃ huṃ phaṭ phaṭ Svāhā", whereas, the Mantras for Mārīcī are "Oṃ Mārīeyai māṃ huṃ Svāhā" or "Oṃ Vajravetāli huṃ phaṭ". Śāntideva gives the Dhāraṇī for Mārīcī but the Dhāraṇī never gives her the name of Vajravārāhī. Lastly, the conception of Mārīcī has a greater antiquity than the conception of either Vajravārāhī or Heruka. The union of Heruka and Vajravārāhī is the subject-matter of the Vajravārāhī Tantra but no Tantra is assigned to Mārīcī. Vajravārāhī stands in the Ardhaparyaṅka in a dancing attitude on a corpse, but Mārīcī stands almost always in the Ālīdha attitude, moves in a chariot but never has the dancing attitude. Vajravārāhī has been called a Ḍākinī, or in other words, an *abbess* who has attained perfection (*siddhi*), and has become a deified woman; but Mārīcī is a goddess and was never less than a goddess.

In view of these wide differences in form and character we do not see how the identity of the two goddesses, Mārīcī and Vajravārāhī, can be established. The only points of agreement between them are that both of them are emanations of Vairocana, and both sometimes have two arms and two legs.

Sixteen Sādhanas in the Sādhanamālā describe six distinct forms of Mārīcī. She may have one, three, five or six faces and two, eight, ten or twelve arms. She is generally accompanied by her four attendants, Varttālī, Vadālī, Varālī and Varāhamukhī. She is recognized generally by the sow face and the seven pigs that run her chariot. The needle and string are her characteristic symbols by which she is believed to sew up the mouths and the eyes of the wicked. Images of Mārīcī are rather common in India. In her two-armed form of Aśokakāntā she accompanies Khadiravanī-Tāra; among the other varieties of Mārīcī, the form with three faces and eight arms are extensively met with in sculptures.

(i) Aśokakāntā.

Vāhana—pig. Colour—yellow.
Āsana—standing. Mudrā—Varada.
Distinctive feature—left hand touching the Aśoka bough.

Ordinarily Mārīcī has two arms and one face. She is called Aśokakāntā when she holds the bough of an Aśoka tree in the left hand and exhibits the Varada Mudrā in the right hand ; but she will be called Ārya-Mārīcī if she carries the needle and the string in her two hands. The Dhyāna describing the form of Aśokakānta is stated below :—

" Hemābhāsūkarārūḍhāṃ taptakāñcanabhāsurāṃ ।
Līlayorddhvasthitāṃ [caiva] candrāmbhoruhasaṃsthitāṃ ॥
Aśokavṛkṣaśākhāgravilagnāṃ vāmapāṇinā ।
Bibhratī varadākāraṃ dakṣiṇakarapallavāṃ ॥
Dīptaratnopaśobhena maulinā Buddhaśekharā ।
Svetavastrāṃ namasyāmi Mārīcīṃ abhayapradāṃ." ॥

Sādhanamālā. A—161, N—146, C—130.

"I bow to Mārīcī who rides the sow of golden colour, whose complexion is like the colour of molten gold, who stands in a sportive attitude on the moon over the lotus, holds with her left hand the bough of an Aśoka tree, and displays the Varada pose in the right ; who bears the image of the Dhyānī Buddha [Vairocana] on the crown, is decorated with bright jewels, wears white garments and bestows assurance [to the world.] "

(ii) Ārya-Mārīcī.

Symbols—needle and the string.

Ārya Mārīcī is identical in all other respects with Aśokakāntā and can only be distinguished by the symbols she bears in her hands. As already stated, Aśokakāntā has the Aśoka bough and the Varada pose but Ārya-Mārīcī carries the needle and the string.*

* Cf. the description in the Sādhanamālā—
" Cintayet Ārya-Mārīcīṃ sūcīsūtradharāṃ rūpāṃ ॥"
Ms. A—161.

(iii) Mārīcīpicuvā.

Faces—three. Arms—eight.

Mārīcīpicuvā is also called Aṣṭabhujapīta-Mārīcī (or Saṃkṣipta-Mārīcī). These two names denote two distinct varieties of Mārīcī, but they are both endowed with three faces and eight arms and carry similar weapons in their hands. One Sādhana only is devoted to Mārīcīpicuvā and it is not mentioned whether she should be accompanied by the four goddesses, as usual. She holds the needle and the string in the first pair of hands, the Aṅkuśa and the noose in another pair, the bow and the arrow in the third pair, and the Vajra and the Aśoka flower in the fourth pair. She has three faces, each displaying three different sentiments (Rasa). The Dhyāna in verse runs as follows :—

" Śṛṅgāravīrasaddharṣair-jāmbūnadasamaprabhāṃ ı
Madhyendranīlavaraṇāsyāṃ bhayabībhatsaraudrakaiḥ ıı
Karuṇādbhutaśāntaiśca sphaṭikenditarānanāṃ ı
Trivimokṣamukhaistryakṣo dharmasambhoganirmitāṃ ıı
Pitākṣaraṇasadvastrāṃ mayūkhasukhavāsinīṃ ı
Sūcyākṣāsyāni sīvantīṃ bandhantīṃ mukhacakṣuṣī ıı
Hṛdgale'ṅkuśapāśābhyāṃ bindhantīṃ bāṇakārmukaiḥ ı
Vajreṇa duṣṭahṛdbhitvāśokenāsecanaparāṃ ıı
.. ..
Prajñopāyapadākrāntāṃ Mārīcīṃ bhāvayed-vratī ıı

Mārīcīpicuvāsādhanaṃ." Sādhanamālā. A—156-7, N—142. C—126.

" The worshipper should conceive himself as Mārīcī-[Picuvā], who displays the sentiments of Śṛṅgāra, Vīra and Harṣa in one of her faces which is of the colour of Jāmbūnada (gold) ; in the middle face which is of the colour of Indranīla gem, the sentiments of Bhaya, Bībhatsa, and Raudra are displayed ; and in the third face of crystal colour, the sentiments of Karuṇā, Adbhuta and Śānta appear. She has three eyes in all the three faces, which give freedom from the three great evils. Her essence is made up of the Dharmakāya and Sambhogakāya. She is clad in garments of yellow colour and resides happily in the mass of rays. She sews up the eyes and the mouths of the wicked by the needle and secures them with a string. She strikes their heart with the Aṅkuśa, draws them by the neck with the noose, pierces them by the bow and the arrow, and by rending their heart to pieces with the Vajra, sprinkles water with the leaves of Aśoka....she tramples under her feet Prajñā and Upāya."

Aṣṭabhuja-Mārīcī or Saṃkṣipta-Mārīcī is yellow in colour, wears red garments, is decked in various ornaments, bears the image of Vairocana on the crown and resides within the cavity of a Caitya. Her three faces display three different sentiments. The first or the principal face displays amour and has the colour of gold. The second or the left face is distorted sow-like, has the colour of the Indranīla gem, displays wrath and looks terrible with bare fangs and protruding lips. The third or the face to the right is of deep red colour, glows in heavenly splendour and displays the sentiment of Śānta. She rides the chariot drawn by seven pigs, stands in the Ālīḍha attitude and appears as a virgin in the fulness of youth. Below the seven sows is the fierce Rāhu who devours the sun and the moon. She is surrounded by the four attendant goddesses, Varttālī, Vadālī, Varālī and Varāhamukhī.

(i) Varttālī has red complexion, the sow-face, four arms, wears red garments, is decked in all ornaments and carries the noose and the Aśoka in the left hands and the Vajrāṅkuśa and the needle in the right.

(ii) Vadālī has many features in common with Varttālī with the difference that her colour is yellow and she carries the noose and the Vajra in the left hand and the Aśoka and the needle in the right.

(iii) Varālī is identical with Vadālī in many respects except that the former holds the Vajra and the needle in the right hand and the noose and the Aśoka in the left.

(iv) Varāhamukhī wears the same garments and the same ornaments as the two previous ones. But she is red in complexion and carries the Vajra and the arrow in the right hand and the Aśoka and the bow in the left.

It is very curious that nearly all the images of Mārīcī we have come across, up till now, belong to this variety. In actual images instead of Rāhu, sometimes a lady charioteer without legs may be seen. Some images, again, retain the charioteer as well as the Rāhu. Two images of the eight-armed variety of Mārīcī are in the Dacca Museum, two are in the Indian Museum, (Plate XXX,c-d) Calcutta ; and the one (Plate XXXI,a) * that is frequently represented in many works of art, was discovered at Sārnāth and is now deposited in the Lucknow Museum ; a sixth has been discovered in Orissa. Besides these, several more images of Mārīcī hail from the museums at Rajshahi and Sarnath. All these images are three-faced and eight-armed, and some of them are very fine specimens of art. In the more artistic and accurate images the three sentiments have actually been depicted by the sculptors. A study of these images will show that though the sculptors generally follow the Sādhana in all the details, yet they do not always follow it in the case of the four attendant gooddesses. Sometimes they are two-armed, and sometimes, though four-armed, they do not carry the symbols prescribed by the Sādhanamālā.

* The remarkable feature of this image is that it bears on the crown a miniature figure of the Dhyānī Buddha Amitabha instead of Vairocana, the parental Buddha, as required by the Sādhana. The reason for this anomaly is that this particular image belongs to the cult of Amītabha, the followers of which considered Amitābha as the Ādi Buddha and made all their gods emanate from him.

(iv) Ubhayavarāhānana-Mārīcī.*

Faces—three.	**Arms—twelve.**
Āsana—Ālīḍha.	**Distinctive mark—two sow-faces.**

She has been given this name as her two faces to the right and left of the principal one are both depicted sow-like, unlike any other three-faced variation of Mārīcī. She is clad in decent tiger-skin, has red complexion, bejewelled headdress, red scarf and is decked in all ornaments. She resides within the womb of a Caitya, stands in the Ālīḍha attitude and is endowed with three faces and twelve arms. The principal face smiles with delight, is peaceful in appearance and displays the sentiment of amour. The two side ones are distorted sow-like, all three faces having three eyes in each. The face to the left is red and paid homage to by a deity carrying Vajra and Mudgara. The face to the right has a reddish effulgence like that of the Saindhava salt and is paid homage to by Purandara (Indra) who carries the Vajra and the noose. In her six left hands she shows the Tarjanī against the breast, the Aśoka bough, the Vajrāṅkuśa, the Kapāla, the head of Brahmā and the vessel, and in the six right hands the needle, Aṅkuśa, the Bhiṇḍipāla (spear), the sword, the Kartri and the Staff surmounted by a Vajra. She bears the image of Vairocana on her crown, and tramples under her feet the Hindu gods, such as, Hari (Viṣṇu), Hara (Śiva), Hiranyagarbha (Brahmā) and others. The guardians of the quarters all pay homage to this goddess.

It may be pointed out here that the Sādhana is reticent about the chariot, the seven sows that run it, and about the four attendant goddesses, Varttālī, Vadālī, Varālī, and Varāhamukhī.

(v) Daśabhujasita-Mārīcī.

Faces—five.	**Colour—white.**
Arms—ten.	**Legs—four.**

Two Sādhanas in the Sādhanamālā describe her form with ten arms, which shows that she is one of the white variations of Mārīcī. The most important feature of this variety is that she is endowed with four legs. She has five faces and ten arms. The principal face is white, the one to the right is blue, the other to the left is red and distorted sow-like, the face behind is green and the face above is yellow and bears the Triśikhā (three tufts of

* The name is mine.

hair) and the crown of chignon. The five right hands hold the sun, the blue Vajra, the arrow, the goad and the needle. The hands to the left carry the moon, the bow, the Aśoka bough, the noose with the Tarjanī and the string. She rides a chariot drawn by seven pigs and tramples under her feet the four Hindu gods, Indra, Śiva, Viṣṇu and Brahmā, and bears the effigy of Vairocana on the tiara.

The Sādhanas further add that she should be accompanied by three other goddesses. The first among them is of blue complexion, and rides upon a Makara. Her face is distorted like that of a sow and she carries the Vajra in one hand and shows the Tarjanī in the other.

The second goddess appears to the right of Mārīcī, wears celestial ornaments, is of red colour with one face distorted sow-like. She carries in her four hands, the goad, the needle, the noose with the Tarjanī and the string.

The third goddess appears to the left of Mārīcī. She is also of red colour with one face distorted sow-like and four arms. The two principal hands are engaged in drawing full the bow charged with an arrow, while the rest hold the Vajra in the right and the Aśoka bough in the left.

Below the seven pigs drawing the chariot are the Navagrahas or the Nine Planets and various diseases and disasters in human shape lie flat on the ground.

The Sādhanas do not give the names of the attendant deities, which are only three in number. It is possible that these three are the members of the Varttālī group. The illustration in Plate XXXI,b represents a Nepalese drawing of this variety of Mārīcī.

(vi) Vajradhātvīśvarī Mārīcī.

Faces—six.	Āsana—Ālīḍha.
Arms—twelve.	Appearance—terrible.

When six-faced and twelve-armed, Mārīcī is invoked in three different varieties, under the three different names, Vajradhātviśvari-Mārīcī, Odiyāna-Mārīcī and Vajravetālī. As there are very slight differences amongst the three they have been classed together. The difference, however, lies in the different weapons that are held in their hands. Excepting Vajravetālī, who is represented singly, each of the two others is accompanied by a deity, who serves as the charioteer.

The features that are common to all the three may be summarised from the Sādhanas as follows. They are all endowed with six faces and twelve arms. The first five faces have respectively the red, blue, green, yellow and white colour. The face on the top is distorted sow-like and has the blue colour. All the three are said to reside in the womb of a Caitya, they stand in the Ālīḍha attitude and bear the image of Vairocana on the crown. They present a terrifying appearance with three eyes, protruding tongue, bare fangs, the ornaments of serpents, and garments of tiger-skin.

Vajradhātvīśvarī carries in her six right hands the sword, the Mūṣala, the arrow, the goad, the Vajra, and the Paraśu, and in the six left show the noose,* the Kapāla, the Aśoka bough, the head of Brahmā, the bow and the Triśūla. Oḍiyāna Mārīcī holds the Cakra in the right instead of the goad, and the Khaṭvānga-Kapāla in one of the left hands instead of Kapāla only. Vajravetāli in one of her right hands holds the crossed double thunderbolt instead of the goad or the Cakra ; and in one of the left, the noose instead of Kapāla or the Khaṭvānga-Kapāla. All the other hands carry the same weapons in all the three cases.

2. Uṣṇīṣavijayā.

Colour—white. Faces—three.
Arms—eight. Identification mark—Buddha on lotus.
Symbols—*right* Visvavajra, Buddha on lotus, arrow, Varada Mudrā.
left bow, Tarjanī and noose, Abhaya Mudrā, Kalaśa.

Like Mārīcī, Uṣṇīṣavijayā is also said to bear the image of Vairocana on the crown and to reside within the womb of a Caitya. She is one of the most popular deities of the Pantheon and almost every temple in Nepal has got her image in it. The most artistic specimen, however, belongs to the Indian Museum, Calcutta. A miniature Caitya on the top of the image of Uṣṇīṣa-vijayā signifies that she is a presiding deity of the sanctum of the Caitya. Several Sādhanas describe her form and we quote below the Dhyāna contained in one of these :—

" Śuklāṃ trimukhāṃ trinetrāṃ navayauvanāṃ nānālaṅkāradharāṃ aṣṭabhujāṃ Bhagavatīṃ cintayet ; pītakṛṣṇadakṣiṇetaravadanāṃ ; dakṣiṇa-caturbhujaih viśvavajra-padmastha-Buddha-bāṇa-varadamudrādharāṃ, Vāma-caturbhujaih cāpa-tarjanīpāśa-abhayahasta-pūrṇakumbhāḥ; caityaguhāgarbha-sthitāṃ Vairocanamukuṭinīṃ niṣpādya.... "

Uṣṇīṣavijayāsādhanaṃ."

Sādhanamālā. A—210, Na—14, C—168.

* She also carries the Tarjanī with the noose in one of the left hands instead of the noose only.

(a) Aṣṭabhuja Mārīcī
(Lucknow Museum)

(b) Daśabhujasīta-Mārīcī

(d) Uṣṇīṣavijayā

(c) Uṣṇīṣavijayā
(Indian Museum)

(e) Sītātapatrā Aparājitā

Plate XXXI

" The worshipper should conceive himself as [Uṣṇīṣavijayā] who is white in complexion, three-faced, three-eyed, is youthful, and decked in many ornaments ; whose right and left faces are respectively of yellow and blue colour, whose four right hands carry the Viśvavajra, Buddha on lotus, arrow and the Varada pose, and the four left hands show the bow, the noose with the Tarjanī, the Abhaya pose and the well-filled water-vessel ; who resides in the womb of the interior of the Caitya, and bears the image of Vairocaṅa on the crown. Thus meditating...."

The specimen (Plate XXI,c) * of Uṣṇīṣavijayā in the Indian Museum, Calcutta agrees almost in all details with the description given in the Sādhana. The attitude in which she sits here is the Vajraparyaṅka attitude.

The other illustration (Plate XXXI,d) is the reproduction of a painting contained in an illuminated manuscript of Pañcarakṣā. In it, the right hand whieh ought to have carried the Viśvavajra or the crossed thunderbolt, carries the jewel instead. In all other respects the painting follows the description of the Sādhana most accurately.

3. Sitātapatrā Aparājitā.

Faces—three. Arms—six.
Symbols—*right* Cakra, Aṅkuśa, bow.
left white Vajra, arrow and Tarjanīpāśa.

One Sādhana only is devoted to the worship of this deity. The word, " Vairocananāyakāṃ " in the Sādhana shows that she also belongs to the family of the Dhyānī Buddha Vairocana. She is otherwise of a mild nature except for the eyes which display anger. The Dhyāna describes her form in the following manner :—

"Sitātapatrāparājitāṃ Bhagavatīṃ trimukhāṃ ṣaḍbhujāṃ, pratimukhaṃ trinayanāṃ, śuklanīlāruṇadakṣiṇavāmamukhīṃ, cakrāṅkuśadhanurdhārī dakṣiṇakarāṃ, śitavajraśarapāśatarjanīdharavāmakarāṃ sakrodhadṛṣṭikāṃ sarvagrahavidhvaṃsinīṃ divyālaṅkāravastravatīṃ Vairocananāyakāṃ dhyātvā...."

Sādhanamālā. A—210, Na—14, C—169.

* The image was first illustrated in Foucher : *L'Iconographie Bouddhique de L'Inde*, parte 2, Fig. 6. The Dhyānī Buddha over her head is here Akṣobhya instead of Vairocana. The reason is that the image belonged to the Akṣobhya cult, which did not acknowledge the superiority of Vairocana.

" The worshipper should conceive himself as goddess Sitātapatrā Aparajītā who is three-faced, six-armed, and has three eyes in all faces ; who is of white complexion ; whose faces to the right and left are respcctively of blue and red colour ; who carries in the right hands the Cakra, the goad, and the bow, and in the left the white Vajra, the arrow and the noose with the Tarjanī ; who has angry looks, destroys all sorts of evil spirits (Grahas, *lit.* Planets), wears celestial ornaments and garments, and is looked after by Vairocana. Thus meditating...."

This goddess is called Sitatapatrā, meaning " of white parasol ", and should be distinguished from the other Aparājitā,* who has an entirely different form and is represented without the figure of any Dhyanī Buddha on the crown. The illustration (Plate XXXI,e) represents a Nepalese drawing of Sitātapatrā.

4. Mahāsāhasrapramardanī.

Colour—white. Arms—six.
Symbols—*right* sword, arrow, Varada Mudrā.
left bow, noose, axe.

Mahāsāhasrapramardanī is another of the Pañcarakṣā group and is assigned to Vairocana exactly in the same way as Mahāsitavatī and Mahāmantrānusāriṇī are affiliated respectively to Amitābha and Akṣobhya. Her form is different from the form in which she is worshipped in the Pañcarakṣā Maṇḍala. Here the Dhyāna describes her form in the following terms :—

" Mahāsāhasrapramardanīṃ ātmānaṃ dhyāyāt ; śuklāṃ ekamukhīṃ ṣaḍbhujāṃ ; dakṣiṇatribhujeṣu khaḍgabānavaradamudrāḥ, vāmatribhujeṣu dhanuḥpāśaparaśavaḥ ; vicitrālaṅkāradharāṃ rūpayauvanaśṛṅgāravatīṃ Vairocanakirīṭayuktāṃ padmacandrāsanaprabhāṃ."

Sādhanamālā. A—214-15, Na—17, C—171.

" The worshipper should conceive himself as Mahāsāhasrapramardanī who is of white complexion, one-faced, six armed, carries in her three right hands the sword, the arrow and the Varada pose, and in the three left the bow, the noose and the Paraśu ; who is decked in variegated ornaments, is young and beautiful, displays the sentiment of passion, has the figure of Vairocana on her tiara, sits on the moon over the lotus and has moonlike effulgence."

* See *Infra*, Chapter XII, (ii), No. 2.

5. Vajravārāhī.

Āsana—dancing in Ardhaparyaṅka.
Charateristic feature—excrescence near the right ear.

The union of Vajravārāhī with Heruka is the cult of the celebrated Cakrasamvara Tantra and the Vajravārāhī Tantra. One of the Sādhanas give her the epithet of "Śrī-Herukadevasyāgramahiṣī," that is, the first queen of the god, Śrī-Heruka. She is also called a Ḍākinī and in the Buddhist Tantra, it signifies any Śakti with whom the Yuganaḍdha (yab-yum) worship may be performed. It will not be out of place to mention here that Heruka is also associated with Vajrayoginī and their union is the subject of the great Heruka Tantra. But as they differ considerably in form, we do not venture to combine them into one. If Vajravārāhī is the first queen of Heruka there is no reason to suppose that Vajrayoginī may not be another. Vajravārāhī is represented as nude and as displaying the intense sentiment of amour and passion. The word, Vajravārāhī means in English "the Adamantine Sow" for the simple reason that she had an excrescence to her right which resembles the face of a sow.* Getty's story† regarding the attack of Yun-gar on the abbess and the monastery does not, in all probability, refer to Mārīcī, but to this Vajravārāhī; for, when Mārīcī has one face it may be distorted sow-like but Vajravārāhī has an excresence just near the right ear, which is a natural one, and for which the Sādhanas give her the epithet of Vajraghoṇā (adamantine excrescence). Another argument in favour of this is that, while Vajravārāhī is called a Ḍākinī, and is associated with four other Ḍākinīs, she may, very well, be an abbess, and therefore, an ordinary woman deified, and not a goddess. But Mārīcī is decidedly a goddess, she is Vajradhātvīśvarī, and the consort of a Dhyānī Buddha.

Several Sādhanas, long and short, describe the procedure of her worship discriminating two distinct forms of Vajravārāhī, who is also designated as Buddhaḍākinī and Vajravairocanī. She is either two-armed or four-armed. Even among the two-armed forms, some varieties are noticed. In one Sādhana only is she said to emanate from the family of Vairocana, and to bear the double Vajra on head, but others are silent as to her crest.

* Almost all the Sādhanas give her the epithet of Ghoṇā or Vajraghoṇā, which means "of adamantine excrescence;" and the images of Vajravārāhi, whether in paintings or in sculpture,—all agree in attributing her a sow-like excrescence near the right ear.

† Getty: *Gods of the Northern Buddhism*, p. 117 *et. sqq.*

(i)

Colour—red. Appearance—nude. Arms—two.
Symbols—Vajra-Tarjanī and Kapāla. Distinctive feature—Khaṭvāṅga to the left.
Āsana—Pratyālīḍha.

Several Sādhanas describe the two-armed varieties of Vajravārāhī and let us take up a specimen Dhyāna, which will give a general idea as to her form.—

" Ātmānaṃ Bhagavatīṃ Vajravārāhīṃ dāḍimakusumaprakhyāṃ dvibhujāṃ ekānanaṃ trinetrāṃ muktakeśāṃ ṣaṇmudrāmudritāṃ digambarāṃ pañcajñānātmikāṃ sahajānandasvabhāvāṃ ; dakṣiṇena vajratarjanīkākarāṃ vāmena karoṭakakhaṭvāṅgakarāṃ ; pratyālīḍhapadākrānta-bhairava-Kālarātrikāṃ sārdramuṇḍamālālaṅkṛtagātrāṃ, sravadrudhiraṃ pivantīṃ, bhāvayet.'

Sādhanamālā. A—230, Na—65, C—182.

The worshipper should conceive himself as goddess Vajravārāhī whose complexion is red like the pomegranate flower ; who is two-armed, one-faced and three-eyed, has dishevelled hair, is endowed with the six auspicious symbols, and is nude; whose essence is the five spiritual knowledges,* who is of the nature of the Sahaja pleasure, who shows in the right hand the Vajra together with the Tarjanī, and bears the Kapāla and the Khaṭvāṅga in the left ; who stands in the Pratyālīḍha attitude, tramples upon the fierce Kālarātri, is decked in garlands of wet heads, and who drinks of the blood trickling therefrom."

The Sādhana further adds that the four leaves of the lotus on which she stands are occupied by Ḍākinī, Lāmā, Khaṇḍarohā and Rūpiṇī on the four cardinal points beginning from the right. The four companions are respectively of blue, green red and white colour and they are all one-faced and four-armed and carry the Khaṭvāṅga, Kapāla, Ḍamaru and the Kartri in the right and left hands.

(ii)

Symbols—Kartri and Kapāla. Āsana—Dancing in Ardhaparyaṅka.
Vāhana—corpse (lying on its breast.)

This variety of Vajravārāhī is invoked in the rite of bewitching men or women and is very popular now-a-days in Nepal and other Buddhist countries. In all respects she is identical with the one described

* The five spiritual knowledges are Rūpa, Saṃjñā, Samskāra, Vedanā and Vijñāna, or in other words, the five Skandhas.

(a) Vajravārāhī

(b) Vajravārāhī

(c) Khadiravāṇī Tārā
(Indian Museum)

(d) Khadiravāṇī Tārā
(Mahobā)

(e) Khadiravāṇī Tārā
(Dacca Museum)

(f) Khadiravāṇī Tārā
(Indian Museum)

Plate XXXII

before, except that here she wields the Kartri in the right hand and carries the Kapāla in the left. The Khaṭvāṅga, as usual, hangs from her left shoulder in the same way as Heruka carries it. She stands in the attitude of dancing on a corpse.

The drawing of Vajravārāhī (Plate XXXII,a) is quite in keeping with the Sādhana ; but the other image (Plate XXXII,b)* now in Germany is somewhat different. The corpse on which she dances in the Ardhaparyaṅka attitude is lying on its back, instead of, on its breast. We may add that the image is a Tibetan bronze and as Tibet had a different iconographical development, it does not follow the Sanskrit Sādhana, in all details.

(iii) Āryavajravārāhī.

Symbols—*right* Vajra and Aṅkuśa.	*left* Kapāla and Tarjanīpāśa.
Appearance—terrible.	Attitude—Ālīḍha.

The four-armed form of Vajravārāhi is also similar to the forms mentioned before and is called Āryavajravārāhī. The difference lies only in the attitude, number of arms and the symbols carried in her hands. She carries in the two right hands the Vajra and the goad, and in the two left the Kapāla and the Tarjanī with the noose. She is one-faced, three-eyed and appears terrible with contortions of the brows, the adamatine excrescence, and the protruding tongue, teeth and belly. She stands in the Ālīḍha attitude on the corpse, unlike other forms of Vajravārāhī. The Khaṭvāṅga hangs from her left shoulder as usual.†

* Published in Grunwedel : *Die Geschichten vierundachtzig Zauberer* in *Baessler-Archiv*, Fig. 5.

† Extracts from the Dhyāna may be quoted as follows :—

" Pretāsanasthāṃ ālīḍhapadāṃ nagnāṃ ūddhvakeśāṃ Kapālamukuṭāṃ.... caturbhujāṃ, dakṣiṇe Vajrāṅkuśadharāṃ, vāme Kapālakhaṭvāṅgatarjanīpāśadharāṃ...... Vajraghoṇāṃ.... "

Sādhanamālā. A—236.

CHAPTER VIII.

EMANATIONS OF AMOGHASIDDHI.

Like the emanations of Vairocana, the deities emanating from Amoghasiddhi also are entirely feminine in character. In the whole of the Sādhanamālā only seven deities are expressly stated to bear the image of the Dhyānī Buddha Amoghasiddhi on the crown. Amoghasiddhi is distinguished from the other Dhyānī Buddhas by the green colour of his body, and the Abhaya Mudrā he displays in his right hand.

1. Khadiravanī-Tārā.

Colour—green.	Mudrā—Varada.
Symbol—Utpala.	Companions—Aśokakāntā and Ekajaṭā.

Tārā is the common name applied to a large number feminine divinities in the Buddhist Pantheon. In the Sādhanamālā, Jāṅgulī, Parṇaśavarī, Mahācīnatārā, Ekajaṭā and many others are called Tārās. Khadiravanī is also designated as a Tārā in the Sādhanamālā and is endowed with two hands, which show the Varada Mudrā in the right and the Utpala in the left. She can be recognized by the figures of the two attendant deities, Aśokakāntā Mārīcī and Ekajaṭā. One Sādhana in the Sādhanamālā describes her form and the Dhyāna is quoted as follows :—

" Haritāṃ Amoghasiddhimukuṭīṃ varadotpaladhārīdakṣiṇavāmakarāṃ Aśokakāntā-Mārīcy-Ekajaṭāvyagradakṣiṇavāmadigbhāgāṃ divyakumārīṃ dhyātvā...."

Khadiravanī-Tārāsādhanaṃ."

Sādhanamālā. A—93, N—65, C—72.

The worshipper should conceive himself as Khadiravanī-Tārā of green colour, who bears the image of Amoghasiddhi on her tiara, shows the Varada pose and the Utpala in the right and left hands respectively ; whose right and left sides are occupied by Aśokakāntā Mārīcī and Ekajaṭā, and who appears a celestial virgin. Thus meditating...."

She is commonly known as Śyāmā-Tārā because of her green colour, and as the Sādhana does not mention the particular Āsana, she may be represented in any attitude, either sitting (Plate XXXII,d) or standing (Plate XXXII,c). The sitting image (Plate XXXII,f) belonging to the Indian Museum, represented with the Dharmacakra Mudrā and two companions, Aśokakāntā Mārīcī and Ekajaṭā, may also be identified as Khadiravanī. She bears the stems of the Utpala and the lotus under her two armpits. The Dharmacakra Mudrā displayed in the image, however, may point to its identification as Prajñāpāramitā, but in that case, we fail to explain the presence of the two companions, Aśokakāntā and Ekajaṭā.

The Dacca Museum image of Khadiravanī-Tārā illustrated in Plate XXXII,e is a very interesting specimen. In it we find that the principal goddess, in addition to the two divinities Aśokakāntā and Ekajaṭā, is accompanied by eight more goddesses, four to the right and four to the left. They are identical in all respects with the principal figure. It seems probable that they represents the eight letters of the Tārā Mantra exactly in the same way as Dhanada Tārā is said to be accompanied by eight attendant deities in the Sādhana, each originating from a letter of the Mantra for her invocation. It may be remarked by the way that the Tārā Mantra does not consist of eight syllables but ten. When eight goddesses are present, it must be understood that Uṣṇīṣavijayā and Sumbhā originating from the last two letters of the Tārā Mantra, "Svā" and "hā", have not been represented.

2. Vaśyatārā.

Āsana—Bhadrāsana.	Symbol—lotus.
Mudrā—Varada.	Colour—green.

Vaśyatārā is also known by the name of Āryatara, and only one Sādhana in the Sādhanamālā is assigned to her. There is practically no difference in her form with that of Khadiravanī-Tārā in as much as both display the Varada Mudrā in the right hand and carry the Utpala in the left. Both have the green colour and both bear the image of Amoghasiddhi on the crown. In the case of Khadiravanī-Tārā it is not mentioned in what attitude she should stand or sit, but here it is expressly mentioned that Vaśyatārā should be seated in the Bhadrāsana, which represents the European fashion of sitting with two legs dangling below. This Āsana or the attitude of sitting alone distinguishes Vaśyatārā from all other ordinary Tārās carrying the Utpala in the left and exhibiting the Varada Mudrā in the right. The other point of difference between Khadiravanī-Tārā and Vaśyatārā is, that the former is accompanied by two goddesses, Aśokakāntā Mārīcī and Ekajaṭā; whereas, the latter is absolutely unattended. Khadiravanī may have any attitude, but the Sādhana prescribes that Vaśyatārā must show the Bhadrāsana only.

The accompanying sketch (Plate XXXIII,a) represents Vaśyatārā as she is pictured in Nepal. The sketch is important in showing the Bhadrāsana attitude in which the goddess sits.

3. Ṣaḍbhuja Sitatārā.

Faces—three. Arms—six. Colour—white. Āsana—Ardhaparyaṅka. Symbols—*right* Varadamudrā, rosary and arrow ; *left* Utpala, lotus, and bow.

There are many Sādhanas for Sitatārās, or the Tārās of white colour, but in none of them it is mentioned that they should bear the image of Amoghasiddhi on the crown. It is only in this case that the crest of the Dhyānī Buddha is expressly mentioned. This white Tārā is three-faced and six-armed, and the Dhyāna describes her in the following terms :—

" Sitatārāṃ trimukhāṃ ṣaḍbhujāṃ pītanīladakṣiṇetaramukhīṃ pratimukhaṃ trinetrāṃ varadākṣasūtraśaradharadakṣiṇatrikarāṃ utpalapadmacāpadharavāmapāṇitrayāṃ ardhaparyaṅkaniṣaṇṇāṃ candrāsanacandraprabhāṃ jaṭāmukuṭasthit-Āmoghasiddhiṃ pañcamuṇḍavibhūṣitamastakāṃ ardhacandrakṛtaśekharāṃ nānālaṅkāradharāṃ dviraṣṭavarṣākṛtiṃ aṣṭaśmaśānamadhyasthitāṃ. . . . vicintya."

Ṣaḍbhujaśukla-Tārāsādhanaṃ."

Sādhanamālā. A—115, N—82, C—89-90.

The worshipper should conceive himself as Sitatārā who is three-faced and six-armed ; whose faces to the right and left are yellow and blue in colour and are endowed with three eyes ; whose three right hands show the Varada Mudrā, the rosary and the arrow, and the three left carry the Utpala, the lotus and the bow ; who sits in the Ardhaparyaṅka attitude, sits on and glows like the moon, and bears the image of Amoghasiddhi on the crown of chignon ; whose head is embellished by the five heads and the crescent ; who is decked in many ornaments, is twice eight years old, is situated in the midst of the eight cremation grounds. Thus meditating. . . ."

The accompanying sketch (Plate XXXIII,b) shows how she is represented in Nepal. It tallies in all respects with the description given in the Sādhana, except that here she is represented in Vajraparyaṅka instead of Ardhaparyaṅka as required by the Sādhana.

(a) Bhadrāsana Tārā

(b) Ṣaḍbhuja-Sītatārā

(c) Dhanada-Tārā

(d) Parṇaśavarī (Vikrampur, Dacca)

Plate XXXIII

4. Dhanada-Tārā.

Arms—four. Symbols—*right* rosary, Varada pose ; *left* Utpala, book.

Dhanada-Tārā is one of the four-armed varieties of Tārā. The special features of this goddess are that she rides an animal and that, like Vajratārā, she is surrounded by eight goddesses, originating from the eight syllables of the famous Mantra "Oṃ Tāretuttāreture Svāhā". The symbols that are held in her four hands are also different from all other varieties of four-armed Tārā. The Dhyāna describing her form runs as follows :—

"Tārāṃ Bhagavatīṃ ātmānaṃ bhāvayet ; candrāsanaprabhāṃ saumyāṃ sattvaparyaṅkasthāṃ haritaśyāmāṃ ekavadanāṃ dvilocanāṃ caturbhujāṃ akṣasūtravaradotpalapustakadharāṃ vicitravastrālaṅkāravatīṃ......Locanādibhir-devībhiḥ abhiṣiktāṃ ātmānaṃ Amoghasiddhimukuṭāṃ dhyāyāt."

Dhanada-Tārāsādhanaṃ."

Sādhanamālā, A—116, N—83-4, C—91.

The worshipper should conceive himself as goddess Dhanada-Tārā, who has the seat and the radiance of the moon, is benign in appearance, sits on an animal, has green complexion, one face, two eyes, and four arms showing the rosary, the Varada pose, the Utpala and the book, wears variegated ornaments and garments.....The worshipper should further conceive himself as being offered homage by the goddesses, Locanā and others, and as bearing the image of Amoghasiddhi on the crown."

It is not mentioned in the Sādhana on what animal the goddess should sit. The Newari artists represent her as seated on a human being (Plate XXXIII,c).

5. Parṇaśavarī.

Colour—green.	Identification mark—angry laugh.	Faces—three.
Arms—six.	Vāhana—Diseases (in human form).	Āsana—Pratyālīḍha.

One form of Parṇaśavarī with yellow colour has already been discussed under the feminine emanations of the Dhyānī Buddha Akṣobhya. But here her colour is green, which is probably due to the green colour of the Dhyānī Buddha Amoghasiddhi, from whom she is said to emanate. The Mantra, designates her as a 'Piśācī,' and as 'Sarvamāripraśamanī' or the destroyer of all diseases and epidemics. In form, she is almost identical with the form that has been described previously except that here her colour is green and that she bears the image of Amoghasiddhi on the crown, instead of Akṣobhya. She carries the same weapons as the previous one, but her faces instead of displaying the pleasant smile, depict angry laugh. As the two specimens of Parṇaśavarī discovered in East Bengal both bear the image of Amoghasiddhi on the crown, we consider it necessary to quote the Dhyāna in this case also, for a comparison of the details with the images illustrated :—

" Parṇaśavarīṃ haritāṃ trimukhāṃ trinetrāṃ ṣaḍbhujāṃ kṛṣṇaśukla-dakṣiṇavāmānanāṃ vajraparaśuśaradakṣiṇakaratrayāṃ kārmukapatracchaṭā-sapāśatarjanīvāmakaratrayāṃ sakrodhahasitānanāṃ navayauvanavatīṃ sapatramālāvyāghracarmanivasanāṃ īṣallambodarīṃ ūrddhvasaṃyatakeśīṃ adho aśeṣarogamāripadākrāntāṃ Amoghasiddhimukuṭīṃ ātmānaṃ jhaṭiti niṣpādya...."

Sādhanamālā. A—161-2, N—121, C—131.

The worshipper should conceive himself as Parṇaśavarī, who has green complexion, three faces, three eyes, and six arms ; whose right and left faces have blue and white colour respectively ; who carries in her three right hands the Vajra, Paraśu and the arrow, and in the three left, the bow, the cluster of leaves and the Tarjanīpāśa ; whose faces depict angry laugh, who is in fulness of youth, is decked in tiger-skin and the apron of leaves, has a slightly protruding belly, and hair tied up above ; who tramples under her feet various diseases and pestilences and bears the image of Amoghasiddhi on the crown. Thus meditating....."

The two images of Parṇaśavarī illustrated in Plate XXXIII,d and XXXIV,a have been discovered by Mr. N. K. Bhaṭṭaśālī, Curator of the Dacca Museum, and they hail from Parganna Vikrampur in the District of Dacca. These two images follow the Sādhana most accurately in all details ; the angry laugh has been correctly depicted in the three faces, and the belly slightly protrudes. To the right and left are two divinities, who are Hayagrīva, the Hindu god of Fever, and Sitalā, the Hindu goddess of Small-pox. They are represented in the images as flying in opposite directions to escape the wrath of Parṇaśavarī. The prostrate figures under the feet are the Diseases and Pestilences in human shape. The figure under the right leg, apparently, is a man attacked with small pox, as we can judge from the circular marks all over his body. The other figure under the left foot is probably attacked with some fatal disease. Both the images of Parṇaśavarī are decidedly very fine specimens of the Bengal School of Art.

6. Mahāmāyūrī.

Colour—green. Faces—three.
Arms—six. Āsana—Ardhaparyaṅka.

Mahāmāyūrī is another goddess of the Pañcarakṣā group and is assigned to Amoghasiddhi in the same way as other members of the group affiliate themselves to one or the other of the Dhyānī Buddhas. She is different in form when worshipped in the Pañcarakṣā Maṇḍala which will be described later. When she bears the image of Amoghasiddhi on the crown she is three-faced and six-armed. But she may have another form with one face, two arms and yellow complexion, in which case she will hold the tail of a peacock in the right hand and display the Varada Mudrā in the left. The three-faced and six-armed form of Mahāmāyūrī has been described in the Sādhanamālā as follows :—

"Mahāmāyūrīṃ haritavarṇāṃ trimukhāṃ ṣaḍbhujāṃ pratimukhaṃ trinetrāṃ kṛṣṇaśukladakṣiṇetaravadanāṃ ; dakṣiṇatrihasteṣu yathākramaṃ mayūrapicchabāṇavaradamudrāḥ ; tathā vāmatrihasteṣu ratnacchaṭācāpotsaṅgasthakalaśāḥ ; vicitrābharaṇāṃ, śṛṅgārarasāṃ, navayauvanāṃ, candrāsane candraprabhāvatīṃ, ardhaparyaṅkinīṃ Amoghasiddhimukuṭīṃ bhāvayet ātmānam."

Sādhanamālā. A—214, Na—17, C—171.

"The worshipper should realize himself as Mahāmāyūrī, who has green complexion, six arms, and three faces, each endowed with three eyes ; whose right and left faces respectively have blue and white colour ; who shows in her three right hands the tail of a peacock, the arrow and the Varada Mudrā, and similarly in the three left hands the jewel, the bow and the water-vessel on the lap ; who is decked in wonderful ornaments, displays the sentiment of amour, is youthful, has the seat and radiance of the moon, sits in the Ardhaparyaṅka attitude and bears the image of Amoghasiddhi on the crown."

7. Vajraśṛṅkhalā.

Colour—green. Faces—three.
Arms—eight. Āsana—Lalita.
Identification mark—chain.

Three Sādhanas in the Sādhanamālā are devoted to the worship of Vajraśṛṅkhalā. Her colour is green, and as she emanates from Amoghasiddhi she bears the image of that Dhyānī Buddha on the crown. "Śṛṅkhala" means a chain, and as the goddess carries the adamantine chain, she is called

Vajraśṛṅkhalā. The chain, therefore, is her characteristic sign and should be paid particular attention to, in identifying her images, if they ever come to light. One of the Dhyānas describes her form in the following manner :—

"Haritāṃ trimukhīṃ aṣṭabhujāṃ ; prathamamukhaṃ īṣaddhāsarasaṃ ; dakṣiṇaṃ kapilaṃ, kapilalocanaṃ ca ; vāmaṃ raktaṃ bhṛkuṭīdaṃṣṭrākarālaṃ ; dakṣiṇeṣu catuḥkareṣu abhaya-vajra-vajraśṛṅkhala-śaradharāṃ ; vāmacatuḥkaraiḥ rudhirapūrṇakapāla-tarjanī-pāśa-cāpadharāṃ ; lalitākṣepāsanasthāṃ, mārjjāracarmottarīyāṃ, Amoghasiddhibhūṣitorddhvapiṅgalakeśāṃ vicintya......

Vajraśṛṅkhalāsādhanaṃ."

Sādhanamālā. A—223, Na—3, C—177.

"The worshipper should realize himself as [Vajrasṛṅkhalā] of green complexion with three faces and eight arms ; whose first face is gently smiling, the right face is of brown colour with brown eyes, and the left is of red colour and appears terrible with contortions of the brows and bare fangs ; who shows in the four right hands the Abhaya pose, the Vajra, the Vajraśṛṅkhala and the arrow, and in the four left, the Kapāla full of blood, the Tarjanī, the noose and the bow ; who sits in the Lalita attitude, has the scarf of a cat's skin ; whose brown hair rises upwards and is decorated with the image of Amoghasiddhi. Thus meditating........"

Vajraśṛṅkhalā may have, according to the Sādhanas, another form with three faces and six arms in which case she carries the Vajra, the Vajraśṛṅkhala and the arrow in the three right hands ; and the Tarjanī, the noose and the bow in the three left hands. The illustration (Plate XXXIV,b) shows this form of the goddess as drawn by the native Citrakāras of Nepal.

(a) Parṇaśavarī
(Vikrampur, Dacca)

(b) Vajraśṛṅkhalā

(d) Jambhala
(Vikrampur, Dacca)

(c) Jambhala (Nepal)

(e) Jambhala
(Vikrampur, Dacca)

Plate XXXIV

CHAPTER IX.

EMANATIONS OF RATNASAMBHAVA.

I. GODS.

Ratnasambhava is a comparatively late incorporation into the Pantheon of the Northern Buddhists, and this is evident from the small number of deities that emanate from him. In the Sādhanamālā two male and two female divinities only are affiliated to this Dhyānī Buddha. It has already been pointed out that Jambhala and Vasudhārā were known long before the Dhyānī Buddhas were ushered into existence, and it appears therefore, that Jambhala has been made an emanation of Ratnasambhava at a very late period. Jambhala is connected with wealth and is said to distribute gems, jewels and riches to his devotees. Again, Ratnasambhava means 'born of jewels' and whom else might Jambhala, the god of wealth, call his sire than the Dhyānī Buddha born of jewels ? If one or two forms of Jambhala emanate from Ratnasambhava, it may reasonably be expected that at least one or two forms of his consort Vasudhārā, should also originate from the same source. In spite of all this the Buddhists were divided in their opinion as to the sire of Jambhala. The followers of the Akṣobhya cult held that he must have originated from Akṣobhya.

Mahāpratisarā, another of his emanations, belongs to the Pañcarakṣā group, and affiliates herself to Ratnasambhava in the same way as other members of the group affiliate themselves to one or the other of the five Dhyānī Buddhas. Curiously enough, we do not see a single god or goddess strictly and individually bearing an independent stamp of Ratnasambhava. The reason, we venture to think, is the very late incorporation of Ratnasambhava into the Pantheon as a Divine Buddha. He is distinguished from the other Dhyānī Buddhas by his yellow colour and the Varada Mudrā he displays in his right hand.

The male deities that emanate from Ratnasambhava are Jambhala and Ucchuṣma-Jambhala, the latter being regarded as a terrible form of Jambhala.

1. JAMBHALA.

Varieties—Single and yab-yum.

Several of Jambhala's forms are noticed in the Sādhanamālā, which states that the god may emanate either from Akṣobhya or from Ratnasambhava or from Vajrasattva or from a combination of the five Dhyānī Buddhas. The form that emanates from Akṣobhya has already been described. The characteristic features of Jambhala emanating from Ratnasambhava is that he carries the mongoose in his left hand and the citron in the right. The mongoose is supposed to be the receptacle of all gems and jewels and when Jambhala presses the two sides of the mongoose it vomits forth the riches. By noticing this mongoose in actual representations it is easy to recognize the possessor to be Jambhala. As an emanation of Ratnasambhava he may be represented alone or in the embrace of his Śakti in yab-yum. In the Sādhanamālā he is described as single in three Dhyānas only. When represented in yab-yum he sits on the moon under which is the double lotus of eight petals. He wears all sorts of ornaments, his complexion is golden yellow and he has a protruding belly. He carries the citron and the moongoose in the right and the left hand respectively and wears a garland of yellow lotus, and remains in yab-yum with Vasudhārā. The eight petals of the lotus seat are occupied by the eight Yakṣas, to wit, Maṇibhadra, Pūrṇabhadra, Dhanada, Vaiśravaṇa Kelimālī, Civikuṇḍalī, Sukhendra and Carendra. These attendant Yakṣas, are identical in all respects with the principal figure. The Yakṣas are all accompanied with a Śakti with whom they remain in yab-yum in the same way as Jambhala remains with Vasudhārā. The Yakṣiṇīs are eight in number and they are Citrakālī, Dattā, Sudattā, Āryā, Subhadrā, Guptā, Devī, and Sarasvatī. The Yakṣiṇīs are identical in form with Vasudhārā who is yellow in complexion, carries the ears of corn and shows the Varada Mudrā in her two hands.

When single, Jambhala is of golden complexion and carries the mongoose in the left hand and the citron in the right.* The illustration (Plate XXXIV,c) represents a stone image from Nepal which is in the possession of Paṇḍit Siddhiharṣa. Here the god is represented as sitting in the Lalita attitude. Two other specimens (Plate XXXIV,d-e) from Vikrampur in Eastern Bengal, depict the god in the same attitude ; and they are some of the finest products of the Bengal School of Art.

* Cf.—" Śrī-Jambhalaṃ pītavarṇaṃ dvibhujaṃ, dakṣiṇahaste vījapūrakadharaṃ vāmahastena ratnapravarṣamāṇa-nakulīdharaṃ. . . ."

Sādhanamālā. A—310.

2. Ucchuṣma Jambhala.

Āsana—Pratyālīḍha. Appearance—terrible. Identification mark—nude.
Arms—two. Vāhana—Kuvera.

One of the forms of Ucchuṣma Jambhala has already been discussed along with the other male emanations of Akṣobhya. Even when he emanates from Ratnasambhava his form is the same as has been described before. When we are on the subject of Ucchuṣma Jambhala, we should refer to a stone image of this god, that was unearthed during the excavations carried on at Sarnath, and which is now preserved in the Museum of Archaeology there. This unique image (Plate XXXV,a) has been described by Rai Bahadur Dayā Rām Sāhni in the Museum Catalogue under No. B (*e*) 1. In terms of the Sādhana the image should bear on its crown either the image of Akṣobhya or of Ratnasambhava, but neither of them is to be found. It is Amitābha who is there. We cannot, however, reject the identification on this ground only : for, dressed in celestial garments and ornaments, the Hindu God, Kuvera, lying flat on the ground, is pressed down by the two heavy legs of Ucchuṣma and vomits out all the jewels he had in his stomach. As a matter of fact we notice, even in the photograph, a stream of jewels flowing out of his mouth. Also in accordance with the Sādhanas, Ucchuṣma stands in the Pratyālīḍha attitude with his left leg stretched forward on the forehead of Kuvera while the right tramples upon his two legs. He has a terrible appearance with protruding belly, bare fangs and the ornaments of snakes. He holds the Kapāla full of blood, against his breast and looks eagerly towards it with his three eyes. The left hand, though broken, doubtless held the mongoose near his thigh, which must have vomitted forth the jewels when pressed by the god. We have no means to ascertain why the Dhyānī Buddha in this case is Amitābha and not Akṣobhya or Ratnasambhava. Should we explain this anomaly by holding that it is due to a mistake or whim of the sculptor ? Or that the proper Sādhana has not been recorded in the Sādhanamālā ? The latter proposition may be correct, for, in the sculpture we notice the headless yet graceful figure of Vasudhārā, not required by the Sādhanas at all. The existence of a separate cult of Amitābha may be responsible for putting in a figure of its supreme Buddha, where the figures either of Akṣobhya or Ratnasambhava might reasonably have been expected.

II. GODDESSES.

Now that we have done with the male emanations of Ratnasambhava, let us proceed to deal with the two goddesses emanating from this Dhyānī Buddha. Both of them are benign in character, and graceful in appearance, and like the Dhyānī Buddha himself have yellow complexion.

1. Mahāpratisarā.

Varieties— 1. Three-faced, ten-armed.
2. Four faced, eight-armed.

Mahāpratisarā is one and the first member of the Pañcarakṣā group. Her worship is widely prevalent amongst the Tāntric Buddhists,* and she is represented either singly or in a Maṇḍala in the company of four other Pañcarakṣā deities. She is generally yellow when worshipped independently and occasionally white when worshipped in the Maṇḍala of the five goddesses. She may be represented with four faces and eight arms, or with three faces and ten arms in accordance with the Sādhanas. But in actual representations she may have three faces and eight arms. The form with three faces and ten arms, is said to bear the image of Ratnasambhava on the crown. The other yellow form may also be assigned to this Dhyānī Buddha. The Sādhana describes the former in the following terms :—

Mahāpratisarā pītā trimukhī pratimukhaṃ† trinayanā daśabhujā kṛṣṇa-sitadakṣiṇetaravadanā dakṣiṇapañcabhujeṣu yathākramaṃ khaḍga-vajra-bāna‡-varada-hṛdayaśāyīhastacchatrāni tathā vāmapañcabhujeṣu cāpa-dhvaja-ratnacchaṭā§-paraśu-śaṅkhāḥ Ratnasambhava-mukuṭī kṛṣṇakañ-cukaraktottarīyā ca ardhaparyaṅka-lalitākṣepadivyābharaṇavastrabhūṣitā ceti."

Sādhanamālā. A—215, Na—18, C—171.

Mahāpratisarā has yellow complexion, three faces, each with three eyes, ten arms with the right and left faces having blue and white colour ; she carries in her five right hands the sword, the Vajra, the arrow, the Varada Mudrā, and the umbrella held against her breast, and the five left hands similarly

* It is perhaps for this reason, Mahāpratisarā was incorporated by the Tāntric Hindus in their Pantheon. In the annual worship of Durgā oblations are offered to Mahāpratisarā in the beginning and her Mantras are muttered.

† A read pītamukhaṃ.

‡ For -bāṇa A has -pāśa.

§ For -cchatā A reads -cchattrā.

(a) Ucchuṣma-Jambhala (Sārnāth)

(b) Mahāpratisarā (Dacca Museum)

(c) Mahāpratisarā (Dacca Sāhitya Pariṣat)

(d) Vasudhārā (Nepal)

Plate XXXV

hold the bow, the banner, the jewel, the Paraśu and the coneh ; she bears the image of Ratnasambhava on the crown, has a blue bodice and a red scarf, sits in the Ardhaparyaṅka or the Lalita attitude and wears celestial ornaments and garments."

The form with four faces and eight arms will be described hereafter under the head, Pañcarakṣā Maṇḍala. But there is another form which is worshipped independently, in which case she is almost identical with the preceding one in all respects expect that she is endowed with four faces and eight arms. The principal face is yellow, the right white, the left red, and the face behind blue. She carries in her four right hands the sword, the Cakra, the Triśula and the arrow, and in the four left the Paraśu, the bow, the noose and the Vajra.

Two photographs (Plate XXXV,b-c) represent this form of the goddess and these tally with the Sādhana in all other respects, but that instead of four they have only three faces.

2. Vasudhārā.

Colour—yellow. Symbols—*right* Varada pose. *left* ears of corn and vessel.

Vasudhārā is the consort of Jambhala and bears the image either of Akṣobhya or of Ratnasambhava on the crown. Several Sādhanas in the Sādhanamālā describe her form, which is always two-armed. As none of the Sādhanas mention the Āsana, she may be represented in any attitude standing or sitting. She is decently decked in ornaments and is invariably accompanied by her confidents. Her complexion is always yellow and she carries in her left hand, the ears of corn with the vessel that showers gems while the right hand exhibits the Varada Mudrā. The short Sādhana may be quoted as follows :—

" Pīta'vaṃ'kārapariṇataṃ dvibhujaikamukhīṃ pītāṃ navayauvanābharaṇavastravibhūṣitāṃ dhānyamañjarīnānāratnavarṣaghaṭavāmahastāṃ dakṣiṇena varadāṃ anekasakhī janaparivṛtāṃ visvapadmacandrāsanasthāṃ Ratnasambhavamukuṭinīṃ [dhyāyāt].

Vasudhārāsādhanaṃ."

Sādhanamālā, A—228—9, Na—2, C—181.

The worshipper should conceive himself as [Vasudhārā] who originates from the yellow germ syllable ' Vaṃ,' she is two-armed, one-faced, has yellow complexion, is in the fulness of youth and is decked in all ornaments and garments, carries in her left hand the ears of corn with the vessel showering gems, while the right exhibits the Varada Mudrā ; she is surrounded by her various companions, rests on the moon over the double lotus, and bears the image of Ratnasambhava on the crown. . . . "

Images of Vasudhārā are not generally to be met with in sculpture. She accompanies Ucchuṣma in the unique Sārnath image already referred to. The other image from Sārnath*, is mutilated beyond recognition. In both cases, however, she has been represented as standing.

Vasudhārā is sometimes represented as one-faced and six armed, and as sitting in the Lalita attitude. In the three right hands she exhibits the Namaskāra Mudrā, and the Varada Mudrā and the ears of corn. The first left hand has the book, the second the ears of corn, and the third on the lap carries the vessel containing jewels. Her hair rises upwards in the shape of a flame, she is beautifully decked in ornaments and displays a truly peaceful appearance. The image reproduced (Plate XXXV,d) represents this variety of the goddess and is a fine specimen of Newari art but shows a considerable influence of the Bengal School.

* Sarnath Catalogue Plate XV(*b*).

CHAPTER X.

EMANATIONS OF THE FIVE DHYĀNI BUDDHAS.

I. GODS.

Vajrasattva is not included in the group of five Dhyānī Buddhas. He appears to be a later addition. The emanations of the five Dhyānī Buddhas are said to bear the images of Vairocana, Amitābha, Akṣobhya, Ratnasambhava and Amoghasiddhi on the crown ; but when represented, they are either painted or carved on the aureole behind the heads of the emanated deities. The five Dhyānī Buddhas, as has already* been pointed out, are supposed to represent the five Skandhas and the essence of their emanations consists of a combination of all the five.

Besides several forms of Mañjuśrī and one form of Avalokiteśvara, two gods only are said to emanate from a combination of the five Dhyānī Buddhas. The first is Jambhala, (also regarded as an emanation of either, Akṣobhya, or Vajrasattva), and the second Mahākāla.

1. Jambhala.

Symbols—citron and mongoose.

Almost all his different forms mentioned in the Sādhanamālā have already been described under the emanations of Akṣobhya and Ratnasambhava ; the form emanating from Vajrasattva will be described later. Jambhala as an emanation of the five Dhyānī Buddhas is two-armed, carries the citron and the mongoose in his two hands and tramples upon two semi-human beings Śaṅkhamuṇḍa and Padmamuṇḍa apparently in the Ālīḍha attitude.

* Ante, p. 2.

2. Mahākāla.

Appearance—terrible.

Colour—blue. Āsana—Pratyālīḍha.

The reason why Mahākāla has been classified under the emanations of the five Dhyānī Buddhas is that one of the numerous Sādhanas for the worship of Mahākāla gives him the epithet of "Pañcabuddhakirīṭinam," that is "bearing the images of the five Dhyānī Buddhas on the crown." He may have one face with two, four, or six arms, or eight faces with sixteen arms, He is one of the many terrible deities described in the Sādhanamālā, with ornamemts of snakes, canine teeth, protruding belly and garments of tiger-skin. At least six Sādhanas describe the two-armed variety of Mahākāla. One Dhyāna from among them is quoted below :—

"Śrī-Mahākālabhaṭṭārakaṃ dvibhujaṃ ekamukhaṃ kṛṣṇavarṇaṃ trinayanaṃ mahājjvālaṃ kartrikapāladhāriṇaṃ dakṣiṇavāmabhujābhyāṃ muṇḍamālālaṅkṛtorddhvapiṅgalakeśopari pañcakapāladharaṃ daṃṣṭrābhīmabhayānakaṃ bhujaṅgābharaṇayajñopavītaṃ kharvarūpaṃ sravadrudhira mukhiṃ ātmānaṃ jhaṭiti niṣpādya...."

Sādhanamālā. A—223, C—246*.

The worshipper should conceive himself as Śrī Mahākāla Bhaṭṭāraka, who is two armed, one-faced, and of blue complexion ; who is three eyed, has fiery radiance, carries the Kartri and the Kapāla in the right and left hands bears the five skulls on the hair which is brown, and which rises upwards on the head, and is decorated with a row of [severed] heads ; who is terrible with awful fangs, is decked in ornaments of serpents and the sacred thread of a snake ; who is short and from whose mouth trickles forth blood. Thus quickly meditating...."

Images of Mahākāla abound in Nepal and are found in large numbers in Buddhist temples, monasteries and even in the streets. Sometimes only the head is represented. The image (Plate XXXVI,a) is the finest specimen of Mahākāla ever discovered belonging to Pandit Siddhiharṣa of Nepal. It is carved out from a block of fine black stone, so beautifully polished as to be mistaken for metal. Here the god tramples upon two human beings representing two dead bodies, as required by some of the Sādhanas assigned to him, wields the menacing Kartri in the right hand and the kapāla full of blood in the left.

(ii) When four-armed he resembles the two-armed variety, with the difference that the former variety carries the Kartri and the Kapāla in the first pair of hands and the sword and the Khaṭvāṅga in the second pair.

* Omitted in N.

(a) Mahākāla (Nepal)

(b) Vajratārā (Indian Museum)

(c) Prajñāpāramitā (Indian Museum)

(d) Vajratārā (Orissa)

Plate XXXVI

(iii) When six-armed he appears like the one previously described, with the difference that he carries in his three right hands, the Kartri, the ro ary and the Ḍamaru, and in the three left, the Kapāla, the Śūla, and the Vajrapāśa.

(iv) When sixteen-armed, he is eight-faced and represented in yab-yum in the embrace of his Śakti, and what is strange he is also four-legged. The Sādhana describes his form in the following terms :—

" Ātmānaṃ Bhagavantaṃ ṣoḍaśabhuja-Mahākālaṃ bhāvayet ; aṣṭavadanaṃ caturviṃśatinetraṃ catuṣcaraṇaṃ ṣoḍaṣabhujaṃ ; dakṣiṇakaraiḥ kartri-vajra-gajacarma-mudgara-triśūla-khaḍga-yamadaṇḍāh, vāmakaraiḥ raktapūrṇakapāla-gajacarma-ghaṇṭā-aṅkuśa-svetacāmara-ḍamaru-naraśiro dadhānaṃ, śeṣabhujābhyāṃ Prajñāliṅgitaṃ ; kharvakṛṣṇaṃ hāhāhīhīhehepūritamukhaṃ mahāraudraṃ trikāyātmyakaṃ pañca-Buddhamukuṭinaṃ naramuṇḍamālābharaṇaṃ bhayasyāpi bhayaṅkaraṃ "

Sādhanamālā, A—330—1, C—251.*

The worshipper should conceive himself as Mahākāla with sixteen arms and eight faces, twenty-four eyes, four legs, sixteen arms, who carries in his [seven] right hands the Kartri, the Vajra, the elephant-hide, the Mudgara, the Triśūla, the sword and the staff of Yama, and in the [seven] left hands the Kapāla full of blood, elephant-hide, the bell, the goad, the white chowrie, the Damaru and human head ; while the two remaining hands are engaged in embracing the Prajñā ; who is short and blue in complexion, utters laughing sounds such as, hā hā, hī hī, he he ; who is terribly fierce, is the essence of the Three Kāyas, bears the images of the five Dhyānī Buddhas on the crown, is decked in garlands of heads as ornaments, and who is more awe-inspiring than Awe itself."

The Sādhana further adds the information that Mahākāla should be surrounded by seven goddesses, three in the three cardinal points, (fourth being occupied by himself) and the other four in the four corners.

To the East is Mahāmāyā, wife of Maheśvara, who stands in the Ālīḍha attitude and rides a lion, who has four arms, out of which the two left hands carry the Kapāla and the Ḍamaru, and the Kartri and the Mudgara in the two right. She is blue in complexion, has dishevelled hair, three eyes and protruding teeth.

To the South is Yamadūtī, who is of blue complexion and has four arms. She carries in her two right hands the staff of lotus stalk and the Kartri, and in the two left the bowl of blood and the fly-whisk. She stands in Ālidha attitude, rides the buffalo and has dishevelled hair.

* Omitted in the Nepal ms.

To the West is Kāladūtī, who carries in her two left hands the Kapāla and the cow's head and in the two right the Mudgara and the Triśūla. She rides a horse and stands in the Ālīḍha attitude, has a red complexion and dishevelled hair.

All these deities are terrible in appearance with protruding teeth and ornaments made of serpents.

The four corners are occupied by the following goddesses. Kālikā in the S. E. corner is blue in complexion, has two arms carrying the Kapāla and the Kartri and stands on a corpse in Ālīḍha attitude. Carcikā in the S. W. corner has a red complexion, carries the Kartri and the Kapāla in her two hands and is similar to Kālikā in all others respects. Caṇḍeśvarī in the N. W. corner has a yellow complexion, rides a corpse and carries in her two hands the grass and the deer, and stands in the Ālīḍha attitude. Kuliśeśvarī in the N. E. corner has white complexion, carries the Vajra and the staff, rides a corpse and stands in the Ālīḍha attitude. These four deities are nude, and terrible with bare fangs, three eyes and dishevelled hair.

Surrounded by all these deities Mahākāla should be meditated upon as trampling upon Vajrabhairava in the form of a corpse.

Mahākāla is a ferocious god who is generally worshipped in the Tāntric rite of Māraṇa for the destruction of enemies. Mahākāla was also regarded as a terrible spirit, and was calculated to have inspired awe in the minds of those Buddhists, who were not reverential to their Gurus, and did not care much for the Three Jewels ; Mahākāla is supposed to eat these culprits raw, and the process of eating has been minutely detailed in almost all the Sādhanas. The Sādhanas generally states the following ślokas in order to show the terrible nature of Mahākāla :—

Acāryye yaḥ sadā dveṣī kupito Ratnatraye'pi yaḥ ।
Anekasattvavidhvaṃsī Mahākālena khādyate ॥
Cchedayet svāṅgamāṃsāni pivedrudhiradhārayā ।
Śirasi viniveśyaiva tilamātrañca kartayet ॥*

He who hates his preceptor, is adversely disposed to the Three Jewels, and destroys many animals is eaten up raw by Mahākāla.

He, [Mahākāla] cuts his flesh to pieces, drinks the blood, and [after] entering into his head breaks it into minute fragments."

* Sādhanamālā. A—323, C—246 (omitted in ms. N.)

II. GODDESSES.

Four female deities emanate from a combination of the five Dhyānī Buddhas. They are Vajratārā, Sitatārā, Prajñāpāramitā and Kurukullā. Excepting Sitatārā all other goddesses are widely worshipped. The Sādhanamālā shows unusual devotion to Vajratārā in as much as five long Sādhanas are assigned to her, and in all cases the same details of worship are recorded. Her worship is supposed to bring success in all Tāntric rites including the six cruel ones. One of the forms of Prajñāpāramitā and one of Kurukullā are said to bear the images of the five Dhyānī Buddhas on the crown.

1. Vajratārā.

Faces—four. Arms—eight. Colour—yellow. Āsana—Vajraparyaṅka.
Symbols—*right* Vajra, Pāśa, Śaṅkha and arrow ;
left Vajrāṅkuśa, Utpala, bow and Tarjani.

We know of at least three images of Vajratārā, one, in the Indian Museum discovered in the District of Bhagalpore, the second, in Orissa, described in N. N. Vasu's *Mayurbhanj Archæological Survey*, and the third in Nepal. The Indian Museum bronze of Vajratārā is in the form of a lotus and represents the complete Maṇḍala with all the attendant deities. It is constructed in such a way as to be opened or closed at will. The petals are eight in number and each has a deity figured on it. There are several Sādhanas describing the form of Vajratārā, who is said to bear on the crown the images either of the five Dhyānī Buddhas or four of them. The Dhyāna describing her form with the five Dhyānī Buddhas on the crown is as follows :—

" Mātṛmaṇḍalamadhyasthāṃ Tārādevīṃ vibhāvayet ı
Aṣṭabāhuṃ caturvaktrāṃ sarvālaṅkārabhūṣitāṃ ıı
Kanakavarṇanibhāṃ bhavyāṃ kumārīlakṣaṇojjvalāṃ ı
Pañca-Buddhamahāmukuṭīṃ vajrasūryyābhiṣekajāṃ ıı
Navayauvanalābaṇyāṃ calatkanakakuṇḍalāṃ ı
Viśvapadmasamāsīnāṃ raktaprabhāvibhūṣitāṃ ıı
Vajrapāśatathāśaṇkhasaccharodyatadakṣiṇāṃ ı
Vajrāṅkuśotpaladhanustarjanīvāmadhāriṇīṃ ı
Vajraparyaṅkayogena sādhayet bhuvanatrayaṃ ıı

Sādhanamālā. A—95, N—67, C—73—4.

The worshipper should conceive himself as [Vajra]-Tārā who is in the midst of the circle of the Eight Mothers, is eight armed, four-faced, and decked in all ornaments ; whose complexion is like the colour of gold, who is graceful, and resplendent with the auspicious marks of a virgin ; who bears the images of the five Dhyānī Buddhas on her great tiara, and is born of the offerings to the Vajra and the sun ; who is effulgent in her blooming youth, has the dangling ear-ornaments, sits on the double lotus, and sends out radiance of red colour ; who carries in her right hands the Vajra, the noose, the conch, and the quick arrow, and in the left the Vajrāṅkuśa, the Utpala, the bow and the Tarjanī. Thus conceiving her as sitting in the Vajraparyaṅka attitude [the worshipper] may gain the three worlds."

The Sādhana further goes on to describe the deities constituting the Maṇḍala. In the four cardinal points there should be four goddesses on the four petals of the lotus on which Vajratārā sits.—

Pūrveṇa Puṣpatārāṃ tu sitavarṇāṃ manoramāṃ ।
Oṃkārākṣaraniṣpannāṃ puṣpadāmakarākulāṃ ।
Dvibhujāṃ ekavaktrāñca sarvālaṅkārabhūṣitāṃ ॥

" On the East is Puṣpatārā, who is white and elegant in appearance, is born of the syllable ' Oṃ,' carries the garland of flowers, is two-armed, one-faced and is decked in all ornaments.

Dakṣiṇe Dhūpatārām tu kṛṣṇavarṇāṃ surūpiṇīṃ ।
Dhūpaśākhākaravyagrāṃ sarvālaṅkārabhūṣitāṃ ॥

On the South is Dhūpatārā, who is of blue colour, of elegant appearance, carries the Dhūpa (incense) stick and is decked in all ornaments.

" Paścime Dīpatārāñca dīpayaṣṭikarākulī ।
Pītavarṇāṃ mahābhūṣāṃ calatkanakakuṇḍalāṃ ॥ "

On the West is Dīpatārā, who carries the light stick in her hands, is of yellow complexion, profusely ornamented and has dangling ear-ornaments.

" Uttare Gandhatārāṃ tu gandhaśaṅkhakarākulāṃ ।
Raktavarṇanibhāṃ devīṃ bhāvayet garbhamaṇḍale ॥"

On the North is Gandhatārā, who carries in her hands the conch of scents, has a red complexion, and all these [goddesses] should be situated in the inner circle."

The Sādhana further says that the following Guardians of the Gates should also be meditated upon round the principal goddess, apparently not in the same circle with the four described above.

" Pūrvadvāre Vajrāṅkuśīṃ ekavaktrāṃ dvibhujāṃ vajrāṅkuśotpalahastāṃ vikṛtavadanāṃ kṛṣṇavarṇāṃ...."

In the Eastern Gate should be Vajrāṅkuśī, who is one-faced, two armed, carries the Vajrāṅkuśa and the Utpala, has a distorted face and blue colour.

" Dakṣiṇadvāre Vajrapāśī pītavarṇāṃ vikṛtānanāṃ ekavaktrāṃ dvibhujāṃ vajrapāśahastāṃ...."

In the Southern Gate is Vajrapāśī of yellow complexion, with one distorted face, and two arms carrying the adamantine noose.

" Pascimadvāre Vajrasphoṭīṃ raktavarṇāṃ ekavaktrāṃ dvibhujāṃ vikṛtavadanāṃ vajrasphoṭahastāṃ...."

In the Western Gate is Vajrasphoṭī, who has a red complexion, one distorted face, two arms, and clapping hands.

" Uttaradvāre Vajraghaṇṭāṃ śvetavarṇāṃ ekavaktrāṃ dvibhujāṃ vikṛtavadanāṃ vajraghaṇṭāhastāṃ...."

In the Northern Gate is Vajraghaṇṭā, who is white, one-faced, two-armed, has a distorted face and carries a bell surmounted by a Vajra."

All these goddesses stand in the Ālīḍha attitude, with the right leg stretched forward, on the seat of the sun. They have sun-like radiance, are surrounded with a fiery halo and are decked in ornaments of snakes. The upper region is occupied by Uṣṇiṣavijayā and the lower by Sumbhā.*

The reason why Vajratārā is surrounded by these goddesses is that each of these goddesses originates from each of the ten letters of the Mantra of Vajratārā, which is 'Oṃ Tāre tuttāre ture Svāhā', consisting of ten syllables. Each syllable brings forth a goddess, and these goddesses are said to be the embodiments of the Ten Pāramitās† of the Mahāyāna doctrine.

The following are some of the instances in which the Mantra of Vajratārā might be applied with success. A knot should be tied at the end of the cloth over which the Mantra has been recited seven times. If any man wearing this cloth goes even to the most inaccessible regions of the Vindhya mountains he will not be molested. Tigers, thieves, crocodiles, lions, snakes, elephants, baffaloes, bears, bulls and the like will fly away or even be destroyed at the mere recital of the name of the goddess. If one hundred and eight blue lotuses are offered into the fire with this Mantra any woman would be subdued. The feather of a crow over which this Mantra has been recited thirty-two times, if kept concealed within the house of an enemy, will destroy it mysteriously in course of a week. It is useless to multiply instances. In fact, in all matters Vajratārā is sure to ensure success to the worshipper and that is the reason why she is so popular among the Vajrayānists.

Among the three extant images of Vajratārā the one (Plate XXXVI,b) in Calcutta may be identified with this variety of Vajratārā. As the Dhyānī

* Cf. " Ūrddhve Uṣṇīṣvijayāṃ adhaḥ Sumbhāṃ Vibhāvayet."

† Cf. " Daśākṣarair-daśadevatyo daśapāramitāśrayaḥ."

Buddhas are not given she may, however, be regarded as an emanation of the four Dhyānī Buddhas also. The Orissa image belongs to the combination of four Dhyānī Buddhas, while the third also belongs to another variety of Vajratārā also emanating from four Dhyānī Buddhas.

2. PRAJÑĀPĀRAMITĀ.

Mudrā—Dharmacakra. Distinctive feature—Book on lotus on either side. Āsana—Vajraparyaṅka.

This variety of Prajñāpāramitā is identical in all respects with one of the forms that has been described previously under the emanations of Akṣobhya, except that here she exhibits the Dharmacakra Mudrā with her two hands and from under her left and right armpits rise two lotuses bearing the Prajñāpāramitā Scripture. She is of golden complexion and bears the images of the five Dhyānī Buddhas on the crown*. The form of Prajñāpāramitā described in Plate XXVIII,c, has only one lotus bearing the book in her left, but the Indian museum stone image (Plate XXXVI,c) with two lotuses on either side bearing the book, belongs most assuredly to this variety of Prajñāpāramitā.

3, MĀYĀJĀLAKRAMA KURUKULLĀ.

Āsana—Vajraparyaṅka. Arms—six. Colour—red.

The form of Kurukullā bearing the effigies of the five Dhyānī Buddhas on the crown is called Mayājālakrama-Kurukullā as the Sādhana is said to have been restored from the now lost Māyājāla Tantra by the Tāntric author† Kṛṣṇācārya. Several forms of Kurukullā have already been described under the female emanations of Amitābha. The six-armed variety only emanates from the combination of five Dhyānī Buddhas. In accordance with the

* The Dhyāna is quoted as follows :—

" Bhagavatī Prajñāpāramitā pītavarṇā dvibhujaikamukhī pañca-Tathāgatamakuṭī, vyākhyānamudrāvatī, viśvadalapadme candrāsanāsīnā, sarvālaṅkāravastravatī, vāmadakṣiṇapārśve utpalastha-Prajñāpāramitāpustakadhāriṇī."

Sādhanamālā. A—163-4, N—123, C—132.

† Cf. the Colophon—" Srīman Māyājālamahāyogatantrāt ṣoḍaśasāhasrikāt ākṛṣṭa-Kurukullā-sādhanaṃ samāptaṃ."

Sādhana she sits in the Vajraparyaṅka attitude, on the sun over the red lotus of eight petals. She has a red complexion, is clad in red garments, exhibits the Trailokyav jaya Mudrā in the first pair of hands, shows the Abhaya Mudrā and the sprout of a white Kunda flower in the second, and the rosāry and the Kamaṇḍalu in the third, bears the images of the five Dhyānī Buddhas on the crown,* and sits on the back of Taksaka. She has another form with six arms, which is not expressly called the Māyājāla Kurukullā, described in a separate Sādhana. According to this Sādhana, she exhibits the Trailokyavijaya Mudrā in the first pair of her hands, the Aṅkuśa and the red lotus in the second pair, and the full drawn bow charged with an arrow in the third.* We have not yet been able to find out images of any of the two varieties of Kurukullā mentioned above.

4. Sitatārā.

Colour—white. Arms—four. Symbol—Utpala.
Mudrā—Utpalamudrā in the first two hands and the Varada Mudrā in the third.

Sitatārā, as the name implies, is a Tārā of the white variety, with one face and four arms. She is accompanied by two goddesses, Mārīcī and Mahāmāyūrī. It may be remembered that Khadiravanī is also accompanied by Mārīcī and Ekajaṭā ; but the difference is that Khadiravanī is two-armed whereas Sitatārā is four-armed. The Dhyāna contained in the only Sādhana in the Sādhanamālā describes her form in the following terms :—

Tārābhagavatīṃ śuklāṃ trinetrāṃ caturbhujāṃ Pañca-Tathāgatamukuṭīṃ nānālaṅkārāṃ, bhujadvayena utpalamudrāṃ dadhanāṃ, dakṣiṇabhujena cintāmaṇiratnasaṃyuktavaradāṃ, sarvasattvānāṃ āśāṃ paripūrayantīṃ, vāmenotpalamañjarīṃ vibhrāṇāṃ dhyāyāt.

Tasya dakṣiṇapārśve Mārīcīṃ pītāṃ candrāsanāṃ nīlāṃbarāṃ dvibhujāṃ ; vāmena raktāśokapallavadharāṃ, dakṣiṇena sitacāmaradharāṃ ; raktakañcukābharaṇāṃ.

Vāmapārśve Mahāmāyūrīṃ priyaṅguśyāmāṃ dvibhujāṃ ; vāmena mayūrpicchadharāṃ, dakṣinena cāmaradharāṃ, evaṃ vicintya...."

Ṣādhanamāla. A—114, N—82, C—89.

* The Dhyāna may be quoted as follows :—

"....Vajraparyaṅkaniṣaṇṇāṃ,.....ṣaḍbhujām, savyāvasavyaprathamabhujābhyāṃ Trailokyavijayamudrādharāṃ, dvitīyadakṣiṇavāmakarābhyāṃ aṅkuśaraktotpaladharām, pariśiṣṭakaradvayena ākarṇapūritadhanuḥśarāṃ....pañca-Tathāgatamukuṭāṃ."

Sādhaṇamālā. A—207, N—115, C—162.

" The worshipper should meditate in himself the goddess [Sita]-Tārā, of white complexion with three eyes and four arms ; who bears the images of the five Dhyānī Buddhas on the crown, is decked in many ornaments, exhibits the Utpala Mudrā in the first pair of hands, displays the Varada Mudrā along with the Cintāmaṇi in the right, and carries the Utpala bud in the left, and fulfils the prayers of all beings.

To her right is Mārīcī, who is yellow in complexion, sits on the moon, is clad in blue garments, is two-armed, and carries the bough with red Aśoka flowers in the left hand and the *fly-whisk* in the right, and who wears red bodice and ornaments.

To her left is Mahāmāyūrī of green complexion like the Priyaṅgu fruit, who is two-armed and carries the tail of a peacock in the left hand and the *fly-whisk* in the right. Thus meditating...."

CHAPTER XI.

§ 1. EMANATION OF FOUR DHYĀNI BUDDHAS.

Vajratārā.

Vajratārā is the only emanation of a combination of four Dhyānī Buddhas, but she has another form emanating from five. Here also she is accompanied by the usual eight goddesses (Mothers), in the four cardinal points and in the four intermediate corners. While the upper regions is occupied by Uṣṇīṣavijayā, Sumbhā remains below. Here also the Mantra is the same and each syllable of the Mantra brings forth one of the surrounding deities. In essence she is the same as has been previously described and she performs very nearly the same functions, and is invoked in the same rites including the six cruel Tāntric ones.

Several Sādhanas describe two distinct forms of this goddess. In one she will be identical with the form described before under the emanations of the five Dhyānī Buddhas, with the difference that she should have the crest of the four Dhyānī Buddhas only instead of five. The Orissa image (Plate XXXVI,d) of Vajratārā belongs to this variety, although all the ten goddesses constituting the Maṇḍala are not represented. It has four companions only and these probably represent the four deities of the four cardinal points, Puṣpatārā, Dhūpatārā, Dīpatārā and Gandhatārā. The deity sitting below to the left of the principal goddess may be identified with Gandhatārā who is required by the Sādhana to hold the conch-shell full of scents ; for, this figure clearly shows the conch over the two hands held in the Samādhi Mudrā.

(ii) The second form differs a little from the above as the weapons are not the same, or in the same order either. She carries in her four left hands the Utpala, the bow, the Aṅkuśa, and the Tarjanīpāsā, and in the four right the Vajra, the arrow, the conch and the Varada pose.*

* Prof. Foucher has quoted the Dhyāna of this variety of Vajratārā in explaining and identifying the Indian Museum bronze (fig. 5) illustrated in Plate XXXVI,b of this book. *L'Iconographie Bouddhique*, II, p. 70 *et sqq.* I fail to understand, why the learned Professor chose this Dhyāna for quotation leaving the one with which the bronze accurately agrees. *Supra ch.* X.

One stone image (Plate XXXVII,a) of this second variety of Vajratārā has been discovered at the Sarasvatīsthān close to the Svayambhū Temple in Nepal. It represents the goddess in the Vajraparyaṅka attitude with a form and weapons identical with the one described above. Though the crest of the four Dhyānī Buddhas is not present, yet, as this form agrees in all details with the Vajratārā emanating from the combination of the four Dhyānī Buddhas, we may reasonably regard the identification as correct.

One of the Sādhanas of Vajratārā enumerates the four Divine Buddhas, and it is curious that Ratnasambhava is not one of them. This fact, again, points to his late incorporation into the brotherhood of the Divine Buddhas.

§ 2. EMANATIONS OF VAJRASATTVA.

That Vajrasattva is the latest incorporation into the brotherhood of the Divine Buddhas in amply borne out by the Sādhanamālā, in the whole of which only two deities are said to bear the image of Vajrasattva on the crown. One is a god and the other a goddess. It is not necessary, however, to repeat the description of Vajrasattva, who may be represented both singly and in yab-yum. He sits in the Vajraparyaṅka attitude, carries the Vajra in the right hand with palm upwards against the breast and the Ghaṇṭā in the left near the waist.

1. Jambhala.

Variety—yab-yam. Faces—three.
Arms—six. Attitude—Vajraparyaṅka.

Jambhala is the only male deity who is said to bear the image of Vajrasattva. The Sādhana describes his form with three faces, six arms and the image of Vajrasattva on the crown. From a study of the Sādhana we gather the following details about his form. He is white in complexion, and his two faces to the right and left of the principal one, are red and blue. He sits in the Vajraparyaṅka attitude and embraces Vasudhārā, his Svābhā Prajñā. With the two principal arms he embraces the Prajñā and remains in yab-yum ; he carries in his two right hands the mongoose and the jewel, and in the two left the citron and the sword. In all other respects he is identical with the form discussed under the emanations of Akṣobhya.

(a) Vajratārā (Nepal)

(b) Cūṇḍā (British Museum)

(c) Mahāpratisarā

(d) Mahāsāhasrapramardanī

Plate XXXVII

2. Cundā.

Colour—white. Arms—four.
Symbols—*first pair*—vessel ; *right* Varada Mudrā ; *left* book on lotus.

According to the Sādhanamāla, Cundā is the only feminine emanation of Vajrasattva, bearing the image of this Divine Buddha on the crown. Cundā is variously spelt as Cuṇḍā, Cundrā, and Cuṇḍrā, to whom three Sādhanas are assigned. One of the Sādhanas describes her form in the following words :—

" Ārya-Cundāṃ śaraccandrābhāṃ ekamukhāṃ caturbhujāṃ varada-dakṣiṇabhujāṃ pustakāṅkitapadmavāmabhujāṃ pātradhāriśeṣabhujadvayāṃ nānābharaṇavastravibhūṣitāṃ Vajrasattvamukuṭāṃ [dhyāyāt.]"

Sādhanamālā. A—142, Na—6, C—113.

" The worshipper should conceive himself as Ārya-Cundā, who is radiant as the autumn moon, is one-faced and four-armed ; who exhibits the Varada Mudrā in the right hand and carries the lotus bearing the book in the left, while the other two hands are engaged in holding the bowl ; who is decked in many ornaments and garments, and bears the image of Vajrasattva on the crown."

Professor Foucher has discovered perhaps the only extant image (Plate XXXVII,b) of Cundā which is the nearest approach to the Sādhana though it does not follow it accurately. The photograph has already been reproduced in his *l'Iconographie Bouddhique de l'Inde,* parte 1*. In this image, Cundā sits in the Paryaṅka attitude and carries in one of her right hands the rosary instead of showing the Varada Mudrā as required by the Sādhana. Over her head is a parasol and on the aureole are noticed two figures of Amitābha. Another Sādhana says that she should sits on an animal on the moon over lotus. Another form, not described in the Sādhanamālā, with sixteen arms is said to have been installed in the Cundāvarabhavana at Paṭṭikerā in Bengal. This has also been reproduced by Prof. Foucher.†

We cannot agree however with the identification of the Java figure given on Pl. XLIV and explained on p. 265-6 in the " Beginnings of Buddhist Art " as that of Cundā. The stone image does not follow the Sādhana in important details. We venture to suggest that the figure is a male one and we should search for its identification in the direction of Lokeśvara or Mañjuśrī.

* Op. cit. Part I. fig. 24.

† Op. cit. Part 1, fig. 25 is a stone image of Cundā with sixteen arms.

In the same way we cannot agree also with the identification of a bronze* offered by Dr. Coomaraswamy in J. R. A.S. 1909, as it does not follow the Sādhana in important details.

§ 3. THE PANCHARAKSA MANDALA.

The deities constituting the Pañcarakṣā Maṇḍala are called Mahāpañcarakṣā deities and are five in number, to wit, Mahāpratisarā, Mahāsāhasrapramardanī, Mahāmantrānusāriṇī, Mahāmāyūrī and Mahāsitavatī. They are said to affiliate themselves to the five Dhyānī Buddhas and their forms have already been described under the feminine emanations of the different Dhyānī Buddhas. When they are worshipped in the Maṇḍala, their forms differ to some extent, and we shall presently describe these forms.

The Mahāpañcarakṣā deities are very popular with the Mahāyāna Buddhists inasmuch as every Buddhist priest keeps a copy of the Pañcarakṣā manuscript, which is neatly written, sometimes in gold and silver and with illustrations. That their worship was much in vogue is evident from the fact that every Vihāra in Nepal possesses images of these deities either in stone or in bronze.† The miniatures that are reproduced with this have been taken from a manuscript of Pañcarakṣā which is now in the possession of an American Anthropologist, Dr. W. Y. Evans Wentz, Ph.D. (Oxford).

The reason why the Pañcarakṣā deities are so popular are enumerated in the Sādhana named in the Colophon as "Pañcarakṣāvidhānaṃ" in the Sādhanamālā. The five deities when worshipped grant long life; they protect kingdoms, villages, and meadows; and protect men from evil spirits, diseases, and famines, and from all possible dangers that may befall humanity.

Prof. Foucher has given‡ only a general idea about the Pañcarakṣā deities. The following is an attempt to describe them more elaborately from the

* Op. cit, 1909, p. 297, Pl. III, Fig. 1.

† In several of the Vihāras we made an attempt to photograph a series of bronzes but their inconvenient position did not allow us to do so with success.

‡ In his *Etude sur L'Iconographie Bouddhique de L'Inde*, II, p. 99 *et sqq*. Prof. Fucher has quoted two Dhyānas of Mahāsitavatī and Mahāsāhasrapramardanī, as emanations respectively of Amitābha and Vairocana. But it may be pointed out that the two forms, such as has been described there, are not worshipped in the Pañcarakṣā Maṇḍala.

Dhyānas given in the Sādhanamālā, and to give an idea as to their respective positions in the Maṇḍala. It may be pointed out that all the five goddesses excepting Mahāsāhasrapramardanī, are peaceful in appearance, and each of them is distinguished by the foliage of a tree under the shade of which she rests. Mahāsāhasrapramardanī, as will be seen from the description given below, is terrible and awe-inspiring with bare fangs, three eyes rolling in anger and the ornament of human bones and skulls.

In the middle should be Mahāpratisarā, who is all white in complexion, of twice eight years, has the Caitya on the crown and the moon as her seat. She resides in the orb of the sun and sits in the Vajraparyaṅka attitude. She has three eyes, eight arms, dangling ear-ornaments, necklace, Nūpura, golden armlets, girdle of gold and all other ornaments. She is four-faced ; the first face is white, right blue, left red and the fourth behind is yellow. She holds in her four left hands the Vajrapāśa, the Triśūla, the bow and the axe, and in the four right hands the Cakra the Vajra, the arrow and the sword. Over her head is the foliage of the Bodhi tree with various flowers and fruits* (Plate XXXVII,c).

To the East of Mahāpratisarā is Mahāsāhasrapramardanī, who has blue complexion, brown hair rising upwards in the shape of a flame, and is decked in garlands of skulls. Her faces look terrible with contortions of the brows and canine teeth ; her seat is the burning sun on which she sits in the Lalita attitude, and tramples upon the evil spirits, the Bhūtas and the Yakṣas. She has golden armlets, necklace, Nūpura and other ornaments, is four-faced and eight-armed. The first right hand shows the Varada Mudrā, and the other three carry the Vajra, the Aṅkuśa and the sword. The four left hands carry the Tarjanīpāśa, the axe the bow and the sixteen jewels on the lotus. Her principal face is blue, the right white, the left green and the fourth behind yellow. Over her head is the foliage of the Bo-tree† (Plate XXXVII,d).

* The text is as follows :—

" Mahāpratisarā gauravarṇā dviraṣṭavarṣākṛtī caityālaṇkṛtamūrdhā candrāsanasthā, suryyamaṇḍalālīḍhā vajraparyaṅkinī trinetrā, aṣṭabhujā, calat-kuṇḍalaśobhitā hāranūpura-bhūṣitā kanakakeyūramaṇḍitamekhalā sarvālaṅkāradhāriṇī. Tasyā Bhagavatyāḥ prathamamukhaṃ gauravarṇaṃ, dakṣiṇaṃ kṛṣṇaṃ pṛṣṭhe pītaṃ vāme raktaṃ. Dakṣiṇaprathamabhuje cakraṃ, dvitīye vajraṃ, tṛitīye śaraḥ, caturthe khaḍgaḥ ; vāmaprathamabhuje vajrapāśaḥ dvitīye triśūlaṃ, tṛtīye dhanuḥ, caturthe paraśuḥ ; Bodhivṛkṣopaśobhitā, nānāpuṣpaphalādyalaṅkṛtā."

Sādhanamālā, A—217—18.

† Compare Text—Tasyā Mahāpratisarāyāḥ pūrvasyāṃ diśi........Mahāsāhasrapramardanī Kṛṣṇavarṇā piṅgalorddhvakeśā narakapālālaṅkṛtā bhrūbhṛkuṭīdaṃṣṭrākarālavadanā......lalitākṣepena mahābhūtamahāyakṣamākramamāṇā......tasyā dakṣiṇaprathamabhuje varadavajraṃ, dvitīye aṅkuśaḥ tṛtīye śaraḥ caturthe khaḍgaḥ, vāmaprathamabhuje tarjanīpāśaḥ, dvitīye paraśuḥ, tṛtīye dhanuḥ, caturthe padmopari ṣoḍaśaratnaṃ........Vaṭavṛkṣopaśobhitā. *Ibid*, A—218.

To the right of Mahāpratisarā is Mahāmāyūrī who is yellow in complexion, rests on the orb of the sun and unlike others rides an animal. She is three-faced, three-eyed, and eight-armed ; she has jewels on the crown and wears all sorts of ornaments. The first right hand exhibits the Varada pose, the second the vessel of gems, the third Cakra, and the fourth the sword. The first left hand carries the fruit* on the bowl, the second the peacock's feather and the third the Ghaṇṭā surmounted by a Viśvavajra and the fourth the bejewelled banner. Her principal face is yellow, the right blue, and the left red. Over her head is the foliage of the Aśoka tree† (Plate XXXVIII,a).

To the West of the principal goddess Mahāpratisarā, is Mahāmantrānusāriṇī, who has white complexion, twelve arms, three faces each with three eyes, resides in the orb of the sun and wears the jewel on the crown. She is youthful and is decked in various ornaments. Her first pair of hands exhibits the Dharmacakra Mudrā, and the second the Samādhi Mudrā ; the remaining hands show the Varada and Abhaya poses, the Vajra and the arrow in the four right hands ; and carry the Tarjanīpāśa, the bow, the jewel, and the lotus on the vessel in the four left hands. The principal face is white, the right blue and the left red. Flowers are strewn on all sides of the goddess, and over her head is the foliage of the Śirīṣa tree‡ (Plate XXXVIII,b).

To the North of Mahāpratisarā is Mahāsitavatī who has green complexion, resides in the orb of the sun, has three eyes, three faces and six arms, bears the image of the Tathāgata [Amitābha] on the crown, wears celestial ornaments, and garments. Her first right hand displays the Abhaya pose, the second has the Vajra and the third arrow, while the first left carries the

* In two Mss. the expression is " pātropari bhikṣuḥ" meaning "the mendicant on the bowl," which I do not approve of. In the miniature the thing on the bowl seems to be a kind of fruit. It is, therefore, such a hazardous translation has been made.

† Compare Text—" Tato Mahāpratisarāyā dakṣiṇadigbhavane....Mahāmāyūrī pītavarṇā sūryyamaṇḍalālīḍhā sattvaparyaṅkinī. trimukhā....aṣṭabhujā......tasyā dakṣiṇaprathamabhuje varada[ṃ], dvitīye ratnaghaṭadharā, tṛtīye cakraṃ, caturthe khaḍgaḥ ; vāmaprathamabhuje pātropari bhikṣuḥ (?), dvitīye mayūrapicchaḥ, tṛtīye ghaṇṭopari viśvavajraṃ, caturthe ratnadhvajaṃ......Aśokavṛkṣopaśobhitā...."

Op. cit.—A—219.

‡ Compare Text—" Tasyā Pratisarāyā paścimadiśi......Mahāmantrānusāriṇīṃ bhāvayet, śuklavarṇāṃ dvādaśabhujāṃ trimukhāṃ....sphuratsūryyamaṇḍalālīḍhāṃ ......Śirīṣavṛkṣopaśobhitāṃ ; tasya prathamabhujābhyāṃ dharmacakramudrā, dvitīyabhujābhyāṃ samādhimudrā, tṛtīye varadaḥ, caturthe abhayaḥ, pañcame vajraṃ, ṣaṣṭhe śaraḥ ; tṛtīye tarjanīpāśaḥ, caturthe dhanuḥ, pañcame ratnacchaṭā, ṣaṣṭhe padmāṅkitakalasaḥ (*sic.* Kamalaḥ, which is absurd)...."

Op. cit, A—219.

(a) Mahāmāyūrī

(b) Mahāmantrānusāriṇī

(c) Mahāsītavatī

(d) Prasanna Tārā

Plate XXXVIII

noose with the Tarjanī, the second the bow and the third the bejewelled banner. Over her head is the foliage of the Campaka tree* (Plate XXXVIII,c).

The illustrations represent all the goddesses in the Vajraparyaṅka attitude except Mahāsāhasrapradanī, whose attitude is Lalita. They tally in all respects with the descriptions given in the Pancarakṣāvidhāna section of the Sādhanamālā, referred to before.

§ 4. THE TĀRĀS.†

I. ORDINARY.

Symbols—*right* Varada Mudrā ; *left* lotus.

To Professor Foucher we are indebted for the classification of the various Tārās in accordance with colour. Strictly speaking, only those should be designated as Tārās, to whom the Mantra, Oṃ Tāre tuttāre ture Svāhā, is assigned, and there are seven different variations of Tārā carrying the Utpala in the left hand and exhibiting the Varada Mudrā in the right. Out of these seven, two only bear the image of Amoghasiddhi on the crown and the others do not bear any image of a Dhyānī Buddha. It is, therefore, difficult to identify the representations of the latter especially in stone when no colour is present. So a special attention should be paid not only to the particular pose in which the Tārās sit, but also to their companions if present, in order to arrive at a correct identification. In this section attempt would be made to indicate the characteristic features of each of the seven varieties for correct identification.

* Compare Text—" Tato Mahāpratisarāyā uttarasyāṃ diśi....Mahāsitavatī, haritavarṇā sūryyamaṇḍalālīḍhā trimukhā trinetrā ṣaḍbhujā.... ; tasyā prathamabhuje abhayaḥ, dvitīye vajraṃ, tṛtīye śaraṃ ; vāmaprathamabhuje tarjanīpāśaḥ, dvitīye dhanuḥ, tṛtīye ratnadhvajaṃ......Campakavṛkṣopaśobhitā (*sic*-śobhitaṃ).

Ms. A—220.

† In the Sādhanamālā a very large number of goddesses has been designated as Tārās, some with the crest of the Dhyānī Buddhas and others without. In order to clearly distinguish between their forms it is necessary that they should be treated separately. I have classifisd them under two heads. The ordinary Tārās showing the Varada Mudrā in the right hand and carrying the Utpala or the lotus in the left ; while the extraordinary forms of Tārā will embrace all goddesses designated as Tārās in the Sādhanamālā.

(i) Green Tārā.

Amongst the green varieties of Tārā, Khadiravanī and Vaśyatārā have already been noticed under the feminine emanations of Amoghasiddhi. (*i*) Khadiravanī can be identified by the presence of Mārīcī and Ekajaṭā. (*ii*) Vaśyatārā has, as her characteristic feature, the European fashion of sitting (Bhadrāsana). It may be noticed, however, that she is described as single and is not accompanied by any other god or goddess. (*iii*) The characteristic features of Āryatārā are that she sits in the Ardhaparyaṅka attitude and like the aforementioned one, is entirely alone. (*iv*) Mahattarī Tārā (Plate XXXIX,a) may be distinguished by the Vajraparyaṅka attitude in which she sits and also by the fact of her being represented without any companion. (*v*) Varada Tārā sits in the Ārdhaparyaṅka like Āryatārā, but she can be easily recognized by the presence of four goddesses, Aśokakāntā Mārīcī, Mahāmāyūrī, Ekajaṭā and Jāṅgulī.

(ii) White Tārā.

Under this head two varieties may be noticed, one is Aṣṭamahābhaya Tārā and the other is Mṛtyuvañcana Tārā, also called Sitatārā or Vajratārā. (*i*) The distinguishing feature of Aṣṭamahābhaya Tārā is that she sits in the Ardhaparyaṅka attitude and is surrounded by the goddesses, originating from the ten syllables of the Tārā Mantra, identical with the principal figure in appearance. (*ii*) As regards Mṛtyuvañcana Tārā, the only distinctive feature of this goddess is that she bears a wheel on her breast. She is absolutely unattended and sits in the Vajraparyaṅka attitude.

II. EXTRAORDINARY TĀRĀS.

The seven different varieties of Ordinary Tārās carrying the Utpala in the left hand and showing the Varada Mudrā in the right have already been described. The other varieties of Tārā classified according to colour will now be dealt with. Their Mantra, however, is not necessarily the famous "Oṃ Tāre tuttāre ture Svāhā" for, in this section have been included all the female deities called in the Sādhanamālā by the name of Tārā.

(i) Green Tārā.

1. Durgottāriṇī Tārā. She has green complexion, lotus as her seat, and garments of white colour; she has four arms carrying in the first pair, the noose and the goad, and showing in the second the lotus and and Varada Mudrā.

2. Dhanada Tārā. She carries the book and the rosary in the first pair of hands, while the second pair carries objects similar to those held by Durgottāriṇī. She has an animal for her Vāhana and is accompanied by eight goddesses originating from the eight syllables of her Mantra, and bears the image of Amoghasiddhi on the crown.

3. Jāṅgulī. She emanates from Akṣobhya and may have three different colours, yellow, white and green. When green, she is four-armed and carries the Triśūla, the peacock's tail, and a snake, and exhibits the Abhaya Mudrā in the fourth.

4. Parṇaśavarī. When green, she emanates from Amoghasiddhi, and from Akṣobhya when yellow, and as such, both of her forms have already been described. She is generally three-faced and six-armed, but in rare cases may have four arms. The peculiarity of the green variety is that all the three faces are depicted as irritated but smiling (sakrodha-hasitānanām).

(ii) White Tārā.

1. Caturbhuja Sitatārā. As she bears the images of the five Dhyānī Budhas on the crown, her form has already been described. She has four arms which exhibit in the first pair, the Utpala Mudrā, and the rosary and the Varada pose in the second. She may be recognized by the presence of two goddesses, Mahāmāyūrī and Mārīcī.

2. Ṣaḍbhuja Sitatārā. As she bears the image of Amoghasiddhi on the crown, her form has already been described. She is three-faced and six-armed and has no companions.

3. Viśvamātā. She has been described in the Sādhanamālā as one-faced, with the white complexion of the moon, white garments and a white serpent as her Vāhana. She carries the white lotus in the left hand and exhibits the Abhaya pose in the right. She has not been described as bearing any image of her sire.

4. K u r u k u l l ā as an emanation of Amitābha of red colour generally assumes the red colour. But when she is two-armed, she has according to the Sādhanamālā, the white colour, and her form has already been described. She carries the rosary and the bowl of lotus, and her Vahana is an animal.

5. J ā ṅ g u l ī as an emanation of Akṣobhya ought to be of blue colour. But according to the Sādhanamālā she may have three colours, white, yellow or green. When white, she is one-faced and four-armed and plays on the Vīṇā in the first pair of hands, and shows the white serpent and the Abhaya pose in the second.

(iii) Yellow Tārā.

1. V a j r a t ā r ā. She is yellow, has four faces, eight arms bearing the images of four or five Dhyānī Buddhas on the crown. Both the forms of Vajratārā have been described previously. She is accompanied by ten goddesses when worshipped in the Maṇḍala.

2. J ā ṅ g u l ī. The yellow variety of Jāṅgulī has three faces and six arms, and bears the image of the Dhyānī Buddha Akṣobhya on the crown. This form has already been described.

3. P a r ṇ a ś a v a r ī. When yellow, Parṇaśavarī is an emanation of Akṣobhya, and has three faces and six arms, and a pleasant smile instead of the irritated expression in her faces. This form of Parṇaśavarī has also been described under the feminine emanations of Akṣobhya.

4. B h ṛ k u ṭ ī is yellow and emanates from Amitābha. She is one-faced and four-armed, shows the Varada Mudrā and the rosary in the two right hands and carries the Tridaṇḍī and the Kamaṇḍalu in the two left.

5. P r a s a n n a T ā r ā. She is also yellow and her form has not been described before as she is an independent goddess without the figure of any Dhyānī Buddha on the crown. The Mantra assigned to her, calls her by the epithets of Amṛtamukhī and Amṛtalocanā, and as a matter of fact, except the face on the top, all the seven faces are represented as having charmingly sweet appearance. She is unlike the other Tārās, benign and peaceful ; she is more like Vidyujjvālākarālī, a form of Ekajaṭā, than anybody else. The Dhyāna describes her form in the following terms :—

Hemavarṇāṃ mahāghorāṃ Tārādevīṃ maharddhikāṃ trinetrāṃ aṣṭavadanāṃ bhujaṣoḍaśabhūṣitāṃ ūrddhvapiṅgalakeśāṃ sārdraśatārdhamuṇḍamālākṛtahārāṃ jagattrāṇāṃ mahāvalāṃ pratyālīḍhapadopetāṃ hasantīṃ navayauvanāṃ vicitravastranepathyāṃ pradhānamukhaṃ pītaṃ, dakṣiṇaṃ dvitīyaṃ nīlaṃ, tritīyaṃ śyāmaṃ, caturthaṃ gaganaśyāmaṃ, vāmaṃ, kundasannibhaṃ, dvitīyam raktaṃ, tritīyaṃ gaganaśyāmaṃ, ūrddhvāsyaṃ dhūmravarṇābhaṃ mahāghoraṃ vikaṭotkaṭaṃ; dakṣiṇakareṣu khaṭvāṅga-utpala-śara-vajra-aṅkuśa-daṇḍa-kartri-abhayadharāṃ; vāmabhujeṣu sapāśatarjanī-kapāla-dhanuḥ-khaṭvāṅga-vajrapāśa-Brahmaśiraḥ-ratnakalasadharāṃ; viśvapadmacandrasthāṃ sūryyaprabhāvibhūṣitāṃ; vāmapādena Indraṃ, dakṣiṇapādena Upendraṃ, padadvayamadhye Rudraṃ Brahmāṇaṃ ca ākramya sthitāṃ, sarvamāravināśinīṃ bhāvayet yogī.

Prasannatārāsādhanaṃ."

Sādhanamālā, A—127-8, N—92, C—101.

"The worshipper should conceive himself as [Prasanna Tārā] who is of golden complexion, of terrible appearance, bestows prosperity, is three-eyed, eight-faced and sixteen-armed; whose brown hair rises upwards, whose bracelet is constituted of half a hundred heads wet with blood, who emanacipates the universe and is irresistible, stands in the Pratyālīḍha attitude, has smiling faces, is in fulness of youth; whose garments are of variegated colours; whose first face is yellow, the second to the right is blue, the third green, and the fourth blue like the sky; the face to the left is white like the Kunda flower, the second red, and the third blue like the sky; the face on the top is of the colour of smoke, terrible in appearance and is distorted and disfigured; in whose right hands are the Khaṭvāṅga, the Utpala, the arrow, the Vajra, the Aṅkuśa, the staff, the Kartri and the Abhaya pose, and in the left, the noose with the Tarjanī, the Kapāla, the bow, the Khaṭvāṅga, the Vajra, the noose, the head of Brahmā, and the vessel of gems; who stands on the moon over the double lotus, is radiant with the glow of the sun, tramples under her left foot Indra, under the right Upendra, and presses Rudra and Brahmā between the two, and who destroys all the Māras."

The accompanying sketch (Plate XXXVIII,d) shows how she is represented by the artists of Nepal in modern days, and it agrees with the description of the Sādhana in all important details.

(iv) Blue Tārā.

1. E k a j a ṭ ā. She may have several forms with the blue colour and bears the image of her sire Akṣobhya on the crown in all cases. All her forms have been described previously under the emanations of Dhyānī Buddha Akṣobhya including the terrible form which goes by the name of Vidyujjvālākarālī with blue colour, twelve faces and twenty-four arms.

2. M a h ā c ī n a T ā r ā. She also bears the image of Akṣobhya on the crown and has already been described under the feminine emanations of the Dhyānī Buddha. She gets the name of Mahācīna Tārā as she is believed to have come from Mahācīna, the place where she was originally worshipped.

She is the subject of the Mahācīnakrama-Tantra and has been incorporated wholly into the Hindu Tāntric Pantheon.

(v) RED TĀRĀ.

There are not many red Tārās in the Sādhanamālā and in fact K u r u-k u l l ā is the only one that belongs to the red variety. As she bears the image of red Amitābha on the crown, she gets also the red colour being one of his emanations, though her white forms are by no means rare. Kurukullā may also bear the image of the five Dhyānī Buddhas on the crown but the colour would be red in that case also. She will be white when two-armed, and red when four, six or eight-armed. Only when she is six-armed, she is regarded as an emanation of the five Dhyānī Buddhas. All her forms have also been described.

CHAPTER XII.

INDEPENDENT DEITIES.

I. GODS.

The deities discussed in this chapter are mentioned as Independent, and they do not, according to the Sādhanamālā, bear any image of the Dhyānī Buddhas on the crown. It is therefore impossible to classify them in the way as we have hitherto done*. The reason why the Sādhanamālā is silent about their sires is not known. Either these deities were foreign to Buddhism and incorporated later on, as in the cases of Gaṇapati and Sarasvatī, or it may be, that the compilers of the Sādhanamālā did not think it worth their while to mention the sires in all cases having already described many typical ones. But our ignorance does not allow us to find out the secret. Otherwise why should some of the deities with the same Mantra 'Oṃ Tāretuttāreture Svāhā' bear the image or images of the Dhyānī Buddhas, while others are without them. It is not proposed to deal here with the deities of whom identical parallels have already been discussed. But we will take up only those that are absolutely independent and have not been described previously. It may be remarked that the images and paintings of gods do not generally bear the images of their sires on the crown, and when the latter is not present, what does it matter if they are emanated or independent ? At least for the purpose of identification it has practically no value.

In the Sādhanamālā there are six male gods who could not be assigned to their sires. This number is increased by one if we include Paramāśva, another form of Hayagrīva without crest, who emanates from either Amitābha or Akṣobhya. Not knowing to whom Paramāśva may be assigned†, he is dealt with under the independent deities. If we add Nāmasaṅgīti from Dharmakoṣasaṃgraha of Amṛtānanda, the number rises to eight.

* We may, however, suggest a tentative classification in accordance with colour and assign the gods or goddesses to the five Dhyānī Buddhas with five different colours. Thus the deities with blue colour may be assigned to Akṣobhya, yellow to Ratnasambhava, white to Vairocana and so on.

† Paramāśva cannot be dealt under the emanations of Amitābha because of his red colour, as Hayagrīva when an emanation of Akśobhya even has the red colour.

1. Gaṇapati.

Colour—red. Arms—twelve. Vāhana—mouse.
Āsana—Dancing in Ardhaparyaṅka.

Only one Sādhana in the Sādhanamālā describes the form of Gaṇapati. He is twelve-armed and one-faced and rides his favourite Vāhana, the mouse. The Dhyāna describes him in the following terms :—

" Bhagavantaṃ Gaṇapatiṃ raktavarṇaṃ jaṭāmukuṭakirīṭinaṃ sarvābharaṇabhūṣitaṃ dvādaśabhujaṃ lambodaraikavadanaṃ arddhaparyaṅkatāṇḍavaṃ trinetraṃ api ekadantaṃ savyabhujeṣu kuṭhāra-śara-aṅkuśa-vajra-khaḍga-śūlañca ; vāmabhujeṣu mūṣala-cāpa-khaṭvāṅga-asṛkkapāla-śuṣkamāṃsakapāla-phaṭkañca raktapadme mūṣikoparisthitam dhyāyāt."

Sādhanamālā. A—328, C—249*

" The worshipper should conceive himself as god Gaṇapati of red complexion, wearing the crown of chignon, who is decked in all ornaments, has twelve arms, protruding belly and one face, stands in the Ardhaparyaṅka in a dancing attitude, is three-eyed, and has one tusk ; who carries in his right hands the Kuṭhāra, the arrow, the goad, the Vajra, the sword and the Śūla, and in the left hands the Mūṣala, the bow, the Khaṭvāṅga, the Kapāla of blood, the Kapāla of dried meat and the Phaṭka†; and who rides the mouse on the red lotus."

2. Bighnāntaka.

Āsana—Pratyālīḍha. Colour—blue.
Symbols—Tarjanīpāśa and Vajra.

Bighnāntaka is closely associated with three other gods, Padmāntaka, Yamāntaka and Prajñāntaka, who are generally represented as guardians of the gates in Maṇḍalas. Bighnāntaka is represented in various forms. The name is significant as the word " Bighna" or "obstacle" refers to the Hindu god, Gaṇeśa. Only one short Sādhana in the Sādhanamālā describes his form in the following terms :—

" Ātmānaṃ pratyālīḍhapadasthitaṃ ekamukhaṃ dvibhujaṃ nīlavarṇaṃ vāmakareṇa tarjanikāpāśam, dakṣiṇakareṇa udyatavajraṃ bhayānakaṃ, piṅgalorddhvakeśaṃ....viśvadalakamalopari sūryyasthaṃ bhāvayet.

Bighnāntakasādhanaṃ." Sādhanamālā. A—306, Na—45 C—235.

* Omitted in Ms. N.

† It is not clear, however, what this word ' Phaṭka' means. The broken tusk in one hand is almost compulsory for all images of Gaṇeśa. May the word here stand for the broken tusk ?

"The worshipper should conceive himself as [Bighnāntaka], who stands in the Pratyālīḍha attitude, is one faced, two-armed, has blue complexion, carries in his left hand the Tarjanīpāśa, and weilds the Vajra in the right ; is terrible in appearance, has brown hair rising upwards,...., whose seat is on the sun supported by the lotus."

This Sādhana is silent about the prostrate figure of Gaṇesa whom he tramples under his feet, thereby giving a significance to his name as already indicated. It may be pointed out here that the god Gaṇesa, whom the Hindus consider as the remover of all obstacles, is regarded as the most dangerous obstacle by the Buddhists. As to the origin of this god there runs a Nepālese legend* that at a certain time an Oḍiyāna Paṇḍit was performing certain Tāntric rites on the bank of the Bāghmatī river near Kāthmāṇḍu in order to obtain a particular Siddhi (perfection). Gaṇeśa, it is said, being strongly opposed to the idea, began throwing dangerous obstacles on the way of the performance of the rite. The Oḍiyāna Paṇḍit without seeing any succour invoked the god Bighnāntaka, the destroyer of all obstacles, and lo! Bighnāntaka instantly appeared in a terrible and fierce form, armed with many destructive weapons. He gave a hot chase to Gaṇesa who was, by this time, flying in terror, and in no time overcame the latter.

In the representation it may be seen how Bighnāntaka is pressing Gaṇeśa with his heavy legs, and the latter in order keep up the reputation of his godhead, exhibits the Abhaya pose even in the agony of pain. The form in which Bighnāntaka is said to have appeared before the Oḍiyāna Vajrācāryya has six arms. He carries in the two principal arms the Kartri and the Kapāla against the breast ; the rest carry the Ḍamaru and the goad in the right, and the Triśūla and the noose with the Tarjanī in the left (Plate **XXXIX**,b).

This image was bought from Nepal and is now deposited in the Museum of the Vaṅgīya Sāhitya Pariṣat at Calcutta.

3. Vajrahuṅkāra.

Appearance—terrible. Symbols—Vajra and Ghaṇṭā.
Mudrā—Vajrahuṅkāra. Arms—two.
Āsana—Pratyālīḍha. Vāhana— iva.

Only one short Sādhana in the Sādhanamāla describes the form of the god Vajrahuṅkāra, who is so-called because his two hands carrying the Vajra and the Ghaṇṭā exhibit the Vajrahuṅkāra Mudrā. The Sādhana says that the god originates from the sacred syllable 'Huṃ', which is irresistible like the

* The story has been recorded a little differently in the Dharmakoṣasaṃgraha, A. S. B. Ms. Fol. 106.

Fire of Destruction, is blue in clour and strongly radiant. The Sādhana adds further :—

" Tadutpannaṃ mahāraudraṃ Vajrahuṅkārasaṃjñakaṃ ı
Aṭṭahāsaṃ mahāraudraṃ kṣepayantaṃ tridhātukaṃ ıı
Ghaṇṭāvajraprayogena mudrābaddhakaradvayaṃ ı
Pratyālīḍhapadenaiva Bhairavākrāntabhīkaraṃ ıı"

Sādhanamālā. A—278, Na—31, C—216.

" The worshipper should conceive himself as the god of the name of Vajrahuṅkara, who originates from that syllable [Huṃ], who is terribly fierce in appearance, laughs horribly, is wrathful, and disturbs the three Worlds ; whose two hands carrying the Ghaṇṭā and the Vajra are locked in the Vajrahuṅkāra Mudrā ; who tramples upon Bhairava in the Pratyālīḍha attitude, and inspires awe."

It may be pointed out that though Vajradhara also displays the Vajrahuṅkāra Mudrā and carries the Ghaṇṭā and the Vajra exactly in the same way as Vajrahuṅkāra does, there are too many differences between their forms. Vajradhara sits in the Vajraparyaṅka attitude on a lotus and has a peaceful and a graceful appearance. But Vajrahuṅkāra stands in the Pratyālīḍha attitude, tramples upon Bhairava, a form of the Hindu god, Śiva, and has a terrible appearance. No connection can, however, be established between the two.

4. Bhūtaḍāmara.

Colour—black as collyrium. Appearance—terrible.
Arms—four. Symbols—Vajra and Tarjanī.
Mudrā—Bhūtaḍāmara Mudrā.

Three Sādhanas in the Sādhanamālā describe the form of Bhūtaḍāmara, who is terrible and awe-inspiring with ornaments of snake, canine teeth, and garlands of skulls. The Dhyāna runs as follows :—

" Ātmānaṃ paśyet raudraṃ ca jvālāmālākulaprabhaṃ ı
Caturbhujaṃ mahākrodhaṃ bhinnāñjanasamaprabhaṃ ıı
Dakṣiṇe vajramullālya tarjayan vāmapāṇinā ı
Daṃṣṭrākarālavadanaṃ nāgāṣṭakavibhūṣitaṃ ıı
.. ..
Kapālamālāmukuṭaṃ trailokyaṃ api nāśanaṃ ı
Aṭṭahāsaṃ mahānādaṃ trailokyādhiṣṭhitaṃ prabhuṃ ıı
Pratyālīḍhasusaṃsthānaṃ ādityakoṭitejasaṃ ı
Aparājitapadākrāntaṃ mudrābandhena tiṣṭhati ıı

Bhūtaḍāmarasādhanaṃ." Sādhanamālā. A—285, C—221, Na—91.

(a) Mahāttarī Tārā (Nepal)

(b) Bighnāntaka (Baṅgīya Sāhitya Pariṣat)

(c) Trailokyavijaya (Bodh-Gayā)

(d) Paramāśva

Plate XXXIX

The worshipper should conceive himself as [Bhūtaḍāmara] who is wrathful in appearance, round whose person radiate fiery flames, who is four-armed, terribly angry, and is resplendent like a broken lump of collyrium, weilds the Vajra in the right hand and shows the Tarjanī in a threatening attitude in the left ; whose face appears terrible with bare fangs ; who is decked in ornaments of eight serpents ;......has the garland of skulls on the crown, is capable of destroying the three Worlds, laughs horribly, trumpets loudly and is the lord of the three Worlds ; who stands firmly in the Pratyālīḍha attitude, is resplendent like myriads of suns, and tramples under his feet, the god, Aparājita and exhibits (in his two other hands) the (Ḍāmara) Mudrā.

So from the Dhyāna it appears that the god in his two principal hands exhibits the Bhūtaḍāmara or the Ḍāmara Mudrā, while the other two carry the menacing Vajra in the right and exhibits the Tarjanī in the left. The description of this Mudrā appears in the same Sādhana.*

5. VAJRAJVĀLĀNALĀRKA.

Colour—blue. Faces—four.
Arms—eight. Āsana—Ālīḍha.
Vāhana—Viṣṇu and his wife.

Only one Sādhana in the Sādhanamālā describes his form. He is four-faced, eight-armed, stands in the Ālīḍha attitude, and tramples upon Viṣṇu, who is accompanied by his wife. He has blue complexion and presents a terrible appearance. The Dhyāna describes him in the following terms :—

" Vajrajvālānalārkaṃ nīlavarṇaṃ jvālāmālākulaprabhaṃ caturmukhaṃ aṣṭabhujaṃ śṛṅgāra-vīra-bībhatsa-karuṇānvitacaturmukhaṃ, caturbhir-dakṣiṇakarair-vajra-khaḍga-cakra-bāṇadharaṃ caturvāmakarair-ghaṇṭā-cāpa-pāśa-khaṭvāṅgāsaktavicitrapatākādharaṃ jvaladanalakapilaśikhākalāpaṃ atibhīṣaṇamahāhivalayakaṅkana-kaṭisūtranūpura-kaṇṭhikā-kuṇḍala-mukuṭābharaṇaṃ Mahāmāyācakravaraṇacaturaṃ sapatnīkaṃ Viṣṇuṃ ālīḍhapadena ākramya avasthitaṃ bhāvayet."

Sādhanamālā. A—342, Na—33, C—217.

" The worshipper should conceive himself as Vajrajvālānalārka of blue complexion, round whose person radiate fiery flames, who is four-faced and eight-armed ; whose four faces display the sentiments of amour, heroism, disgust and compassion ; who carries in his four right hands the Vajra, the sword, the Cakra and the arrow, and in the four left the Ghaṇṭā, the bow,

* The description of the Mudrā is given in the following verse in the Sādhanamālā—
"Anāmikādvayaṃveṣṭya tarjanīdvayaṃ kuñcayet ।
Kaniṣṭhāṃ madhyamāñcaiva jyeṣṭhāṅguṣṭhena cākramet ॥"

noose, and the Khaṭvāṅga surmounted by the banner of variegated colours ; whose brown hair resembles a burning flame ; who is decked in ornaments of bracelet, armlet, girdle, nūpura, torque, earing and tiara consisting of the [eight] great lords of frightful serpents ; who stands in the Ālīḍha attitude and tramples upon Viṣṇu with his consort who are expert in choosing the discus of Mahāmāyā."*

6. TRAILOKYAVIJAYA.

Colour—blue.	Faces—four.
Arms—eight.	Āsana—Pratyālīḍha.

Vāhana—Gaurī and Siva.

Trailokyavijaya has also the blue colour, is terrible in appearance, and inspires awe. Two images of this divinity have been noticed by Prof. Foucher ; one hails from Java,† and the other is preserved in the monastery of the Hindu Mohānta at Bodh Gaya (Plate XXXIX,c)‡. The Dhyāna describes his form in the following words :—

" Trailokyavijaya-Bhaṭṭārakaṃ nīlaṃ caturmukhaṃ aṣṭabhujaṃ ; prathamamukhaṃ krodhaśṛṅgāraṃ, dakṣiṇaṃ raudraṃ, vāmaṃ bībhatsaṃ, pṛṣṭhaṃ vīrarasaṃ ; dvābhyāṃ ghaṇṭāvajrānvitahastābhyāṃ hṛdi vajrahuṅkāramudrādharaṃ ; dakṣiṇatrikaraiḥ khaṭvāṅgāṅkuśabāṇadharaṃ, vāmatrikaraiḥ cāpapāśavajradharaṃ ; pratyālīḍhena vāmapādākrānta-Maheśvaramastakaṃ dakṣiṇapādāvaṣṭabdha-Gaurīstanayugalaṃ ; Buddhasragdāmamālādivicitrāmbarābharaṇadhāriṇaṃ ātmānaṃ vicintya...."

Sādhanamālā. A—341, Na—32—33, C—217.

" The worshipper should realize himself as Trailokyavijaya Bhaṭṭāraka of blue complexion, four-faced and eight-armed ; the first face displays the sentiment of wrathful passion, the right displays rage, the left disgust, and the face behind the sentiment of heroism ; who exhibits the Vajrahuṅkāra Mudrā with the two hands bearing the Ghaṇṭā and the Vajra against the breast ; and carries in his three right hands the Khaṭvāṅga, the goad, and the arrow, and in the three left, the bow, the noose and the Vajra ; who, standing

* The expression "Mahāmāyācakravaraṇacaturaṃ" seems to establish a connection between this god and Mahāmāyā.

† *Beginnings of Buddhist Art*, pl. XIII, 2. See also the masterly refutation of Dr. Pleyte's identification by the author on p. 268, which is simply enjoyable.

‡ The photograph representing Trailokyavijaya has been taken from M. Foucher's *Etude sur L'Iconographie Bouddhique de L'Inde*, parte 2. It may be noticed that the two prostrate figures of Maheśvara and Gaurī are in yab-yum.

in the Pratyālīḍha attitude, tramples upon the head of Maheśvara with his left leg, while the right presses upon the bosom of Gaurī ; who wears garments of variegated colours, and many ornaments and garlands pertaining to (the respective) Buddhas. Thus meditating...."

7. Paramaśva.

Faces—four. Arms—eight.
Legs—four. Vāhana—four gods and four goddesses.

We have already said that Paramāśva is another form of Hayagrīva, as the word "aśva" in Paramāśva indicates. In the Sādhana it is said that he should have four faces, but in reality he has seven faces, for one of his faces, is said to be Brahmamukha, or the face of Brahmā, who is credited with four faces. The other peculiar feature of this god is that he has four legs and each leg tramples upon two deities. The Dhyāna contained in the Sādhanamālā is quoted below :—

"Paramāśvaṃ raktaṃ caturmukhaṃ aṣṭabhujaṃ catuścaraṇaṃ ; prathamamukhaṃ krodhaśṛṅgāraṃ trilocanaṃ, dakṣiṇaṃ raudraṃ, vāmaṃ Brahmamukhaṃ, mūrdhni lalitoddhūlitoṣṭhaṃ haritāśvamukhaṃ ; ekena dakṣiṇatripatākādharakareṇa viśvavajrasahitenottiṣṭhābhinayaṃ kurvantaṃ ; ekena vāmakheṭakahastena viśvapadmaṃ dhārayantaṃ ; punardakṣiṇatripatākākareṇa uttiṣṭhābhinayaṃ kurvantaṃ ; punarvāmakareṇa śaktim dhārayantaṃ ; punardakṣiṇakarābhyāṃ khaḍgam bāṇañca, avaśiṣṭavāmakarābhyāṃ daṇḍaṃ cāpañca dhārayantaṃ. Pratyālīḍhena dakṣiṇapādaikena Indraṇīṃ Śriyañca ākramya sthitaṃ, dvitīyadakṣiṇacaraṇena Ratiṃ Prītiñca, vāmaprathamapādena Indraṃ Madhukarañca, vāmadvitīyapādena Jayakaraṃ Vasantañca, ityātmānaṃ dhyāyāt....

Iti Paramāśvasādhanaṃ."

Sādhanamālā, A—280, Na—32. C—217-18.

"The worshipper should meditate on himself as Paramāśva, who has red complexion, is four-faced, eight-armed and four-legged. The first face with three eyes displays angry passion, the second depicts wrath, the third is the face of Brahmā, and the fourth on the top is green, distorted like a horse with its lower lip beautifully protruding. He weilds the double Vajra, in one of his right hands with three fingers erect (Tripatākā) and in one of his left hands carries the staff with the double lotus. Another right hand, with three fingers erect, is raised upwards, and the other left carries the Śakti (dart). The remaining two right hands carry the Khaḍga and the arrow, and the remaining left carry the staff and the bow. He stands in the Pratyālīḍha attitude, and tramples with one of the right legs upon Indrāṇī and Śrī, and with the second Rati and Prīti ; with one of the left legs Indra and Madhukara, and with the other left Jayakara and Vasanta."

Paramāśva is illustrated in the accompanying drawing (Plate XXXIX,d) prepared by a native Citrakāra of Nepāl. Though it does not correspond to all the details of the Sādhana still it is important as showing many minor details without which the Sādhana becomes practically unintelligible.

8. Nāmasaṅgīti.

Āsana—Vajraparyaṅka. Arms—twelve. Colour—white.

Mudrās—two Abhayas, Añjali, Kṣepaṇa and Samādhi and two Tarpaṇas.

Symbols—*right* sword on double lotus ; *left* Khaṭvāṅga surmounted by a Vajra.

Paṇḍit Amṛtānanda's Dharmakoṣasaṃgraha gives the description of a very interesting god, who goes by the name of Nāmasaṅgīti, and thus enables us to identify his images which are scattered about in Nepal in large numbers. He should be distinguished from the Nāmasaṅgīti Mañjuśrī who has been described before,* as the former seems to us to be the Deification of the Nāmasaṅgīti literature in exactly the same way as Prajñāpāramitā is regarded as a goddess. Paṇḍit Amṛtānanda characterises him as a Buddha, but from the description and the illustration given it would appear that he cannot be a Buddha but a Bodhisattva, for among other things we cannot expect to find the magical instrument, the Khaṭvāṅga as also the destructive weapon like the sword in the hands of any Buddha. As there is no mention of the crest in the Dhyāna he is dealt with as Independent. Images of Nāmasaṅgīti are to be found in large numbers in Nepal either in stone (Pl. XL,a)† or in bronze (Plate XL,b), and he is also extremely popular in Tibet. Getty‡ erroneously designates this divinity as a " Dogmatic Form of Avalokiteśvara" and erroneous also are the names given by her of the series of the Mudrās

* Supra p. 23.

† Some of the arms in the stone image are broken ; the image hails from the Sarasvatīsthān in Nepal. The bronze is in the collection of Paṇḍit Siddhiharṣa.

‡ *The Gods of Northern Buddhism*, p. 63.

(a) Nāmasaṅgīti (Nepal)

(b) Nāmasaṅgīti (Nepal)

(c) Ārya-Sarasvatī

(d) Vajraśāradā

(e) Vajraśāradā (Nālandā)

Plate XL

that are exhibited by the god. The Dhyāna as given in the Dharmakoṣa-saṃgraha is quoted as follows :—

" Nāmasaṅgītināma [Bodhisattvaḥ].*

Ekavaktraḥ śvetavarṇaḥ dhyānanayanaḥ smerānanaḥ jaṭāmukuṭadharaḥ nānālaṅkārālaṅkṛtaḥ ṣaṇmudrālaṅkṛtaḥ dvādaśabhujaḥ prathamābhyāṃ savya-dakṣābhyāṃ hṛdayapradeśe abhyamudrādvayaṃ, dvāyābhyāṃ mukuṭopari kṛtāñjalimudrāṃ, dakṣatṛtīyena viśvavajropari khaḍgaṃ, savyavāmacaturthā-bhyāṃ tarpaṇamudrādvayaṃ, savyavāma-pañcamābhyāṃ pātrasthāṃṛtakṣe-paṇamudrāṃ, ṣaṣṭhasavyavāmābhyāṃ sapātradhyānamudrāṃ vāmatṛtīyena savajrakhaṭvāṅgaṃ dadhānaḥ, kamalopari vajrāsanaḥ."

Dharmakoṣasaṃgraha (A.S.B. Ms.) : Fol. 91.

The [Bodhisattva] Nāmasaṅgīti.

"He is one-faced, white in colour, has eyes (half-closed) in meditation, smiling countenance, the crown of chignon and various ornaments, is decked in the six auspicious ornaments, and twelve-armed. He exhibits in the first pair of right and left hands the two Abhaya Mudrās against the breast, and in the second pair the Añjali (clasped hand) Mudrā over the crown. The third right hand carries the sword on the double lotus. The fourth pair exhibits the Tarpana Mudrās, the fifth pair shows the Mudrā of sprinkling nectar from the vessel (Kṣepana) and the sixth pair exhibits the Samādhi Mudrā on which is the vessel (of nectar) ; the third left hand carries Khaṭvāṅga surmounted by the Vajra ; and he sits in the meditative pose on the lotus."

The image reproduced by Getty† has lost the sword on the double lotus and the Khaṭvāṅga surmounted by the Vajra‡ carried in the third pair of hands by Nāmasaṅgīti.

II GODDESSES.

The feminine deities that are not directly or indirectly expressed in the Sādhanamālā to be the emanations of any Dhyānī Buddha or a combination of four or five of them, are four§ in number, and if we include the three deities mentioned in the Dharmakoṣasaṃgraha of Amṛtānanda, the number would be increased to seven. A tentative classification may also be suggested in

* The A. S. B. and Nepal Mss. both read " Buddhaḥ."

† Getty and Deniker's *The God of Northern Buddhism*, Plate XX bearing the label " Dogmatic form of Avalokiteśvara."

‡ I have seen in some of the paintings of Nāmasaṅgīti, the Book on lotus instead of the Khaṭvāṅga topped by a Vajra, in one of the hands of the third pair, which carries in that case the sword and book on lotuses—the two symbols of Mañjuśrī. It is therefore not unreasonable to suppose the two to be of a similar nature. We may even go so far as to call Nāmasaṅgīti, a variety of Mañjuśrī.

§ Prasanna Tārā, as an independent goddess, has been described under section 4 : Chapter XI. If she is included the number is five.

these cases according to the colour of the Dhyānī Buddhas. But in view of the insufficiency of materials, it is not proper to have recourse to such a classification. To illustrate the statement let us take up a concrete example. We know Jāṅgulī is an emanation of Akṣobhya, and she is credited in the Sādhanamālā with three different colours, except the blue one, the colour of Akṣobhya. Supposing for argument's sake the crest of the Dhyānī Buddha had not been mentioned in the Sādhanamālā in this case, should we not be misled by assigning to three different Dhyānī Buddhas (excepting her own sire Akṣobhya), the three varieties of Jāṅgulī ?

1. Sarasvatī.*

Sarasvatī is the name of an ancient river now dried up in the sands of Rajputānā, and on the banks of this river the Vedic Aryans originally settled after their migration to India. As the banks of the river were occupied by the Vedic Aryans who composed many hymns, and were the scene of many sacrifices, the river was, later on, inthe Paurāṇic age, deified as the goddess of Learning. The Buddhists borrowed this Hindu goddess, incorporated her bodily into their Pantheon in the Tāntric age, when she was equally popular amongst the Hindus as well as the Buddhists,—and modified her form in various ways. The Buddhist Sarasvatī may have one face with two arms, or three faces with six arms. When two-armed, she has four different variations. As her worship is widely prevalent among the Buddhists owing to the belief that like Mañjuśrī and Prajñāpāramitā, she confers wisdom, learning, intelligence, memory, etc., a comparatively large number of Sādhanas are assigned to her in the Sādhanamālā.

(i) Mahāsarasvatī.

Symbols—*right* Varada Mudrā ; *left* lotus. Colour—white.

She has white complexion and shows the Varada pose in the right hand and carries the white lotus in the left. The Dhyāna describes her form in the following terms :—

" Bhagavatīṃ Mahāsarasvatīṃ anuvicintayet ; śaradindukarākārāṃ sitakamlopari candramaṇḍalasthāṃ ; dakṣiṇakareṇa varadāṃ, vāmena sanālasitasarojadharāṃ smeramukhīṃ atikaruṇāmayāṃ śvetacandanakusumavasanadharāṃ muktāhāropaśobhitahṛdayāṃ nānāratnālaṅkāravatīṃ dvādaśavarṣākṛtīṃ muditakucamukuladanturorastaṭīṃ sphuradanantagabhastivyūhāvabhāsitalokatrayāṃ. . . . "

Sādhanamālā. A—172, C—128, C—140.

* The Java image illustrated in Fig. 199, p. 264 and identified as " Saraswatī enthroned " in Vincent A. Smith's monumental work, *A History of Fine Arts in India and Ceylon*, is in reality an image of Jambhala, for, it shows clearly the mongoose in the left hand.

"The worshipper should concieve himself as goddess Mahāsarasvatī, who is resplendent like the autumn moon, rests on the moon over the white lotus, shows the Varada Mudrā in her right hand, and carries in the left the white lotus with a stalk ; who has a smiling countenance, is extremely compassionate, wears garments decorated with white sandal flowers ; whose breast is decorated with the pearl-necklace, who is decked in many ornaments, appears as a girl of twelve years, whose chest is uneven with half-developed breasts like flower-buds ; and who illumines the three worlds with the immeasurable light that radiates from her body."

This is the general appearance of Sarasvatī, and all the other varieties unless otherwise stated, are identical in appearance with the one just described. The distinctive feature of this goddess Mahāsarasvati is that she shows like the ordinary Tārās the Varada Mudrā in the right hand and carries the lotus in the left, (Plate XL,c)* and is accompanied by four deities identical in form around her. Prajñā is in her front, Medhā to her right, Smṛti in the left, and Mati in the West.† These four divinities may also accompany other varieties of Sarasvatī. As the Sādhana is silent about the particular Āsana, she may be represented in any attitude, sitting or standing.

(ii) Vajravīṇā Sarasvatī.

Colour—white. **Symbol—Vīṇā.**

Vajravīṇā Sarasvatī, like Mahāsarasvatī, is also white in complexion, peaceful and benign in appearance. She is also two-armed, but the distinguishing feature in this case is that she carries in her two hands the Vīṇā, a kind of stringed instrument and plays upon it. She may also be represented as accompanied by the four devinities as in the previous case.

(iii) Vajraśāradā.

Symbols—*right* lotus ; *left* book.

According to the Dhyāna in the Sādhanamālā she rests upon a pure white lotus, and a crescent decorates her headdress ; she is three-eyed and two-

* First published in the A. S. I. Central circle : Annual Report, 1919-20, Plate IV, fig. *a*.

† Compare Text—

"Tataḥ purato Bhagavatīṃ Prajñāṃ, dakṣiṇato Medhāṃ, paścimato Matiṃ, vāmataḥ Smṛtiṃ—etāḥ svanāyikā-samānavarṇādikāḥ sammukhamavasthitāḥ cintānīyāḥ." Op. cit. A—17.

armed, and carries the book in the left hand and the lotus in the right. The accompanying illustration (Plate XL,d) shows how she is pictured by Nepalese artists. She may, however, be accompanied by the four attendants, Prajñā and others. As the Sādhana is silent about the Āsana, she may have any attitude. The Nālanda image (Plate XL,e), which has been identified as that of Koṭiśrī (?) is probably a stone representation of this goddess. Vajraśāradā here sits in Bhadrāsana and her companions also have the same attitude. All the figures in the group are mutilated, but at least one among them carries the Utpala and the book, in the right and left hands.

(iv) Āryasarasvatī.

Symbol.—*left* **Prajñāpāramitā on lotus.**

Āryasarasvatī is another variation of Sarasvatī and is also designated as Vajrasarasvatī, which seems to be the common name of Sarasvatī of the Vajrayānists. She appears as a girl of sixteen years, is in the fulness of youth, has white complexion, and carries in the left hand the stalk of a lotus on which rests the Prajñāpāramitā Book. The Dhyāna is silent about the symbol carried in the right hand which may or may not remain empty. The Āsana is not mentioned also, which fact shows that she may be represented in any attitude. In the drawing illustrated, (Plate XLI,a) she holds the stem of a lotus in the right hand.

(v) Vajrasarasvatī.

Faces—three. Arms—six.
Āsana—Pratyālīḍha.

The name Vajrasarasvatī is given to this goddess in order to distinguish her from the other four varieties of Sarasvatī, with four different names given in the Sādhanas. It has already been said that Sarasvatī has a form with three faces and six arms. In all other respects her form is identical with Mahāsarasvatī. The difference here is that her hair is brown and rises upwards, and she stands in the Pratyālīḍha attitude on the red lotus. Three Sādhanas in the Sādhanamālā are assigned to her worship, and according to these, she has the red colour, with the right and left faces of blue and white colour respectively. She carries in her three right hands the lotus on which is the Prajñāpāramitā book, the sword and the Kartri, and in the three left the Kapāla of Brahmā, the jewel and the Cakra. Instead of the book on lotus and Brahmakapāla, she may hold the lotus and the Kapāla. The illustration (Plate XLI,b) belongs to the latter variety.

(a) Mahāsarasvatī

(b) Vajrasarasvatī

(c) Aparājitā

(d) Aparājitā (Nālandā)

Plate XLI

2. Aparājitā.

Identification mark—trampling upon Gaṇeśa.
Symbols—Tarjanīpāśa and Capeṭādāna-Mudrā.

The name of Aparājitā occurs in the Dhyāna for the Aṣṭabhujā Kurukullā already quoted and translated.* There she is said to bear the image of Ratnasambhava on the crown, and to carry in her four hands the staff and the goad, and the bell and the noose. The reason why this Aparājitā has not been dealt along with the other emanations of Ratnasambhava will be amply borne out by the description that follows. It will be noticed that except the colour, the two Aparājitās have nothing in common.

Aparājitā is a very interesting Buddhist goddess. She tramples upon Gaṇeśa and one of her hands is raised in the attitude of dealing a slap and her parasol, according to the Sādhana, is held by important Hindu gods. A very short Sādhana is devoted to her worship and the Dhyāna contained in the Sādhana describes the form of Aparājitā in the following terms :—

"Aparājitā pītā dvibhujaikamukhī nānāratnopaśobhitā Gaṇapatisamākrāntā capeṭadānābhinayadakṣiṇakarā gṛhītapāsatarjanīkahṛdayasthitavāmabhujā atibhayaṅkarakarālaraudramukhī aśeṣamāranirdalani(aṃ) Brahmādiduṣṭaraudradevatāparikarocchritacchatrā ceti."

Sādhanamālā. A—216, Na—18, C—172.

"Aparājitā is yellow in complexion, two-armed, one-faced, is decked in various gems, and tramples upon Gaṇeśa. Her right hand is raised in displaying the attitude of dealing a slap, while the left carries the Tarjanīpāśa against the breast ; her face appears awful, terrible and ferocious ; she is the destroyer of all Māras, and her parsol is raised over her head by the host of wicked and ferocious gods, Brahmā and others."

In the Sādhana it may be noticed there is a word Gaṇapatisamākrāntā, which means "who tramples upon Gaṇapati." The word 'ākrānta, comes from the original root 'kram' to trample.* In the Sādhanamālā again, the root *kram* is invariably used in the sense of trampling and not in its ordinary sense of attacking. On the strength of this argument the Nālanda fragment (illustrated in Plate XLI,d) was identified with Aparājitā. In it, the

* *Supra*, Chapter IV, p. 58.

† *Cf.*—Kramū pādavikṣepe.

figure to the right of the principal goddess seems to be Indra, and the rod held by him seems to be the handle of the parasol required to be held by the gods beginning with Brahmā.* The upper part of the Nālanda image is unfortunately lost. If it were not so, we could reasonably have expected the Capeṭadāna Mudrā in the right hand of the goddess and the Tarjanīpāśa in the left, and a parasol above her head in continuation of the broken handle. This identification was later on confirmed when a traditional drawing (Plate XLI,c) of Aparājitā was secured from the native Citrakāras of Nepal. Subsequently, at the Indian Museum, we came across an image (Plate XLII,a) slightly mutilated, but complete, which resembled the Nalanda fragment in the lower portion while the whole image exactly followed the directions given in the Sādhana quoted above. This new discovery, however, left no room for doubting the identification.†

3. Vajragāndhārī.

Faces. six.	Arms—twelve.
Colour—blue.	Āsana—Pratyālīḍha.

The name of Vajragāndhārī has already been mentioned in connection with the Maṇḍala of the eight-armed Kurukullā.‡ There Vajragāndhārī is said to bear the image of Amoghasiddhi on her tiara. As the two forms of Vajragāndhārī vary widely, she could not be dealt with under the emanations of Amoghasiddhi. She is one of the terrible feminine deities without any crest of a Dhyānī Buddha, is endowed with six faces and twelve arms. A short Sādhana in the Sādhanamālā describes her form as follows :—

" Vajragāndhārī kṛṣṇā ṣaṇmukhī dvādaśabhujā ūrddhvapiṅgalakeśī pratyālīḍhapadā daṃṣṭrākarālavadanā, pratimukhaṃ trinetrā, dakṣiṇaṣaḍbhujeṣu yathākramaṃ vajra-vajraghaṇṭā-khaḍga-triśūla-bāṇa-cakrāṇi ; vāmaṣaḍbhujeṣu khaṭvāṅga-aṅkuśa-dhanuḥ-paraśu-pāśa-hṛttarjanyaḥ ; prathamamukhaṃ kṛṣṇaṃ, aparāṇi mukhāni pañcavarṇāni viśvapadmasūryyāsanā ceti."

Sādhanamālā. A—216, Na—18—19, C—172.

* The gods commencing from Brahmā are four in number, to wit: Brahmā, Viṣṇu, Śiva and Indra, often designated by the Tāntric Buddhists as the four Māras or Evil Ones. Brahmā has four faces and both Siva and Viṣṇu have four arms each. As this figure, attendant on Aparājitā, is endowed with two hands only, I propose to identify it with Indra. The identification is further strengthened by the fact that in some Buddha images, it is Indra who holds the parasol above the Lord's head.

† The image had long been hidden from public gaze, as it was kept in an obscure corner on the left side of the marble staircase leading from the Galleries to the office of the Archaeological Section, Indian Museum. The staircase, I may add, is inaccessible to the public.

‡ Supra, Chapter IV, p. 58.

Vajragāndhārī is blue, six faced, twelve-armed, with brown hair rising upwards, stands in the Pratyālīḍha attitude and has faces terrible with bare fangs and three eyes; she carries in her six right hands, the Vajra, the Vajraghaṇṭā the sword, the Triśūla and the Cakra, and in the six left hands the Khaṭvāṅga, the goad, the bow, the Paraśu, the noose with the Tarjanī against the breast; her first face is blue, and other five faces are of five different colours; she rests on the sun supported by the double lotus."

The Dhāraṇī quoted in the Sādhanamālā gives her the epithets of Yoginī and Bhīṣmabhaginī, and she is believed to be the consort of the Yakṣa general, Caṇḍavajrapāṇi by name.

4. Vajrayoginī.

(i) She is another of the important and popular goddesses, who do not seem to bear the image of any of the Dhyānī Buddhas on the crown. Four Sādhanas describe her form, which consists of two entirely different types. In one case, she has no head on the neck, but carries it in her hand, and in another, she has her head intact.* In the former she is identical in appearance with the Hindu goddess Cchinnamastā belonging to the group of the ten Mahāvidyās. Our conclusion therefore is that this Buddhist goddess has been borrowed and incorporated wholly by the Hindus into their Pantheon.† She is always accompanied by the two Yoginīs on either side of her, who are called Vajravairocanī and Vajravarṇanī. The Sādhana describing her form without head is as follows:—

"Bhaṭṭārikāṃ Vajrayoginīṃ....pītavarṇāṃ śvayameva svakartri-kartita-svamastaka-vāmahastasthitāṃ dakṣiṇahastakartrisahitāṃ, ūrddhva-vistṛtavāmabāhuṃ, adhonamitadakṣiṇabāhuṃ, vāsaśūnyāṃ, prasāritadak-ṣiṇapādāṃ saṅkucita-vāmapādāṃ, bhāvayet. Kavandhānnisṛtyāsṛkdhārāśca mukhe praviśati, apare ubhayoḥ pārśvayoginyoḥ mukhe praviśati iti bhāvayet.

Vāmadakṣiṇapārśvayoḥ śyāma-Vajravarṇanī-pitavarna-Vajravairocanyau vāmadakṣiṇahastakartrisahite, dakṣiṇavāmahastakarpparasahite, prasārita-vāmapādaprasāritadakṣiṇapāde muktakeśyau bhāvayet. Ubhayoḥ pārśvayoḥ, ubhayoḥ yoginyoḥ madhye antarīkṣe atibhayākulaṃ śmaśānaṃ bhāvayet."

Sādhanamālā. A—245, Na—76, C—193.

* The headless form is designated in the Mantra as Sarvabuddhaḍākinī, while the other form is called in the Mantra as Vajrayoginī.

† The most powerful augment in favour of this conclusion is that the Hindus retained the same Buddhist Mantra, though they changed the name of the principal deity and all Buddhist flavour into Hindu. But owing to religious fear they did not venture to change the Mantra.

The worshipper should conceive himself as Bhaṭṭārikā Vajrayoginī.... of yellow complexion, who carries in her left hand her own head severed by herself with her own Kartri held in her right hand ; whose left hand is raised upwards while the right is placed below ; who is nude, and whose right leg is stretched while the left is bent down. He, (the worshipper), should also meditate on the streams of blood issuing out from the severed body as falling into her mouth and into the mouths of the two Yoginīs on either side of her.

He (worshipper) should also conceive the two Yoginīs to the left and right [of the principal goddess], the green Vajravarṇanī, and the yellow Vajra-vairocani, both of whom carry the Kartri in the left and right hands respectively, and the cup of skull in the right and left hands respectively ; whose left and the right legs respectively are stretched forward and who have dishevelled hair. On all sides between the two Yoginīs and in the firmament are stretched the awful cremation ground."

(ii). The other form is also as terrible as the one described above, and she is surrounded on all sides by the terrible burning grounds. She stands in the Ālīḍha attitude on the sun, is in the fulness of youth, and has red complexion. She rides the corpse, is nude, has three eyes, red and round, contorted brows, protruding belly and tongue, and possesses the six auspicious symbols. She carries the Kapāla in the left hand and the Vajra in the right, while the Khaṭvāṅga hangs form her left shoulder. This form of Vajrayoginī is similar in many respects to the forms of both Nairātmā and Vajrāvarāhī so much so, that a confusion is likely to occur in the identification of their images. If an image shows the dancing attitude in Ardhaparyaṅka, it may be identified as Nairātmā or Vajravārāhi, but if it shows the Ālīḍha attitude, it must be identified as Vajrayoginī. The excrescence near the right ear and the corpse lying on its breast is peculiar only to Vajrāvarāhī ; while the absence of the excrescence, and the presence of the corpse lying on its back point to the identification of Nairātmā. The Ālīḍha attitude is peculiar only to Vajrayoginī.

She may have a yellow form, and according to the Sādhana, she will carry the Kartri and the Kapāla, and in other respects she will be indentical with the one just described. Another Sādhana adds the information that the Kāpala should be filled with the blood of the Devas (gods) and the Asuras (demons), and that the hand carrying the Kartri may show the Tarjanī also.

Vajrayoginī is one of the consorts of Heruka, who remains with her in the yab-yum, and their union is the subject of the celebrated Heruka Tantra. The temple of Vajrayoginī at Sāṅku (Plate XLII,b)

(a) Aparājitā (Indian Museum)

(b) Vajrayoginī Temple at Sāṅku

(d) Gaṇapatihṛdayā

(c) Grahamātṛkā

(e) Vajravidāraṇī

Plate XLII

in Nepal does not contain an image of any of these varieties of Vajrayoginī. It contains, within it, the image of Ugratārā or more popularly known as the Mahācīna-Tārā, which is believed to have been carried over there by Bengali priests from a place of the same name in the District of Dacca, about A.D. 1350, when the Muhammadans carried their victorious arms over Eastern Bengal.

* * * * * *

In the Sādhanamālā we do not find any Sādhana for the goddesses that are mentioned below. Paṇḍit Amṛtānanda's Dharmakoṣasaṅgraha, which embodies later developments than those recorded in the Sādhanamālā gives us descriptions of some of these deities. We give below descriptions only of those that are generally represented in art. The pictures reproduced, were photographed from an illuminated manuscript of Pañcarakṣā, which is now in the possession of an American Anthropologist, Dr. W. Y. Evans Wentz. The Ms. and therefore the miniatures, may be taken to be four hundred years old on Palæographical evidence.

5. Grahamātṛkā.

Faces—three. Arms six.
Mudrā—Dharmacakra. Āsana—Vajraparyaṅka.

She has been described in the Dharmakoṣasaṅgraha in the following terms :—

" Grahamātṛkā trimukhaśvetapītaraktā ṣaḍbhujā dakṣe dharmacakra-mudrā-vajra-śara ; vāme kamalacāpa ; sahasradalapadme vajrāsanā."

Dharmakoṣasaṅgraha, Fol. 44A.

" Grahāmatṛkā has three-faces of white, yellow and red colours, and six-arms, displaying the Dharmacakra-Mudrā (in the principal pair of hands) and carrying the Vajra and the arrow in the two right hands and in the two left the lotus and the bow. She sits in Vajrāsana on a lotus of thousand petals." (Plate XLII,c).

6. Gaṇapatihṛdayā.

Āsana—dancing. Arms—two.
Mudrās—Abhaya and Varada.

Like Gaṇapati himself Gaṇapatihṛdayā, who, in all probability, is his Śakti, does not bear any image of a Dhyānī Buddha. She is described in the work as :—

" Ganapatihṛdayā ekamukhā dvibhujā varadā abhayā nṛtyāsanā."

Dharmakoṣasaṅgraha, Fol. 43.

" Gaṇapatihṛdayā is one-faced, two-armed, exhibits the Varada and the Abhaya poses, and a dancing attitude."

The miniature, (Plate XLII,d) however, does not tally with the above description. In this miniature she has sixteen arms and one face. The symbols, beings indistinct, cannot be recognised in all details.

7. Vajravidāraṇī.

Vajravidāraṇī has been described in the above-named work as follows :—

" Vajravidāraṇī, pañcamukhī, daśabhujā ; dakṣe aṅkuśa-khaḍga-śara-vajravaradā ; vāmẹ pāśa-carma-dhanu-dhvaja-abhayā pratyālīḍhāsanā."

Dharmakoṣasaṇgraha, Fol. 44A.

" Vajravidāraṇī is five-faced, ten-armed, carries in the right hands the goad, the sword, the arrow, the Vajra, and the Varada Mudrā, and in the left, the noose, the armour, the bow, the flag and the Abhaya pose ; she stands in the Pratyālīḍha attitude." (Plate XLII,e.)

CONCLUSION.

There is no evidence to show that the Sādhanas existed before the time of Indrabhūti (*Cir.* 700-750 A. C.) who, with the materials now before us, may be regarded as the founder of the Vajrayāna System. But when the Sādhanamālās were cempiled, in about the middle of the 12th Century, we find no less than 300 Sādhanas recorded in them. It cannot be denied that after Indrabhūti, during these four hundred years, this System underwent a rapid development, which is due mostly to time, and space, as well as to the temperament and idiosyncracies of the followers of that System.

The Sādhanas of the Sādhanamālā were composed by men distinguished in the Mediaeval ages as great Tāntric scholars, and we have been able to find out thirty-three names of such authors. The Dhyānas contained in the Sādhanas laid down the essential features of different gods, and the sculptors prepared images with the help of those general directions. The Dhyānas left much scope for the exercise of imagination on the part of the sculptors and the products of their chisels were also very greatly influenced by the spirit of the age in which they flourished, as well as by the geographical situation of the area in which they worked. Ornaments, dress and even the expressions of the face in the images reflected local colouring to a great extent, over which particular Tāntric rites in which the images were used, had also a modifying influence.

We have seen that the most important factor in the identification of images is the miniature figure of the Dhyānī Buddha on their crown. In rare instances, however, the Dhyānī Buddhas are absent. In such cases, we have to look out for other marks of identification. Even when the Dhyānī Buddhas are present, there may arise difficulties. Sometimes all the five Dhyānī Buddhas are carved on the aureole. In cases like these, the principal figure may be an emanation of the five Dhyānī Buddhas as in the case of the Birbhum figure of Mañjuvara, or, it may be, that the principal figure is the emanation of that particular Dhyānī Buddha, who appears right above its head, such as, we find in the cases of the Indian Museum standing figure of Khadiravanī Tārā or the Vikrampur figures of Parṇaśavarī. They are both emanations of Amoghasiddhi, whose effigy appears right above the heads of the goddesses. The figures of all other Dhyānī Buddhas are not required either by the Sādhanas or for identification. Their presence can only be explained by a reference to the Sādhana, prescribing the worship of all the Buddhas before the commencement of the offering of oblations, or of the worshipper conceiving himself as the principal deity, to whom the Sādhana is devoted. Sometimes again, the Dhyānī Buddhas appear on the image only to serve artistic purposes ; for instance, in the case of the Dacca Museum image of Arapacana Mañjuśrī, who is regarded as independent in the Sādhanamālā. Four companions, identical in appearance with himself, appear round his image. The Java figure of Arapacana is of this kind. But in the Dacca Museum image we find four Dhyānī Buddhas while the central position above the head is occupied by one of the companions of Arapacana. The Dhyānī Buddhas are not required by the Sādhana and are, therefore, more ornamental than otherwise.

But the most serious difficulty arises when instead of the Dhyānī Buddha mentioned in the Sādhana some other Buddha appears on the crown of any figure, contrary to the prescription of the Sādhanas. For instance, in the Sarnath image of Ucchuṣma Jambhala we could reasonably have expected according to the Dhyānas, the figures either of Akṣobhya or of Ratnasambhava on its crown. But we find instead the effigy of Amitābha on the crown of Ucchuṣma Jambhala. Again, take for instance, the Lucknow Museum figure of Mārīcī, who ought to have shown, in agreement with the Sādhana, the figure of Vairocana on her crown ; but we find instead that of Amitābha. Again, we notice over the head of the Indian Museum image of Uṣṇīṣavijayā, the figure of the parental Buddha Akṣobhya, instead of her own sire Vairocana. We leave out of discussion the image of Cundā who bears two miniature images of Amitābha on her crown instead of the parental Buddha Vajrasattva,—because the figure does not tally with the Sādhana in important details.

It is difficult to surmise the true reason for these discrepancies. The most reasonable suggestion seems to be that we have still to discover many texts, and that the Sādhanamālā is not the only collection of the Sādhanas. It is difficult to believe, however, that a new Sādhana for either Mārīcī or Uṣṇīṣavijayā will be forthcoming. In the Sādhanamālā itself a large number of Sādhanas are devoted to their worship, but nowhere do we find mention of any parental Buddha other than Vairocana. When we consider that there are existent nine or ten different recensions of the Sādhanamālā or Sādhanasamuccaya, the hope of discovering further Sādhanas prescribing other parental Buddhas than Vairocana, seems to be far distant.

The second alternative presupposes the existence of different cults according as one or the other of the Dhyānī Buddhas are believed to be the principal or the Ādi-Buddha. The Buddhists of Nepal, even now are divided into so many different cults,—some regard Vairocana as the Ādi-Buddha, others regard Akṣobhya or Amitābha as the Ādi-Buddha.* But we have not yet been able to find out a single instance where Amoghasiddhi or Ratnasambhava are believed to be the Ādi Buddha. Now, though the Sādhanas prescribe the figure of the parental Buddha Vairocana for Mārīcī, yet the followers of the Amitābha cult are at liberty to make her emanate from the same Buddha, whom they consider as the Ādi Buddha. Similarly Ucchuṣma Jambhala, being regarded as the offspring of Amitābha, is made to bear an image of that Dhyānī Buddha on the crown of the Sarnath figure already referred to. It is unnecessary to multiply instances.

In identifying Buddhist images, the student of Iconography should guard himself against taking unnecessary figures in the image as principal ones, or a necessary one as unnecessary. A full-fledged Buddhist icon shows in the first place, the principal god, an effigy of his sire on the crown, and the Dhyānī Buddhas on the aureole. The icon may show further miniature figures of the companions of the principal god, some worshippers, mythical figures, and the three, seven or sixteen jewels. The figure of Vajrasattva seems to be a favourite device with the artists. He appears on many Buddhist images, and is perhaps conceived as a sort of general guardian of Buddhism and Buddhist worship. For the purpose of identification the principal figure, the figure of the Dhyānī Buddha on the top and the companions are the necessary parts of the image. Examine, for instance, the Dacca Museum image of Arapacana in which besides the four companions there are present four Dhyānī Buddhas, Vairocana, Akṣobhya, Amitābha and Ratnasambhava, two mythical figures supporting the lotus seat, and two worshippers on the extreme left of the pedestal. All these figures are redundant for the purpose of identification, and their absence in the Java figure does not affect it. But if, for instance, the companions are confused with the worshippers, as has been done in the case of the Mahoba figure of Vajrāsana†, the identification must be regarded as incomplete. In it, the figures flanking the principal figure of Buddha in the Bhūmiṣparśa Mudrā are clearly Maitreya and Avalokiteśvara according to the Sādhana, but they have been described as worshippers. Thus the identification of the whole image has been vitiated.

* The theory of Ādi-Buddha originated in the Nalanda monastery about the beginning of the 10th. century and was accepted first in Kālacakrayāna, a later form of Vajrayāna. See Csoma: *The Origin of the Theory of Adi Buddha*, in J.A.S.B. Vol. II (1833) p. 57 *et sqq.* See also my paper on *Buddhist Iconography* in J. B. O. R. S., March, 1923.

† *See* K. N. Dikshit, *Six Sculptures from Mahoba.*

Another difficulty arises in identifying images where the letters of the Mantra of the god represented are deified and appear on the image. We have seen in the case of Vajratārā that she should be surrounded by ten goddesses, who are the ten Pāramitās and originate from the ten syllables of the Tārā Mantra, " Oṃ Tāre-tuttāre-ture svāhā"; also, we have seen how from the the five letters of the name Arapacana originated five deities including the principal one, Mañjuśrī. The Dacca Museum image of Kadiravanī Tārā is a particular instance of the deification of the Mantra. The main figure, in accordance with the Sādhana, carries the Utpala in the left hand and shows the Varada Mudrā in the right, and is flanked on either side by Aśokakāntā and Ekajaṭā. But on the aureole there are eight female figures identical in appearance with the principal figure. They represent none but the eight syllables of the Tārā Mantra " Oṃ Tāretuttāreture," the two others, Uṣṇīṣavijayā and Sumbhā being omitted.

Sometimes in the images of the Buddhist gods and goddesses we notice the presence of Gaṇeśa, who is regarded by the Hindus as " Siddhidātā" or the Bestower of Perfection or success in Tāntric rites. The Buddhists in order to display their aversion to the followers of the Brahmanical faith, made their gods trample upon Gaṇeśa. Thus in the Indian Museum images of Parṇaśavarī and Aparājitā, the Vaṅgīya Sāhitya Pariṣat image of Bighnāntaka, etc., the deities have been represented as trampling upon Gaṇeśa under their feet. In the two Vikrampur images of Parṇaśavarī and the Dacca Sāhitya Pariṣat image of Mahāpratisarā,* Gaṇeśa appears below the lotus seat lying prostrate on the ground, under the pressure of the Buddhist deities. The Buddhists thus showed their animosity against the Hindu god, Gaṇeśa, and gave him the epithet of *Bighna* or Obstacle. Their animosity may be further illustrated by the following features of the Sādhanas. The four Hindu gods, Brahmā, Viṣṇu, Śiva and Indra have been designated uniformly as the four Māras or Wicked Beings and several Buddhist gods have been described as trampling them under their feet. The Sādhanas of Prasanna-Tārā, Vajrajjvālānalārka, Vidyujjvālākarālī, and the like, are instances in point. Trailokyavijaya has been represented as trampling upon the prostrate forms of Śiva and Gaurī. Nārāyaṇa has been made a Vāhana or vehicle by Hariharihari-

*Unfortunately, the disadvantageous position of this image did not permit me to photograph the whole pedestal. The figure of Gaṇeśa has therefore been omitted in the photograph.

vāhana. Poor Brahmā has been more severely handled by the Buddhists. The severed head of Brahmā or the Brahmakapāla is carried by a number of Buddhist deities. According to the Hindu tradition, Brahmā should be very old, with grey beards and four heads, and the Buddhist deities mercilessly hold the heads by the matted hair and flourish them in their hands. This is how the Buddhists attempted to exhibit the superiority of their gods over those of the Brahmanical faith. It is a matter of satisfaction, however, that the Hindus never disgraced any gods belonging to the alien faith in this manner. On the contrary, they placed Buddha among the ten Avatāras of Viṣṇu.

A deep spiritual significance is attached to the colour, the weapons, and Āsanas of the Buddhist gods, who are represented either singly or in yab-yum. The conception of yab-yum images, however, is much more complicated than the single ones.

It has been stated in the Sādhanamālā that a single deity may take any colour according as he is worshipped in different Tāntric rites. For instance, in Śāntikavidhi or propitiatory rite the god will take the white or yellow colour, in Pauṣṭikavidhi or protective rite the yellow colour, in Vaśyavidhi or bewitching and Ākarṣaṇa or the rite of forcible attraction the yellow, green or red colour, and in Ucāṭana (destruction of dwelling houses) and Māraṇa (destruction of enemies), the god will be generally blue. It may be pointed out here that the word ' Kṛṣṇa' in the Sādhanamālā always signifies blue colour and not black. Except in very exceptional circumstance, we meet with black colour in paintings of gods, but always the blue colour. It was not because the Buddhists had no perception of black, but it seems that there was some religious prejudice against using the black colour in paintings of gods. It may be pointed out here that whenever the deity gets the blue colour his appearance becomes terrible with protruding teeth, tongue and belly, garland of heads, ornaments of serpents or bones, and the garment of tiger-skin.

The Āsanas have likewise a spiritual significance. The Vajraparyaṅka attitude signifies meditation, the Ardhaparyaṅka and Lalitāsana signify serenity, the Ālīḍha heroism, the Pratyālīḍha destruction and loathsomeness, and the dancing attitude in Ardhaparyaṅka signifies wrath and horror.

A reference here is necessary to the yab-yum representations. The Tibetan *yab* means the honourable father, and *yum* the honourable mother. Therefore the word yab-yum means the honourable father in the company of the honourable mother. A yab-yum image has a deep spiritual significance. It signifies that the god, the embodiment of Śūnya represents perfection having attained Śūnya (Karuṇā) and therefore the highest stage of Nirvāṇa.

The conception of Śūnya in Vajrayāna took the concrete shapes of a god and a goddess. Śūnya took the shape of Heruka when a male divinity, and became otherwise known as Nairātmā when a goddess. That Śūnya took the form of a deity does not seem strange in Vajrayāna where we find conceptions, such as Saṅgha, Dharma, Prajñāpāramitā, the ten Parāmitās, and the Skandhas,—deified in the Buddhist Pantheon. The conception of Śūnya in the form of a god or a goddess is therfore quite in keeping with the traditions of the Vajrayāna System. When the Bodhi Mind attains Nirvāṇa it merges in Śūnya and there remains in eternal bliss and happiness. And when Śūnya was made a goddess, it was easily understood, as to how eternal bliss and happiness was possible after the attainment of Nirvāṇa. The yab-yum figures, representing Śūnya in the form of Heruka in the embrace of Śūnya in the form of Nairātmā,* were held up before the mass as ideals, and they readily attracted them and helped them in their conception of a bright and definite spiritual prospect.†

Buddhists of the Vajrayāna considered Śūnya as the Ultimate Reality, and they believed that the host of gods and goddesses including the Dhyānī Buddhas are Śūnya in essence, ‡ that is, are gods about whom neither existence, nor non-existence, nor a combination of the two, nor a negation of the two may be predicated. The innumerable gods and goddesses of the Vajrayāna Pantheon thus, are all manifestations of the Śūnya. The gods have no real existence, the images have no real existence, and therefore, we may

* The Nairātmā is also known by the names of Prajñā Śakti, Svābhā Prajñā, Vidyā, Svābhā-Vidyā and the like. But Nairātmā and Heruka both have their stereotyped forms described before.

† The perfected Bodhicitta in the embrace of Śūnya or Nairātmā as represented in yub-yum figures is likened by Saraha as salt and water. As salt cannot be taken out from water, so the two yub-yum figures are eternally united into one. This is what the Buddhists call " Advaya" where all conception of a duality ceases. This is Heruka represented as single.

‡ The whole of the Buddhist Tāntric literature is full with ideas of this kind ; for instance, in Advayavajra we find—"The divinities are manifestations which are naturally non-existent. Whenever there is manifestation, it must be Śūnya in essence."—

" Spurtiśca devatākarāḥ niḥsvabhāvo svabhāvataḥ ।

Yadā yadā bhavet sphurtiḥ sā tathā śūnyatātmakā ॥ "

Mahāsukhaprakāśa in Advayavajrasaṅgraha. Fol, 33.

be positive in saying, that a true Vajrayānist never worshipped any image or god. Because, the images, the paintings, or even the divinities themselves have no real existence. They are the different manifestations of the Śūnya. But that the images had some utility can never be denied. The form presented in images in accordance with the Dhyānas, no doubt, facilitated the conception of the deities, who were to be identified with the worshipper himself. As they had no real existence, the deities had to be drawn from unknown regions in the firmament by the luminous rays of light issuing out from the Vījamantras uttered by the worshiper. The Śūnya transforms itself in the form of a divinity in accordance with the germ-syllable uttered, and exists only as a positive idea in the mind of the worshipper who identifies himself with that transformation of Śūnya.

The question may be raised as to the necessity of a variety of gods and goddesses, when one Śūnya would have been sufficient. In answer to this we have to consider a number of things. First, that Śūnya which was identified with Compassion by the Vajrayānists, was concieved as manifesting itself in different forms in accordance with the different functions discharged. For instance, if any disease is to be cured, Śūnya takes the form of Siṃhanāda ; when it is the question of snake-bite, Śūnya becomes Jāṅgulī ; when destruction of the wicked is needed the Śūnya takes the form of Mahākāla. When again, diseases and pestilences are to be prevented, Śūnya is conceived in the form of Parṇaśavarī, for success in love-affairs, Śūnya is invoked in the form of Kurukullā, and when forcible submission is required in love-affairs, Śūnya becomes Vajrānaṅga. When finally Buddhahood is wanted by the worshipper he should conceive himself as Heruka. From the above it appears that the conception of the multitude of Buddhist deities emerges from the one grand conception of Śūnya according as it is believed to discharge different functions as a mark of compassion towards the Buddhists.

Secondly, the number of deities increases according as Śūnya is taken to depict the different " Rasas" or sentiments, numbering nine. For instance, Śūnya will be Khadiravanī or Lokanātha when benign (Karuṇā) ; it will be Mārīcī when heroic (Vīra) ; Bighnāntaka, Heruka or Mahākāla when awe-inspiring (Bhaya) Aparājitā when wrathful (Raudra) ; Vajracarcikā in disgust and loathsomeness (Bībhatsa) and Prajñāpāramitā when peaceful (Śānta), and so on.

Thirdly, the number of deities increases also in accordance with the three Kāyas, the four Ānandas, the five Skandhas, the ten Pāramitās, and so on.

As all these deities centre round the one grand conception of Śūnya the different weapons held by them also centre round the one grand conception of Bodhicitta*, which is also of the essence of Śūnya. As these weapons are required to discharge different functions, the Bodhicitta manifests itself into so many different forms. For instance, when the darkness of ignorance is to be dispelled, Bodhicitta becomes the sword, which spreading its rays destroys darkness ; when destruction is needed of the host of wicked beings it manifests itself also in the form of a sword, which cuts them through. Bodhicitta becomes Aṅkuśa when the heart of the wicked is to be wrung with pain. It is conceived as the noose when the Māras are to be bound securedly ; it becomes the needle and the string when the eyes and the mouths of wicked are to be sewn up. Bodhicitta will be the Kartri when chopping, a Bhiṇḍipāla when the Māras are to be destroyed from a distance, the bow and the arrow when the distance is much greater, and so on.

The Mudrās also are nothing but the manifestations of the Bodhicitta. If protection is needed, Bodhicitta is conceived as the Abhaya Mudrā ; when it is the question of boon, it becomes Varada ; when instruction in Buddhist Law is required, it becomes Dharmacakra, and so on.

The Bodhicitta or the Mind determined upon obtaining the Bodhi is that state of Mind which has already acquired the potentiality of dissolving itself in Sūnya. As a matter of fact, without Bodhicitta Śūnya or Nirvāṇa cannot be obtained. Like the Śūnya, Bodhicitta exists in the mind only and therefore has no real existence. It is the Bodhicitta which contributes to the attainment of Śūnya, and ultimately it is the Bodhicitta which merges itself in Śūnya.

The gods of the Buddhist Pantheon are conceived as carrying the Bodhicitta in their hands both being of the nature of Śūnya. It is with the help of this Bodhicitta that the god is supposed to confer Buddhahood or success in Tāntric rites upon the worshipper. The yab-yum conception of deities

* Compare Jñānasiddhi by Indrabhūti—

Bodhicittaṃ bhavedvajraṃ Prajñāt ghaṇṭā vidhīyate |
Cakramajñānacchedāt Ratnantu durlabhādapi ||
Bhavadoṣairaliptatvāt Jñānaṃ tat padmamucyate || etc. etc. etc.

Fol. 61 (MS in the possession of M.M. H. P. Shastri).

is still more complicated. The god Heruka, the embodiment of Śūnya, carrying weapons, the embodiments of Bodhicitta also of the nature of Sūnya, is embraced by Nairātmā, whose essence is also Śūnya, carrying weapons also of the nature of Śūnya. Thus Void with Void commingles. This is the highest state—the Anupādhiśeṣa-Nirvāṇa.

Farewell Mighty Gods!

Kṛto vaḥ sarvasattvārthaḥ
siddhirdattā yathānugā ।
Gacchadhvaṃ Buddhaviṣayaṃ
punarāgamaṇāya Muḥ ॥

॥ शुभमस्तु सर्व्वजगतां ॥

APPENDIX A.

KIÑCIT-VISTARA-TĀRĀ-SĀDHANA.

Text.

Prathamaṃ tāvat mantrī mukhacaraṇādikaṃ prakṣālya pavitrībhūya vijane mano'nukūle sugandhopalipte surabhikusumāvakīrṇe ca bhūpradeśe sukhāsanopaviṣṭaḥ svahṛdaye prathamasvarapariṇataṃ śītāṃśumaṇḍalaṃ vicintya tanmadhye kamanīyanīlanīrajaṃ tatkiñjalke niṣkalaṅkaśaśāṅkamaṇḍalaṃ tadupari pīta-Tāṅkāravījaṃ paśyet tato'pi pīta-Tāṅkāravījāt niḥsṛtya jaganmohāndhakārāpahāribhiḥ mayūkhasamūhaiḥ daśasu dikṣu ye ca aparyantā lokadhātavo vidyante tān sarvān avabhāsya tatrasthān api asaṅkhyeyān aprameyān Budda-Bodhisattvāṃśca ākāśadeśe api ānīya avasthāpyante. Tadanu teṣāṃ ākāśadeśāvasthitānāṃ mahākāruṇikānāṃ Buddha-Bodhisattvānāṃ divyapuṣpa-dhūpa-gandha-mālya-vilepanacūrṇacīvaracchatradhvajaghaṇṭāpatā kādibhir-mahatīṃ pūjāṃ kṛtvā pāpadeśanāṃ kuryyāt.

Yatkiñcit anādisaṃsāre saṃsaratā mayā pāpakaṃ karma kāyena vā manasā api kṛtam kāritaṃ kriyamāṇaṃ anumoditaṃ vā tatsarvaṃ prati-

Translation.

The worshipper after leaving the bed in the morning, should wash his face and feet, and purifying himself go to a place which is lonely, is agreeable to him, is besmeared with scents, is strewn with fragrant flowers, and then sit in an easy pose. Then he should meditate on his heart the orb of the moon, which is originated from the first vowel "A" and notice a blue lotus which is beautiful ; on the filaments of the lotus he should meditate on the orb of the spotless moon, on which is the yellow germ syllable "Tām." Then from the yellow germ "Tām" issue rays of light, which destroy the darkness of ignorance of the world, and illumine the innumerable worlds that exist in the ten quarters, and bring from the the firmament innumerable and inconceivable Buddhas and Bodhisattvas. Then after an elaborate worship of these great compassionate Buddhas and Boddhisattvas [situated] in the firmament, by means of celestial flowers, incense, scents, garlands, unguents, powders, mendicant dress, umbrellas, flags, bells, banners and the like, he should make a confession of sins in the following manner (by saying)—Whatever sinful deeds I have done, caused to be done or consented

deśayāmi ityanena vidhinā pratideśya punaḥ akaraṇasamvaraṃ pratigṛhya puṇyānumodanām kuryyāt. Sugata-pratyekaśrāvakajinānāṃ tatsutānāṃ api Bodhisattvānāṃ sadevasa-Brahma kalokānāṃ yat kuśalaṃ tat sarvaṃ anumodayāmīti. Tadanu Ratna-trayaśaraṇagamanaṃ—

Buddhaṃ śaraṇaṃ gacchāmi
yāvadābodhimaṇḍataḥ ı
Dharmaṃ śaraṇaṃ gacchāmi
yāvadābodhimaṇḍataḥ ı
Saṃghaṃ śaraṇaṃ gacchāmi
yāvadābodhimaṇḍataḥ ıı

iti. Paścāt mārgāśrayaṇaṃ mārgāḥ Tathāgatoktāḥ sa ca āśrayaṇīyaṃ mayā nānya iti. Tadanu adhyeṣaṇāṃ kuryyāt. Jagadarthaṃ āsaṃsāraṃ kurvanto Bhagavantaḥ Tathāgatāḥ tatsutā api tiṣṭhantu māṃ pariṇirvāntu iti. Tadanu yācanā. Tādṛśiṃ niruttarāṃ dharmadeśanām Bhagavantaḥ Tathāgatāḥ deśāyantu yayā jhaṭityeva saṃsāriṇaḥ sattvāḥ bhavabandhanāt nirmuktāḥ bhavanti iti. Tadanantaraṃ puṇyapariṇāmanāṃ kuryyāt. Sapta-vidh-ānuttara-pūjā-pāpadeśanā kuśalamūlaṃ upajātaṃ tat sarvaṃ samyaksambodhaye pariṇāmayāmi iti. Athavā samāsataḥ saptavidhā-

to be done in this endless cycle of creation—everything I confess. Again, meditating on the restraint of wrong deeds he should give his assent to meritorious deeds (of others) with the words—I assent to the virtues of the Sugatas, Pratyekas, Śrāvakas, the Jinas and their sons the Boddhisattvas, and of the world with all the gods and Brahmā. After this refuge in the Three Jewels should be taken with the words—" I take refuge in Buddha so long as the Bodhi essence subsists ; I take refuge in Dharma so long as the Bodhi essence subsists, and I take refuge in Saṅgha so long as the Bodhi essence subsists." After this, adherence to the path (of the Tathāgata) should be done with the words—"By me should be followed the path indicated by the Tathāgata, and naught else. Then solicitation should be done with the words—" The gods the Tathāgatas and their children, who have created everything in this world, for the benefit of the world, be constant to me, and emancipate me." Then begging should be done with the words,—" The gods, the Tathāgatas instruct me with such incontrovertible advices on Law, by which the beings of the world may be freed from the bonds of the world quickly. Then he should meditate on the results of his meritorious deeds with the following words—" Whatever merit I have acquired by the seven kinds of extraordinary worship like the confession of sins—all that I devote to gain, at the end, the final Sambodhi."

uttarapujāsūcakaṃ ślokaṃ enaṃ paṭhet.—

Sarvaṃ pāpaṃ ahaṃ diśāmi paramaṃ prītyānumode śubhān
Nājanmasthitaye'rthaye Bhagavataḥ Saddharmaratnasya ca ।
Ratnānaṃ trayamabhyupaimi śaraṇaṃ Bodhau dadhe mānasaṃ
Tanmārgañca samāśraye śubhavidhīn Sambodhaye nāmaye ॥

Ityanena saptavidhānuttarapujāṃ vidhāya Oṃ Āh Muḥ iti visarjayet. Athavā.—

Śīlacandanaliptānāṃ dhyānaprāvaraṇāvṛtāḥ ।
Bodhyaṅgakusumākirṇāḥ viharadhvaṃ yathāsukhaṃ ॥

ityanena. Tadanantaraṃ catur-Brahmavihāraṃ.—Maitrī-Karuṇā-Mudit-Opekṣāsaṃjñakaṃ vakṣyamāṇakrameṇa bhāvayet. Tatra keyaṃ Maitrī ?

Sarvasattveṣu ekaputraprematā lakṣaṇā. Athavā hitasukhopasaṃhārākarā iti. Karuṇā punaḥ kīdṛśī. Duḥkhāt duḥkhahetoḥ samuddharaṇakāmatā. Triduḥkhaduḥkhamahānalaprajjvalitasaṃsāralohabhavanapraviṣṭān jantūn tato'pi samuddharāmi iti adhyāsayo vā karuṇā. Athavā triduḥkhaduḥkhitānāṃ sattvānāṃ aṃsārāmbudheḥ samuddharaṇ-

Otherwises briefly he should recite the following ślokas which indicate the seven kinds of extraordinary worship. "All sins I confess and gladly assent to the merits of others. For the reason of not remaining till the next birth, I take refuge in the Lord Buddha and the jewel of Good Law, or the Three Jewels and direct my thoughts to Bodhi. I follow His path and devote my merits for the attainment of Sambodhi." With this, the seven kinds of extraordinary worship should be performed and then the (gods) should be dismissed with the Mantra "Oṃ Āh Muḥ" or with the following śloka—Thou movest according to Thy will, being besmeared with the sandal of the Śīlas, and wearing the garments of Dhyāna, and strewn with the flowers of the limbs of the Bodhi.

Then he should meditate on the four Brahmas consisting of Friendship, Compassion, Joyousness and Indifference. What is meant by Friendship ? Its indication is the love that exists in all beings like the love towards the only son. or like its fruition in their welfare and happiness. Compassion again is of what kind ? It is the desire to save from misery and from causes that lead to misery. The desire—I shall even save the people who are burnt with the great fire of suffering from the three evils and have entered the prison of Saṃsāra—is Compassion. Or it is the desire to save from the sea of Saṃsāra the beings suffering from the three evils.

ecchā. Muditā tu īdṛśī. Pramodo Muditā. Athavā asadṛśe Buddhatve tadupāye ca sarvā eva saṃsāriṇaḥ sattvā mayā pratiṣṭhāpayitavyā ityadhyāśayo Muditā. Yadvā viśveṣāṃ yāni kuśalāni teṣu tadbhogaiiśvaryādiṣu ca ākṛṣṭacittatā. Kā Upekṣā. Pratighānunaya-nivandhanaṃ apahāya hitāhiteṣu jantuṣu paramahitācaraṇaṃ Upekṣā. Yadvā sarvasmin premānuśayarahitaparahitadharmatāyāṃ svarasavāhinī pravṛttiḥ Upekṣa. Athavā lābhālābha-yaśo'payaśo-nindāstuti-sukha-duḥkhetyādyaṣṭalokadharma-pramukha-sakalāprastutavyāpāropekṣaṇaṃ Upekṣā. Catur-Brahmavihārabhāvanānantaraṃ sarvadharmaprakṛtipariśuddhatāṃ bhāvayet. Sarvā eva dharmāḥ prakṛtyā svabhāvena pariśuddhāḥ ahamapi prakṛtipariśuddhā ityādikaṃ āmukhīkuryyāt. Imāñca sarvadharma-prakṛti-pariśuddhatāṃ anena mantrena adhitiṣṭhet. Oṃ Svabhāvaśuddhāḥ sarvadharmāḥ svabhāvaśuddho'haṃ iti. Yadi prakṛtipariśuddhāḥ sarvadharmāḥ kutaḥ tarhi saṃsāraṃ āvahati. Grāhya-grāhakādimalāvṛtatvāt. Tadvigamopāyaḥ sanmārgabhāvanā. Tayā sa niruddhaṃ syāt. Ataḥ prakṛtipariśuddhāḥ sarvadharmāḥ iti sid-

Muditā (Joyousness) is of the following nature. Muditā is that desire of all beings in this world for the attainment of Buddhahood, which is unlikely to them ; or it is the attraction (of the beings) towards the virtues that exist in this world and to their enjoyment and the spritual powers arising out of them. What is Upekṣā (Indifference) ? Upekṣā is the doing of great welfare to all beings, good or bad, by overcoming adverse requestes and obstacles ; or, it is the desire that comes of its own accord to do good to all beings without the least craving for their love ; or Upkeṣā is the indifference to the eight human institutions of gain and loss, fame and notoriety, blame or praise, pleasure and pain, and all unusual activities (deeds). After meditating on the four Brahmas the natural purity of all Phenomena should be meditated. All Phenomena indeed, are by nature, pure and therefore he the (worshipper) should think himself pure by nature. This natural purity of all Phenomena should be established by the charm "Oṃ svabhāvaśuddhāḥ sarvadharmāḥ svabhāvaśuddho'haṃ. If all Phenomena are naturally pure where then is the possibility of the cycle of existence ? Because of its being covered up with the impurity of the thought-categories, such as the Subject and the the Object. The way of purging off (this impurity) is the meditation on the good path. By that it is restrained. Therefore, is established the essential purity of all Phenomena.

dhaṃ. Sarva-dharma-prkṛti-pariśuddhatāṃ vibhāvya sarvadharmaśūnyatāṃ vibhāvayet. Tatrcyaṃ śūnyatā. Grāhyagrāhakādi-sakalakalpanā-prapañca-vañcitacitrādvaitaprakāśamātrātmyakaṃ sacarācaraṃ viśvaṃ iti cintayet. Imāṃ eva śūnyatāṃ anenāpi mantreṇa adhitiṣṭhet. Oṃ Śūnyatājñānavajrasvabhāvātmyako'haṃ iti.

Tadanu purvahṛdisthaṃ mṛgāṅkamaṇḍalamadhyavartilasannīlotpalakiñjalkābhyantarasthitaniṣkalaṅkaniśānāthamaṇḍalopari sthitāt pītaTāṅkāravījāt Bhagavatīm Āryatārāṃ....[bhāvayet].

Evaṃ rūpāṃ Bhagavatīṃ yāvat icchati tāvat vibhāvayet. Tadanantaraṃ asyā eva Bhagavatyā hṛdisthahimāṃśumaṇḍalamadhyāvasthitamañjunīlasarojakiñjalkāntargatakalaṅkavarjitakumudabāndhavamaṇḍala-madhy-āvalīna-pīta-Tāṃ'kāravījavinirgatānekamarīcimālābhiḥ trailokyālokakāriṇībhiḥ gatvā anādisaṃsiddhā Bhagavatī jñānasattvarūpā api ākāśāt ānīyate. Ānīya tāṃ ākāśādeśe api avasthāpya ratnabhājanāvasthitasugandhitoyena surabhikusumena ca tasyā eva Bhagavatyāḥ caraṇārghyaṃ dattvā divyapuṣpa-

After meditating on the purity of all Phenomenal existence the voidness of all Phenomena should be meditated upon. Here void means this. He should concieve the entire universe with its mobile and immobile creations as the clear manifestation of non-duality when the mind is devoid of all the extensions of such thought categories as Subject and Object. This very voidness should be established by the charm "Oṃ Śūnyatājñanavajrasvabhāvātmyako'haṃ."

Then, as previously stated, on the heart should be meditated the goddess Āryatārā who originates from the yellow germ syllable, 'Tāṃ' placed on the orb of the spotless moon, which again is inside the filament of a blooming blue lotus, which is within the orb of the moon with the deer on its lap..........

The goddess of this description should be conceived as long as desired. Then the eternally accomplished Bhagavatī should be drawn out by spreading rays that illumine the three worlds—the rays which issue forth out of the yellow germ syllable 'Tāṃ,' contained in the orb of the spotted moon, which is again within the filament of a beautiful blue lotus. After thus discovering her, she should be placed on the firmament and should be worshipped with the offerings of scented water and fragrant flowers contained in the vessel inlaid with gems, at the feet of the Bhagavatī; and should also be worshipped with dhūpadīpanaivedyagandhamālyavilepanacūrṇacīvaracchatradhvajaghaṇṭāpatākādibhiḥ bahuvidhābhiśca tām eva Bhagavatīṃ pūjayet. Punaḥ punaḥ saṃpūjya stuttvā ca mūdrāṃ darśayet......Anayā mudrayā tāṃ eva Bhagavatīṃ jñānasattvarūpāṃ santoṣya atraiva samayasattvarūpāyāṃ Bhagavatyā mantraṃ bhāvayet iti anayor-advaitaṃ adhimuñcet· Tadanu niśīthinīnāthamaṇḍalamadhyaniviṣṭavikacanīlāmbujakiñjalkāntarlīnaniṣkalaṅkendumaṇḍaloparisthitapīta-Tāṃ-kāravījavinirgatāś-ca aparyantāḥ ca Tārādevyāḥ daśadiglokadhātūn samavabhāsya tatsthitānāṃ api sattvānāṃ nānāratnavarṣaṇena dāridryādiduḥkhān apanayanti. Kṣaṇikanairātmādidharmadeśanāmṛtena tān santarpayanti. Punaḥ nānāprakāraṃ jagadarthaṃ kṛtvā viśvaṃ api Tārārūpaṃ niṣpādya tatrāpi pīta-Tāṃ-kāravīje tasyāntar-Bhagavatī ityevamādisphuraṇasaṃharaṇakrameṇa yāvat khedo na jāyate tāvat bhāvayet. Bhāvanātaḥ khinno mantraṃ japet. Tatrāyaṃ mantraḥ Oṃ Tāre-tuttāre ture svāhā. Mahāprabhāva evāyaṃ mantrarājaḥ. Sarvaireva Tathāgatairvanditaḥ pujitaḥ satkṛtaśceti. Dhyānāt vyuthtito yogī jagat-Tārārūpaṃ dṛṣtvā Bhagavatyahaṅkāreṇa yatheṣṭaṃ viharet

various ceremonies, external and internal, by means of flowers, incense, light-stick, food-offerings, scents, garlands, unguents, powders, mendicant dress, umbrella, flags, bell, banner, and and the like. Thus repeatedly worshipping and praising her, the Mudrā should be exhibited..........With this Mudrā after propitiating that very goddess of the essence of knowledge he should commingle her with the goddess of the essence of time, and by so doing, the non-duality of the two is meditated. Then the rays that issue out from the yellow germ syllable 'Tāṃ' which is on the spotless moon (*lit.* the Lover of Night)—the rays illuminating the worlds in the ten quarters,—cause the removal of the poverty and other miseries of the beings that inhabit them, by showers of various gems, and satisfy them by the nectar of advice on realization of temporary Śūnya (Nairātmā) or voidness. After doing good deeds for the world he should meditate on the form of Tārā which is identified with the universe ; again he should meditate repeatedly, until tired, the yellow germ syllable and the Bhagavatī concontained therein. He, who is unable to meditate should mutter the Mantra. The Mantra in that case is "Oṃ Tāre-tuttāre ture svāhā. This lord of all Mantras has great power, and is saluted, worshipped and revered by all the Tathāgatas. Finishing the Dhyāna he should think the world as the form of Tārā and should move about conceiving himself to be the iti. Prāyaḥ amunā krameṇa Bhagavatīṃ bhāvayato aṣṭamahāsiddhayaḥ caraṇayoḥ nipatanti. Kiṃ punaḥ anyāḥ siddhayaḥ. Api tu tāśca sutarāṃ eva. Yaśca vijanagiriguhāsīnaḥ san Bhagavatīṃ bhāvayet, sa khalu pratyakṣataḥ eva tāṃ paśyati. Svayaṃ eva Bhagavatī tasyā śvāsapraśvāsādikaṃ dadāti. Kimbahu vaktavyaṃ, paramadurllabhaṃ Buddhatvaṃ api karatalagataṃ tasya avatiṣṭhate.

Iti kiñcit-vistara-Tārā-sādhanaṃ samāptaṃ.

Kṛtiriyaṃ paṇḍita-sthavira-Anupamarakṣitānāṃ.

Sādhanamālā ? A—106-110,
N—75-79, C—82-86.

Bhagavatī.

Generally those who meditate on the Bhagavatī in this manner all the eight great perfections (Siddhi) fall at their feet. Not to speak of other smaller perfections, which come as a matter of course. Whosoever meditate upon the Bhagavatī in the lonely cave of the mountains, espies her with his own eyes ; the Bhagavatī herself gives him his breath. Not to say more, even the Buddhahood which is most difficult to attain, comes to him as if it is in the palm of his hand.

Here ends the somewhat long procedure for the worship of Tārā.

The author of this Sādhana is Anupama Rakṣita, the Sthavira.

APPENDIX B.

Descriptions of one hundred and eight forms of Avalokiteśvara *appearing in the Macchandar Vahal, Kathmandu, Nepal.*

(Plates XLIII—LXIX)

1. **Hayagrīva Lokeśvara.** The god sits in the Vajraparyaṅka attitude on a lotus. He has four hands, out of which the two principal ones exhibit the Vyākhyāna pose. The second pair holds the rosary in the right hand and the lotus in the left. He is accompanied by six other gods and a dragon.

2. **Mojaghāñjavala (?) Lokeśvara.** He stands in the Samabhaṅga pose on a lotus with his two hands showing the Abhaya Mudrā in the right and the lasso in the left.

3. **Hālāhala Lokeśvara.** He sits in the Lalita attitude on a lotus with his Śakti on the lap. He has three faces and six arms. The face above represents probably the head of the Dhyānī Buddha, the effigy of whom he ought to bear on the crown. In his three right hands he shows the sword, the rosary and the Varada pose. In the three left hands he carries the lotus, the noose and the Utpala. The hand holding the noose passes round the Śakti in the act of embracing. The Śakti exhibits the Varada Mudrā in the right hand and the Abhaya in the left.*

4. **Harihariharivāhana Lokeśvara.** Lowermost is the snake, on it is the lion ; over the lion is Garuḍa. Nārāyaṇa rides Garuḍa and on his shoulder sits Lokeśvara. The Garuḍa has two hands in the Añjali Mudrā. Nārāyaṇa has four hands, out of which the first pair is engaged in forming the Añjali against the breast while the second pair has the Cakra in the right hand and the Gadā in the left. Lokeśvara sits in Vajraparyaṅka, and has six arms ; the three right hands show the rosary, the Cakra and the Varada pose while the three left carry the Tridaṇḍī, the noose and the Utpala.†

5. **Māyājālakrama Lokeśvara.** He has five faces and twelve arms. The head on the top probably represents Amitābha. He stands in the Ālīḍha attitude, wears the tiger-skin and the garland of heads, but his faces do not present a fearful appearance. The six right hands carry the Tridaṇḍī, the

* Described in the Sādhanamālā.

† Also described to the Sādhanamālā.

Khaṭvāṅga, the jewel, the Khaḍga, the Vajra and the rosary, and the six left the noose, the Kapāla, the Utpala, the fruit, the Cakra and the lotus.*

6. Saḍakṣarī Lokeśvara. He sits in the Vajraparyaṅka attitude. He has four arms and one face. The principal pair of hands are joined against the breast in forming the Añjali. The second pair carries the rosary in the right and the lotus in the left.†

7. Ānandādi Lokeśvara. He shows a standing attitude in the Samabhaṅga, carries the lotus, the stem of which he holds in his right hand while the left displays the Varada pose.

8. Vaśyādhikāra Lokeśvara. He sits in the Vajraparyaṅka attitude carries the bowl with his two hands arranged in Samādhi Mudrā.

9. Potapāda Lokeśvara. He sits also in the Vajraparyaṅka attitude and has four arms. The two principal hands exhibit the Añjali against the breast while the other pair holds the rosary in the right and the noose in the left.

10. Kamaṇḍalu Lokeśvara. He stands in the Samabhaṅga pose and is endowed with six arms. The two principal hands are engaged in drawing the bow to its full length. The other four hands carry the Vajra and the Cakra in the two right and the Ghaṇṭā and the Kamaṇḍalu in the two left.

11. Varadāyaka Lokeśvara. He is one-faced, six-armed and stands on a lotus. The two principal hands join against his breast in forming the Añjali. He shows also the rosary and the Varada pose in the two right hands and the book and a Mudrā (probably Karaṇa) in the two left.

12. Jaṭāmukuṭa Lokeśvara. He is four-armed and one-faced, the head on the top representing the head of Amitābha ; The two right hands show the rosary and the Varada pose while the two left have the lotus and the water-pot. He is represented in a standing attitude.

13. Sukhāvatī Lokeśvara. He is one-faced and six-armed and sits on lotus in the Lalita attitud . The first pair of hands exhibits the Dharma-cakra Mudrā, the second pair carries the rosary and the book and the third pair shows the Varada Mudrā in the right and the water-pot in the left.‡

14. Pretasantarpita Lokeśvara. He is one-faced and six-armed and stands on a lotus. In his three right hands he carries the rosary, the jewel

* Described in the Sādhanamālā.

† Described in the Sādhanamālā.

‡ Described in the Dharmakoṣasaṅgraha of Amṛtānanda.

1. Hayagrīva Lokeśvara

3. Hālāhala Lokeśvara

2. Mojaghāñjavala (?) Lokeśvara

4. Harihariharivāhana Lokeśvara

Plate XLIII

5. Māyājālakrama Lokeśvara

7. Ānandādi Lokeśvara

6. Ṣaḍākṣarī Lokeśvara

8. Vaśyādhikāra Lokeśvara

Plate XLIV

9. Potapāda Lokeśvara

10. Kamaṇḍalu Lokeśvara

11. Varadāyaka Lokeśvara

12. Jaṭāmukuṭa Lokeśvara

Plate XLV

13. Sukhāvatī Lokeśvara

15. Māyājālakramakrodha Lokeśvara

14. Pretasantarpaṇa Lokeśvara

16. Sugatisandarśana Lokeśvara

Plate XLVI

and shows the Varada Mudrā, while the three left carry the Tridaṇḍi and the book and exhibit the Varada Mudrā.*

15. Māyājālakramakrodha Lokeśvara. He presents a very fierce appearance with five faces terrible with protruding teeth, and eyes rolling in anger. His hair rises upwards like flames of fire. He stands in the Pratyālīḍha attitude and wears the tiger-skin. He has twelve arms, out of which the six right carry the sword, the Vajra, the goad, the noose, the Triśūla, and the arrow. The six left have the shield, the Cakra, the Jewel, the deer-skin, the Kapāla and the Tarjanī with the noose.†

16. Sugatisandarśana Lokeśvara. He is one-faced and six-armed and stands on a lotus. In his three right hands he carries the rosary and exhibits the Varada and Abhaya poses. The three left have the Tridaṇḍi, the Utpala and the water-pot.‡

17. Nīlakaṇṭha Lokeśvara. He is one-faced and two-armed, and sits on a lotus in the Vajraparyaṅka attitude. He carries the bowl of gems in his two hands arranged in the Samādhi Mudrā.§

18. Lokanātha-raktāryyāvalokiteśvara. He is one-faced and two-armed and sits in the Lalita attitude on a lotus. The right hand displays the Varada Mudrā while the left holds the stem of a lotus on his lap.||

19. Trilokasandarśana Lokeśvara. He is also one-faced and two-armed and sits in the Vajraparyaṅka attitude. His right hand is raised against the breast with outstretched fingers and the palm inwards. The other hands exhibit exactly the same pose (Karaṇa ?) as displayed in one of the left hands by Varadāyaka Lokeśvara.

20. Siṃhanātha Lokeśvara. He is one faced and four-armed and sits in Bhadrāsana, or the European fashion, on a raised seat placed on the lotus. In his two right hands he carries the sword and the jewel while the two left hold the book and the noose.

* Described on the obverse side of the first leaf of Abhiṣekavidhi, appended to the Nepal palm leaf Ms. of the Sādhanamālā.

† This form seems to have some affinity with the form described under No. 5. The Dhyāna in the Sādhanamālā probably gave rise to two distinct forms in later times.

‡ Also described in Abhiṣekavidhi.

§ Described in the Sādhanamālā.

|| Described in the Sādhanamālā as Lokanātha.

This seems to be quite different from the Siṃhanāda described in the Sādhanamālā.

21. Khasarpaṇa Lokeśvara. He is one-faced and two-armed and sits in the Lalita attitude on a lotus. His right hand exhibits the Varada pose and the left is raised against the breast and holds the stem of a lotus.*

22. Maṇipadma Lokeśvara. He is one-faced and four-armed and sits in the Vajraparyaṅka attitude on a lotus. His two principal hands are joined against his breast in forming the Añjali. The other pair holds the rosary in the right hand and the lotus in the left. He is identical in form with no. 6. described above.

23. Vajradharma Lokeśvara. He is one-faced and two-armed and sits in the Vajraparyaṅka attitude on a lotus. The right hand displays the Abhaya pose and the right on the lap holds the stem of the Utpala.†

24. Pupala Lokeśvara. He is one-faced and four-armed and sits in the Vajraparyaṅka attitude on a lotus. One of the two right hands carries the rosary while the other exhibits the Abhaya pose. One of the two left carries the book and the other displays a Mudrā with the index and little finger pointed forwards (Karaṇa ?).

25. Utnauti (?) Lokeśvāra. He is one-faced and six-armed and sits in Bhadrāsana on the raised seat of a lotus. His three right hands hold the rosary and the Vajra and exhibit the Abhaya pose, while the three left carry the Kapāla, the noose and the water-pot.

26. Vṛṣṇācana Lokeśvara. He is one-faced and six-armed and sits in the Lalita attitude on a lotus. The three right hands show the Utpala, the arrow and the Varada pose while the three left show the book, the bow and the Abhaya pose.

27. Brahmadaṇḍa Lokeśvara. He is one-faced and four-armed, sits in the Lalita attitude on a lotus and is accompanied by his Śakti who sits on his lap. His two right hands show the Tridaṇḍī and the Varada pose, while the two left show the Ratnakalasa (vessel containing jewels) and a Mudrā with the index and little fingers pointed forwards. The Śakti displays the Varada pose in the right hand and the Abhaya in the left.

28. Acāta (?) Lokeśvara—He is one-faced and six-armed and sits in the Lalita attitude. The three right hands carry the sword and the arrow and display the Varada pose ; while the three left hold the Kartri, the bow and display the Abhaya pose.

* Described in the Sādhanamālā. Here the four companions have not been given.

† Described in the Sādhanamālā ; but the form presented in this figure does not agree with the one described in chapter III.

17. Nīlakaṇṭha Lokeśvara

19. Trilokasandarśana Lokeśvara

18. Lokanātha-Raktāryyāvalokiteśvara

20. Siṃhanātha Lokeśvara

Plate XLVII

21. Khasarpaṇa Lokeśvara

22. Maṇipadma Lokeśvara

23. Vajradharma Lokeśvara

24. Pupala Lokeśvara (?)

Plate XLVIII

25. Utnauti (?) Lokeśvara

27. Brahmadaṇḍa Lokeśvara

26. Vṛṣṇācana Lokeśvara

28. Acāta Lokeśvara (?)

Plate XLIX

29. Mahāvajrasattva Lokeśvara

30. Viśvahana Lokeśvara

31. Śākyabuddha Lokeśvara

32. Śānsāti Lokeśvara

Plate L

29. Mahāvajrasattva Lokeśvara. He is one-faced and eight-armed and sits in the Vajrapaıyaṅka attitude on a lotus. The four right hands exhibit the sword, the rosary, the Cakra and the Abhaya pose while the four left carry the noose, the Tridaṇḍī, the conch and the bowl of gems on the lap.

30. Viśvahana Lokeśvara—He is one-faced and six-armed and sits in the Vajraparyaṅka attitude on a lotus. The three right hands carry the sword, the arrow and the Cakra, while the three left carry the noose, the bow and display the Abhaya pose.

31. Śākyabuddha Lokeśvara—He is one-faced and four-armed and is represented in a standing attitude on a lotus. His two right hands carry the arrow and the Khaṭvāṅga, while the two left hold the bow and exhibit the Tarjanī.

32. Sāntāsi Lokeśvara. He is one-faced and six-armed and stands on a lotus. The two principal hands join against the breast in forming the Dharmacakra Mudrā. The other four hands show the rosary and the Varada pose in the right and the book and the Abhaya pose in the left.

33. Jamadaṇḍa Lokeśvara. He is one-faced and six-armed and sits in the Lalita attitude on a lotus. The three right hands carry the sword, the lotus and the Vajra while the three left carry the fruit, the bowl of gems and exhibit a Mudrā (Karaṇa ?).

34. Vajroṣṇīṣa Lokeśvara. He is one-faced and six-armed and is represented as standing on a lotus. His three right hands show the rosary, the Tridaṇḍī and the Abhaya pose, while the three left show the book, the noose and the Varada pose.

35. Vajrahuntika Lokeśvara. He is one-faced and twelve-armed and stands in Ardhaparyaṅka in a dancing attitude. He carries the Utpala in all his twelve hands.*

36. Jñānadhātu Lokeśvara. He is one-faced and eight-armed and stands on a lotus. Two of his hands join in forming the Añjali against the breast ; the second pair exhibit what is called the Kṣepaṇa Mudrā. The remaining hands carry the rosary and the Tridaṇḍī in the right and the book and the noose in the left.

* This form may be a later development of the conception of Padmanarttеśvara, who is also sometimes represented as eighteen-armed, carrying the double lotus in all his hands.

37. Kāraṇḍavyūha Lokeśvara. He is one-faced and two-armed and sits in the Vajraparyaṅka attitude on a lotus. He carries the Vajra in the right hand and the book against his breast in the left.*

38. Sarvaṇivaraṇaviṣkambhī Lokeśvara. He is one-faced and two-armed and sits in the Vajraparyaṅka attitude on a lotus. He carries the stem of a lotus on which appears the sword in the right hand and the Vajra against his breast in the left.

39. Sarvaśokatamonirghāta Lokeśvara. He is one-faced and four-armed and sits in the Vajraparyaṅka attitude on a lotus. The two principal hands exhibit the Abhaya poses against his breast and the other two hands carry the rosary in the right and the Utpala in the left.

40. Pratibhānakakūṭa Lokeśvara. He is one-faced and two-armed and sits in Vajraparyaṅka attitude on a lotus. He carries the noose against his breast in the right hand and holds the bowl of gems in the left.

41. Amṛtaprabha Lokeśvara. He is also one-faced and two-armed and sits in the Vajraparyaṅka attitude on a lotus. He carries the double Vajra on his lap in the right hand and the lotus on a water-vessel in the left.

42. Jālinīprabha Lokeśvara. He is also one-faced and two-armed and sits in the Vajraparyaṅka attitude on a lotus. He holds the sword on a lotus in the right hand and the stem of a lotus against his breast in the left.

43. Candraprabha Lokeśvara. He is also one-faced and two-armed and sits in the Vajraparyaṅka attitude on a lotus. He exhibits the Vitarka Mudrā in the right hand and carries the stem of a lotus against the breast in the left.

44. Avalokita Lokeśvara. He is also one-faced and two-armed and sits in the same attitude. He weilds the sword in his right hand and holds the stem of a lotus against his breast in the left.

45. Vajragarbha Lokeśvara. He has got also the same number of hands and faces like no. 44. He carries the Vajra in the right hand and the stem of a lotus in the left.

46. Sāgaramati Lokeśvara. He is in all respects identical to No. 44 with the difference that he carries the double Vajra in his right hand.

* This form ought to have been the same as the Ṣaḍakṣarī Lokeśvara, but it is not so.

33. Yamadaṇḍa Lokeśvara

35. Vajrahuntika Lokeśvara

34. Vajroṣṇīśa Lokeśvara

36. Jñānadhātu Lokeśvara

Plate LI

37. Karaṇḍavyūha Lokeśvara

39. Sarvaśokatamonirghāta Lokeśvara

38. Sarvanivāraṇa-Viṣkambhī Lokeśvara

40. Pratibhānakakūṭa Lokeśvara

Plate LII

41. Amṛtaprabha Lokeśvara

42. Jālinīprabha Lokeśvara

43. Candraprabha Lokeśvara

44. Avalokita Lokeśvara

Plate LIII

45. Vajragarbha Lokeśvara

47. Ratnapāṇi Lokeśvara

46. Sāgaramati Lokeśvara

48. Gaganagañja Lokeśvara

Plate LIV

47. Ratnapāṇi Lokeśvara. He is also identical with No. 44 in all other respects. The difference lies in the fact that he carries the sword in the left hand and displays the Varada Mudrā in the right.

48. Gaganagañja Lokeśvara. He is also identical to No. 44. in all other respects with the difference that he exhibits the Vitarka Mudrā in the right hand and the book in the left.

49. Ākāśagarbha Lokeśvara. He is also identical to No. 44 in all respects with the difference that here the god exhibits the Varada pose in the right hand and the stem of a lotus in the left.

50. Kṣitigarbha Lokeśvara. He is also identical to No. 44 except that here the god carries a tray of gems in the right hand and displays the Varada Mudrā in the left.

51. Akṣayamati Lokeśvara. He is also identical to No. 44 with the difference that this god carries the rosary in the right hand and holds the lotus on a water-vessel against his breast in the left.

52. Sṛṣṭikāntā Lokeśvara. He is one-faced and two-armed and stands on a lotus. He displays the Varada pose in the right hand while the empty left hand rests near his waist. A large number of four armed gods issue out from various points of his body while Amitābha appears over his head.

53. Sāmantabhadra Lokeśvara. He is one-faced and two-armed and sits in the Vajraparyaṅka attitude on a lotus. He exhibits the Varada pose in the right hand and holds the stem of a lotus against his breast in the left.

54. Mahāsahasrabhuja Lokeśvara. In all other respects he is identical to No. 53 with the difference that here the god weilds the sword in his right hand and dispalys the Varada Mudrā in the left.

55. Mahāratnakīrti Lokeśvara. He is three-faced and six-armed and stands on a lotus. He carries the fruit, the Utpala, and the conch in the three right hands, and shows the bow, the whip and the Namaskāra Mudrā in the three left.

56. Mahāsaṅkhanātha Lokeśvara. He is identical in all respects to No. 55 with the difference that the symbols carried by him are different. Here the god shows the Namaskāra Mudrā, and the two Vajras in the three right hands while the three left carry the noose, the arrow and the Ghaṇṭā.

57. Mahāsahasrasūryya Lokeśvara. He is eleven-faced and eight-armed and stands on a lotus. The two principal hands exhibit the Abhaya

poses against the breast. The remaining hands show the rosary, the Cakra and the Varada pose in the three right hands and the Utpala, the bow charged with an arrow, and the vessel in the three left. This form of Lokeśvara is very popular in Tibet.*

58. Mahāratnakula Lokeśvara. He is three-faced and six-armed and stands on a lotus. The head on the top represents that of Amitabha. He carries the sword, the Utpala and the rosary in the three right hands and the book, the lotus and the Utpala in the three left.

59. Mahāpaṭala Lokeśvara. He is also three-faced and six-armed and stands on a lotus. He carries in his three right hands the Vajra, the Viśvavajra and the Utpala and in the three left, the banner, the Ghaṇṭā and the Kamaṇḍalu.

60. Mahāmañjudatta Lokeśvara. In all other respect he is similar to No. 59. But he carries the Ghaṇṭā, the sword and the Ratnapallava in his three right hands and the Vajra, the Ghaṇṭā and the Utpala in the three left hands.

61. Mahācandrabimba Lokeśvara. He is three-faced and six-armed and stands on a lotus. He carries the arrow, the Utpala and the fruit in his three right hands and the bow, the Vajra and the Cakra in the three left. The head on the top probably represents Amitabha.†

62. Mahāsūryyabimba Lokeśvara. He is identical in all respects to No. 61 except that here the god carries two Vajras, and the Cakra in the three right hands and two Utpalas and the bowl of gems in the three left.

63. Mahā-abhayaphalada Lokeśvara. He is also similar in form to No. 61. except that here the god carries the Vajra, the sword and the Utpala in the three right hands and two Ghaṇṭās, and the book in the three left.

64. Mahā-abhayakarī Lokeśvara. He is also similar in form to No. 61, but the symbols held by the hands are diffrent. Here the god carries the book against his breast in the two principal hands, and holds the Vajra and the the rosary in the right and the Ghaṇṭa and the Tridaṇḍī in the left.

* Getty's Avalokiteśvara with 22,000 arms is only a development of this form of Lokeśvara, which appears in the middle of the image. *See* Getty : *Gods of the Northern Buddhism.*

† In the whole of the Sādhanamālā we do not find any deity with four faces and six arms. The arms are generally double the number of faces.

49. Ākāśagarbha Lokeśvara

51. Akṣayamati Lokeśvara

50. Kṣitigarbha Lokeśvara

52. Sr̥ṣṭikāntā Lokeśvara

Plate LV

53. Samantabhadra Lokeśvara

54. Mahāsahasrabhuja Lokeśvara

55. Mahāratnakīrti Lokeśvara

56. Mahāśaṅkhanātha Lokeśvara

Plate LVI

57. Mahāsahasrasūryya Lokeśvara

59. Mahāpaṭala Lokeśvara

58. Mahāratnakula Lokeśvara

60. Mahāmañjudatta Lokeśvara

Plate LVII

61. Mahācandrabimba Lokeśvara

62. Mahāsūryyabimba Lokeśvara

63. Mahā-Abhayaphalada Lokeśvara

64. Mahā-Abhayakarī Lokeśvara

Plate LVIII

65. Mahāmañjubhūta Lokeśvara. He is also similar to No. 61 with the difference that here the god carries the sword, the Vajra and the Kamaṇḍalu in the three right hands, and the rosary, the Utpala and the bell in the three left.

66. Mahāviśvaśuddha Lokeśvara. He is four-faced and eight-armed and stands on a lotus. He carries in his four right hands the sword, the flag, the Vajra and the goad, while the four left hold the Ghaṇṭā, the conch, the Utpala and the lotus.

67. Mahāvajradhātu Lokeśvara. He is identical with No. 66 in all respects but the symbols differ. Here the god carries the Vajra, the bow, the Triśūla and the sword in the four right hands, and the Ghaṇṭā, the arrow, the Kamaṇḍalu and the noose in the four left.

68. Mahāvajradhṛk Lokeśvara. He is also identical in form to No. 66 with the difference that here the god carries the sword, the Vajra, the bow and the Aṅkuśa in the four right hands, and the Utpala, the Ghaṇṭā, the arrow and the noose in the four left.

69. Mahāvajrapāṇi Lokeśvara. He is also identical with No. 66 except that here the god carries the sword, the goad, the Gadā, and the rosary in the four right hands, and the Cakra, the noose, the Utpala and the book in the four left.

70. Mahāvajranātha Lokeśvara. He is three-faced and eight-armed and stands on a lotus. He carries the rosary and the noose and displays the Abhaya and Varada poses in his four right hands. The three left show the book, the Tridaṇḍī, and the lotus, while the empty fourth rests near the waist.

71. Amoghapāśa Lokeśvara. He is four-faced and eight-armed and stands on a lotus. He carries in his four right hands the Vajra, the sword, the goad and the bow, while the three left carry the Ghaṇṭā, the Tridaṇḍī the noose and the arrow.

72. Devadevatā Lokeśvara. He is also similar to No. 71 with the difference that here the god carries the Vajra, the bow, the Triśūla and the sword in the right, and the bell, the arrow, the jewel (?) and the noose in the left.

73. Piṇḍapātra Lokeśvara. He is one-faced and two-armed and stands on a lotus. He carries the Piṇḍapātra (the bowl containing oblations to be offered to the Departed Fathers) in his two hands near the waist.

74. Sārthavāha Lokeśvara. He is similar to No. 73 in all respects except that here the god displays the Varada Mudrā in his right hand and carries the Piṇḍapātra (bowl) in the left.

75. Ratnadala Lokeśvara. He is also similar to No. 73 in all other respects except that here he displays the Varada pose in the right hand while the empty left touches the shoulder.

76. Viṣṇupāṇi Lokeśvara. He is again similar in form to No. 73, except that here he carries the Triśūla in the right hand and a lotus bud in the left.

77. Kamalacandra Lokeśvara. He is also similar to No. 73 except that here he displays the Vitarka Mudrā in both of his hands.

78. Vajrakhaṇḍa Lokeśvara. He is also similar to No. 73 in all other respects except that here the god carries the lotus bud in the right hand and the book against the breast in the left.

79. Acalaketu Lokeśvara. He is also similar to No. 73. But he displays the Abhaya Mudrā in the right hand and the Piṇḍapātra (bowl) in the left. A *chowrie* rests against his right shoulder.

80. Śiriṣarā (?) Lokeśvara. He is also similar to No. 73 in all respects except that here he carries the sword in the right hand and the noose in the left.

81. Dharmacakra Lokeśvara. He is again similar to No. 73 except that here he carries the Vajra in the right hand and the axe in the left.

82. Harivāhana Lokeśvara. He is identical to No. 73 with the difference that here the god carries the Kamaṇḍalu in the right hand and the *chowrie* in the left.

83. Sarasiri (?) Lokeśvara. He is again identical with No. 73. The difference is that here the god carries the Triśūla in the right hand and the lotus in the left.

84. Harihara Lokeśvara. He is also identical with No. 73 in all other respects expect that here he displays the Vyākhyāna Mudrā with his two hands against the breast.

85. Siṃhanāda Lokeśvara. He is again similar to No. 73. But here the god carries the *chowrie* resting against his shoulder in the right hand, while the empty left rests near the waist.

65. Mahāmañjubhūta Lokeśvara

67. Mahāvajradhātu Lokeśvara

66. Mahāviśvaśuddha Lokeśvara

68. Mahāvajradhṛk Lokeśvara

Plate LIX

69. Mahāvajrapāṇi Lokeśvara

70. Mahāvajranātha Lokeśvara

71. Amoghapāśa Lokeśvara

72. Devadevatā Lokeśvara

Plate LX

73. Piṇḍapātra Lokeśvara

74. Sārthavāha Lokeśvara

75. Ratnadala Lokeśvara

76. Viṣṇupāṇi Lokeśvara

Plate LXI

77. Kamalacandra Lokeśvara

79. Acalaketu Lokeśvara

78. Vajrakhaṇḍa Lokeśvara

80. Ṣiriṣarā Lokeśvara

Plate LXII

86. Viśvavajra Lokeśvara. He is also similar to No. 73 with the difference that here the god displays the Varada pose in the right hand and carries a snake in the left.

87. Amitābha Lokeśvara. He is again similar to No. 73 in all other respect except that here the god carries the *chowrie* in the right hand and the wheel in the left.

88. Vajrasattvadhātu Lokeśvara. He is similar to No. 73 except that here he carries the Cakra in the right hand and the conch in the left.

89. Viśvabhūta Lokeśvara. He is similar to No. 73 in form ; but here he carries the rosary in the right hand and the lotus in the left.

90. Dharmadhātu Lokeśvara. He is again identical with No. 73 in form except that here the god carries in his two hands the water-pot held near the waist.

91. Vajradhātu Lokeśvara. He is identical with No. 73 except that here the god displays the Varada Mudrā in the right hand and carries the lotus in the left.

92. Śākyabuddha Lokeśvara. He is also similar to No. 73 with the difference that he carries the Vajra in the right hand while the empty left is held near the waist.

93. Cittadhātu Lokeśvara. He is also similar to No. 73 with the difference that he carries the image of a Jīna (probably Amitābha) in the right hand and displays the Abhaya pose in the left.

94. Cintāmaṇi Lokeśvara. He is also similar to No. 73 except that here he carries the Caitya in the right hand while the empty left is held near the waist.

95. Śāntamati Lokeśvara. He is again similar to No. 73 with the difference that he exhibits the Varada pose in the right hand, and carries the bough of a tree in the left.

96. Mañjunātha Lokeśvara. He is also similar to No. 73 ; but here the god carries the rosary in the right hand and the book against the breast in the left.

97. Viṣṇucakra Lokeśvara. He is also similar to No. 73 except that here he carries the Cakra in the right hand and the Gadā in the left.

98. Kṛtāñjali Lokeśvara. He is also similar to No. 73 with the difference that here the god exhibits the Añjali, which is held against the breast, in his two hands.

99. Viṣṇukāntā Lokeśvara. He is again identical with No. 73 in all other respects except that here the god displays the Varada Mudrā in the right hand and the book against the breast in the left.

100. Vajrasṛṣṭa Lokeśvara. He is also identical with No. 73. The difference lies in the fact that here the god carries the *chowrie* in the right hand and the lotus in the left.

101. Saṅkhanātha Lokeśvara. He is also similar to No. 73 with the difference that here the god carries the conch against his breast in the right hand and the lotus in the left.

102. Vidyāpati Lokeśvara. He is also similar to No. 73 except that here the god shows the empty right hand against his breast while the left carries the lotus. The *chowrie* hangs from his right shoulder.

103. Nityanātha Lokeśvara. He is identical with No. 73 with the difference that here the god carries the rosary in the right hand over the book held in the left.

104. Padmapāṇi Lokeśvara. He is also similar in form to No. 73 with the difference that here the god displays the Varada pose in the right hand and carries the stem of a lotus in the left.

105. Vajrapāṇi Lokeśvara. He is again identical with No. 73 in all other respects except that here the god carries the Vajra on his head in the right hand, while the empty left is held near the waist. The attitude in which he stands is also different. He shows the dancing attitude in Ardhaparyaṅka.

106. Mahāsthāmaprāpta Lokeśvara. He is similar in all respects to Padmapāṇi Lokeśvara (No. 104).

107. Vajranātha Lokeśvara. He is also identical with No. 105, Vajrapāṇi Lokeśvara, with the only difference that here the god holds the lotus in the left hand. Like the previous one, he shows also the dancing attitude in Ardhaparyaṅka.

108. Śrīmadāryāvalokiteśvara. He is one-faced and two-armed and stands on a lotus. He holds the Vajra in his right hand, which rests against the breast, while the left carries the stem of a lotus held near the waist.

81. Dharmacakra Lokeśvara

83. Sarasiri Lokeśvara

82. Harivāhana Lokeśvara

84. Harihara Lokeśvara

Plate LXIII

85. Siṃhanāda Lokeśvara

87. Amitābha Lokeśvara

86. Viśvavajra Lokeśvara

88. Vajrasattvadhātu Lokeśvara

Plate LXIV

89. Viśvabhūta Lokeśvara

91. Vajradhātu Lokeśvara

90. Dharmadhātu Lokeśvara

92. Śākyabuddha Lokeśvara

Plate LXV

93. Cittadhātu Lokeśvara

94. Cintāmaṇi Lokeśvara

95. Śāntamati Lokeśvara

96. Mañjunātha Lokeśvara

Plate LXVI

97. Viṣṇucakra Lokeśvara

99. Viṣṇukāntā Lokeśvara

98. Kṛtāñjali Lokeśvara

100. Vajrasṛṣṭa Lokeśvara

Plate LXVII

101. Śaṅkhanātha Lokeśvara

103. Nityanātha Lokeśvara

102. Vidyāpati Lokeśvara

104. Padmapāṇi Lokeśvara

Plate LXVIII

105. Vajrapāṇi Lokeśvara

107. Vajranātha Lokeśvara

106. Mahāsthāmaprāpta Lokeśvara

108. Śrīmad-Āryāvalokiteśvara

Plate LXIX

GLOSSARY.

Abhaya—Mudrā, or the gesture of protection. Any hand showing this Mudrā should be slightly elevated and bent with the palm turned outward, the fingers being outstreched and elevated. This Mudrā should be distinguished from the Varada Mudrā in which case the hand is stretched downwards with the fingers, instead of being elevated, pointed downwards; and also, from the Capeṭadāna Mudrā, which shows the right hand menacingly extended upwards, just as we do in dealing a slap.

Akṣamālā—or *Mālā,* is the string of beads such as is carried by the Roman Catholic priests. The beads consist of a kind of dried fruit, called in Sanskrit, Rudrākṣa.

Alīḍha—a particular Āsana, or attitude of legs, in all respects similar to the attitude adopted in drawing the bow charged with an arrow. The right leg is outstretched while the left is slightly bent. This attitude should be distinguished from the *Pratyālīḍha* attitude, in which case the left leg is outstretched while the right is slightly bent and placed behind.

Añjali—name of a Mudrā also known as the *Sarvarājendra* Mudrā or the *Saṃpuṭāñjali.* It is the Mudrā in which the two hands are clasped palm to palm, both of which are extended upward with all fingers erect or slightly bent. This is the characteristic Mudrā of Ṣaḍakṣarī Lokeśvara and is also exhibited by Nāmasaṅgīti.

Aṅkuśa—elephant goad. *See* the weapon, for instance, in the image of Parṇa-śavarī. When the goad is surmounted by a Vajra, it is called *Vajrāṅkuśa.*

Anuvyañjanas—see *Lakṣaṇas.*

Ardhaparyaṅka—also called *Mahārājalīlā,* is a particular Āsana of sitting. Both the legs are on the same pedestal; one of the knee is raised while the other is bent in the usual position of a Buddha. This Āsana should be distinguished from the *Lalitāsana* in which case one of the legs is pendent, while the other is bent in the usual position of a Buddha. When both the legs are pendent, the attitude is called the *Bhadrāsana.*

Āsana—The word in Sanskrit may mean a seat, a mystic or any attitude exhibited in the lower limbs. The word *Padmāsana* means the seat of a lotus. Similarly *Siṃhāsana* means the lion-throne or the seat of a lion. The word *Sukhāsana* means any easy attitude of sitting. It may be the Paryaṅkāsana, the Lalitāsana or the Ardhaparyaṅkāsana. In fact, in the Sādhanamālā, the word Sukhāsana has has not been used in a technical sense. When used in a technical sense *Āsana* always signifies a particular mystic position of the lower limbs of the body. This Āsana may be of various kinds, such as, the Paryaṅkāsana, Vajraparyaṅkāsana, Lalitāsana, Ardhaparyaṅkāsana, Bhadrāsana, Ālīḍhāsana, Pratyālīḍhāsana or the Nāṭyāsana, a variety of Ardhaparyaṅka.

Aśoka—the absence of sorrow; but the word is always used to designate a particular kind of tree which blossoms forth red flowers. From time immemorial, this tree is regarded as sacred in India. It is believed that kicks at the tree by chaste women cause it to blossom.

Bāṇa—see *śara*.

Bhūmisparśa—also called *Bhūmisparśana* or the *Bhūsparśa* is the name of a Mudrā. The right hand exhibiting this Mudrā has the palm turned inward and the fingers outstretched with the tips touching the ground. This Mudrā should be distinguished from the *Varada* Mudrā in which case the tips do not touch the ground and the palm instead of being turned inward is turned outward. The deity showing the Bhūsparśa Mudrā must sit in the Vajraparyaṅka attitude.

Bhūtas—a class of mischievous spirits or hobgoblins who, without any provocation whatever, are supposed to injure men and destroy them mysteriously.

Bīja—see *Vīja*.

Brahmakapāla—or the *Brahmaśirah*, is the severed head of Brahmā who is credited with four faces with grey beards in all of them and the crown of grey chignon. The Buddhist gods, carrying triumphantly the severed head of Brahmā, display the aversion of the Buddhists towards the Hindus, as well as, the superiority of their gods to the gods of the alien faith.

Brahmamukha—the face of Brahmā containing four faces. The Brahmamukha is super-imposed on the head of Paramāśva.

Brahmaśirah—see Brahmakapāla.

Caitya—or the *Stūpa*, which represents the Buddhist Universe, is the Buddhist sanctuary, sometimes square and sometimes round, with spires or steps in the capital. Each spire or step represents a heaven, the uppermost portion being a point which is supposed to be the highest peak of Mount Sumeru, a mythical mountain, whence the Bodhicitta loses itself in Śūnya. On the four sides of the Caitya the figures of the Dhyānī Buddhas appear. Vairocana is sometimes present or sometimes absent. The intermediate corners are sometimes occupied by the figures of the Divine Buddhaśaktis or their symbolic representations in the form of Yantras. The Caitya may show further, in the four cardinal points, the Caturmahārājikas or the Guardains of the quarters, namely, Vaiśravaṇa, Virūpākṣa, Virūḍhaka and Dhṛtarāṣṭra. See *Stūpa* and Plate II.

Cakra—wheel or disc. It is the characteristic symbol of the Hindu god Viṣṇu or Kṛṣna.

Cāmara—Chowrie or the fly-whisk consisting of the tail of a *Yak*.

Cāpa—also called *Dhanu*, is the bow. It is generally carried in the left hand. With the bow and the arrow Mārīcī inflicts pain to the Māras or wicked beings.

Caṣaka—the same as *Kapāla. See Kapāla.*

Caturmudrā—See *ṣaṇmudrā.*

Cintāmaṇi—the gem that satisfies all desires. The jewel is sometimes represented in the form of small round object and sometimes in the shape of a flame.

ḍākinī—same as *śakti*. See *śakti.*

ḍamaru—small drum, such as is carried by the Hindu god. Śiva. *See ḍamaru* in the image of Bighnāntaka.

Daṇḍa—the staff or the mace carried by Hayagrīva. It cannot be translated as the magic wand, as the Khaṭvāṅga serves that purpose. When the staff is surmounted by a Vajra, it is called a *Vajradaṇḍa.*

Dhāraṇī—meaningless conglomeration of syllables, occasionally containing one or two intelligible words, used as a charm or prayer. There are Dhāraṇī-Saṃgrahas or collections of Dhāraṇīs in the Nepal Library, with an astonishingly large number of Dhāraṇīs devoted to the different deities. The list given in the *Nepal Catalogue*, Vol. II, App. p. 251 *et sqq*. may be consulted.

Dharmacakra—or *Vyākhyāna* Mudrā is that gesture of hands exibited by Lord Buddha while preaching his first sermon at Sarnath. This pose is depicted variously but the most artistic and correct representation of this Mudrā is to be found in the celebrated Prajñāpāramitā image from Java (Plate XXVIII,c) *See* Getty: *The Gods of Northern Buddhism*, p. 168.

Dhanu—same as *Cāpa*. See *Cāpa*.

Dhūpa—incense stick, which when burns, emits fragrance.

Dhyāna—meditation ; it refers generally to that portion of the Sādhana in which instruction is given as to the description of the deity with whom the worshipper is to identify himself.

Dhyāna—or *Samādhi Mudrā ;* the position of hands while in meditation. The hands with palm upwards lie one upon the other on the lap with all the fingers stretched. This is the characteristic Mudrā of Amitābha.

Dhyānāsana—or *Vajraparyaṅkāsana*, or *Vajrāsana*, is the meditative pose, the two legs being firmly locked with both the soles apparent—the characteristic sitting attitude of the Dhyānī Buddhas. Sometimes a small thunderbolt, shown on the seat of the god, indicate the meditative attitude. Dhyānāsana should be distinguished from the *Paryaṅka* attitude in which case the legs are placed one upon the other with both the soles invisible.

Dīpa—lamp ; the sacred lamp fed with *ghee*.

Gadā—mace.

Garuḍa—mythical bird supposed to be the destroyer of all serpents. The Hindus regard him as the Vāhana of Viṣṇu. Garuḍa is represented as a huge bird with a human body, two wings and sharp beaks, generally with hands clasped against the breast.

Ghaṇṭā—bell ; when the bell is surmounted by a Vajra, it is called *Vajraghaṇṭā*, which is a symbol of Vajrasattva.

Jaṭāmukuṭa—the crown of chignon. The hair is tied up above the head in such a way so as to resemble a crown or a tiara.

Kalasa—is the ordinary water-vessel of metal or earth. It is different from *Kamaṇḍalu* or *Kuṇḍikā*, which is smaller in size and in which there is a projecting pipe for discharging water.

Kamaṇḍalu—See *Kalasa.*

Kapāla—either (i) severed head of a man, or (ii) the cup made of a skull, or (iii) a bowl. The skull cup is of two kinds ; when it is filled with blood it is called *Asṛkkapāla*, and when with human flesh it is called *Māṃsa-kapāla.* The deities are supposed to partake of the blood or the flesh carried in these cups.

Karaṇa—Mudrā. Any hand showing this Mudrā is outstretched with the index and the little fingers erect, while the thumb presses the two remaining fingers against the palm of the hand.

Karppara—same as *Kapāla.* See *Kapāla.*

Kartri—or *Karttari* signifies a small knife ; sometimes the edge of it is uneven like the edge of a saw. It is called *Vajrakartri* when surmounted by a Vajra.

Khaḍga—sword. The sword in the hand of Mañjuśrī is called the Prajñākhaḍga or the Sword of Wisdom, which is believed to destroy the darkness of ignorance by the luminous rays issuing out from it.

Khaṭvāṅga—magic wand ; the stick is generally surmounted either by the Vajra, or the Kapāla, or the Triśūla, or the banner, or all of them. In any case, for a Khaṭvāṅga the skulls are necessary and it will be so called even if nothing else is present.

Kṣepaṇa—The Mudrā of sprinkling, exhibited by Nāmasaṅgīti. The two hands are joined palm to palm with fingers all stretched, the tips of which are turned downwards and enter into a vessel containing nectar.

Kuṇḍikā—same as *Kamaṇḍalu.* See *Kalasa.*

Lakṣaṇas—auspicious marks ; the thirty-two special marks of a Buddha, enumerated in *Dharmasaṃgraha* attributed to Nāgārjuna. The Lakṣaṇas are also enumerated in Getty : The *Gods of Northern Buddhism*, p. 170 *et sqq.* Another class of minor marks are called *Anuvyañjanas*, eighty in number, also enumerated in the *Dharmasaṃgraha.*

Mālā—same as *Akṣamālā ;* see *Akṣamālā.*

Maṇḍala—the magic circle containing mystic figures and diagrams, and figures of gods and goddesses constituting the Maṇḍala. In the Niṣpanna-yogāmbara Tantra, Kriyāsamuccaya and the Vajrāvalī-nāma-maṇḍalo-pāyikā there are descriptions of no less than a score of Maṇḍalas, each containing a number of deities.

Maṇi—same as Cintāmaṇi ; see ***Cintāmaṇi***.

Mantra—mystic syllables, sometimes containing one or two intelligible words, but shorter than the *Dhāraṇīs*. The Mantras are believed to be a contracted form of the Dhāraṇīs and are meant for the mass to obtain an easy salvation, by simply muttering them. In many instances, the Mantra gives the name of the divinity or his attributes, and these are most important in determining the names of different gods when the Colophons of Sādhanas are not reliable.

Mayūra—peacock ; and *Mayūrapiccha* is the tail or feathers of a peacock.

Mudgara—hammer ; it may also mean a staff or a mace.

Mudrā—mystic pose of hand or hands. Some of the Mudrās can be shown by one hand, such as the Varada, Abhaya, Namaskāra, etc. ; others require both the hands, such as the Añjali, Dharmacakra and many others. In the Sādhanamālā there are descriptions of an everwhelming number of Mudrās. But it is very difficult to comprehend them unless actually explained by the priests.

Mūṣala—pestle.

Nāga—serpent. They have the character of water-spirits and are believed to dwell in the springs, lakes and tanks and have the power to yield rain. But if they are roused to anger, they hurl down rocks from the mountain tops and destroy fair cities. The gods of the Sādhanamālā are fond of ornaments of eight lords of snakes. For their names and ornaments constituted by each of them, see *supra* p. 56.

Nakulī—mongoose ; the characteristic animal of Jambhala. The mongoose is believed to be the receptacle of all gems and when the god of Wealth presses the animal, it vomits forth all the riches.

Namaskāra—the Mudrā assumed by the Bodhisattvas when paying homage to the Buddhas or Tathāgatas, or by the minor deities to the principal one. The hand, slightly bent, is raised above in a line with the shoulder with fingers outstretched or slightly bent and palm turned upwards. The description given in *Getty*, p. 172 is a description of the *Añjali Mudrā*.

Nūpura—anklet ; small bells are attached to the ornament so that when the leg moves, it chimes melodiously.

Padma—lotus, which may be any colour except blue. The blue lotus is designated by the word *Utpala* or *Nīlotpala.* It is regarded as especially sacred by all classes of Indians. See Getty : *The Gods of Northern Buddhism,* p. 172. When the lotus shows petals in both the upper and lower directions it is called the *Viśvapadma* or the double lotus.

Paraśu—axe.

Paryaṅka—see *Dhyānāsana.*

Pāśa—noose or lasso ; when a Vajra is attached at the end of it, it is called the *Vajrapāsa* or the adamantine noose. The noose is required to bind the host of the Māras and all other wicked beings.

Pātra—begging bowl or bowl, generally found in the images of the five Dhyānī Buddhas and of Buddha Śākyasiṃha. Sometimes the *Kapāla* is used in the Sādhanamālā to designate a bowl. See *Kapāla.* Getty records a Buddhist legend as to how a Pātra came in the possession of Buddha. *Op. cit.* p. 173 *et sqq.*

Prañjā—see *śakti.*

Preta—or *Mṛtaka,* or *śava* always mean a corpse in Indian Buddhist Iconography.

Pustaka—book in the form of a Sanskrit Manuscript which represents the Prajñāpāramitā or the Book of Transcendental Knowledge. Nāgārjuna is said to have restored the Scripture from the nether regions. The book is carried by several Buddhist gods, notably, Prajñāpāramitā, Mañjuśrī and Sarasvatī.

Ratna—jewel ; the word Triratna signifies the three Jewels, Buddha, Dharma and Saṅgha. Similarly there are different groups of jewels, such as the seven jewels or the sixteen jewels. For the enumeration of the seven jewels, see Getty : *The Gods of Northern Buddhism* p. 174. See also *Cintāmaṇi.*

Sādhana—the procedure of worship for the invocation of Buddhist gods, and not 'charm' as translated by C. Bendall. For the translation of a complete Sādhana see Appendix A. The Sādhanamālā or the Sādhanasamuccaya is a collection of more than three hundred Sādhanas.

śakti—or ***Prajñā, Vidyā, Svābhā Prajñā*** or ***Svābhā Vidyā***, the female counterpart of a Bodhisattva. All goddesses are regarded as female counterparts of one or the other of the Bodhisattvas. The Śaktis are either represented singly or in *yab-yum*, i.e. in the actual embrace of the god to whom she is affiliated as a Śakti. This female counterpart may be "Svābhā" (own shadow) when she carries the same symbols and is in all respects similar, unless otherwise stated, to the god she embraces.

Samādhi—meditation ; "the deepest form of abstract meditation." For a description of the *Samādhi Mudrā* see *Dhyāna Mudrā.*

śaṅkha—conch-shell ; it is especially given as a symbol to the gods as the sound vibrated through a shell penetrates far and wide. The conch-shell seems to have been extensively used in wars by ancient Indians.

ṣaṇmudrā—the six Mudrās, the meaning of this Mudrā being quite different from the Mudrā meaning mystic gestures. It has been translated as auspicious ornaments or symbols. The six ornaments are enumerated in the following verse in the Sādhanamālā—

Kaṇṭhikā rucakaṃ ratnamekhalaṃ bhasmasūtrakaṃ ı
Ṣaṭ vai pāramitā etā mudrārūpena yojitāḥ ıı

"The torque, the bracelet, the jewel, the girdle, the ashes and the sacred thread are ascribed to the gods in the form of Mudrās (ornaments), which represent the six Pāramitās."

These ornaments or symbols are generally of human bones, the Khaṭvāṅga being the sacred thread. When one of the six is absent, they are called *Pañcamudrā*, and *Caturmudrā*, when two.

śara—or *Bāṇa* is the arrow. It is generally carried in the right hand, while the corresponding left shows the Dhanu.

śava—see *Preta.*

Siddhas—or *Siddhapuruṣas* are saints who have already attained Siddhi or perfection in a Tāntric rite and have acquired superhuman powers. Two groups of Siddhas are generally recognized, one consisting of eight and another of eighty-four. They were famous in the mediaeval ages for their magical powers and prodigious deeds. Most of them were Bengalees.

Siṃha—lion. The word *Siṃhāsana* means the lion-seat or the lion-throne, but does not designate a special attitude of sitting such as the Vajrāsana, Ardhaparyaṅkāsana, and so forth. See *āsana.*

śṛṅkhala—chain, also called the *Vajraśṛṅkhala,* or the adamantine chain, which is the characteristic symbol of Vajraśṛṅkhalā.

Stūpa—see *Caitya,* and pictures of three celebrated Stūpas of Nepal in Plate II.

Sūci—Mudrā used generally in the act of dancing, though it is to be seen in other cases also. All the fingers are stretehed with the tips joining at the end, so as to resemble a needle (*sūci*).

śūnya—translated as ' Void' in the absence of a suitable and more expressive word. It signifies a stage of the mind after Nirvāṇa, about which neither existence, nor non-existence, nor a combination of the two, nor a negation of the two can be predicated. This Śūnya in Vajrayāna is identified with Compassion which transforms itself in the form of divinities, of the nature of Śūnya, for the welfare and happiness of men (*śunyatā-karuṇābhinnā*).

Sūryya—the sun or the disc of the sun, which is held in one of her hands by Mārīcī and which is the seat of many Buddhist gods and goddesses. Rāhu is said to devour the sun and the moon.

Svābhā Prajñā—see *śakti.*

Tarjanī—Mudrā ; the pose of the raised index finger in a menacing attitude. In the hand, showing this Mudrā, the index finger only is raised while the other fingers are locked up in the fist. If a *pāśa* or noose appears round the index finger it is called *Tarjanipāśa.* The word *Vajratarjanī* signifies the Vajra held in the fist while the index is raised in a menacing attitude.

Tarjanīpāsa—see *Tarjanī.*

Tarpaṇa—Mudrā of doing homage to the Departed Fathers ; the Mudrā of Nāmasaṅgīti. Any arm showing this gesture is bent and is raised upward in a line with the shoulder. The palm of the hand is turned inward with fingers slightly bent and pointed towards the shoulder.

Tathāgatas—the Buddhas who have attained the highest stage of perfection according to the Buddhists. In the Sādhanamālā, the word is invariably used in the plural number always with reference to the five Dhyānī Buddhas, but does not even signify Vajrasattva or Vajradhara. The Buddhas are innumerable and have a hierarchy among them ; the different orders are, *Pratyeka, śrāvaka, Samyak-Sambuddha, Jina, Arhat, Tathāgata,* and the like.

Trailokya—pertaining to the three worlds, the terrestrial, the celestial and the infernal.

Triśūla—trident. The Hindu god Śiva is believed to carry the trident and hence it is popular among the Tantra symbols as most of the Tantras are in the form of a dialogue between Śiva and Pārvatī.

Utpala—see *Padma.*

Vāhana—vehicle or the mount of gods ; the mount may be any animal including men, demons and corpses. Sometimes even the gods of an alien faith serve as Vāhanas.

Vajra—thunderbolt. When two thunderbolts are crossed, it is called a *Viśva-Vajra,* or a double Vajra. In Buddhist Tantra the word generally designates Śūnya or Void, which cannot be cut, cannot be destroyed, but which destroys all evils.

Vajradaṇḍa—see *Daṇḍa.*

Vajraghaṇṭā—see *Ghaṇṭā*

Vajrahuṅkāra—Mudrā. The wrists are crossed at the breast with two hands holding the Vajra and the bell, both of which are turned inwards. But if the two symbols and the hands are turned outward the Mudrā will be called the *Trailokyavijaya Mudrā.*

Vajrakartri—see *Kartri.*

Vjrāṅkuśa—see *Aṅkuśa.*

Vajraparyaṅka—see *Dhyānāsana.*

Vajrapāśā—see *Pāśa.*

Vajrāsana—see *Dhyānāsana.*

Vajraśṛṅkhala—see *śṛṅkhala.*

Vajratarjanī—see *Tarjanī.*

Varada—Mudrā ; the gesture of hand shown by gods while bestowing boons. The hand showing this gesture is pendent with its palm outward and fingers all stretched. Sometimes a jewel is seen stamped on the hand showing the Mudrā ; it is known as the ***Ratnasaṃyukta Varada***, that is, the gift-bestowing attitude together with a jewel. The Mahoba figure of Khadiravanī is an example of this kind.

Vīja—also ***Bīja***. In Tantra the word means the germ-syllable, the radiance of which illumines all the innumerable worlds and the darkest regions, and attract the deity which is the transformation of Śūnya. See ***Conclusion***.

Vījapūraka—citron ; the characteristic symbol of Jambhala.

Viśvapadma—the double conventional lotus. See ***Padma***.

Viśvavajra—the double conventional Vajra. See ***Vajra***.

Vitarka—Mudrā assumed in discussion. This Mudrā is altogether unknown in the Sādhanamālā and seems to be a later development. It is, nevertheless, shown by a number of forms of Avalokiteśvara treated of in Appendix B, all of which are more or less influenced by Tibetan art and Iconography. This Mudrā is represented with the right arm bent and all fingers erect except either the index or the ring finger which touches the thumb so as to resemble a ring. The hand is extended forward with the palm outward.

Vyākhyāna Mudrā ;—see ***Dharmacakra***.

Yab-yum—It is a Tibetan word consisting of two particles, ***yab*** and ***yum***. The word ' Yab' in Tibetan means the honourable father and ' yum' means the honourable mother. The combined word therefore means the father in the company of the mother, or in her embrace. For the spiritual significance of the conception of yab-yum, see ***Conclusion***.

Yakṣas—The Yakṣas are misshapen dwarfs who guard the treasures of the northern mountains and their Chief is Kuvera, the god of Wealth. They are usually malignant in disposition and they occasionally feed on human flesh. But the benign influence of Buddha's teaching makes them forego their cruel habits.

BIBLIOGRAPHY

ABHAYAKARA GUPTA—*Niṣpannayogāmbara Tantra* (manuscript in the possession of the author.)

ADVAYAVAJRA—*Advayavajrasaṃgraha* consisting of nineteen small works. Copied from Nepal Durbar Library palm-leaf MS. III. 360 C. Copy in the library of M. M. Haraprasād Śāstrī.

BEAL (S.)—*Si-yu-ki* or the Buddhist Records of the Western World translated from the Chinese of Hiuen Thsang, London, 1906. 2 Vols.

BENDALL (C.)—*Śikṣā-Samuccaya* of Śāntideva in the Bibliotheea Buddhica Series, St. Petersburg, 1897.

2. *Catalogue of the Buddhist Sanskrit Manuscripts in the University Library, Cambridge.* Cambridge, 1883.

3. *A Historical Introduction to H. Sāstri's Nepal Catalogue*, Vol. I. Calcutta 1905.

BURGESS (J.) AND FERGUSSON (J.)—*The Cave Temples of India. London*, 1880.

COOMARASWAMY (DR. A. K.)—*Mahayana Buddhist Images from Ceylon and Java* (with three plates). J. R. A. S. April, 1909.

CORDIER (P.)—*Catalogue du Fonds Tibetain de la Bibliotheque Nationale*, 2e partie, Index du Bstan-Hgyur (1909), 3e partie (1915). Paris.

CSOMA (ALEX. DE KOROS)—*Note on the Origin of the Kāla-Cakra and Adi-Buddha Systems* in J. A. S. B. Vol. II, 1833, 57ff.

2. *Notices on the different systems of Buddhism extracted from Tibetan authorities* in J. A. S. B. Vol. VII, 1838, Part I, 142ff.

CUNNINGHAM (A.)—*The Bhilsa Topes or Buddhist monuments of Central India.* London, 1854.

DAVIDS (W. RHYS)—*Early Buddhism.* London, 1908.

DIKSHIT (K. N.)—Six Sculptures from Mahoba, *Memoirs* of the ASI No. 8.

FERGUSSON (J.)—*See* Burgess (J.)

FOUCHER (A.)—*Etude sur l'Iconographie Bouddhique de l'Inde* 1st partie. Paris, 1900. 2e partie 1905.

2. *The Beginnings of Buddhist Art* and other essays in Indian and Central Asian Archæology, translated by L. A. Thomas and F. W. Thomas with a preface by the latter. Oxford, 1917.

GRUNWEDEL (A.)—*Buddhist Art in India,* translated from German by Agnes Gibson, revised and enlarged by J. Burgess. London, 1901.

INDRABHUTI—*Jñānasiddhi* (MS with the author.)

KERN (H.)—*Manual of Indian Buddhism.* Strassbourg, 1896.

LEGGE (J.)—*A Record of Buddhistic Kingdoms being an account of the Chinese monk Fa-Hien of his Travels in India,* (A. D. 399-414). Oxford, 1886.

MAX MULLER (F.), KASAWARA (K.) and WENGEL (H.)—*The Dharma-Saṃgraha* attributed to Nāgārjuna. Oxford, 1885.

MITRA (R.)—*The Sanskrit Buddhist Literature of Nepal.* Calcutta, 1882.

MONIER WILLIAMS (SIR M.)—*Buddhism in its Connexion with Brahmanism and Hinduism and in its contrast with Christianity.* London, 1889.

OLDFIELD (H. A.)—*Sketches from Nepal.* Vol. II. London, 1880.

RAO (T. A. GOPINATHA)—*Elements of Hindu Iconography.* Vols. I. and II. Madras, 1916.

SAHNI (D. R.)—*Catalogue of the Museum of Archæology at Sarnath.* Calcutta 1914.

SAMASRAMI (S.)—Ed. *Kāraṇḍa-Vyūha.* Calcutta.

SASTRI (H.)—Eighteen articles in vernacular on " *Bauddhadharma* " published in the Monthly Magazine *Nārāyaṇa.* Calcutta.

2. *Introduction* to N. N. Vasu's " *The Modern Buddhism and its Followers in Orissa.*" Calcutta, 1911.
3. *A Catalogue of Palm-leaf and Selected paper Manuscripts belonging to the Durbar Library, Nepal.* Vol. I (1905) and Vol. II (1915). Calcutta.
4. *A Descriptive Catalogue of Sanskrit MSS. in the Government Collection under the care of the Asiatic Society of Bengal,* Vol. I. *Buddhist MSS.* Calcutta, 1917.
5. *Buddhists in Bengal* in the *Dacca Review,* Vol. II, No. 7 pp. 91-104. Dacca, 1922.
6. *Discovery of Living Buddhism in Bengal.* Calcutta.
7. *Bauddha Gan O Doha* (in vernacular). Sāhitya Parisat Granthāvalī No. 55. Calcutta B. S. 1323.
8. *Bāṅgālār Purāṇa Akṣara* (in vernacular) in the Journal of the Vaṅgīya Sāhitya Pariṣat. B. S. 1327.
9. *The Discovery of a work by Āryadeva in Sanskrit* in JASB 1898, p. 175 foll.

SASTRI (H. KRISHNA)—*South Indian Images of Gods and Goddesses.* Madras, 1916.

SENART (E.)—*Le Mahavastu* Vol. 3. Part I. Paris, 1882.

SMITH (V. A.)—*A History of Fine Arts in India and Ceylon.* Oxford, 1911.

SUJUKI (D. T.)—*The Outlines of Mahayana Buddhism*, London, 1907.

UI (H.)—*The Vaiśeṣika Philosophy*, edited by F. W. Thomas, Oriental Translation Fund, New Series. Vol. XXIV. London, 1917.

VASU (N. N.)—*The Modern Buddhism and its Followers in Orissa.* Calcutta, 1911.

2. *The Archaeological Survey of Mayūrbhañja.* Calcutta.

VOGEL (J. PH.)—*Catalogue of the Archæological Museum at Mathura*, Allahabad 1910.

2. *Introduction* to D. R. Sahni's Sarnath Catalogue, *See*—Sahni (D. R.).

3. The *Mathura School of Sculpture*, contributed to the ASI Annual Report 1906-7, pp. 137-160.

WADDEL—(L. A.)—*The Indian Buddhist Cult of Avalokita and his Consort Tārā, the 'Saviouress,' illustrated from the remains of Magadha.* JRAS 1898.

2. *The Buddhism of Tibet or Lamaism.* London 1895.

WRIGHT (D.)—*History of Nepal.* Cambridge 1877.

INDEX

A

Abhiṣeka, 23.
Abhiṣekavidhi ; source of the Sādhana of Sugatisandarśana Lokeśvara, 49 : of Pretasantarpita Lokeśvara, 50 ; two pages illustrated, XXIV, a.
Acala, name of Caṇḍaroṣaṇa, 60, 61.
Acalaketu Lokeśvara, described, 186.
Acāta (?) Lokeśvara, described, 180.
Adhyeṣaṇā, the process described, 170.
Ādi Buddha 15 ; manifestation of, 16 ; becomes Vajradhara when represented in human form, xxviii ; origin of the theory of, 161n, xxvii ; theory accepted in Vajrayāna, xxviii.
Advaya, an advanced stage of Yab-yum when all duality ceases, 164n ; meaning of the word in Vajrayāna, 164n.
Advayavajra, his time, xxixn ; discovery of one of his manuscripts, xiff ; on Nirvāṇa, xvin.
Advayavajrasaṅgraha, passage on Śūnya and its manifestations cited, 164n.
Ajayā, accompanies Buddhakapāla, 64.
Akaraṇasamvaraṇa, the process described, 170.
Ākarṣaṇa, a Tāntric rite, 69.
Ākāśagañja, Mortal Bodhisattva, 12.
Ākāśagarbha Lokeśvara, described, 183.
Akṣayamati Lokeśvara, described, 183.
Akṣobhya, a Dhyānī Buddha. 2 ; his antiquity, 4 ; described, 4 ; Dhyāna cited, 4n ; significance of his blue colour, 60 ; his stone images noticed, 4n ; representations of, VII, b, c ; gods emanating from, 60ff ; goddesses emanating from, 76ff ; character of his emanations, 60, 76 ; Mañjuśrī as an emanation of, 17, 19ff ; his effigy on the crown of Caturbhuja Heruka, 63 ; Dhvajāgrakeyūrā, 89 : Ekajaṭā, 81 : Hayagrīva, 53, 69 : Heruka, 62 : Jambhala, 74, 114 : Jāṅgulī, 80 : Mahācīnatārā, 77 : Mahāmantrānusāriṇī, 87 : Mahāpratyaṅgirā, 88 : Mañjughoṣa, 20 : Nairātmā 91 : Nāmasaṅgīti Mañjuśrī, 23 : Parṇaśavarī, 83, 84, 109 : Raktayamāri, 70 : Saṃvara, 65 : Siddhaikavīra, 21, 20 : Sita-Prajñāpāramitā, 85 : Hindu goddess Tārā, 78 : Ucchuṣma Jambhala, 74, 75 : Vajracarcikā, 86 : Vajrānaṅga, 22 : Vajrasattva, 6 : Vajravetālī, 58 : Vasudhārā, 90 : Vidyujjvālākarālī, 83 : Yamāri, 73 ; significance of his image on the crown of the Indian Museum figure of Uṣṇīṣavijayā, 101n.
Alphabet, letters of the ; represented by the Dhyānī Buddhas, 7A.
Amitābha, a Dhyānī Buddha, 2 ; described, 3 ; Dhyāna cited, 3n ; duty and character of, 3 ; representations of, VII, a ; Bhadrakalpa, the cycle of, 32 ; his emanations, 52ff, 55ff ; spiritual father of Avalokiteśvara, 32 ; his image in the Dacca figure of Arapacana, 28 ; Mañjuśrī as an emanation of, 17 ; Amitābha and Nīlakaṇṭha distinguished, 48 ; Amitābha and Vāk distinguished, 18 ; his effigy on the crown of Aṣṭabhuja Kurukullā 57 : 14 varieties of Avalokiteśvara, 33 : Bhṛkuṭī 59 : Dharmadhātu Vāgīśvara, 17, 19 : Ekajaṭā, 58 : Khasarpaṇa, 37 : Lokanātha 40 : Mahāvala, 53 : Padmanartteśvara, 42, 43 : Rakta Lokeśvara, 47 : Saptaśatika Hayagrīva, 53, 54 : Tārodbhava Kurukullā, 56 : on the tongue of Vāk, 17, 18 : instead of Vajrasattva on the British Museum figure of Cundā, 131 : instead of the parental Buddha on the crown of the Sarnath figure of Ucchuṣma Jambhala, 115 : instead of Vairocana on the Lucknow Museum figure of Mārīcī, 97.
Amitābha Lokeśvara, described, 187.
Amitābha Mañjuśrī, name of Vāk, *see* Vāk.
"Amitāyus Sūtra," *see* "Sukhāvatī Vyūha."
Amoghapāśa Lokeśvara, described, 185.
Amoghasiddhi, a Dhyānī Buddha, 5 ; another form of Amitābha, 5 ; described, 5 ; Dhyāna cited, 5n ; stone image of, 4n ; representations of, VIII, b-c ; character of his emanations, 106 ; his emanations, 106ff ; his effigy on the crown of Dhanada Tārā, 109 : Khadiravanī Tārā 106 : Mahāmāyūrī 111 : Parṇaśavarī 83, 110, 109 : Saḍbhuja Sitatārā, 108 : Vajragāndhārī, 58 : Vajraśṛṅkhalā, 112 : appears in the Dacca image of Arapacana, 28.
Amṛtalocanā, epithet of Prasanna Tārā, 138.
Amṛtamukhī, epithet of Prasanna Tārā, 138.
Amṛtānanda, author of "Dharmakoṣasaṅgraha," 50, 33.
Amṛtaprabha Lokeśvara, described, 182.
Ānanda, disciple of Buddha Śākyasiṃha, 12 ; Mortal Bodhisattva, 12 ; first recipient of the knowledge of Jāṅgulī, 78.
Ānandas, four ; data for increase in the number of deities, 165.
Ānandādi Lokeśvara, described, 178.
Anaṅga, name of Madana, *see* Madana.
Ananta, name of a serpent lord, 56.
Añjali Mudrā, exhibited by Maṇidhara, 34 : Nāmasaṅgīti, 149 : Saḍakṣarī Lokeśvara, 33 : Saḍakṣarī Mahāvidyā, 34 : Sudhanakumāra, 38 ; *see* Glossary.
Anupadhiśeṣa Nirvāṇa, explained, 167.
Anupama Rakṣita, author of "Kiñcitvistara-Tārāsādhana," 175.
Anuttara Vajrasattva, yab-yum form of Vajrasattva, 6.
Aparājitā, an independent goddess, 153ff, 102 ; described, 153 ; Dhyāna cited, 153 ; her interesting features, 153 ; her Nālanda image identified, 153 ; illustrated, XLI, d ;

Nepalese drawing illustrated, XLI, c; discovery of her complete image, 151; Indian Museum image illustrated, XLII, a; accompanies Kurukullā as a minor goddess, 153, 58; why she is not an emanation of Ratnasambhava, 153.
Aparājitā, Sitātapatrā *see* Sitātapatrā.
Apron of leaves, special recognition symbol of Parṇaśavarī, 84.
Arapacana; significance of the word, 28; a variety of Mañjuśrī, 17; an independent god, 27, 28; described, 29; Dhyāna cited, 29; origin of Arapacana and his four companions, 29; his Sādhanas, 28; character of his representations, 28; images illustrated, XVI, d, XVII, a-b-c; peculiarities of his Nepal bronze, 28; Arapacana and Siddhaikavīra distinguished, 21; called Prajñācakra when seated on an animal, 28.
Ardhaparyaṅka, name of an Āsana; its two varieties, 42; dancing in, *see* Dancing.
Ārolika, occurs in the Mantra of Amitābha, 3n.
Art, Buddhist; its evolution with regard to time and space, xxiff.
Āryā accompanies Jambhala, 114.
Āryadeva, 1; a disciple of Nāgārjuna, 1n; regarded as a Bodhisattva, 17; called a Bodhisattva, 8; author of "Catuḥśatikā," 1.
Ārya Mārīcī, variety of Mārīcī, described, 95. Ārya Mārīcī and Aśokakāntā distinguished, 95.
Ārya Sarasvatī; variety of Sarasvatī, 152; described, 152; Nepalese drawing illustrated, XL, e.
Āryatārā, Divine Buddhaśakti, 7; illustrated, XI, a.
Āryatārā, variety of Green Tārā, 136; another name of Vaśyatārā, 107.
Āryavajravārāhī, variety of Vajravārāhī, 105; extracts from her Dhyāna cited, 105n.
Āsanas, all have a deep spiritual significance, 163; for the meaning *see* Glossary.
Asaṅga; regarded as a Bodhisattva, 17; his connection with Maitreya, 13; composer of a Sādhana for Prajñāpāramitā, 84; introduces Tantra into Mahāyāna, xviii.
Aśoka bough, special symbol of Mārīcī, 95; carried by Vajrānaṅga, 22.
Aśokakāntā, variety of Mārīcī, 95; described, 95; Dhyāna cited, 95; *see* Ārya Mārīcī; accompanies Khadiravanī 94; 106.
Aśoka tree; Raktalokeśvara appears under, 46; special symbol of Mahāmāyūrī, 134.
Aṣṭabhuja Kurukullā, eight-armed variety of Kurukullā, 57ff; described, 58; Dhyāna cited, 57ff; Maṇḍala given in the Sādhana, 57.
Aṣṭabhuja Mārīcī, eight-armed variety of Mārīcī, 96; described, 96; several images noticed, 97; *see* Mārīcīpicuvā.
Aṣṭamahābhaya Tārā, variety of White Tārā, 136.
Aśvaghoṣa; regarded as a Bodhisattva, 17; called a Bodhisattva, 8; his conception of Nirvāṇa, xvin.
Avalokita, significance of the word, 52.
Avalokita Lokeśvara, described, 182.
Avalokiteśvara, Bodhisattva, 32ff; emanation of Amitābha 53; antiquity of the conception of, 51; the period of his activity, 32; his character, moral teachings and miracles, 32; his refusal of Nirvāṇa, 32; an abstract idea, 17; origin of, 17; his functions, 8; Sādhanas of, 32; his dogmatic form is really Nāmasaṅgīti, 148; antiquity of his images, 52; varieties of, enumerated and described, 33ff; 108 forms of, 33; reason of his having 108 forms, 33; his 108 forms enumerated and described, 177ff; illustrated, XLIII-LXIX; date and character of the paintings of 108 forms, 33; their discovery, 33; importance of the discovery, 33.
Āvenika Dharmas, eighteen, 10.
Āyadeva, another name of Āryadeva, author of *Cittaviśuddhiprakaraṇa*, 1n.

B

Balas, ten, 10.
Bara in the District of Birbhum, 25.
Bauddhanātha Temple; coloured image of Saḍakṣarī Lokeśvara to be found in, 35.
Bendall, C; quoted, xviii; criticized, iv.
Bengal School of Art; its existence not yet recognized, xxiii; its excellences and flourishing period, xxiiff; its excellence exemplified, 110.
Bewitching; the process described, 22.
Bhadrakalpa, the cycle of Amitābha, 3, 32.
Bhadrāsana, special attitude of Vaśyatārā, 107.
Bhairava, name of Hindu god Śiva; trampled by Vajrahuṃkāra, 144.
Bhasma, one of the six auspicious symbols, 91; *see* Saṇmudrā.
Bhattacharyya, B. C.; his identification of Mahākālī criticized, 91.
Bhaṭṭaśālī, N. K., 38n; discoverer of the image of Dvibhuja Heruka, 62; of Khasarpaṇa, 38; of the two Vikrampur images of Parṇaśavarī 110.
Bhīmā, accompanies Buddhakapāla, 64.
Bhiṇḍipāla (spear), 98.
Bhīṣmabhaginī, epithet of Vajragāndhārī, 155.
Bhṛkuṭī, 37; emanation of Amitābha, 55; described, 59; Dhyāna cited, 59; Getty's image of Bhṛkuṭī should be identified as Grahamātṛkā, 59; a variety of Yellow Tārā, 138; her description as a minor deity, 38; accompanies Avalokiteśvara, 59; Khasarpaṇa, 38, 36, 59; Padmanarteśvara, 42, 43; Rakta-Lokeśvara, 46.
Bhūmisparśa Mudrā, described, 4; *see* Glossary.
Bhūriṇī, accompanies Padmanartteśvara, 43.
Bhūtas, trampled by Mahāsāhasrapramardanī, 133.
Bhutaḍāmara, an independent god, 144ff; described, 145; Dhyāna cited, 144.
Bhuvaneśvarī, Hindu goddess; Mañjuvara identified as, 25n.
Bighna; significance of the word, 142; represented by Gaṇeśa, 84; trampled by Parṇaśavarī, 84.
Bighnāntaka, an independent god, 142ff;

associated with three other 'Antaka' gods 142 ; described, 143 ; Dhyāna cited, 142 ; his legendary origin, 143 ; tramples upon Gaṇeśa, 84n ; his image illustrated, XXXIX, b.
Bīrbhum, image of Mañjuvara found in, 25 ; image of Saḍakṣarī group found in, 34 .
Bīrbhum Vivaraṇa, 25n.
Blue, significance of the colour, 60.
Blue Tārās (Extraordinary) ; enumerated with leading characteristics of each, 139.
Bodh Gayā, 14 ; image of Trailokyavijaya found in, 146.
Bodhicaryyāvatāra, work of Śāntideva, xxv.
Bodhicitta, mind which has acquired the potentiality of dissolving in Śūnya, 166 ; is Śūnya in essence, 166 ; has no real existence, 166 ; its transformation in the form of Mudrās, 166 ; its transformation in the form of weapons, 166.
Bodhisattva, derivation of the word and meaning, xvn ; significance of the term, 8, xv ; application of the term in Hiuen Thsang's time, 8 ; Buddhas, Buddhaśaktis and, 1ff.
Bodhi Tree, characteristic sign of Mahāpratisarā, 133.
Bodhi Trees, of the 24 Past Buddhas, 10.
Book, symbol of Mañjuśrī, 17.
Bo-tree, special sign of Mahāsāhasrapramardanī, 133.
Bowing, attitude shown by Bhṛkuṭī, 38 ; by Hayagrīva, 38.
Bowl, found in images of Dhyānī Buddhas, 3.
Brahmā, Hindu God ; his position in the Buddhist Pantheon, 83n ; trampled by Daśabhujasita Mārīcī, 99 : by Ubhayavarāhānana Mārīcī, 98 : disgraced by Prasanna Tārā 139 ; his severed head flourished by Ubhayavarāhānana Mārīcī, 98 : by Prasanna Tārā, 139.
Brahmas, four ; enumerated, 171 ; *see* Caturbrahmavihāra.
Brahmadaṇḍa Lokeśvara, described, 180.
Brahmakapāla (severed head of Brahmā) ; mercilessly flourished by Buddhist deities, 163 : by Vajrasarasvatī, 152 ; *see* Brahmā.
Brahmamukha, one of the faces of Paramāśva, 147.
Brahmānanda, author of *Tārārahasya*, 77 ; his time, 77n.
Buddha, Gautama, 11ff, 34 : his divinity acknowledged in Mahāyāna, xiv ; his first statue in Gandhāra School, xxi ; *see* Gautama.
Buddha, significance of the term used in the Sādhanamālā, 26 ; external characteristics of a, 9 ; mental characteristics of a, 10 ; description of a, 9 ;.
Buddha on lotus, characteristic symbol of Uṣṇīṣavijayā, 101.
Buddha in Vajrāsana, 11ff ; described, 11 ; Dhyāna cited, 11 ; his image illustrated, XIII, a.
Buddhas, Buddhaśaktis and Bodhisattvas, 1ff ; Mānuṣī or Mortal, 10ff ; twenty-four Past, 10 ; Mortal, *see* Mortal Buddhas ; Dhyānī or Divine, *see* Dhyānī Buddhas.
Buddhaḍākinī, name of Vajravārāhī, 103 ; Śakti of Mahāmāyā, 67 ; described, 68 ; Dhyāna quoted, 68n.
Buddhahood, conferred by Heruka when worshipped, 61.
Buddhakapāla, variety of Heruka, 60, 63 ; an emanation of Akṣobhya, 63 ; described, 64 ; Dhyāna cited 63ff ; his Maṇḍala described, 64 ; his companions described, 64 ; his Nepalese drawing illustrated, XXV, b.
Buddhaśaktis, Buddhas and Bodhisattvas, 1ff ; *see* Mortal and Divine Buddhaśaktis.
Buddhism, a brief historical survey of, ixff ; its condition when Buddha was alive, ix ; schisms in, ixff ; rise of different schools of, xff.
Buddhists, their attitude towards the Hindu gods, 162ff.
Buffalo, characteristic Vāhana of Yamāri, 70 ; Kṛṣṇayamāri, 71 ; of Yamadūti, a minor goddess, 121.

C

Caitya, residence of Aṣṭabhuja Mārīcī, 96 ; on the crown of Maitreya, 13 ; what it signifies, 14 ; *see* Stūpa.
Cakrasamvara Tantra treats of the union of Heruka and Vajravārāhī, 103.
Campaka Tree, special tree of Mahāsitavatī, 135.
Caṇḍamahāroṣaṇa Tantra, 61.
Caṇḍaroṣaṇa, an emanation of Akṣobhya, 60ff ; his alternative form emanating from the five Dhyānī Buddhas, 60n ; described, 61 ; Dhyāna cited, 60 ; drawing illustrated, XXV, a.
Caṇḍavajrapāṇi, a Yakṣa general, 155.
Caṇḍeśvarī, accompanies Mahākāla, 122 ; described, 122.
Candraprabha, accompanies Arapacana, 28, 17 : Siddhaikavīra, 21.
Candraprabha Lokeśvara, described, 182.
Capeṭadāna Mudrā, exhibited by Aparājitā, 154 ; *see* Glossary.
Carcikā, accompanies Mahākāla, 122 ; described, 122.
Carendra, accompanies Jambhala, 114.
Catuḥśatikā, work of Āryadeva, 1n.
Caturbhuja Heruka, variety of Heruka, 63 ; described, 63.
Caturbhuja Sitatārā, a variety of White Tārā, 137.
'Caturbhuj Lokeśwara,' name given to Saḍakṣarī Lokeśvara by Waddell, 34.
Caturbrahmavihāra, the process described, 171.
Chain, *see* Śṛṅkhala.
Chhinnamastā, Hindu name of Vajrayoginī, 155 ; reasons for thinking her to be a Buddhist goddess, 155n.
China, Mañjuśrī hailed from, 15.
Cintāmaṇi Datta, author of the Sādhana of Vādirāṭ, 31.
Cintāmaṇi Lokeśvara, described, 187.
Citrakālī accompanies Jambhala, 114.
Citrasenā, Śakti of Buddhakapāla, 63 ; described, 64.
Citron, symbol of Jambhala, 114.

Cittadhātu Lokeśvara, described, 187.
Cittaśodhanaprakaraṇa, 1n; *see Cittaviśuddhiprakaraṇa.*
Cittaviśuddhiprakaraṇa, Vairocana mentioned in, 4; its date discussed, 1; mentions Dhyānī Buddhas and therefore later than 700 A. D., xxivn.
Civikuṇḍalī, accompanies Jambhala, 114.
Colour, has a spiritual significance, 163.
Comilla, image of Dvibhuja Heruka found in, 62.
Confession of sins, the process described, 169.
Coomaraswamy, Dr. A.; on Cundā, 132; criticized, 132.
Corpse lying on its breast, prescribed for Dvibhuja Heruka, 62n.
Cults; origin and nature of cults in Vajrayāna, xxviiiff; responsible for discrepancy of parental Dhyānī Buddhas in images, 160ff.
Cundā, different spellings of her name, 131; an emanation of Vajrasattva, 131; described, 131; Dhyāna cited, 131; her Java figure does not follow Sādhana, 131; as a minor goddess described, 58.
Cundāvarabhavana, containing a 16-armed image of Cundā, 131.

D

Dacca Museum contains image of Arapacana, 28; Dvibhuja Heruka, 62; Khadiravanī Tārā, 107; Mārīcī, 97.
Ḍākinī, name of Vajravārāhī, 94, 103.
Ḍākinī accompanies Vajravārāhī, 104.
Dāmara Mudrā, described, 145n.
Dancing attitude in Ardhaparyaṅka exhibited by Buddhakapāla, 64; his companions, 64; Dvibhuja Heruka, 62; Nairātmā, 90; Vajracarcikā, 86; Vajravārāhī, 94, 105.
Daṇḍa, characteristic weapon of Hayagrīva, 54.
Daśabhujasita Mārīcī, 98ff; described, 98ff; her companions described, 99; Nepalese drawing illustrated, XXXI, b.
Dattā accompanies Jambhala, 114.
Deification of the letters of the Mantra of Vajratārā, 125, 129.
Deities, Buddhist; their scientific classification, vii; data for their increase in numbers, xxix, 165; are transformations of Śūnya, 165; how they are attracted from the rays of the Vījamantra, 165.
Deities, Hindu; how disgraced by Buddhist deities, 162ff.
Devadevatā Lokeśvara, described, 185.
Devī accompanies Jambhala, 114.
Dhanada, name of Hindu Kuvera; trampled by Ucchuṣma Jambhala, 75.
Dhanada accompanies Jambhala, 114.
Dhanada Tārā, a variety of Green Tārā, 137; an emanation of Amoghasiddhi, 109; described, 109; Dhyāna cited, 109; Nepalese drawing illustrated, XXXIII, c.
Dhāraṇīs; first citation in *Śikśāsamuccaya*, xxv.
Dharma, member of the Holy Triad, 34; described, xxn.
Dharmacakra Lokeśvara, described, 186.
Dharmacakra Mañjuśrī, name given to Mañjuvara by the Nepalese, 26n.
Dharmacakra Mudrā, described, 4ff, *see* Glossary.
Dharmadhara, Mortal Bodhisattva, 12.
Dharmadhātu Lokeśvara, described, 187.
Dharmadhātu Vāgīśvara, variety of Mañjuśrī, 17; an emanation of Amitābha, 17, 18ff; described, 19; Dhyāna cited, 19.
Dharmākara, king of China, 16.
Dharmakoṣasaṅgraha, a work of Amṛtānanda, 6n; source of the Dhyāna of Nāmasaṅgiti, 149; Sukhāvatī Lokeśvara, 50; of three independent goddesses, 157.
Dharmasaṅgraha, work of Nāgārjuna, 10, 9; its date discussed, xxivn.
Dharmaśaṅkhasamādhi, name of Vāk, *see* Vāk.
Dhyānas in Sādhanas; most important in identifying images, V; relation between Dhyānas and images, 159. For the meaning of Dhyāna, *see* Glossary.
Dhyānāsana, exhibited by the Dhyāni Buddhas, 2, *see* Glossary.
Dhyānī Buddhas, their antiquity, 1ff; order and enumeration, 2; different theories about their origin, 2; character of, 1; general appearance of the, 2; represented on the Stūpas, 3; nature of their representations, 2; miniatures of, 3n; hints for identifying their images, 6ff; most important factor in identifying images, 159; what their presence in images indicates, 159; reasons why parental Dhyānī Buddhas are sometimes different, 160; if prescribed Dhyānī Buddhas are not present in images, 160; tabular statement showing the relation between Buddhaśaktis, Bodhisattvas and, 9.
Dhyānī Buddhas, five; enumerated, 119, 2; their emanations 119ff, 123ff; their emanations enumerated, 119, 123; Mañjuśrī as an emanation of, 17, 24ff; their images on the aureole behind Maitreya figures, 14; Caṇḍaroṣaṇa as an emanation of, 60n; their images on the crown of Dharmadhātu Vāgīśvara, 18n; Mahākāla, 121; Mañjuvara, 25; Mañjuvajra, 26; Jambhala, 114; Māyājālakrama Kurukullā, 127; Sitatārā, 128; Vajradharma, 57, 47, 33; Vajratārā, 124.
Dhyani Buddhas, four; Vajratārā only emanation of, 129.
Dhūpā accompanies Lokanātha, 38.
Dhupatārā accompanies Vajratārā, described, 124.
Dhvajāgrakeyūrā, emanation of Akṣobhya, 88; two varieties, 88; Dhyāna of the 1st. variety cited, 88; described, 89; 2nd variety described, 89; illustrated, XXIX, d.
Dikshit, K. N.; Mahoba image of Siṃhanāda described by, 36; on the Birbhum image of Saḍakṣarī Lokeśvara, 34; criticized, 35.
Dīpā, companion of Lokanātha, 38.
Dipatārā accompanies Vajratārā, described, 124.
Diseases; Siṃhanāda, curer of, 35.
Divine Buddhas, *see* Dhyānī Buddhas.
Divine Buddhaśaktis, 7; enumerated, 7; character of, 7; described, 7; hints for

identifying their images, 7ff ; illustrated, X, XI, a ; source of the illustrations, 8n ; tabular statement showing their relation with the Dhyānī Buddhas and Bodhisattvas, 9.
Divine Bodhisattvas, 8 ; their duties, 8 ; enumerated, 8 ; attempt to connect them with the last five Mortal Buddhas criticized, 10 ; hints for identifying their images, 8 ; illustrated, XI, b-f ; tabular statement showing their connection with the Dhyānī Buddhas and Buddhaśaktis, 9.
Dragons, a pair of ; Vāhana of Vairocana, 4, 5.
Drawings illustrated in this book are ancient and therefore authoritative as material for study, vii.
Durgā, a Hindu goddess, 116n.
Durgottāriṇī Tārā, variety of Green Tārā, 137.
Durjayā accompanies Buddhakapāla, 64.
Dvibhuja Heruka, variety of Heruka, 61ff ; described, 62 ; Dhyāna cited 62 ; corpse lying on its breast prescribed for, 62n.

E

Ears of corn, special symbol of Vasudhārā, 117.
Ekajaṭā, 106 ; an emanation of Akṣobhya, 80ff ; her character and functions, 80 ; described 81 ; first three varieties distinguished, 81 ; Dhyāna cited, 80 ; illustrated XXVII, d, XXVIII a ; a variety of Blue Tārā, 139 ; accompanies Aṣṭabhuja Kurukullā as a minor goddess, 58 : Khadiravanī Tārā, 106.
Elephant, Vāhana of Akṣobhya, 4 ; appears in drawings of Hariharihariväahanodbhava, 45.
Ellora, images of Mortal Buddhas in the Cave Temples at, 10n.
Evans Wentz, Dr. W. Y., 3n ; indebtedness to, 132, 157.
Excrescence to the right ear ; characteristic sign of Vajravārāhī, 103.

F

Fa-Hien, Buddhist gods mentioned by, xxv ; Mañjuśrī mentioned by, 15 ;
Foucher, Prof., Dr. A. ; the only systematic worker in the field of Indian Buddhist Iconography, 1ff ; criticized, 129n, 131, 132n ; varieties of Avalokiteśvara recorded by, 32 ; on Tārās, 135.
Future Buddha, Maitreya, *see* Maitreya.

G

Gaganagañja accompanies Lokanātha, 38.
Gaganagañja Lokeśvara, described, 183.
Gandhā accompanies Lokanātha, 38.
Gāndhāra Art, its time, xxi ; images of Mañjuśrī absent in, 15 ; images of Maitreya found in, 13.
Gandhatārā accompanies Vajratārā, 124.
Gaṇapati, name of Gaṇeśa, 153 ; an independent god, 142 ; described, 142 ; Dhyāna cited, 142.
Gaṇapatihṛdayā, an independent goddess, 157 ; described, 157 ; Dhyāna cited, 158 ; illustrated, XLII d.
'Gaṇapatisamākrāntā,' meaning of the word, 153.
Gaṇeśa, legendary story of his struggle with Bighnāntaka, 143 ; his defeat, 143 ; his presence in Buddhist images, 162 ; trampled by Aparājitā, 153 : Parṇaśavarī, 84.
Garuḍa, Vāhana of Amoghasiddhi, 5 : of Hariharihariväahana, 44.
Gaurī, trampled by Trailokyavijaya, 147.
Gaurītārā accompanies Aṣṭabhuja Kurukullā, 58.
Gautama Buddha, 11ff ; last in the group of the Seven Mortal Buddhas, 11 ; his images are an independent study, 11 ; his disappearance, 13, 8.
Germany, image of Vajravārāhī in, 105.
Getty, Miss Alice, author of *The Gods of Northern Buddhism ;* on the iconography of Maitreya, 13 ; on Vajravārāhī, 103 ; on the origin of Yamāri, 69 ; criticized, 59 ; calls Nāmasaṇgīti a ' Dogmatic form of Avalokiteśvara,' 148.
Ghaṇṭā carried by the Indian Museum image of Vāgīśvara, 24.
Ghaṇṭāpāṇi, a Divine Bodhisattva, 8 ; and Vajrapāṇi distinguished, 9.
Ghoṇā, *see* Vajraghoṇā.
Ghoracaṇḍī accompanies Saptākṣara, 66.
Grahamātṛkā, an independent goddess, 157 ; described, 157 ; Dhyāna cited, 157 ; illustrated, XLII, c ; Miss Getty's Bhṛkuṭī should be identified as, 59.
Green Tārās, Ordinary ; 136 ; enumerated with leading characteristics of each, 136 ; Extraordinary, enumerated with leading characteristics of each, 137.
Guhyasamāja, Abhiṣekavidhi part of, 49.
Guṇakāraṇḍavyūha ; character, moral teachings and miracles of Avalokiteśvara described in, 32.
Guptā accompanies Jambhala, 114.

H

Hālāhala Lokeśvara, variety of Avalokiteśvara, 40ff ; described, 41, 177 ; Dhyāna cited, 41 ; his Śakti, 40 ; his Śakti described, 41 ; character of his images, 40 ; illustrated, XXII, c.
Hara, *see* Śiva.
Haraprasād Shāstrī, Mahāmahopādhyāya ; on Tantra, xviii.
Hari, *see* Viṣṇu.
Hari, different meanings of the word, 44.
Harihara Lokeśvara, described, 186.
Hariharihariväahanodbhava Lokeśvara, variety of Avalokiteśvara, 44ff ; significance of his name, 44 ; special characteristics of, 44 ; Dhyāna cited, 44 ; described 44ff, 177 ; illustrated, XXIIf, XXIII, a-b ; special features of his drawings, 45 ; peculiarity of his Pāṭan image, 45.
Harivāhana Lokeśvara, described, 186.

Hayagrīva, 37, 60 ; his different forms, 53 ; an emanation of Akṣobhya, 68ff ; described, 69 ; Dhyāna quoted, 68 ; illustrated, XXV, d ; as a minor deity, 38 ; accompanies Khasarpaṇa, 36, 38 ; Lokanātha, 37, 38, 39 ; Padmanartteśvara, 42.
Hayagrīva, Hindu God of Fever, 110.
Hayagrīva Lokeśvara, described, 177.
Hayagrīva, Saptaśatika, *see* Saptaśatika.
Heruka, 1n, 42, 60, 93 ; an emanation of Akṣobhya, 61ff ; varieties of, 61 ; his Namaskāra cited, 63 ; becomes Buddhakapāla when embraced by Citrasenā, 63 ; Mahāmāya when embraced by Buddhaḍākinī, 67 ; Vajraḍāka when embraced by Vajravārāhī, 64 ; his union with Vajravārāhī, 103 ; his consort Vajrayoginī, 156.
Heruka, Caturbhuja *see* Caturbhuja Heruka.
Heruka Tantra treats of the union of Vajrayoginī with Heruka, 103.
Herukī accompanies Saptākṣara, 66.
Hevajrakrama Kurukullā, variety of Kurukullā 55.
Hīnayāna, *see* Mahāyāna.
Hīnayānists, Maitreya worshipped by, 13.
Hindu gods ; how disgraced by the Buddhists, 162ff ; examples 162ff.
Hindus, their attitude towards Buddha, 163.
Hiraṇyagarbha, *see* Brahmā.
Hiuen Thsang ; famous Buddhists regarded as Bodhisattvas in his time, 17 ; Buddhist gods mentioned by, xxv ; on the image of Maitreya in Udyāna, 13 ; Mañjuśrī mentioned by, 15.
Horse, Vāhana of Kāladūtī.

I

Icon, its conception and representation in Buddhism, xiii ; Buddhist icon analyzed, 161.
Iconography, Buddhist ; its importance, i ; difficulties of the investigator, i ; previous workers in the field, i ; materials for the study of, ii ; dependent upon the doctrine of Sūnyatā, xiii.
Identification of Buddhist images ; hints for, 159 ; grounds of, vii ; its pitfalls exemplified, 161 ; when parental Buddha is different, 160ff.
Images of Buddhist deities, their antiquity, vi ; their extent and find spots, viff ; hints for their identification, 159ff ; how modified, 159 ; their utility 165 ; never worshipped by a true Vajrayānist 165.
Independent Deities, 141ff ; reasons for a separate chapter, 141 ; their proposed classification, 141n ; their number, 141 ; their nature and description, 141ff.
Independent Goddesses, 149ff ; their number, 149 ; impossibility of classifying them according to colour, 150.
Indian Museum, image of two-armed Ekajaṭā deposited in, 81 ; Khadiravanī 106ff ; Mañjuvara, 26 ; Mārīcī, 97 ; Seven Mortal Buddhas, 10 ; Nairātmā, 91 ; Saḍakṣarī Lokeśvara, 34 ; Uṣṇīṣavijayā, 100 ; Vāgīśvara, 24 ; Vajrāsana Buddha, 11.
Indra, why the attendant of Aparājitā should be identified as, 154n ; holds the parasol of Aparājitā, 154 ; trampled by Daśabhujasita Mārīcī, 99 ; by Paramāśva, 148 ; Prasanna Tārā, 139 ; pays homage to Ubhayavarāhānana Mārīcī, 98.
Indrabhūtī, king of Uḍḍiyāna, 1 ; a Siddhācāryya, 57 ; probably founder of the Vajrayāna System, 159.
Indrāṇī trampled by Paramāśva, 147.
I-Tsing, Buddhist gods mentioned by, xxv ; Mañjuśrī mentioned by, 15.

J

Jālinīprabha, companion of Mañjuśrī, 17 ; of Siddhaikavīra, 21 ; *see* Sūryyaprabha.
Jālinīprabha Lokeśvara, described, 182.
Jamadaṇḍa Lokeśvara, described, 181.
Jambhala, the Buddhist God of Wealth, 60 ; his antiquity, 73 ; a parallel of Mañjuśrī 73 ; discrepancy as to his parental Buddha, 73, 113 ; better antiquity than his parental Buddhas, 113 ; varieties, 114, 119 ; an emanation of Akṣobhya, 73ff ; how assigned to Ratnasambhava, 113 ; emanation of Vajrasattva, 130 ; emanation of five Dhyānī Buddhas, 119 ; only peaceful deity emanating from Akṣobhya, 60 ; his Dhyāna cited, 74 ; described, 114, 119, 130 ; sometimes represented with Sakti, 114 ; his Sakti, 74 ; hints for identifying his images, 114 ; his images illustrated, XXXIV, c-d-e, XXVI, c ; his image to be found in all schools of art, 73 ; his Java image erroneously identified by Vincent Smith as Sarasvatī, 150n.
Jāṅgulī, 106 ; her antiquity, 78 ; goddess of snake-bite, 78ff ; variety of Green Tārā, 137 ; variety of White Tārā, 138 ; variety of Yellow Tārā, 138 ; an emanation of Akṣobhya 78 ; three varieties, 78ff ; first variety described, 79 ; second variety, 79 ; third variety, 79ff ; Dhyāna of the first variety cited, 78ff ; third variety, 79 ; first variety illustrated, XXVII, c.
Jaṭāmukuṭa Lokeśvara, described, 178.
Java, image of Pita-Prajñāpāramitā found in, 86 ; Java image of Cundā does not follow Sādhana, 131.
Java Art, indebtedness to Bengal Art, xxiii.
Jayā accompanies Buddhakapāla, 64.
Jayākara trampled by Paramāśva, 148.
Jayatārā accompanies Aṣṭabhuja Kurukullā, described, 58.
Jinajika, name of Vairocana, 5n.
Jinas, Dhyānī Buddhas called as, 2.
Jñānadhātu Lokeśvara, described, 181.
Jñānasiddhi, work of Indrabhūti, cited, 166n.

K

Kakudvatī, Mortal Buddhaśakti, 12.
Kāladūtī accompanies Mahākāla, described, 122.
Kālarātri trampled by Samvara, 65 ; by Saptākṣara, 66 ; Vajravārāhī, 104.
Kālihrada, lake in Nepal, 16.
Kālikā accompanies Mahākāla, described, 122.

Kalpokta Kurukullā, variety of Kurukullā, 55.
Kāmadeva and his wife appear under the seat of Tārodbhava Kurukullā, 56.
Kamalacandra Lokeśvara, described, 184.
Kamaṇḍalu Lokeśvara, described, 178.
Kāminī accompanies Buddhakapāla, 64.
Kanakamuni, Mortal Buddha, 10.
Kanakarāja, Mortal Bodhisattva, 12.
Kaṅkelli flowers, carried by Vajrānaṅga, 22.
Kaṇṭhamālinī, Mortal Buddhaśakti, 12.
Kaṇṭhikā one of the six auspicious symbols, *see* Saṇmudrā.
Kapālinī accompanies Buddhakapāla, 64.
Karaṇa Mudrā correctly represented in XXV, d.
Kāraṇḍavyūha, 52 ; characteristics of Avalokiteśvara recorded in, 32 ; cited 32n ; Dhyāna of Ṣaḍakṣarī Lokeśvara restored from, 34.
Kāraṇḍavyūha Lokeśvara, described, 182.
Kāriṇī accompanies Buddhakapāla, 64.
Karkkoṭaka, name of a serpent lord, 56.
Karṇatārā accompanies Aṣṭabhuja Kurukullā, described, 58.
Karuṇā, defined, 171.
Kaśyapa, Mortal Buddha, 10 ; his connection with Maitreya, 14.
Kauverī accompanies Buddhakapāla, 64.
Kāyas, three ; data for increase in number of deities, 165.
Kelimālī accompanies Jambhala, 114.
Kern, Dr. H. ; criticized, xivn.
Keśinī, accompanies Mañjuśrī, 17 ; Siddhaikavīra, 21 ; Arapacana, 28 ; appears in the image of Mañjuvara, 26.
Khadiravanī Tārā, emanation of Amoghasiddhi 106ff ; a variety of Green Tārā, 136 ; described, 106 ; Dhyāna cited, 106 ; illustrated, XXXII, c-d-e ; and Sitatārā distinguished, 127.
Khagarbha accompanies Lokanātha, 38, 40.
Khaṇḍarohā accompanies Vajravārāhī, 104.
Khasarpaṇa, variety of Avalokiteśvara, 36 ; very popular amongst the Mahāyānists, 36 ; described, 180, 37 ; Dhyāna cited, 37 ; and Lokanātha distinguished, 39 ; 37 ; illustrated, XX, c, XXI.
Khaṭvāṅga, special for Dvibhuja Heruka, 62.
Knowledges (Skandhas), five spiritual, enumerated, 104n, *see* Skandhas.
Kot-bar, 16.
Krakucchanda, Mortal Buddha, 10.
Kṛṣṇa, significance of the word in Buddhist Iconography, 163.
Kṛṣṇayāmāri, 60 ; a variety of Yamārī, 71ff ; three varieties noticed, 71 ; first variety described, 71 ; second variety 72 ; third variety, 73 ; Dhyāna of the first variety cited 71 ; second variety 72 ; third variety, 73 ; illustrated, XXVI, a ; third variety illustrated, XXVI, b.
Kṛtāñjali Lokeśvara, described, 188.
Kṣepaṇa Mudrā, exhibited by Nāmasaṅgīti, 149.
Kṣitigarbha accompanies Lokanātha, 38, 40.
Kṣitigarbha Lokeśvara, described, 183.
Kukkurīpāda, author of *Mahāmāyāsādhana*, 67.
Kukkuṭapāda, mountain marking the place of Kaśyapa Buddha, 14.
Kulika, name of a serpent lord, 56.
Kuliśseśvarī accompanies Mahākāla, described 122.
Kurukulla, name of a mountain ; residence of Kurukullā, 56.
Kurukullā, emanation of Amitābha, 55 ; variety of White Tārā, 138 ; the only red Tārā, 140 ; varieties of, 55 ; a resume of her different forms, 140 ; Mantra cited, 55 ; her Tibetan forms, 55n.
Kurukullā, Aṣṭabhuja, *see* Aṣṭabhuja Kurukullā
Kurukullā, Kalpokta, *see* Kalpokta Kurukullā.
Kurukullā, Māyājālakrama, *see* Māyājālakrama Kurukullā.
Kurukullā, Oḍiyāna *see* Oḍiyāna Kurukullā.
Kurukullā, Tārodbhava, *see* Tārodbhava Kurukullā.
Kurukullā, Śukla, *see* Śukla Kurukullā.
Kuvera, name of a Hindu god ; trampled by Ucchuṣma Jambhala, 115 ; *see* Dhanada.
Kva Vahal, a Vihāra at Patan in Nepal, 45.

L

Lakṣmīṅkarā, daughter of Indrabhūti, xxvin, 57 ; founder of Sahajayana, 57.
Lāmā accompanies Vajravārāhī, 104.
Laugh, angry ; indication of Parṇaśavarī as an emanation of Amoghasiddhi, 110.
Lion, Vāhana of Mañjughoṣa, 19, 20 ; Mañjuvara, 25 ; Siṃhanāda, 35, 36 ; Ratnasambhava, 5 ; Vāgīṣvara, 24.
Locanā, and others offer homage to Dhanada Tārā, 109 ; Divine Buddhaśakti, 7 ; illustrated, X, b.
Lokanātha, 38ff ; described, 39 ; Dhyāna cited, 39 ; his companions enumerated and described 38ff ; illustrated, XX, d, XXII, a-b ; earliest image found at Sarnath, 40 ; and Khasarpaṇa distinguished, 37, 39 ; and Siddhaikavīra distinguished, 21 ; his Maṇḍala described, 40, 39 ; constitution of the Maṇḍala, 39.
Lokanātha-raktāryy-Avalokiteśvara, described, 179.
Lokeśvara, companion of Vajrāsana, 11 ; *see* Avalokiteśvara, 32.
Love, Buddhist god of, 22 ; Hindu god of, 22 ; distinction between the Hindu and Buddhist gods of, 22.
Lucknow Museum, Sarnath image of Mārīci in the, 97.

M

Macchandar Vahal, name of a Vihāra in Nepal, 50 ; paintings of 108 forms of Avalokiteśvara discovered at, 33.
Madana and Vajrānaṅga distinguished, 22.
Mādhavācāryya on Nirvāṇa, xvin.
Madhukara trampled by Paramāśva, 148.
Mahā-abhayakarī Lokeśvara, described, 184.
Mahā-abhayaphalada Lokeśvara, described, 184.
Mahācaṇḍaroṣaṇa, *see* Caṇḍaroṣaṇa.
Mahācandrabimba Lokeśvara, described, 184.

Mahācina Tantra, source of Mahācinatārā Sādhana, 77.
Mahācinatārā, emanation of Akṣobhya, 76ff ; 106 ; a variety of Blue Tārā, 139 ; described, 77 ; Dhyāna cited, 76 ; borrowed by the Hindus, 77 ; illustrated, XXVII, a-b.
Mahākāla, emanation of the five Dhyāni Buddhas, 120 ; his popularity, 120 ; his terrible functions, 122 ; varieties, 120 ; Dhyāna cited, 120 ; four-armed variety described, 120 ; six-armed variety described, 121 ; sixteen-armed variety described, 121 ; Prajñā accompanies when 16-armed, 121 ; Dhyānas cited, 120, 121 ; illustrated, XXXVI, a ; his Maṇḍala described, 121ff.
Mahāmañjubhūta Lokeśvara, described, 185.
Mahāmañjudatta Lokeśvara, described, 184.
Mahāmantrānusāriṇi, an emanation of Akṣobhya, 87, 76 ; Dhyāna cited, 87 ; described, 87 ; a Pañcarakṣā goddess, 87 ; extracts from her Dhyāna cited, 134n ; described, 134 ; illustrated, XXXVIII, b.
Mahāmati, Mortal Bodhisattva, 12.
Mahāmāyā, variety of Vajraḍāka, 64, 67ff ; described, 67ff ; Dhyāna cited, 67n ; his Maṇḍala described, 67n ; his companions described, 68.
Mahāmāyā, consort of Maheśvara, accompanies Mahākāla, described, 121.
Mahāmāyūrī, emanation of Amoghasiddhi, 111 ; described, 111 ; Dhyāna cited, 111 ; as a Pañcarakṣā goddess described, 134 ; extracts from her Dhyāna cited, 134n ; illustrated, XXXVIII, a ; accompanies Sitatārā, 127 ; described, 128.
Mahāpadma, name of a serpent lord, 56.
Mahāpañcarakṣā Deities ; their popularity, 132 ; *see* Pañcarakṣā.
Mahāpaṭala Lokeśvara, 184.
Mahāpratisarā, emanation of Ratnasambhava, 113, 116, 117 ; varieties of, 116 ; described, 116ff ; Dhyāna cited, 116 ; her images illustrated, XXXV, b-c ; worshipped in Maṇḍala as a Pañcarakṣā goddess, 116, 133 ; described, 133 ; extracts from her Dhyāna cited, 133n ; illustrated, XXXVII, c ; worshipped by the Hindus in the annual festival of Durgā, 116n.
Mahāpratyaṅgirā, emanation of Akṣobhya, 87ff ; described, 88 ; Dhyāna cited, 88 ; illustrated, XXIX, a-b-c.
Mahārājalīlā, same as Ardhaparyaṅka, *see* Glossary.
Mahārājalīlā Mañjuśrī, *see* Vāgīśvara.
Mahāratnakīrti Lokeśvara, described, 183.
Mahāratnakula Lokeśvara, described, 184.
Mahāsahasrabhuja Lokeśvara, described, 183.
Mahāsāhasrapramardanī, emanation of Vairocana, 102 ; described, 102 ; Dhyāna cited, 102 ; described as a Pañcarakṣā goddess, 133 ; extracts from her Dhyāna cited, 133n ; illustrated, XXXVII, d.
Mahāsahasrasūryya Lokeśvara, described, 183ff.
Mahāsāṅghikas ; forerunners of the Mahāyāna, x ; first conceived Avalokiteśvara, 51.
Mahāśaṅkhanātha Lokeśvara, described, 183.
Mahāsarasvatī, variety of Sarasvatī, 150ff ; described, 151 ; Dhyāna cited, 150 ; illustrated, XL, c ; her Maṇḍala, 151n.
Mahasitavatī, emanation of Amitābha, 55, 87 ; described, 59 ; Dhyāna cited, 59 ; described as a Pañcarakṣa goddess 134 ; extracts from her Dhyāna cited, 135n ; illustrated, XXXVIII, c.
Mahāsthāmaprāpta Lokeśvara, described, 188.
Mahāsukha combined with Vijñāna gives rise to Vajrayāna. xiff.
Mahāsūryyabimba Lokeśvara, described, 184.
Mahattarī Tārā, variety of Green Tārā, described, 136.
Mahāvajradhātu Lokeśvara, described, 185.
Mahāvajradhṛk Lokeśvara, described, 185.
Mahāvajranātha Lokeśvara, described, 185.
Mahāvajrapāṇi Lokeśvara, described, 185.
Mahāvajrasattva Lokeśvara, described, 181.
Mahāvala, emanation of Amitābha, 53 ; described, 53 ; Dhyān acited, 53.
Mahāvastu Avadāna ; first reference to Avalokiteśvara is found in, 51.
Mahāviśvaśuddha Lokeśvara, described, 185.
Mahāyāna and Hīnayana ; points of agreement, xiv ; points of difference, xivff.
Mahāyaśā accompanies Buddhakapāla, 64.
Maheśvara, trampled by Trailokyavijaya, 147 ; *see* Śiva ; his consort Mahāmāyā, 121.
Mahīdharā, Mortal Buddhaśakti, 12.
Mohoba, image of Siṃhanāda discovered at, 36.
Mahodadhi accompanies Buddhakapāla, 64.
Maitreya, the Future Buddha, 13ff, 32 ; now remains in the Tuṣita Heaven, 8 ; described, 11, 14 ; Dhyāna cited, 14 ; his images, 13 ; illustrated, XIII, b ; sometimes represented as a Buddha, 14 ; appears in the image of seven Mortal Buddhas, 10 ; description as a minor god, 14 ; accompanies Lokanātha, 38, 40 ; Vajrāsana, 11.
Maitreyanātha Bodhisattva, 8.
Maitrī, defined, 171.
Makara, Vāhana of a companion of Mārīci, 60.
Māmakī, Divine Buddhaśakti, 7 ; illustration X, c.
Manasā, Hindu goddess akin to Jāṅgulī, 80.
Maṇḍala of Buddhakapāla, 64 ; Lokanātha, 39, 40 ; Mahāmāyā, 67ff ; Siddhaikavīra, 21.
Maṇibhadra accompanies Jambhala, 114.
Maṇidhara accompanies Ṣaḍakṣarī Lokeśvara, 33 ; described, 34.
Maṇipadma Lokeśvara, described, 180.
Mañjughoṣa, variety of Mañjuśrī, 17 ; an emanation of Akṣobhya, 19 ; his Mantra, 20n ; described, 19ff ; Dhyāna, cited, 20 ; distinction between Mañjuvara and, 19 ; accompanies Lokanātha, 38, 40. ;
Mañjukumāra, variety of Mañjuśrī, 17 ; his parental Buddha, 27 ; an emanation of the fiye Dhyānī Buddhas, 27 ; described, 27 ; Dhyāna cited, 27 ; illustrated, XVI, c.
Mañjunātha, independent form of Mañjuśrī described, 31, 17 ; Dhyāna cited, 31n.
Mañjunātha Lokeśvara, described, 187.
Mañjupattana, Vihāra made by Mañjuśrī, 16.
Mañjuśrī Bodhisattva, 15ff ; his place in the

Buddhist Pantheon, 15 ; his antiquity, 15, 28 ; his mention in Fa-Hien, 15n ; merits arising out of his worship, 15 ; his life, 15ff ; his activities in Nepal, 16 ; Sādhanas of, 17 ; his origin and parental Buddha, 27ff, 28 ; varieties enumerated, 17, as an emanation of Akṣobhya 17, 19ff : of Amitābha, 17, 53 : of five Dhyānī Buddhas, 17, 119, 24 ; as an independent deity, 17, 27ff ; his images in different schools of art, 15 ; their identification not properly done, 31 ; distinction between Prajñāpāramitā and, 31 ; Siṃhanāda Lokeśvara and, 36 ; assumes the form of Yamāntaka, 70.
Mañjuśrī Hill or Svayambhūkṣettra in Nepal, 15.
Mañjuvajra, variety of Mañjuśrī, 17 ; an emanation of the five Dhyānī Buddhas, 26 ; his parental Buddha, 26 ; described and Dhyāna cited, 26.
Mañjuvara, variety, of Mañjuśrī, 17 ; an emanation of the five Dhyānī Buddhas 25, described, 25 ; Dhyāna cited, 25 ; images noticed, 26 ; illustrated, XV, b-c-d, XVI, a-b ; identified as Bhuvaneśvarī, 25n ; as Siṃhanāda Lokeśvara, 25n ; distinction between Mañjughoṣa and, 19.
Mantras, our chief guide in determining different names of Mañjuśrī, 17 ; their deification,—a pitfall in identification, 162 ; deification exemplified, 162 ; of Vajratārā deified, 125, 129 ; efficacy, 125.
Mantrayāna, its antiquity, xviin.
Mānuṣī Buddhas, *see* Mortal Buddhas.
Māras, four, 154n ; under the seat of Vajrāsana, 11 ; trampled by Vidyujjvālākarālī, 82 ; by Prasannatārā, etc., 162.
Mārgāśrayaṇa, the process described, 170.
Mārīcī, the chief emanation of Vairocana, 4, 93ff ; her connexion with the Sun-god, 93 ; worshipped in Tibet, 93 ; general remarks about her form, 94 ; her Dhāraṇī given by Śāntideva, 94 ; described, 128 ; character of her images, 97 ; accompanies Sitatārā, 127 ; distinguished from Vajravārāhī, 93ff, 103 ; two different goddesses, 93.
Mārīcī, Ārya, *see* Ārya Mārīcī.
Mārīcī, Aśokakāntā, *see* Aśokakāntā Mārīcī.
Mārīcī, Aṣṭabhuja ; images noticed, 97 ; illustrated, XXX, c-d, XXXI, a ; *see* Aṣṭabhuja Mārīcī.
Mārīcī, Daśabhujāsita, *see* Daśabhujasita Mārīcī.
Mārīcī, Ubhayavarāhānana, *see* Ubhayavarāhānana Mārīcī.
Mārīcī, Vajradhātvīśvarī, *see* Vajradhātvīśvarī Mārīcī.
Mārīcīpicuvā, variety of Mārīcī, 96 ; special characteristics noted, 96 ; Dhyāna cited, 96 ; described, 96.
Māriṇī accompanies Buddhakapāla, 64.
Mathura sculptures ; images of Mañjuśrī absent in, 15.
Māyājālakrama Avalokiteśvara, the only fierce form of Lokeśvara, 47ff ; Māyājāla Tantra, the source of his Sādhana, 47 ; Dhyāna cited, 47 ; described, 47, 177ff ; his image illustrated, XXIII, d.
Māyājālakramakrodha Lokeśvara, described, 179.
Māyājālakrama Kurukullā, fierce form of Kurukullā, 57, 126ff ; described, 126ff ; extracts from Dhyāna cited, 127n.
"Māyājāla Tantra," source of the Sādhana of Māyājālakrama Avalokiteśvara, 47 : of Kurukullā, 126.
Medhā accompanies Mahāsarasvatī, 151.
Mekhalā, one of the six auspicious symbols, 91 ; *see* Saṇmudrā.
Mirror carried by Vajrānaṅga, 22.
Mojaghāñjavala (?) Lokeśvara, described 177.
Monasteries, Buddhist ; destroyed by Muhammadans, xxiin.
Mongoose, characteristic symbol of Jambhala, 114 ; Ucchuṣma Jambhala, 75, 115.
Mortal Boddhisattvas, 12 ; enumerated, 12 ; tabular statement, 13.
Mortal Buddhas, seven, 10 ; enumerated, 10 ; standing image of, XII, d ; tabular statement , 13.
Mortal Buddhaśaktis, 12 ; enumerated, 12 ; tabular statement, 13.
Mothers, eight ; accompany Vajratārā, 129, 123 ; enumerated and described, 124ff.
Mother of Six Syllables, name given by Waddel to Saḍakṣarī Mahāvidya, 34.
Mouse, vāhana of Gaṇapati, 142.
Mṛtyuvañcana Tārā, variety of White Tārā, 136 ; described, 136.
Muditā, defined, 172.
Mudrās, five ; giving rise to five Dhyānī Buddhas, 2 ; are nothing but Bodhicitta in essence, 166.

N

Nāgakeśara flower, carried by Maitreya, 11, 14, 40.
Nāgārjuna, 1n ; regarded as a Bodhisattva, 17, 8 ; author of *Dharmasaṃgraha*, 10 ; of the Sādhana of Ekajaṭā, 80 ; Prajñāpāramitā restored by, 84 ; Mañjuśrī not mentioned by, 15.
Nairātmā, significance of the word, 91 ; another word for Śūnya xvii ; a goddess emanating from Akṣobhya, 90ff ; described, 90ff ; Dhyāna cited, 90 ; distinction between Vajravārāhī and, 90 ; Vajrayoginī and, 156 ; images illustrated, XXX, a-b ; accompanies Buddhakapāla, 64.
Nalanda, source of the image of Yamāri, 73.
Nāmasaṅgīti, 141 ; deification of the Nāmasaṅgīti literature, 148 ; not a Buddha but a Bodhisattva, 148 ; an Independent god, 148ff ; described, 149 ; source of his Dhyāna, 149 ; reasons for thinking him to be a variety of Mañjuśrī, 149n ; images illustrated, XL, a-b ; Nāmasaṅgīti—Mañjuśrī is different from, 148.
Nāmasangīti Mañjuśrī, variety of Mañjuśrī, 17 ; an emanation of Akṣobhya, 19, 23ff ; described, 23 ; Dhyāna cited, 23 ; illustrated, XIV, a-b.
—naramuṇḍaruṇḍair—reading discussed, 73n.
Nartteśvara, meaning of, 42.
Navagrahas (Nine Planets), 99.
Needle and string, their function as weapons, 96.
Nepal, refuge of Vajrayānists after the Muhammadan conquest of Bengal, xviii ;

source of the image of Hālāhala, 40 : Harihariváhana Lokeśvara, 44 : Heruka, 63, 62 ; Māyājālakrama Avalokiteśvara, 48 : Nīlakaṇṭha, 49 : Padmanartteśvara, 42 ; Rakta-Lokeśvara, 46 : Sukhāvatī Lokeśvara, 50 : Vajratārā, 130 : Vasudhārā, 118.
Nepal sculptures, wealth of, xxiii.
Nepal Valley, the making of, 16.
Newari Art, its excellence exemplified, 120.
Noose, significance of, 60n.
Nīlakaṇṭha, significance of the name, 48 ; idea borrowed from the Hindus, 48 ; variety of Avalokiteśvara, 48ff ; described, 48 ; Dhyāna cited, 48 ; his image illustrated, XXIII, e ; distinction between Vāk and, 49 ; between Amitābha and, 48 ; agreement between Śiva and, 48.
Nīlakaṇṭha, name of the Hindu God, Siva, 49 ; *see* Śiva.
Nīlakaṇṭha Lokeśvara, 179.
Nirvāṇa, controversy regarding the interpretation of, xvi ; its conception from two standpoints, xv ; its different meanings according to different schools, xviff ; how obtained by a Bodhisattva, xvff ; Aśvaghosa's conception of, xvin ; refused by Avalokiteśvara, 32.
Nirvāṇa, Anupadhiśeṣa, 167 ; *see* Anupadhiśeṣa.
Niṣpanna Tārā, accompanies Aṣṭabhuja Kurukullā, 58.
Nityanātha Lokeśvara, described, 188.

O

Oḍiyāna, name of a place ; its identification, xxvii ; two theories, xxvii ; Indrabhūti, king of, xxvii ; *see* Orissa.
Oḍiyāna Kurukullā, variety of Kurukullā, 55 ; fierce form of Kurukullā, 57 ; described, 57.
Oḍiyāna Lokeśvara, *see* Trailokyavaśaṅkara.
Oḍiyāna Mārīcī, leading characteristics, 100 ; *see* Vajradhātvīśvarī Mārīcī.
Oertel, Mr. ; on the Sarnath image of Saḍakṣarī Lokeśvara, 34.
Orissa, Oḍiyāna to be identified as, xxvii ; a seat of Tāntric learning, 45 ; Kurukullā worshipped in, 57 ; source of the image of Mārīcī, 97.
Ornaments, the six auspicious, *see* Saṇmudrā.
Ostārakī, accompanies Buddhakapāla, 64.

P

Padma, name of a serpent lord, 56.
Padmaḍākinī accompanies Mahāmāyā, 68.
Padmamuṇḍa, trampled by Jambhala, 119.
Padmanarttesvara, variety of Avalokiteśvara, 41ff, 1n ; his three different varieties, 41 ; described, 42, 44, 43 ; Dhyāna cited, 42, 43 ; his images, 42 ; illustrated, XXII, d-e ; his Maṇḍala described, 43 ; his companions, 42.
Padmāntaka, 142.
Padmapāṇi, Divine Bodhisattva, 8, 3 ; duty and character of, 3 ; illustrated, XI, e ; offers Abhiṣeka to Kurukullā, 56 ; *See* Padmapāṇi Lokeśvara and Avalokiteśvara.
Padmapāṇi Lokeśvara, 188.
Padmasambhava, son of Indrabhūti, xxvin.
Padmavāsinī, accompanies Padmanarttesvara, 43.
Pañcākāra, a chapter in *Jñānasiddhi* of Indrabhūti, xxvi ; gives the origin and description of the Dhyānī Buddhas xxvi.
Pañcarakṣā, name of a Buddhist work, 3n.
Pañcarakṣā deities, 55, 102, 116 ; enumerated, 132 ; merits arising out of their worship, 132 ; their character, 133.
Pañcarakṣā Maṇḍala, 102, 132ff.
Pañcaśirṣa in China, the native place of Mañjuśrī, 15.
Pañcavīrakaśekhara, special significance of the term used in connection with Siddhaikavīra, 20.
Pāṇḍarā, Divine Buddhaśakti, 7; illustrated, X, d ; spiritual mother of Avalokiteśvara, 32.
Pāṇḍaravāsinī, Sakti of Padmanarttesvara, 43.
Pantheon, Buddhist ; its gradual expansion xxivff ; evidence of Mahāyāna literature, xxivff ; evidence of Chinese travellers, xxv ; of Śāntideva, xxv.
Pantheons, frequent interchange of deities in the Buddhist Jaina and Hindu, i.
Pāpadeśanā, *see* Confession of sins.
Paramāśva, name of Hayagrīva, 54, 147 ; why comes under the category of Independent deities, 141 ; cannot be classified in accordance with colour 141n ; an Independent god, 147ff ; described, 147 ; Dhyāna cited, 147 ; illustrated, XXXIX, d.
Pāramitās, ten ; data for increase in number of deities, 165 ; ten companions of Vajratārā, the embodiments of, 125.
Parṇaśavarī, 106 ; her functions, 83 ; an emanation of Akṣobhya, 83ff ; an emanation of Amoghasiddhi, 109ff ; why an emanation of two different Dhyānī Buddhas, 83 ; a variety of Greeṅ Tārā, 137 ; different varieties distinguished, 109 ; her four-armed form, 84 ; described, 84, 110 ; Dhyāna cited, 83ff, 110 ; her images illustrated, XXXIII, d, XXXIV, a.
Past Buddhas, thirty-two according to the Mahāyānists, 10.
Pauṣṭika (vidhi), a Tāntric rite, 69.
Peacock, Vāhana of Amitābha, 3 : of Vajradharma, 47, 51 ; its tail, a symbol of Mahāmāyūrī, 111.
Phaṭka, tentative meaning of the word, 142n.
Photographs illustrated in this book ; their source, viii.
Piṇḍapātra Lokeśvara, described, 185.
Piśācī, epithet of Parṇaśavarī, 109.
Pītaprajñāpāramitā, yellow variety of Prajñāpāramitā, 86 ; described, 86 ; illustrated, XXVII, c.
Planets, nine, *see* Navagrahas.
Potapāda Lokeśvara, described, 178.
Potalaka, mount ; residence of Khasarpaṇa, 37.
Prabhākarakīrti, author of the Sādhana of Caṇḍaroṣaṇa, 60.

Pradīpatārā, accompanies Aṣṭabhuja Kurukullā, 58.
Prajñā, embraces Caturbhuja Heruka, 63 : Jambhala, 74 : Kṛṣṇayamāri, 72 : Mahākāla 121 ; Raktayamāri, 70 ; accompanies Hālāhala, 40 : Mañjuvajra, 26 : Sthiracakra, 30 ; trampled by Mārīcīpicuvā, 96.
Prajñā, accompanies Mahāsarasvatī, 151.
Prajñācakra, variety of Arapacana, 28 ; variety of Mañjuśrī, 28.
Prajñādhṛk, name of Amoghasiddhi mentioned in his Mantra, 5n.
Prajñāntaka, 142.
Prajñāpāramitā, 76 ; deified scripture 84 ; Sakti of Vajradhara, xxviii ; a parallel of Mañjuśrī, 85 ; her resemblance to Mañjuśrī, 31 ; an emanation of Akṣobhya, 84ff : of the five Dhyānī Buddhas, 126 ; varieties of, 85 ; Dhyāna cited, 126n ; described, 126 ; illustrated, XXXVI, c ; Bara image of Mañjuvara may be identified as, 25n.
Prasanna Tārā, variety of Yellow Tārā, 138 ; described, 139 ; Dhyāna cited, 138ff ; illustrated, XXXVIII, d ; an Independent goddess, 149n ; accompanies Aṣṭabhuja Kurukullā as a minor goddess, 58.
Pratibhānakakūṭa Lokeśvara, described, 182.
Pretasantarpita Lokeśvara, 50 ; source of his Sādhana, 50 ; described, 50, 178ff ; Dhyāna cited, 50 ; illustrated, XXIV, c.
Prīti, trampled by Paramāśva, 148.
Priyadarśanā accompanies Buddhakapāla, 64.
Puṇyapariṇāmanā, the process described, 170.
Pupala Lokeśvara, described, 180.
Purandara, *see* Indra.
Pūrṇabhadra accompanies Jambhala, 114.
Pūrṇānanda, a Tāntric writer ; his time, 77n.
Purohita, Vajrasattva's function as a, 6.
Puṣpā accompanies Lokanātha, 38, *see* Puṣpatārā.
Puṣpatārā accompanies Vajratārā, 124.

R

Rāhu, 97 ; under the seat of Tārodbhava Kurukullā, 56.
Rajendralal Mittra, Raja ; quoted, xviii.
Rajshahi, images of Mārīcī hailing from, 97.
Rakta Lokeśvara, name why given, 46 ; a variety of Avalokiteśvara, 46 ; described, 46, 47 ; Dhyāna cited, 46 ; illustrated, XXIII, c ; distinction between Vajradharma and, 47.
Raktayamāri, 60 ; variety of Yamāri, 70ff ; described, 70 ; Dhyāna cited, 70 ; embraced by Prajñā, 70.
Rasas, data for the increase in number of deities, 165.
Rati, trampled by Paramāśva, 148.
Ratna, one of the six auspicious symbols, *see* Saṇmudrā.
Ratnaḍākinī, accompanies Mahāmāyā, 68.
Ratnadala Lokeśvara, described, 186.
Ratnadhara, Mortal Bodhisattva, 12.
Ratnadhṛk ; name given to Ratnasambhava in his Dhyāna, 5n.
Ratnapāṇi, Divine Bodhisattva, 8 ; illustrated, XI, d.
Ratnapāṇi Lokeśvara, described, 183.
Ratnasambhava, Dhyānī Buddha, 2, 5 ; a late incorporation into the Pantheon, 113 ; excluded from the group of four Dhyānī Buddhas, 130 ; described, 5 ; Dhyāna cited, 5n ; his emanations, 113ff, 116ff ; source of his stone image, 4n ; illustrated, VIII, d, IX, a ; on the crown of Aparājitā, 58 ; of Jambhala, 114 ; of Vasudhārā, 118 ; appears in the image of Arapacana, 28.
Red Tārā, 140.
Rosary carried by the Mahoba image of Siṃhanāda, 36.
Rucaka, one of the six auspicious symbols, *see* Saṇmudrā.
Rudra, disgraced by Prasanna Tārā, 139.
Rūpiṇī accompanies Buddhakapāla, 64 ; Vajravārāhī, 104.

S

Saḍakṣarī Group ; Dhyāna cited, 33, 35n ; described, 34, 35 ; Birbhum image described and identified, 34ff ; Magadha image, 34 ; Oertel wrongly identifies as Buddha, Dharma and Saṅgha, 34.
Saḍakṣarī Lokeśvara, variety of Avalokiteśvara, 33ff ; varieties described, 33 ; described, 34, 178 ; Dhyāna cited, 33 ; his Mantra and the significance of his name, 34 ; images illustrated, XVIII, a-b-c, XIX, a.
Saḍakṣarī Mahāvidyā, accompanies Saḍakṣarī Lokeśvara, 33 ; described, 34 ; Dhyāna cited, 35n ; Vīrāsana prescribed only for, 35 ; her image illustrated, XIX, b.
Saḍakṣarī Maṇḍala ; guardians of the gates of, 34.
Saḍbhuja Sitatārā, variety of White Tārā, 137, 108 ; described, 108 ; Dhyāna cited, 108 ; illustrated, XXXIII, b.
Sādhana, meaning of the word, iv ; contents, iv, *see* App. A ; language of, ivn ; antiquity, 159 ; its composers, 159 ; authors enumerated, v.
Sādhana, Kiñcit-vistara, text and translation, 169ff.
Sādhanamālā, most important work for the understanding of Buddhist Iconography, ii ; its extent, 159 ; contents, ii ; extent of MS. material, iii ; date of MSS. discussed, iii, iiin.
Sādhanasamuccaya, another name of the *Sādhanamālā*, iii.
Sadyonubhava Arapacana, *see* Arapacana.
Sadyonubhava Mañjuśrī *see* Arapacana.
Sāgaramati Lokeśvara, described, 182.
Sahajayāna ; Lakṣiṃkarā, founder of, 57.
Sahni, Rai Bahadur D. R. ; on the image of Ucchuṣma Jambhala, 115.
Śakamangala, Mortal Bodhisattva, 12.
Śakti, of Mañjuśrī, 17 : Hālāhala, 41 ; represented on the image of Sthiracakra, 30 : of Vajrasattva, 6 ; embraces Caṇḍaroṣaṇa, 61, *see* Prajñā.
Śākyabuddha Lokeśvara, described, 181, 187.
Śākyasiṃha, Mortal Buddha, 10, 2, 32 ; his

disciple Ānanda, 12 ; his wife Yaśodharā, 12.
Sāmantabhadra, Divine Bodhisattva, 8 ; illustrated, XI, b ; variation in his images, 9 ; accompanies Lokanātha, 38.
Sāmantabhadra Lokeśvara, described, 183.
Saṃkṣipta Mārīcī, *see* Aṣṭabhuja Mārīcī *and* Mārīcīpicuvā.
Samvara, 60, 93 ; a variety of Vajraḍāka, 64, 65 ; described, 65 ; Dhyāna cited, 65 ; his Sakti Vajravārāhī, 65.
Saṅgha, 34 ; a member of the Holy Triad, xx ; described, xxn ; illustrated, III. ; the term Bodhisattva synonymous with, 8.
Saṅgharatna, epithet of Avalokiteśvara, 32.
Śaṅkhamuṇḍa trampled by Jambhala, 119.
Saṅkhanātha Lokeśvara, described, 188.
Śaṅkhapāla, name of a serpent lord, 56.
Sāṇku temple of Vajrayoginī, 156ff.
Saṇmudrā, six auspicious symbols or ornaments, *see* Glossary ; explained by quotation from the text, 47n ; prescribed for Saptākṣara, 66 : Vajravārāhī, 104 : Vidyujjvālākarālī, 82 ; group of five Mudrās enumerated, 91 ; five Mudrās prescribed for Nairātmā, 91 : Vajracarcikā, 86.
Śāntamati Lokeśvara, described, 187.
Śāntāsī Lokeśvara, described, 181.
Śāntideva, 16 ; his date discussed, xxv, xxvn ; his evidence regarding the Buddhist Pantheon, xxv : Dhāraṇī of Mārīcī given by, 94.
Śāntikavidhi, a Tāntric rite, 69.
Saptākṣara, significance of the name, 65 ; a variety of Vajraḍāka, 64, 65ff ; described, 65ff, 66ff ; Dhyāna cited, 66n ; embraced by Vajravārāhī, 65 ; his Prajñā described, 67 ; his Maṇḍala described, 66n ; his companions described, 66.
Saptaśatika Hayagrīva, 53ff ; an emanation of Amitābha, 53ff ; described, 54 ; Dhyāna cited, 54 ; *see* Hayagrīva.
Saptaśatika Kalpa, name of a Tāntric work, 54.
Sarahapāda, author of the Sādhana of Trailokyavasaṅkara, 45.
Sarasiri (?) Lokeśvara, described, 186.
Sarasvatī ; her antiquity, 150 ; a river deified, 150 ; popularity of her worship, 150 ; her functions, 150 ; an independent goddess, 150 ; variety of her forms, 150 ; image of Jambhala wrongly identified by Vincent A. Smith as, 150n ; accompanies Jambhala as a minor goddess, 114.
Sarasvatīsthāna, 15.
Sarnath Museum ; contains the earliest image of Lokanātha, 40 ; image of Mārīcī, 97 : Nīlakaṇṭha, 49 : Saḍakṣarī Lokeśvara, 34 : Saḍakṣarī Mahāvidyā, 35 : Siddhaikavīra, 20.
Sārthavāha Lokeśvara, described, 186.
Sarvabuddhaḍākinī, name given to the headless form of Vajrayoginī, 155n.
Sarvamāripraśamanī, epithet of Parṇaśavarī, 109.
Sarvaṇivaraṇaviṣkambhī Lokeśvara, described, 182.
Sarvaśokatamonirghāta Lokeśvara, described, 182.
Śāśvatavajra, author of the Sādhana of Mahācīnatārā, 77.
Seasons, represented by the Dhyānī Buddhas, 7A.
Senses, five ; probable origin of the five Dhyānī Buddhas, 1.
Serpent ; its presence in the stone images of Amoghasiddhi, 5 ; appears in the image of Harihariharivahana, 45 ; two serpents accompany Nīlakaṇṭha, 48 ; the names and functions of the eight lords of serpents, 56.
Siddhaikavīra, variety of Mañjuśrī, 17 ; an emanation of Akṣobhya, 19 ; described, 20ff ; Dhyāna cited, 21 ; his similarity with Arapacana, 21 ; distinction between Lokanātha and, 21 ; illustrated, XIII, d ; his Maṇḍala, 21 ; his companions enumerated and described, 21n.
Siddhapuruṣas, eighty-four ; Saraha one of the, 45.
Siddhiharṣa, Paṇḍit, 40n.
Sikhī, Mortal Buddha, 10.
Śikhimālinī, Mortal Buddhaśakti, 12.
Śikṣāsamuccaya, a work of Śāntideva, xxv.
Siṃhanāda, variety of Avalokiteśvara, 35ff, 42 ; his functions, 35 ; described, 36 ; 186 ; Dhyāna cited, 36 ; his images illustrated, XIX, c-d-e, XX, a-b ; distinction between Mañjuśrī and, 36 ; Mañjuvara wrongly indentified as, 25n .
Siṃhanātha Lokeśvara, described, 179.
Śirīṣa tree, special tree of Mahāmantrānusāriṇī, 134.
Śiriṣarā (?) Lokeśvara, described, 186.
Sītalā, Hindu goddess of small-pox, 110.
Sitaprajñāpāramitā, white variety of Prajñāpāramitā, 85 ; described, 85 ; Dhyāna cited, 85.
"Sitātapatrā," meaning of the word, 102.
Sitātapartā Aparājitā, emanation of Vairocana, 101ff ; described, 102 ; Dhyāna cited, 101 ; Nepalese drawing illustrated, XXXI, e.
Sitatārā, emanation of the five Dhyānī Buddhas, 127ff ; Dhyāna cited, 127 ; described, 128 ; distinction between Khadiravanī and, 127.
Sitatārā, Caturbhuja, *see* Caturbhuja Sitatārā.
Sitatārā, Saḍbhuja, *see* Saḍbhuja Sitatārā.
Śiva trampled by Daśabhujasita Mārīcī, 99 ; by Ubhayavarāhānana Mārīcī, 98 ; counted as a Māra, 154n ; disgraced by Buddhist gods, 162.
Skandhas, probable origin of the five Dhyānī Buddhas 2 ; represented by the five Dhyānī Buddhas, 7A, 119 ; data for the increase in number of deities, 165.
Smile, pleasant ; indication of Parṇaśavarī as emanation of Akṣobhya, 1110.
Smith, Vincent A. ; criticized, 150n.
Smṛti accompanies Mahāsarasvatī, 151.
Śrī, trampled by Paramāśva, 147.
Śrīmadāryyāvalokiteśvara, described, 188.
Śrīvasu, accompanies Vasudhārā, 90.
Śrīvasumukhī, accompanies Vasudhārā, 90.
Śṛṅkhala (chain), special symbol of Vajraśṛṅkhalā, 111.
Sṛṣṭikāntā Lokeśvara, described, 183.
Sthiracakra, variety of Mañjuśrī, 17 ; independent god, 29ff ; peculiarity of the Sādhana devoted to, 29 ; described, 29,

30 ; illustrated, XVII, d ; his image identified, 30n.
Stūpa, symbol of the Buddhist Universe, 3 ; Dhyāni Buddhas represented on the, 3 ; three stupas illustrated, II.
Subhā, accompanies Buddhakapāla, 64.
Subhadrā, accompanies Jambhala, 114.
Subhagā, accompanies Buddhakapāla, 64.
Subhamekhalā, accompanies Buddhakapāla, 64.
Sūcimukha receives nectar from Lokanātha, 37 ; described, 37.
Sudattā, accompanies Jambhala, 114.
Sudhanakumāra, 37, 20n ; described, 38 ; accompanies Khasarpaṇa, 38, 36 : Mañjughoṣa, 20 : Mañjuvara, 25 : Padmanarttesvara, 42.
Sugatisandarśana Lokeśvara, 49ff ; source of his Sādhana, 49 ; described, 49 , 179 ; Dhyāna cited, 49 ; Nepalese drawing illustrated, XXIV, b.
Sujuki, D. T. ; on Nirvāṇa, xvin.
Sukhāvatī Heaven, the residence of Amitābha, 3.
Sukhāvatī Lokeśvara, 50ff ; source of his Sādhana, 33, 50 ; described, 51, 178 ; Dhyāna cited, 50 ; illustrated, XXIV, d.
Sukhāvatīvyūha, 15 ; date of its Chinese translation, xxv, 52n ; Akṣobhya mentioned in, 4 : Avalokiteśvara, 52 : Mañjuśrī, 15 ; also called *Amitāyus-Sūtra*.
Sukhendra, accompanies Jambhala, 114.
Śukla Kurukullā, white variety of Kurukullā, 55 ; described, 56 ; Dhyāna cited, 55 ; is offered Abhiṣeka by Padmapāṇi and others, 56.
Sumālinī, accompanies Buddhakapāla, 64.
Sumbhā, 107 ; accompanies Vajratārā, 125.
Sundarā, accompanies Buddhakapāla, 64.
Sundarī, accompanies Buddhakapāla, 64.
Sun-god ; connection of Mārīcī with, 93.
Śūnya, meaning and significance of the word in Vajrayāna, 164 ; or Void, 2n ; identified with Compassion, 165 ; its two aspects as a god and a goddess, 164 ; expressed by the word Nairātmā, 91 ; all deities are Śūnya in essence, 164 ; different kinds of transformation, 165 ; all Buddhist deities are manifestations of, 164ff ; how it transforms itself in form of deities, 165 ; transforms itself in accordance with different functions discharged, 165.
Śūnyatā ; Buddhist Iconography dependent upon the doctrine of, xiii.
Surakṣiṇī accompanies Buddhakapāla, 64.
Sūryyaprabha, *see* Jālinīprabha.
Sūtra, one of the six auspicious symbols, *see* Saṇmudrā.
Svayambhūkṣettra, 15.
Svayambhūpurāṇam, details about Mañjuśrī to be found in, 15, 16.
Sword, its significance, 60n ; symbol of Mañjuśrī, 17 ; appears in the images of Mañjuvara, 26 ; its function when carried by Sthiracakra, 29 ; symbol of Siṃhanāda, 35.
Śyāmatārā, name given to Khadiravanī Tārā, 106.
Syllables, six ; mother of, 34.
Symbols of Buddha ; objects of Buddhist worship, xx.
Symbols, the six auspicious, *see* Saṇmudrā.

T

Tabular statement showing the relation between Dhyānī Buddhas, their Buddhaśaktis and Bodhisattvas, 9 ; Mortal Buddhas their Buddhaśaktis and Bodhisattvas, 13 ; the attributes of the Dhyānī Buddhas, 7A.
Takṣaka, name of a serpent lord, 56 ; Vāhana of Māyājālakrama Kurukullā, 127.
Tantra, meaning of, xviii ; Asaṅga initiated in the mysteries of, 13 ; introduced by Asaṅga into Mahāyāna, xviii.
Tantrasāra ; the Dhyāna of Hindu Tārā cited from, 77.
Tantrayāna did not exert much influence before the time of Dharmakīrti, xxvi.
Tāntric deities, how represented in art, xviiiff.
Tārā, significance of the name, 106 ; loose application of the term, 135n ; definition of, 135.
Tārās, Ordinary ; 135ff ; Extraordinary, 136ff ; their classification in accordance with colour, 135ff ; Blue, *see* Blue Tārā ; Green, *see* Green Tārā ; Red, *see* Red Tārā ; White, *see* White Tārā ; Yellow, *see* Yellow Tārā.
Tārā Buddhist ; as a minor goddess, 37 ; described, 37ff ; accompanies Khasarpaṇa, 36 : Lokanātha, 38, 39 : Rakta-Lokeśvara, 46 : Padmanarttesvara, 42, 43.
Tārā, Hindu ; a purely Buddhist goddess wholly incorporated into the Hindu Pantheon, 78 ; prototype of Mahācīnatārā, 78 ; significance of the corpse on which she stands, 78 ; *see also* Mahācīnatārā.
Tārā Mantra, its deification, 109 ; example, 107.
Tārānāth, his evidence regarding Tantric learning, xxvi.
Tārārahasya, Dhyāna of Mahācīnatārā to be found in, 77.
Tārodbhava Kurukullā, variety of Kurukullā 56 ; described, 56.
Tarpaṇa Mudrā, exhibited by Nāmasaṅgīti, 149.
Tastes, represented by the Dhyānī Buddhas, 7A.
Tathāgatas, 23 ; Akṣobhya the earliest Tathāgata, 60, 4 ; Mañjukumāra made of the particles of, 27 ; are cited as witnesses by Harihariharivāhana, 44.
Tattvacintāmaṇi, a work of Pūrṇānanda, 77n.
Thunderbolt ; the seat of Vajrāsana stamped with a, 11n .
Tibet ; Ekajaṭāsādhana restored by Nāgārjuna from, 80.
Tiger, Vāhana of Vādirāṭ, 30.
Trailokyākṣepa, Yab-yum variety of Heruka, 63 ; described, 63.
Trailokyavaśaṅkara, a variety of Avalokiteśvara, 45ff ; described, 45 ; Dhyāna cited, 45.
Trailokyavijaya, an Independent god, 146ff ; described, 146 ; Dhyāna cited, 146 ; his images noticed, 146 ; illustrated, XXXIX, c.

Vikāśayantam, different meanings of the word, 47n.
Vikrampur, in the District of Dacca in Bengal ; source of the images of Khasarpaṇa, 38 ; Jambhala, 114 ; Parṇaśavarī, 110.
Vilokinī, accompanies Padmanartteśvara, 43.
Vīnā, etc., offer Abhiṣeka to Kurukullā, 56.
Vipaśyantī, Mortal Buddhaśakti, 12.
Vipaśyin, Mortal Buddha, 10.
Vīrāsana, rare in Buddhist Iconography, 35 ; prescribed for Saḍakṣarī Mahābidyā, 35 ; exhibited by Saḍakṣarī Mahāvidyā, 34.
Viṣahari, Hindu goddess akin to Jāṇgulī, 80.
Visarjana, the process described, 171.
Viṣkambhin, accompanies Lokanātha, 38, 40.
Viṣṇu, trampled by Daśabhujasita Mārīcī, 99 ; Vāhana of Harihariharivāhana, 44 ; trampled by Ubhayavarāhānana Mārīcī, 98 ; Vajrajjvālānalārka, 146.
Viṣṇucakra Lokeśvara, described, 187.
Viṣṇukāntā Lokeśvara, described, 188.
Viṣṇupāṇi Lokeśvara, described, 186.
Viśvabhū, Mortal Buddha, 10.
Viśvabhūta Lokeśvara, 187.
Viśvaḍākinī, accompanies Mahāmāyā, 68.
Visvadharā, Mortal Buddhaśakti, 12.
Visvahana Lokeśvara, described, 181.
Visvamātā, variety of White Tārā, 137.
Viśvapadmā, accompanies Padmanartteśvara, 43.
Viśvapadmeśvarī, accompanies Padmanartteśvara, 43.
Viśvapāṇi, Divine Bodhisattva, 8 ; illustrated, XI, f.
Viśvavajra, symbol of Amoghasiddhi, 5 ; on the head of Samvara, 65 ; Saptākṣara, 66.
Viśvavajra, accompanies Padmanartteśvara, 43.
Viśvavajra Lokeśvara, described, 187.
Void, *see* Śūnya.
Vṛṣṇācana Lokeśvara, described, 180.

W

Waddel, L. A., on the Magadha image of the Saḍakṣarī Group, 34 ; criticized, 34.
Weapons, are nothing but manifestations of Bodhicitta, 166.
White Tārās, Ordinary ; enumerated with characteristic features of each, 136 ; Extraordinary ; enumerated with leading features of each, 137.
Worship, difference between Hindu and Buddhist forms of, v ; merits arising out of, 175.
Worshipper, his duties, enumerated, 169.

Y

Yab-yum, meaning of the Tibetan word, 163 ; conception is of complicated nature, 166ff ; 'Advaya,' an advanced stage of, 164n ; character of yab-yum representations, 61 ; spiritual significance, 163ff ; ideal of a bright and definite spiritual prospect, 164, *see* Glossary.
Yakṣas, trampled by Mahāsāhasrapramardanī, 133.
Yama, Tibetans oppressed by, 70 ; legendary story of his origin, 70.
Yamadūtī, accompanies Mahākāla, described, 121 .
Yamāntaka, *see* Yamāri.
Yamāri, 142 ; story of his legendary origin, 69 ; an emanation of Akṣobhya, 69 ; his forms vary according to different rites, 69 ; connexion of Mañjuśrī to, 70 ; accompanies Mañjughoṣa as a minor god, 19, 20, 20n ; Mañjuśrī, 17 ; Mañjuvara, 25 ; the Śakti of Sthiracakra identified as, 30n ; *see* Kṛṣṇayamāri and Raktayamāri.
Yantras, of Divine Buddhaśaktis, 7.
Yaśodharā, Mortal Buddhaśakti, 12 ; wife of Śākyasiṃha, 12.
Yellow Tārās, enumerated with leading characteristics of each, 138.
Yoginī, epithet of Vajragāndhārī, 155.
Yun-gar, story of his attack on the monastery of Vajravārāhī, 103.